TESI GREGORIANA
Serie Teologia

—————————— 94 ——————————

BABY PARAMBI, VC

THE DISCIPLESHIP OF THE WOMEN IN THE GOSPEL ACCORDING TO MATTHEW

An Exegetical Theological Study of Matt 27:51b-56, 57-61 and 28:1-10

EDITRICE PONTIFICIA UNIVERSITÀ GREGORIANA

Roma 2003

Vidimus et approbamus ad normam Statutorum Universitatis

Romae, ex Pontificia Universitate Gregoriana
die 18 mensis decembris anni 2002

R.P. Prof. ERNEST R. MARTINEZ, S.J.
R.D. Prof. MASSIMO GRILLI

ISBN 88-7652-958-6
© Iura editionis et versionis reservantur
PRINTED IN ITALY

GREGORIAN UNIVERSITY PRESS
Piazza della Pilotta, 35 - 00187 Rome, Italy

ACKNOWLEDGEMENTS

With great joy and satisfaction, I express my sincere love and gratitude to all who have helped me towards the completion of this work. I humbly acknowledge that the divine project for me has been carried out through the cooperation of many persons in different ways.

In presenting this work I am indebted to many but foremost to Rev. Ernest Richard Martinez, SJ, who has been guiding me with patience, understanding, good will and encouragement as well as with corrections and suggestions during the realization of this work. I remember with gratitude Rev. Grilli Massimo, the defence examiner, for his corrections and valuable suggestions to improve the quality and the presentation of this work.

I recall with gratitude my superiors in the Vincentian Congregation, all my friends and well wishers in India, Germany, Italy, England and elsewhere who encouraged me both with moral as well as financial assistance for the realization of this project. I am grateful to all who have read through the drafts of my work with patience and good will.

The authorities of the library of the Gregorian University and of the Pontifical Biblical Institute, Rome, were very generous in permitting me to use their libraries.

My loving parents, now called by God to eternal life, and all the members of my family had a unique presence in my studies.

GENERAL INTRODUCTION

1. Significance and Originality of the Topic

The historical disciples of Jesus and the discipleship theme in the NT, particularly in the Gospel of Matthew, have been a focus of scholarly debate especially in the contemporary world of exegesis and have been studied from various exegetical angles by different categories of authors, Catholic as well as Protestant, male as well as female. A quick glance at the divergent ways the scholars have studied the discipleship theme will provide us with an overview of the most recent developments on this theme in the NT in general, and the Gospel according to Matthew in particular. This will help us to highlight the significance of the theme we are discussing, and the problems inherent in it, thus opening a new window for our understanding of the discipleship of Jesus.

Prominent among those scholars who have studied the discipleship theme making use of the redaction critical method are G. Bornkamm (1948), E. Schweizer (1955, 1974), G. Barth and H.J. Held (1960), R. Hummel (1963), E. Haenchen, H.D. Betz (1967), G. Strecker (1971), U. Luz (1971), W. Trilling (1975), E. Best (1981), R. Gundry (1994), S.C. Barton and M.J. Wilkins (1995)[1].

---

[1] G. BORNKAMM, «Die Sturmstillung», 49-54. The appearance of this essay is generally said to mark the beginning of redaction-critical approaches to Matthean studies in general, and the Matthean discipleship theme in particular; E. SCHWEIZER, *Erniedrigung,* ID., *Matthäus;* G. BARTH, «Das Gesetzesverständnis», 15-54; H.J. HELD, «Matthäus», 155-287; R. HUMMEL, *Die Auseinandersetzung;* H.D. BETZ, *Nachfolge;* E. HAENCHEN, *Der Weg Jesu;* G. STRECKER, *Der Weg;* U. LUZ, «Die Jünger», 141-171; W. TRILLING, *Das Wahre Israel;* E. BEST, *Following Jesus;* ID., *Disciples and Discipleship;* R.H. GUNDRY, «On True and False Disciples», 433-441; ID., *Matthew;* S.C. BARTON, *Discipleship;* M.J. WILKINS, *The Concept.*

Important among those who have studied the discipleship theme from a literary-critical point of view are N.R. Petersen, R.A. Edwards (1985), J.D. Kingsbury (1988), D.R. Bauer (1988), D.J. Weaver (1990) and D.B. Howell (1990)[2].

Through a sociological and anthropological approach to the Matthean disciples and the discipleship theme, M. Hengel (1981), G. Theissen (1981), and M.H. Crosby (1988) have given a new direction to the study of the Matthean disciples[3].

The social dynamics of Jesus and his disciples also stimulated in the decades of the 1980's and early 1990's several exploratory studies on Matthew and his community, which necessarily involved addressing the Matthean disciples[4].

Some recent studies on the Matthean disciples of Jesus have attempted to amend the polarization of methods by undertaking a synthesis of various critical disciplines, with special focus on combining historical, social and literary methods[5].

This quick survey of various studies on the discipleship from divergent exegetical perspectives shows that most of the works come from the Protestant camp. Through this observation, however, we do not wish to overlook some of the important Catholic studies in this field. A major result of the above-mentioned studies is a growing consensus concerning at least three basic characteristics of the NT model of discipleship, which enjoy multiple attestations by the various Gospel traditions. The first characteristic feature of the discipleship of Jesus is a «personal call from Jesus», which is attested by all the Gospel traditions: (the call of the first four disciples, Mark 1:16-20 par Matt 4:18-22; the call of Levi the tax collector, Mark 2:14 par Matt 9:9; the candidate whose father has just died, Matt 8:18-22 par Luke 9:59-60 [Q], 9:61-62 [L]); the call of Philip (John 1:43). The second characteristic feature, which is closely related to the first one, is a literal and physical

---

[2] N.R. PETERSEN, *Literary Criticism*; R.A. EDWARDS, «Uncertain Faith», 47-61; J.D. KINGSBURY, «On Following Jesus», 45-49; ID., «The Verb *Akolouthein*», 56-73; ID., «The Developing Conflict», 57-73; ID., *Matthew*; D.R. BAUER, *The Structure of Matthew's Gospel*; D.J. WEAVER, *Matthew's Missionary Discourse*; D.B. HOWELL, *Matthew's Inclusive Story*.

[3] M. HENGEL, *Nachfolge und Charisma*; G. THEISSEN, «Soziale Schichtung», 232-272; ID., *Soziologie der Jesusbewegung*; M.H. CROSBY, *The House of Disciples*.

[4] A.J. LEVINE, *The Social and Ethnic Dimensions*; M.H. CROSBY, *The House of Disciples*.

[5] See W. CARTER, *Households and Discipleship*.

following with the consequent obligation to renounce family ties and property. It was a call to join the entourage Jesus gathered in Galilee. The purpose of following was to proclaim the «kingdom of God» (Luke 9:59-62) and to be fishers of men (Matt 4:19). The call meant absolute faithfulness to Jesus (Luke 9:62; see Mark 14:50). The third characteristic of NT discipleship concerns the danger and hostility the following of Jesus, and doing God's will, involved. It meant at least the following three things: a) a paradox of loss and gain (Mark 8:35 Matt 16:25; Luke 9:24; John 12:25); b) self-denial and cross bearing (Mark 8:34; Matt 10:38), and c) the possibility of facing hostility from one's own family (Matt 10:34-37; Luke 12:51-53). On the basis of these characteristics, a disciple of Jesus could be defined as one who is marked by obedience to Jesus' peremptory call, denial of self, and exposure to hostility and danger in seeking to do the will of God.

Now such a definition poses an issue that concerns the boundary of discipleship on which NT scholars have not reached a consensus: who form the circle of the historical disciples of Jesus and how are they intended to function within Matthew's Gospel? All the canonical Gospels provide us with a list of the names of some Jewish men who did qualify (Mark 3:13-19; Matt 10:1-4; Luke 6:12-16; see John 1), important among whom are Peter and Andrew, James and John (Mark 1:16-20; Matt 4:18-22). No doubt there are others whose names may have been lost or whose identity remains unknown to us.

In this context, a field that demands more scholarly attention in the Catholic world of exegesis concerns the identity of those women who followed Jesus from Galilee serving him, who witnessed the death and burial of Jesus, and gave witness to his resurrection. It is to these women that the risen Jesus entrusted the responsibility of bringing the resurrection message to the male disciples in Galilee (Matt 28:9-10). Our focus rests on the identity of these women in the Gospel. Can we speak of a discipleship of women in the Gospel of Matthew?

One main reason for the scarcity of attention paid to this issue is perhaps that Catholic exegesis of the past was under the monopoly of the traditional male religious circles. Lack of sufficient material in the Gospels may also be another reason for this. Recent years have witnessed to a sudden flow of literature on this topic. This is seen especially in issues brought up by the contemporary feminist interpretations of the Bible. The following scholars deserve special mention in this field: F. Neirynck (1968-69), H.C. Waetjen (1976), M.S. Cohen (1980), E.M. Tetlow (1980), D. Irvin (1980), J. Schaberg (1987), J.C. Anderson (1987), G.R. Obsorne (1989), E.M. Wainwright (1991), R.S. Kraemer

(1992), J. Levine (1992), and L. Schottroff (1992), J. Dewey (1994), E. Schüssler Fiorenza (1994), E. Cheney (1997), H.M. Keller (1997) and R. Strelan (1999)[6]. Although these studies have thrown new light on the Gospels' ecclesiology in general, and the discipleship theme in particular, on several occasions they seem to end up in an *eisegesis* or a forced exegesis. Notwithstanding the manifold apparent shortcomings of the feminist approach, it has left a strong effect on the contemporary interpretation of Scripture as it seems to force a rethinking of many of the traditional positions, an important one among them being the question of the discipleship of the women. The title of this work itself may be counted as an example in this direction.

Now we find ourselves faced with two realities. On the one hand, the past Catholic exegesis, mainly male religious dominated, often manifests a prejudice against the significance of the women in the Scriptures and their discipleship of Jesus. On the other hand, the contemporary feminist hermeneutics, mainly female dominated, often seem to interpret the biblical passages in favor of certain hypothetical conclusions, the result often being a «forced exegesis». Faced with these divergent contemporary realities, therefore, a balanced and a systematic approach to the issue of the discipleship of the women from an exegetical, theological, biblical-rhetorical viewpoint forms the significance as well as the originality of the entitled theme of this book: *The Discipleship of the Women in the Gospel According to Matthew: An Exegetical Theological Study of Matt 27:51b-56, 57-61 and 28:1-10*.

2. Scope of the Study

It is generally believed that the Gospel according to Luke is the most favorable to the study of the women disciples of Jesus. The Gospel ac-

---

[6] F. NEIRYNCK, «Les femmes au tombeau»,168-190; ID., «John and the Synoptics», 161-187; H.C. WAETJEN, «The Genealogy», 205-230; M.S. COHEN, «Women», 23-29; E.M. TETLOW, *Women and Ministry*; D. IRVIN, «The Ministry of Women», 76-86; J. SCHABERG, *The Illegitimacy of Jesus*; J.C. ANDERSON, «Matthew: Gender and Reading», 3-27; ID., «Mary's Difference», 183-202; G.R. OBSORNE, «Women in the Ministry of Jesus», 259-291; E.M. WAINWRIGHT, *Shall We Look for Another*; ID., *Towards a Feminist Critical Reading*; R.S. KRAEMER, «Monastic Jewish Women», 342-370; ID., *Hellenistic Jewish Women*; ID., *Her Share of the Blessings*; A.J. LEVINE, «Matthew», 252-262; L. SCHOTTROFF, *Let the Oppressed Go Free*; J. DEWEY, «Jesus' Healing of Women»,122-131; E. SCHÜSSLER FIORENZA, *But She Said*; ID., *In Memory of Her*; E. CHENEY, «The Mother», 13-21; H.M. KELLER, *Jesus und die Frauen*; R. STRELAN, «To Sit is to Mourn», 31-45.

cording to Mark, on whom Matthew depends for many of his references to the women in the Gospel, is considered the next best. Our choice of Matthew in preference to Luke and Mark has its reasons. The Gospel according to Matthew is based on a historically Jewish background in which women were not considered valid witnesses in a court of law, and which was bereft of the concept of a woman disciple. In the process of redaction Matthew preserves the major Markan descriptions concerning women, but at times makes some interesting redactional changes which give a very positive portrayal of women in relation to Jesus. The structural features of the Gospel seem to confirm this idea. We limit our study mainly to the pericopes 27:51b-56, 57-61 and 28:1-10 within Matthew for the following three reasons: a) they contain a large concentration of the discipleship vocabulary that draws attention to the group of male and female disciples around Jesus, b) the women are placed as the principles of continuity that keep together the three different pieces of the paschal mystery: the death, burial and resurrection (27:55-56, 61, 28:1-10), and finally c) these passages form the immediate context to the final commission (Matt 28:16-20) which forms the apex of the Matthean discipleship story.

3. Methodology

The methodology used to uncover the message of the Gospel accounts is guided mainly by the exegetical, theological and biblical rhetorical approach. However, we incorporate different approaches wherever they are of assistance in the development of the theme and thus bring out the message of the Gospel texts under our investigation.

4. Limitation of the Study

The multifaceted problems surrounding the death, burial and resurrection episodes are not the object of this study. These themes will be discussed only in as far as they help us to understand the Matthean presentation of the theme of the discipleship of the women. Our attention rests specifically on their discipleship-identity and their role in the Matthean passion and death (27:51b-56), burial (27:57-61) and resurrection narratives (28:1-10).

5. The Plan

Besides a general introduction and a general conclusion, the work will consist of five, chapters arranged under two section. Each chapter will be complete in itself drawing its own conclusions, and at the same giving a transition to the chapter that follows. Especially in the third, fourth and the fifth chapters we will follow a certain pattern where every chapter will begin with discussions on the delimitation of the text followed by a philological analysis, compositional features and the biblical background, all of which will lead to the interpretation of the text.

The first chapter begins with some preliminary discussions on the date and place of the composition of the first Gospel which may help us to locate the *Sitz im Leben* of Matthew. This will be followed by a discussion on the social and religious status of women in the OT, first century Judaism and finally on the emerging Christian house churches, with special reference to the social religious background of first century Antioch, the probable place of the Matthean composition. This will furnish us with the social, religious and cultural background of Matthew, and women's status in this Gospel. The second chapter will begin with a description of the women in the Gospel according to Matthew which will be arranged under four headings: a) women in the direct narrative comments, b) women as imagery, c) women in Jesus' teaching, and finally d) women as characters. This will be followed by a brief discussion of five passages concerning the life and ministry of Jesus: a) women in the genealogy of Jesus (Matt 1:1-17); b) Jesus' healing of Peter's mother-in-law (Matt 8:14-17); c) Jesus' healing of the woman with a hemorrhage (Matt 9:20-22); d) Jesus and the Canaanite Woman (Matt 15:21-28), and finally e) Jesus and the woman at Bethany (26:6-13). This chapter will give an idea of the role of women in the birth and early ministry of Jesus, which will prepare us to understand in depth Matt 27:51b-61 and 28:1-10, and the significance of the female characters in them. In the third chapter, which will discuss Matt 27:51b-56, special attention will be paid to the discipleship vocabulary ἀκολουθέω and διακονέω which helps us understand the women in relation to Jesus. The fourth chapter will discuss Matt 27:57-61, in which special attention will be paid to the vocabulary items μαθητεύω (μαθητής), κάθημαι and the various structural features. The fifth and final chapter will discuss Matt 28:1-10 in relation to Matt 27:51b-61. Special attention will be given to the extraordinary importance given to the women.

Our study will end with a general conclusion that will contain the important observations we have made in the course of our investigation.

CHAPTER I

Women in the Social-Religious Settings of Matthew

1. Introduction

Any research on women in the Gospel of Matthew necessitates an understanding of their status within the immediate social-cultural context in which Jesus lived, and in which the Gospel was composed. To this end we dedicate this chapter to an understanding of the status of women in Hellenistic Judaism (300 BC-100 AD)[1]: the immediate social-cultural background that surrounded the first Christian century, and the status of women in the first Christian house churches. Special reference will be made to the Matthean community. We begin the investigation with some preliminary remarks on the date, place and source of Matthew, which will be followed by an examination of important literature on the topic. Through this we hope to arrive at a comprehensive view of women's status in the period. These preliminary discussions will be followed by a brief survey of the status of women in Hellenistic Judaism, which will be treated under two sub-headings: a) The Social and Religious Status of Women in Hellenistic Judaism; b) The Social and Religious Status of Women in first century Christian Antioch, against the background of the first century Christian house churches.

2. Some Preliminary Remarks

The discussion on the status of women in Matthew prompts us to make some preliminary remarks concerning the date, place and source

---

[1] For a discussion on the period of Hellenistic Judaism see M. HENGEL, *Giudaismo*, 222-227.

of Matthew, as these factors provide us with some interesting data that explain the extraordinary status that women receive in this Gospel, otherwise known as the most Jewish and patriarchal[2].

2.1 *Date of Composition*

We accept the most generally held opinion that the final redaction of the Gospel of Matthew took place in the closing decades of the first century, most probably between 80 and 90 AD[3].

2.2 *Place of Composition*

Although there is less consensus concerning the location of the Gospel, the majority opinion tends towards Syria[4], more specifically

---

[2] It is not within the scope of this study to enter into various issues and problems related to the date, locale and the source of Matthew. Concerning these matters we rely on opinions held by the majority of scholars who base their arguments on both external as well as internal evidence.

[3] While the majority of Matthean scholars support this view, some suggest a pre-70 dating while still others suggest a second century composition. R.E. Brown proposes three arguments that refuse a pre-70 composition.

Matthew cannot be a pre-70 composition. Brown's reasons in favour of a non pre-70 dating are convincing. For him, Matthew's reference to the king burning the city (Matt 22:7) might perhaps reflect the destruction of the Jerusalem Temple in 70 AD. Naturally, if the Gospel of Matthew was written before 70 AD, Matthew could not make reference to these events. See R.E. BROWN, *An Introduction to the New Testament*, 217. Secondly Matthew's reference to Jesus' controversy with the Pharisees and Jesus' condemnation of the free use of the title «Rabbi» well reflects the early rabbinic period after 70 AD. A third reason is Matthew's dependence on Mark, which is believed to have been composed before 70 AD.

Neither can Matthew be a second century composition, as it betrays no awareness of the problem of Gnosticism. Probably Gnosticism was still in its initial stage. If Matthew was composed in the Antioch area, it was probably written before the time of Ignatius (110) for whom gnosticism was a threat. On the other hand Ignatius' Letter to *Ephesus* (19f) reflects a knowledge of Matt 2.2 and his letter to *Smyrna* (1.1) reflects Matt 3:15. Naturally the Gospel of Matthew influenced Ignatius of Antioch. For a discussion of Ignatius' dependence on Matthew, see C. TREVETT, «Approaching Matthew», 59-67, who cites a list of eighteen parallels commonly cited. J.S. SIBINGA, Ignatius and Matthew», 263-283.

These arguments lead us to the view that Matthew is neither a pre-70 composition, nor a second century composition. Therefore the most probable dating could be 80-90 AD. For a list of the opinions of fifty different authors on the date of composition, see W.D. DAVIES – D.C. ALLISON, *The Gospel According to Matthew*, 127-128.

[4] Syria was Rome's most strategic province for two reasons: first it was a center of trade and industry; secondly it was the frontier (together with Cappadocia) against

Antioch[5]. Together with the majority of the scholars, we presume Antioch to be the most probable location for the Gospel of Matthew in this study.

2.3 *Sources of Matthew*

Markand Q are generally accepted to be the two main sources of Matthew, beside which there are sources known to Matthew alone. Matthew seems to have used Q, which he edits to suit his needs[6].

Parthia. The combined district of Syria and Palestine was the most important eastern corridor of trade to the Mediterranean countries. It was rich in grain, fruit, vegetables, textiles and glass, which were important items of export. This made Antioch a trade center and it had, therefore, a close connection with Rome, along with the «capitals of the richest and most prosperous provinces». See M.H. CROSBY, *The House of Disciples*, 37. In 64 BC, Pompey made Antioch the focus of Roman power in the Near East. This encouraged urbanization, a policy of Rome. This urbanization was another reason for the rapid growth and prosperity of Antioch.

[5] Important scholars who hold this view are J.P. MEIER − R.E. BROWN, *Antioch and Rome*, 15-27; CROSBY, *The House of Disciples*, 37. Other scholars have suggested Jerusalem, Palestine, Phoenicia, Caesarea Maritima, or even Alexandria as the possible locale for the Matthean composition. For a survey of various opinions, see J.P. MEIER − R.E. BROWN, *Antioch and Rome*, 15-27; D. SENIOR, *What are they Saying*, 5-15; B.T. VIVIANO, «Where was the Gospel», 533-546; W.D. DAVIES − D.C. ALLISON, *The Gospel According to Matthew*, 138-147; for a detailed discussion on the topic see C.S. KEENER, *A Commentary*, 41; W. CARTER, *Matthew*, 35-50.

In support of the thesis that Matthew was composed at Antioch, the Gospel itself contains some evidence. Matthew's dependence upon Mark is commonly accepted. The Gospel according to Mark is addressed to the Gentiles. But in Matthew the emphasis is shifted to Jewish Christianity. R.E. Brown's observation that «The most plausible interpretation is that Matthew was addressed to a strongly Jewish Church that had become increasingly Gentile in composition» summarizes the situation of first century Antioch. See R.E. BROWN, *An Introduction to the New Testament*, 213. This opinion has the backing of Josephus who suggests that there were more Jews in Antioch than in any place in Syria, and that the Jewish ceremonies there attracted many Gentiles. See JOSEPHUS, *The Jewish War*, VII: 3.3; R.E. BROWN, *An Introduction to the New Testament*, 215.

[6] It is a generally accepted opinion that Mark is the principal source of Matthew, who makes editorial modifications. R.E. Brown points out four characteristics of such an editing. The first characteristic concerns the language. Matthew's language is simpler than the Markan. He sometimes eliminates difficult phraseology and double expressions, an example of which is found in Matt 26:45. He also edits the unrecognizable place-names, for example Δαλμανουθά, «Dalmanutha» of Mark 8:10 into Μαγαδάν («Magadan» NIV, NRS, «Magdala» KJV) in Matt 15:39. Matt 26:45 drops the difficult Greek word ἀπέχει of Mark 14:41. The second characteristic concerns Matthew's omission of certain passages in Mark which could be unfavorable to the

Besides these sources Matthew also contains several OT citations followed by the formula quotation, «All this took place to fulfill what the Lord had spoken by the prophet ...». Mark also contains several OT citations. But Matthew has them more often. Matthew constantly indicates Jesus as the fulfillment of the OT promises of God. Hence Matthew heavily depends on the OT[7].

The data concerning the date (80-90 AD), place (Antioch), and sources (Mark, Q, M, and OT) of Matthew are important for our investigation on the discipleship of the women in the Gospel.

3. Important Research on the Topic

The first Christian communities were surrounded by wider Hellenistic settings on the one side[8], and an immediate Jewish setting on the other (later Judaism).

Major researches on women in antiquity have begun with a discussion on the position of women within the ancient Mediterranean cul-

---

mission of the disciples. Matthew, for example, omits Mark 8:17 where Jesus asks whether the disciples' hearts are hardened. Matthew omits Mark 8:22-26, which dramatizes the slowness of the disciples to comprehend. The third characteristic concerns Matthew's reverence for Jesus, thus avoiding what might make him appear naïve or superstitious. Matt 8:25-26 changes the chiding questions of the disciples of Mark 4:38 and eliminates Jesus' speaking to the sea. Further, in comparison to Mark, Matthew heightens the miraculous element found in Mark. For example Matthew increases Mark's 5,000 in the multiplication of the loaves by adding women and children. For more examples see R.E. BROWN, *An Introduction to the New Testament,* 204; C.S. KEENER, *A Commentary,* 41-42.

Concerning Matthew's use of certain materials proper to himself, some scholars suggest a unique Matthean source called M, which was known to Matthew alone. It is also argued that Matthew inserted his own creative thoughts and experiences.

[7] For literature on such formula citations see J.A. FITZMYER, «The Use», 297-333; R.H. GUNDRY, *The Use;* K. STENDAHL, *The School;* G.M. SOARES-PRABHU, *The Formula Quotations.*

[8] By the Hellenistic setting we mean the geographical Greco-Roman world, i.e. the territory from Greece to the Indus River that came under the sway of Alexander the Great. See M.H. CROSBY, *The House of Disciples,* 21. In the Hellenistic setting the status of women varied from place to place and from culture to culture. Due to the width of the topic and the wide geographical area that the Greco-Roman setting represented, we limit this section principally to an understanding of the status of women in «Hellenistic Judaism», while making reference to other Greco-Roman religions whenever it is pertinent.

tures: Greek, Roman and Jewish[9]. L.J. Swidler[10] was the first to popu-
larize such a pattern, later articulated by J. Jeremias[11] and then carried
forward by scholars E. Stagg and F. Stagg[12], E.M. Tetlow[13],
W.E. Moltman[14], H.C. Kee[15], W. Wink[16] and B. Witherington[17]. Major
encyclopedias within the last three decades have also followed the
same pattern[18].

The important works on the status of women in Hellenistic Judaism
could be grouped under two sections: a) the works that are centered on
women in Judaism and b) the works that are centered on women in
Greco-Roman religions of the first century.

3.1 *The Works Centered on Women in Judaism*

For much of their information concerning the first century background of women in Judaism, scholars normally depend upon biblical
texts and rabbinic material. Well known among such scholars is
J. Neusner who employs some important caveats about the use of rabbinic materials as evidence for the status and role of women in ancient
Jewish communities[19]. Scholars like S.T. Lachs, S. Fuchs, D. Goodblatt, P. Segal, E. Koltun and L. Kuzmack[20] focus their research particularly upon the attitudes towards women in the Hebrew Bible and the
rabbinic literature.

---

[9] The majority of studies on women in the religions of Greco-Roman antiquity
have their origin in the contemporary feminist movement. See D.C. BASS, «Women's
Studies», 6-12.

[10] L.J. SWIDLER, «Jesus was a Feminist», 177-183; ID., *Biblical Affirmations;*
ID., *Women in Judaism;* ID., *Yeshua,* 7-110.

[11] J. JEREMIAS, *Jerusalem,* 359-376.

[12] E. STAGG − F. STAGG, *Woman in the World of Jesus.*

[13] E.M. TETLOW, *Women and Ministry.*

[14] W.E. MOLTMAN, *Liberty, Equality, Sisterhood,* 9-21.

[15] H.C. KEE, «Changing Role of Women», 225-238.

[16] W. WINK, *Engaging the Powers,* 109-137.

[17] B. WITHERINGTON III, *Women in the Ministry of Jesus.* D. M. Scholer is the only
author who uses a different pattern of study. See D.M. SCHOLER, «Women», 880-887.

[18] See R. SCROGGS, «Woman in the New Testament», 966-968; B. WITHERINGTON
III, «Women (NT)», 957-961.

[19] According to J. Neusner only three Jewish groups in late antiquity, the Essenes,
the Temple Priests, and the Rabbis, denied women significant social, political, and
religious roles. See J. NEUSNER, «From Scripture to Mishnah», 135-148.

[20] S.T. LACHS, «The Pandora-Eve Motif», 341-145; S. FUCHS, «The Expansion»;
D. GOODBLATT, «The Beruriah Traditions», 68-85; P. SEGAL, «Elements», 226-244;
E. KOLTUN, ed., *The Jewish Women;* L. KUZMACK, «Aggadic Approaches», 248-56.

While some scholars focus their research on biblical texts and rabbinic literature, others have made use of other Jewish sources such as Jewish Apocrypha and Pseudepigrapha, Philo and Josephus, in order to understand the status of women in Hellenistic Judaism. Prominent among such scholars are L.J. Swidler[21], R.A. Baer[22], B. Brooten,[23] D. Irvin[24] and S. Cohen[25]. Swidler devotes much space to images of women in the Jewish apocrypha and pseudepigrapha, as well as in Philo and Josephus. Swidler's research ends with the observation that ancient Judaism was pervasively misogynist[26]. Baer, on the other hand, analyzes Philo's use of the categories of male and female, although he omits any discussion on the relationship between Philo's use of the categories and their correspondence to the actual social circumstances and relationships[27]. Brooten has studied the inscriptional evidence for women as leaders in Hellenistic synagogues[28], indicating that Jewish women in the Diaspora often financed the construction of public monuments. Brooten's study of the inscriptional evidence for special galleries in first century synagogues was a breakthrough in the understanding of women's status in Hellenistic Judaism[29]. She provides several instances that suggest that women were given the title of «leaders», «elders», and «mothers of synagogues»[30]. Irvin comments on the significance of these inscriptions, although she prefers to use them as possible evidence for women's leadership roles in early Christian communities[31]. Cohen's study deals with the archaeological evidence for women in ancient Synagogues[32].

---

[21] L.J. SWIDLER, *Women in Judaism*.

[22] R.A. BAER, *Philo's Use*.

[23] B.J. BROOTEN, *Women Leaders*.

[24] D. IRVIN, «The Ministry of Women», 76-86.

[25] M.S. COHEN, «Women», 23-29.

[26] L.J. SWIDLER, *Women in Judaism*.

[27] R.A. BAER, *Philo's Use*.

[28] B.J. BROOTEN, *Women Leaders*.

[29] B.J. BROOTEN, «Jewish Women's History», 25; See D.F. SAWYER, *Women and Religion*, 75.

[30] B.J. BROOTEN, «Jewish Women's History», 26. For similar views see R.S. KRAEMER, «Hellenistic Jewish Women», 183-200; ID., «Non-literary Evidence», 85-101; ID., «Monastic Jewish Women», 342-370.

[31] D. IRVIN, «The Ministry of Women», 76-86.

[32] S. COHEN, «Women», 23-29.

3.2 *The Works Centered on Women in the Greco-Roman Religions*

The feminist writer, B. Thurston distinguishes three venues for the practice of Greco-Roman religions: public religion which was observed in the forum and temples; semi-private cults which were practiced in neighborhoods and citizen gatherings; and family practiced religion in the household. In both public and household cultic celebrations, men took the primary sacerdotal duties of priest, magistrate and *paterfamilias*. The primary focus of religious life was perhaps the home, and the *paterfamilias* normally conducted the cultic activities on behalf of those who were under his authority, namely, his wife, children and slaves[33].

There were two basic categories of religion in the public sphere: the native cults that supported the status quo and were, consequently, supported by the state, and the oriental cults that were «imported». The official Roman festivals were the mainstay of religious life and were attended by the *matronae*[34]. The fundamental mythology of these festivals supported the traditional roles for women as wives and mothers under the legal authority of fathers and husbands. On the other hand the oriental religions gave women a status of equality. This may be one reason why foreign oriental religious cults were especially popular among the women[35]. Many scholars speak of the status of women in the Greco-Roman religions in relation to goddesses such as Isis[36] and

---

33 B. THURSTON, *Women in the New Testament*, 24.

34 For a list of such Roman festivals see B. THURSTON, *Women*, 24.

35 B. THURSTON, *Women*, 24.

36 Isis was originally an Egyptian deity from about 2500 BC. She had the attributes traditionally assigned to the male sky god and had dominion over storm and wind. She was considered creator, giver of language, and healer. She was the single supreme goddess with different manifestations and she promised her followers resurrection after death. In its Greco-Roman form the Isis cult emphasized death, mourning, and resurrection. Eroticism and asceticism mingled in her cult. There was neither any male dominance, nor any class stratification. This cult propagated the authority and autonomy of women. See B. THURSTON, *Women*, 27. According to Kraemer, the religion of Isis was the most favorable to women of any Roman cult. R.S. KRAEMER, *Her Share of the Blessings*; See also D.F. SAWYER, *Women*, 66.

According to Sawyer, Isis was an oriental cult imported and incorporated into Roman culture. This cult had particular associations with women in terms of both its priesthood and its popularity. Two central characters in this cult, Isis and Nephthys, were female, and women were given prominence in any ceremony that re-enacted the myth. Its central focus was the relationship between man and woman. For details on the cult of Isis and its history see D.F. SAWYER, *Women*, 66.

Demeter[37], because of the better status enjoyed by the women in these religions than in Judaism[38]. Some prominent scholars, who speak of the status of women in relation to their roles in «Isis cult» are J. Bergmann[39], L. Vidman[40], R.A. Wild[41], J.S. Kloppenberg[42], F. Dunand[43], S.A. Takács[44], E. Guimet[45], S. Heyob[46] and F. Mora[47]. Guimet considers women next to freedmen, as those most captivated by the cult of Isis.[48] Heyob, who studies exclusively women's issues, tries to prove that women «sought Isis out most eagerly to fill a need which the Greek and Roman religions failed to fill»[49]. In other words, Isis' exceptionally outstanding female and motherly characteristics attracted more women than any other female Greco-Roman deities with similar characteristics[50]. The scholars in general hold the view that women had a special attraction to the cult of Isis because of the freedom Isis offered to women, together with the other underprivileged. This attraction to the cult of Isis, according to G. Lafaye, was due to the gradual decline of «the brilliance of the Hellenic mind»[51].

---

[37] Another goddess cult of ancient Greece that belonged to the great mystery religions, and was particularly popular among women, though not exclusively so, was that of Demeter. This was celebrated mainly by Atheanians at Eleusis as well as in ancient Greek colonies such as Sicily. The importance of this cult has been thought to stem from its connections with the seasons and the crucial issue of fertility. In this the centrality of female characters reflects the obvious link between women and childbirth. For more on Demeter cult see D.F. SAWYER, *Women*, 59-61; R.S. KRAEMER, *Her Share of the Blessings*, 71.

[38] Besides the Isis and Demeter cults, there were also several other cults, in which women played important roles. Important among them were the cults of Persephone, Hecate and Dionysus.

[39] J. BERGMANN, *Ich bin Isis*.

[40] L. VIDMAN, *Isis und Sarapis*.

[41] R.A. WILD, *Water*.

[42] J.S. KLOPPENBERG, «Isis and Sophia», 57-84.

[43] F. DUNAND, *Le Culte*.

[44] S.A. TAKÁCS, *Isis and Sarapis*, 2-4.

[45] E. GUIMET, *L'Isis romaine*, 155-160.

[46] S. HEYOB, *The Cult of Isis*.

[47] F. MORA, *Prosopografia Isiaca*.

[48] E. GUIMET, *L'Isis romaine*, 155-160.

[49] S. HEYOB, *The Cult of Isis among Women*, 80.

[50] However, examining the epigraphical material related to the cult of Isis, Heyob notes that women did not form the majority of the cult's participants. S. HEYOB, *The Cult*, 81.

[51] This notion was first introduced by G. LAFAYE, *Histoire du culte*. ID., «L'introduction», 327-329. A similar notion is supported by Burkert who sug-

While referring to the cult of Isis and its impact on the underprivileged in contemporary society, Takács comments:

> Just like the Bacchanalia, Isis stirred the fancy of the underprivileged, those who lacked the prized Hellenic mind, which seems to stand for the ability to check emotions and possible insecurities. Consequently the underprivileged had to be guided by those who possessed this ability[52].

This nature of Isis in a way eased the spread of Christianity, as it also contained elements that provided men and women, the just and the sinners with equal opportunities. On this Takács comments:

> The pagan salvation religion of Isis had unwillingly prepared the population of the *imperium romanum* for the coming of the true *soter* and made the rapid spread of Christianity possible. ... in the end, however, the goddess could not rival Jesus Christ because the religion he had inspired soon developed a strong central organization, a systematic theology, and an acceptable monotheism[53].

While the cult of Isis and women's participation in it have received much scholarly attention, a number of scholars discuss the status of women in the Greco-Roman religions in relation to the «cult of Demeter». Prominent among them are G.E. Mylonas[54], K. Kerényi[55], A.C. Brumfield[56], J. Engelsman[57] and G. Zuntz[58]. These studies in general show that women participated actively in the Greco-Roman religions.

Besides the research centered particularly on Isis and Demeter, studies undertaken by S.B. Pomeroy, H. Temporini, B. Lincoln, R.S. Kraemer, S.G. Cole, J. Dubisch, J.H. Neyrey, V. Burrus, K.E. Corley and B.J. Malina have contributed to the understanding of the status of women in the contemporary Greco-Roman Religions. Pomeroy[59] discusses the general roles of women in Roman religions, while

---

gests that there is a belief that mystery cults were 1) «typical of late antiquity (...)» when the brilliance of the Hellenic mind was giving way to the irrational», 2) «oriental in origin, style, and spirit», and 3) «indicative of a basic change in religious attitude, one that transcends the realistic and practical outlook of the pagan in search of higher spirituality». See W. BURKERT, *Ancient Mystery Cults*, 2-3.

[52] S.A. TAKÁCS, *Isis and Sarapis*, 2.

[53] S.A. TAKÁCS, *Isis and Sarapis*, 2.

[54] G.E. MYLONAS, *Eleusis*.

[55] K. KERÉNYI, *Eleusis*.

[56] A.C. BRUMFIELD, *The Attic Festivals*.

[57] J. ENGELSMAN, *The Feminine Dimension of the Divine*.

[58] G. ZUNTZ, *Persephone*.

[59] S.B. POMEROY, *Goddesses*.

Temporini[60] speaks of the cultic roles and titles of imperial women in the second century. Scholars like Lincoln[61], Kraemer[62] and Cole[63] discuss other various aspects of women's activities in ancient religions. About women in the first century Mediterranean culture, Dubisch reports that a woman's world was centered on her household, and her roles were limited to domestic jobs such as cooking, cleaning, spinning, and looking after children[64]. As Burrus makes clear in her study of the Apocryphal Acts, women could «offend their societies by transgressing the boundaries of the woman's sphere»[65]. To engage oneself in activities outside the household realm was looked on with suspicion. In her study of women in the context of Greco-Roman meals, K.E. Corley has established that the increasing number of Roman women who accompanied their husbands to banquets, would be viewed by some as undermining the «gender and class-based hierarchy of Greco-Roman society, as well as the gender based division of that society into "public" and "private" categories»[66]. For Corley, Greek women who attended banquets were usually associated with prostitution[67]. The fact that the role of women was often limited to their domestic tasks does not mean they wielded no power. Women exercised a great deal of informal power in the family[68].

The works that are centered on women in the Greco-Roman religions point to the fact that the women, despite having enjoyed much religious freedom as expressed in the cults of the goddesses Isis and Demeter, highlight the fact that their sphere of activity was principally relegated to domestic affairs, indicating a certain level of inferiority.

3.3 *Non-literary Sources*

We have seen that for an understanding of the status of women in Judaism, the authors normally make use of literary sources such as biblical texts, rabbinic literature, the writings of Philo and Josephus. In this line, R.S. Kraemer's investigation of the topic finds a new horizon.

---

[60] H. TEMPORINI, *Die Frauen am Hofe Trajans.*
[61] B. LINCOLN, «The Rape», 223-235.
[62] R.S. KRAEMER, «Ecstasy and Possession», 55-80.
[63] S.G. COLE, «New Evidence for the Mysteries of Dionysus», 223-238.
[64] J. DUBISCH, «Culture», 195-214.
[65] V. BURRUS, *Chastity as Autonomy,* 23.
[66] K.E. CORLEY, *Private Women,* 23.
[67] K.E. CORLEY, *Private Women,* 63.
[68] B.J. MALINA, *The New Testament World,* 44.

Kraemer[69] makes use of non-literary sources such as inscriptions and papyrus documents, which have generally been neglected by scholars of ancient Judaism and Christianity. In her study she brings forth two important points. First, contrary to the common assumption of the scholars of this period, there is significant evidence about women in Hellenistic Judaism. Second, the evidence enables us not only to correct the image of women in early Judaism, but also to see in a clearer light the rich diversity of Judaism in antiquity. She comes to the conclusion that contrary to what we find in the Hellenistic writings of Philo, women in the non-literary sources (papyri) are not secluded. They are active participants in the economic and social life of their communities.

We have seen, by means of a brief analysis of selected literature on women, that different researchers focused on various aspects of the issue. In spite of some of the important social and religious roles that women played, scholars are unanimous about the social as well as religious inferiority that women faced in their Greco-Roman religions and in Hellenistic Judaism, an inferiority that often segregated them to the domestic spheres. With this information we move to a closer understanding of the status of women, especially their social and religious status, in Hellenistic Judaism, the immediate context for first century Christianity.

4. The Social and Religious Status of Women in Hellenistic Judaism

For information concerning the behavior pattern of women in Hellenistic Judaism (300 BC – 200 AD)[70], together with the majority of scholars, we rely upon literary sources such as Jewish biblical texts which date, in the main, from the fifth to the second century BC, that is before the Roman pre-eminence, and then rabbinic literature dating from 200-600 AD, with the Talmudim being edited at the end of that time span. Further we make use of materials from Philo of Alexandria and Josephus although their works are apologetic in nature, and although they do not provide us with much information that usefully and

---

69 R.S. KRAEMER, «Non-literary Evidence», 85-101; See also D.M. SCHOLER, «Women», 881.

70 Whenever it is necessary and helpful to comprehend the Jewish women's status, we will also refer to the status of women in other Mediterranean cultures such as the Roman, Egyptian, and Greek which serve as a wider context for the Palestine of Jesus' time.

directly furnishes us with knowledge of the roles of women in Judaism[71].

In order to gain a complete appreciation of their roles in Hellenistic Judaism, however, we must first briefly trace the history of their involvement in the centuries that preceded the period under consideration. Naturally we start with a discussion on the status of women in the OT.

4.1 The Status of Women in the OT

The Role and status of women in ancient Israel varied considerably between different periods and in different social circles, evidence of which is found in various literary genres such as OT laws[72], Proverbs[73] and Historical writings[74]. From the earlier strands of the OT, it is evident that women in the pre-exilic period of Hebrew history (before 587 BC) enjoyed a certain active involvement in the social and religious

---

[71] For various reasons we cannot say that these works give us an exact vision concerning women in first century Judaism: First the Talmud, though it records much material concerning women from early times, was completed only in the fifth century AD. Secondly, the works of Philo and Josephus give only the authors' personal views of women, which do not necessarily give indications of the lifestyle of ordinary people. Still the Mishnah, Talmud, Philo and Josephus are reliable sources that provide us with a background for women in first century Judaism. See M.J. EVANS, *Woman in the Bible*, 33.

[72] According to the OT laws, women were legally dependent upon men: «... you shall not covet your neighbor's wife» (Exod 20:17); «you shall not afflict any widow or orphan. If you do ... your wives shall become widows and your children fatherless» (Exod 22:22-24); «you shall be men consecrated to me ...» (Exod 22:31).

[73] Proverbs describes a woman as either a mother who instructs and nurtures (1:8; 6:20), or a wife who looks after her husband's interests (12:4; 19:14; 11:16), or an adulteress who endangers a man's status and life (2:16; 5:3; cf. 7:22; 9:18; 21:19; 22:14.)

[74] Historical writings amplify greatly the picture of women obtained from the laws and proverbs. They picture women as mothers and wives who are adjuncts of men (Jehosheba, 2Kgs 11:2; Rahab, Josh 2:1-21). They also appear as harlots (1Kgs 3), prophetesses (Deborah, Jdg 4:4-16; Hulda, 2Kgs 22:14-20 and Noadiah, Neh 6:14), temple cult singers (Ezra 2:65; Neh 7:67; 2Chr 25:5), mediums or sorceresses (1Sam 28:7; Exod 22:18), wise women (2Sam 14:2; 20:16), professional mourners or «keening women» (Jer 9:17), midwives (Gen 35:17; 38:28), nurses (Ruth 4:16; 2Sam 4:4; Gen 24:59; Exod 2:7; 2Kgs 11:2) and household servants of kings (1Sam 8:13).
The creation stories recognize a general equality of the sexes which rises above the average women's actual place in ancient Israel (a helper fit for man, Gen 2:18; one with man, Gen 2:23). See P.A. BIRD, «Images», 252.

affairs of society, whereas in the post-exilic period (500-400 BC)[75] they were mostly relegated to an inferior position.

It is a generally held opinion that the OT is predominantly patriarchal[76] and androcentric[77] in nature[78]. One example would be the desire for male children. There are numerous passages that depict the desire for the birth of a male child and the joy brought at the birth of a boy (Gen 4:1; 17:15-16; 30:1-24). Male children were considered blessings from above and only the names of males were enrolled in the OT genealogical list[79]. Two examples help us to comprehend the patriarchal and androcentric nature of the OT.

The first example that illustrates the type of extreme action that could be taken to ensure the continuity of the male line is that of Lot's daughters. Being without any male in company other than their father, they conspire to get him drunk and have sexual relations with him in order to «preserve offspring through our father» (Gen 19:32). The result of these illicit relationships is that both the daughters conceive and both bear sons. Now it is assumed that the reader will understand that the daughters themselves do not count as offsprings. That is to say, only a son could ensure the line of the father.

The second example concerns the post-birth purification regulations. If a woman gives birth to a son she is assumed to be as unclean as she would be at the time of her menstruation for seven days, and then for a further thirty-three days she is restricted from coming into contact with any sort of cult in the temple. If the child is a girl then the period of uncleanness is doubled[80].

---

[75] See M. NOTH, *The Laws*, 8.

[76] By patriarchal we mean normatively ruled by men.

[77] By androcentric we mean normatively male-focused.

[78] See P. MULLINS, «The Public, Secular Roles of Women», 79-111.

[79] Jewish thinkers of the Greco-Roman period similarly reflect this obsession for the birth of sons rather than daughters. According to Philo of Alexandria, the virtue of a good midwife lay specifically in «bringing out the males to birth» (*Legum Allegoria*, 3.3 on the basis of Exod 1:17-21). Josephus witnesses to the Judaean belief that a woman mistakenly suspected of adultery, having undergone the trial of bitter waters (Num 5:14ff), would bear a son ten months after her ordeal as a compensation to her suffering (*Jewish Antiquities*, III: 271). Rabbinic literature also follows the same thought line as the OT and various Jewish writers. According to the traditional school of Shimmai the command to «be fruitful and multiply» (Gen 1:28), was fulfilled once two sons had been sired; there is no mention of daughters in this school (Yev 5:14ff).

[80] See D.F. SAWYER, *Women*, 38.

In spite of its patriarchal and androcentric nature there are numerous biblical passages that view women positively and assign them an important status in society and in religion. The stories of great female figures such as Sarah and Haggar, Rebekkah and Rachel in the history of the Patriarchs (Gen 12:1-23:20; 16:1-16; 21:1-21; 24:15-27:46) picture a closeness and equality of women with men. Both Zipporah and Miriam were close associates of Moses in his early career (Exod 2:16-22; 4:24-31; 18:1-12; Num 12:1-16; 20:1). The occupation and settlement in Canaan was facilitated by the co-operation of women such as Tamar (Gen 38:1-30), Rahab (Josh 2:1-34; 6:22-25) and Dinah (Gen 34:1-31). The OT also presents the stories of Naomi and Ruth (Ruth 1-4) and the trustful acceptance of God's will by Hannah, the mother of Samuel (1Sam 1:1-2:27). Later we find the personal and political involvement of Bathsheba in the establishment of the Davidic monarchy (2Sam 11:1-12:25; 1Kgs 1:11-2:27) and also the treacherous plots of Queens Jezebel (1Kgs 16:29-21:29) and Athaliah (2Kgs 8:26). In subsequent years, whole books were dedicated to the accomplishments of women like Esther and Judith, women who were truly saviors of the Jewish people (Esth 1:1-10:3).

These examples suggest that women's liberties were greater and that they had a respected and commanding social position in ancient Israel. Moreover, the laws and customs of the time confirm this. Divine Law commanded that children respect both the father and the mother (Exod 20:13). Men and women could associate freely in various religious activities. For example men and women feasted together without restriction, shared sacred meals and the great annual feast (Deut 16:11-14). Women, alongside men, could appear at public assemblies and the exposition of the laws (see Exod 35:1f; Deut 29:9f; 31:12-13) and participate fully in the annual cycle of festivals (1Sam 2:19; 2Kgs 23:21; 2Chr 35), often in the role of singers and dancers (Exod 15:20-21; Judg 21:21; Jer 31:4; Psa 68:12, 26-27). They are featured as prophetesses (Judg 4:4ff; 2Sam 20:16) and as persons who generally have a special association with the holy men (Judg 13:6 ff; 2Kgs 4:23f), and are seen in different cultic capacities (Gen 38:8; 1Sam 2:22; Hos 4:13-14)[81].

Women are also depicted as pastors alongside their male counterparts. Elena Bosetti, making use of the pastoral symbolism of the OT,

---

[81] On women's involvement in public affairs see M.C. ASTOUR, «Tamar the Hierodule» 185-196; B.A. BROOKS, «Fertility», 227-253; I.J. PERITZ, «Women», 111-147.

describes both men and women in pastoral imagery. She presents three couples such as Jacob and Rachel, Moses and Miriam and David and Abigail as examples of pastoral imagery in the Bible. The first and the third couples are husband and wife, while the second are brother and sister. All three couples are presented as pastoral imageries[82].

These examples suggest that there existed a certain basic equality between men and women. They cooperated with each other in their day-to-day lives. God used both men and women as the instruments of salvation. J. Neusner, B. Witherington, L.J. Archer and J.B. Segal hold the view that centralized worship at the temple in Jerusalem brought with it several ritual regulations which were not favorable to the women of the time. Affairs connected with the temple were regarded as the sole responsibility of an organized, hereditary male priesthood, dedicated to the service of Yahweh[83]. According to L.J. Archer, the destruction of the Jerusalem Temple in 587 and the Babylonian exile further strengthened the monotheistic attitude. The tragedy was interpreted as the wrath of God and the final proof of the absolute power of Yahweh[84]. Monotheism was rigorously re-affirmed. Importance was given to the peculiar relation which existed between God and His chosen people[85]. In the people's relationship with Yahweh, a ritual purity on both the individual and the communal level became rigorously affirmed[86]. This overemphasis on ritual cleanness sometimes kept the women away from the sanctuary mainly because of the impurity associated with the menstrual cycle and childbirth (Lev 12:2f). Women's restrictions in regard to place and function in the temple are closely associated with the regulations prescribed in Lev 15:19-25[87]:

---

[82] E. BOSETTI, Yahweh, 17.

[83] For various developments in this regard see J. B. SEGAL, «The Jewish Attitude Towards Women», 121-137.

[84] See L.J. ARCHER, «The Role», 275.

[85] We come across these ideas especially in the writings of Deutero-Isaiah (Isa 34-35, 40-45). See J. BRIGHT, A History of Israel, 323-355.

[86] This is because holiness was considered as closely associated with ritual purity. For details see J. NEUSNER, The Idea.

[87] A woman's uncleanness exempted her from those positive ordinances of the Law which were periodic in nature, such as certain feasts, daily appearance in the synagogue to make a quorum and periodical prayers. The same regulations are found in the Mishnah 1.7: «The observance of all ordinances that depend on the time of year is incumbent on men but not on women, and the observance of all positive ordinances that do not depend on the time of year is incumbent both on men and women». B. WITHERINGTON, Women in the Ministry of Jesus, 8.

> When a woman has a discharge of blood that is her regular discharge from her body, she shall be in her impurity for seven days, and whoever touches her shall be unclean until the evening. [20]Everything upon which she lies during her impurity shall be unclean; everything also upon which she sits shall be unclean. [21]Whoever touches her bed shall wash his clothes, and bathe in water, and be unclean until the evening. [22]Whoever touches anything upon which she sits shall wash his clothes, and bathe in water, and be unclean until the evening; [23]whether it is the bed or anything upon which she sits, when he touches it he shall be unclean until the evening. [24]If any man lies with her, and her impurity falls on him, he shall be unclean seven days; and every bed on which he lies shall be unclean. [25]If a woman has a discharge of blood for many days, not at the time of her impurity, or if she has a discharge beyond the time of her impurity, all the days of the discharge she shall continue in uncleanness; as in the days of her impurity, she shall be unclean.

According to some authors, the basic regulations for the menstruant were annotated and interpreted down the centuries, an interpretation that practically divided the community on the basis of gender, segregating women from major religious roles, thus enforcing the male superiority[88]. We do not fully agree with this opinion. It is true that certain religious regulations restricted the women's role in the community. At the same time we have scriptural evidence that similar laws were applicable to men also. Accordingly, a man who has a discharge is also considered unclean (Lev 16-18). However, we can perhaps say that in comparison to women, men enjoyed more freedom.

Another factor that is believed to have kept women inferior to men was the familial structure, which gave rise to a differentiation between male and female social functions. According to L.J. Archer, in the post-exilic Israelite society «the older system of the extended patriarchal family gave way to the nuclear family»[89]. For him, this move towards a nuclear structured family developed an increasing rigidity in attitude towards women and a definition of function within the family group. Here a woman's status in the family was placed firmly in the private sphere of activity as wife, mother and homemaker. On the other side, men were placed in the public sphere as workers and as active participants in social, political and religious affairs (Prov 31:10ff).

---

[88] For contemporary discussion on the menstrual taboo in Israelite and Jewish society see B. GREENBERG, «Female Sexuality», 36.

[89] L.J. ARCHER, «The Role», 276.

These two post-exilic developments, that is, the concentration upon ritual purity and the sharp differentiation between male and female social functions, gradually excluded women from nearly all expressions of public piety[90].

By the Hellenistic period (300 BC- 100 AD) Yahweh's rule was firmly established and the Torah dominated the lives of the Jewish people. To cite an example, *Makkot* 23b describes the laws of Yahweh like this: «Six hundred and thirteen precepts were given to Moses–three hundred and sixty five of them are negative commandments, like the number of days of the solar year, and two hundred and forty eight are positive commandments corresponding to the parts of the human body». Although both men and women were called to observe the God-given laws, the rabbis of the period declared women exempt from nearly all the positive precepts whose fulfillment depended upon the specific time of the day or of the year[91]. Accordingly, women were exempted from the yearly pilgrimage to Jerusalem at the feasts of Passover, Pentecost, and Tabernacles[92]; from living in the ceremonial booths which were erected at the feast of Tabernacles[93]; from shaking the Lulab[94]; from sounding the Shofar at the new year[95]; reading the Megillah at Purim[96]; and from making the daily affirmation of faith[97].

---

[90] LJ. ARCHER, «The Role», 277.

[91] Qid 1:7.

[92] Hag 1:1.

[93] Suk 2:8.

[94] t. Qid 1:10.

[95] t. RHSh 4:1.

[96] t. Meg 2:7.

[97] The Mishnah in Ber 3:3 cites three types of prayers: reciting the Shema, prayer for divine mercy and reciting the grace after meals. Women were exempted from the first form, reciting the Shema, which begins with «Hear O Israel the Lord our God is One...» (Deut 6:4-9; 11:13-21 and Num 15:37-41). Women were exempted from this prayer since it is a time bound *mitzvah*. See R. BIALE, *Women and Jewish Law,* 18.

Although women were exempted from the first form, they were subject to obligations of the prayer of grace after meals (Deut 8:10, «You shall eat your fill and bless the LORD your God for the good land that he has given you»). Women were obliged to recite this prayer, since it is a thanksgiving over the food which they too eat, and because it is not time bound.

While Shema and «grace after meals» are specific, defined prayers, the prayer for divine mercy addressed in the Mishnah is non-specific. It is a prayer in general. For a model of supplicate prayer see 1Sam 2; t. Ber 31a.

Besides these, women were also exempted[98] from the reading[99] and study of the Torah[100], something central to the entire religious system of Israel[101]. This exemption kept the women ignorant of the Torah, a factor that prevented them from having the possibility of giving expression to their unique piety. Again the prominent reason for this exemption, as we saw above, was associated with the menstrual impurity and the practical consideration of women's secluded domestic roles in society[102].

4.2 *Status of Women in Hellenistic Judaism*

Having discussed the OT view of women we now investigate the social-religious status of women in Judaism, with special reference to the first century context. Judaism, as a distinct culture and society in the ancient world, had its own perceptions and practices concerning

---

[98] For women's exemption see Qid 29b; cf. Naz 29a; Er 27a. See R. BIALE, *Women and Jewish Law*, 18.

[99] There exists a dispute over the issue of women reading the Torah. The biblical commandment to assemble the whole people to hear and learn the Torah explicitly includes women (Deut 31:9-12). Many rabbis argue that the reading of the Torah is analogous to the study of the Torah, since both are ways of fulfilling the commandment, «Recite them to your children and talk about them when you are at home and when you are away, when you lie down and when you rise» (Deut 6:7). The *mitzvah* of studying the Torah applies only to men. Thus if the reading of the Torah is part of the *mitzvah* of the study of the law, women are exempt from this. According to m. Sot 20a, women are barred from the study of the Torah. See R. BIALE, *Women and Jewish Law*, 18.

In spite of the manifold restrictions, there were women well versed in the Torah. The most celebrated case is that of Beruriah, the wife of Rabbi Meir. She was the disciple of Rabbi Akiba, who studied Torah, and claimed to be a scholar in her own right. For an analysis of this female Torah scholar, see A. GOLDFELD, «Women as Sources of Torah». See also R. RUETHER – E. MCLAUGHLIN, ed., *Women of Spirit*. D.F. SAWYER, *Women and Religion*, 86.

[100] This exemption does not imply that women were not required to know the law. Since women were bound by most of the laws they were obliged to know them too. What is meant here is that they were not obliged to engage themselves in the study of the Torah as an end in its own right, whether as a form of worship or as a professional pursuit. See R. BIALE, *Women and Jewish Law*, 18.

[101] On the importance of education in the lives of Jewish people see b. Ber 47b, I. EPSTEIN, *The Babylonian Talmud, Zera'imim* I, 286-90; m. Qid 1:10, H. DANBY, *The Mishnah*, 323.

[102] L.J. ARCHER, «The Role», 277; See R. BIALE, *Women and Jewish Law*, 13; S. BERMAN, «The Status», 114-128.

women. The Torah was considered the corner-stone of Judaism[103]. Besides the information found in the Torah, we get much of the contemporary attitudes concerning women from rabbinic literature, Josephus and Philo. For much of the information concerning the status of women, we rely on rabbinic literature, which could be divided into two main categories: Talmud and Midrash[104]. The basis of the Talmud is the Mishnah, the collected sayings of rabbis compiled in AD 200[105]. The Mishnah is divided into six divisions (*Sedarim*), each of which is sub-divided into a number of Tractates, 63 in all. What catches our special attention is the third division, which is called *Nashim* (women). This division consists of 7 *Tractates*. They are *Yevamoth* (Sisters-in-law), *Ketubboth* (Marriage Deeds), *Nedarim* (Vows), *Nazir* (The Nazirite-Vow), *Sotah* (The Suspected Adultress), *Gittin* (Bills of Divorce) *and Qiddushin* (Betrothals). These texts communicate interesting information concerning women's social and religious status in the Hellenistic period.

4.2.1 Social Status

A woman's importance in social matters was confined to her connection to the family, almost the exclusive sphere of influence for Jewish women in the Hellenistic period, especially in the first century AD. This was partly due to the Jewish marital customs of the day, according to which a woman remained the property of a man. As a result the father as well as the husband had extraordinary *patria potestas* over the woman. Naturally the laws concerning inheritance, betrothal and divorce were heavily male biased and therefore a woman was often entitled only to maintenance rather than inheritance[106]. According to R. Ishamel, a woman's unworthiness to inherit the property was due to her poverty[107]. As a minor she did not have any right to own even her own possessions, while the fruit of her labor was considered the prop-

---

[103] D.F. SAWYER, *Women and Religion*, 33.

[104] For details on the Talmud and Midrash see H.L. STRACK – G. STEMBERGER, *Introduction to the Talmud and Midrash*.

[105] See R.T. FRANCE, ed., *A Bibliographical Guide,* 43. Further materials of the same period make up the Tosephta, compiled slightly later, with the same arrangement of Orders and Tractates. For a standard edition see M.S. ZUCKERMANDEL, *Tosephta.*

[106] m. Ket 4.1-12.

[107] m. Ned 9.10.

erty of the father[108]. When she was violated, the compensation money
was not paid to her, but to the father[109]. Her marriage was arranged by
the father, which she could not refuse if she was underage, although she
had an occasion to express her desire to remain home until puberty[110].

A wife, like a Gentile slave could be obtained through sexual inter-
course, money, or writ[111]. It was normal that the wife be paid *ketubbah*
even when the husband went into debt[112]. But this was not as strict as it
might have been since a woman could be put away without her *ketubah*
on certain grounds[113]. The laws concerning divorce were similarly male
biased as the husband could divorce his wife if she caused an «impedi-
ment» to the marriage, but not vice versa.

In spite of the numerous negative views concerning the position of
women in first century Judaism, there exist also a number of positive
comments concerning women's status. On several occasions rabbinic
literature reiterates the OT maxim (Exod 20:12; Lev 19:3) that the
mother is to be honored equally with the father[114]. The Mishnah teaches
that both parents are to be revered equally as God is revered[115], while
the Talmud instructs a man to love his wife as himself and to respect
her more than himself[116]. Domestic jobs such as grinding flour, baking
bread, washing clothes, breast-feeding the children, making the bed,
working in wool[117], preparing food for the husband, washing his face,
feet and hands were assigned to women[118]. The divine commandment
to be fruitful and multiply was extended equally to man and woman,

---

[108] m. Ket 4.4.

[109] m. Ket 4.1.

[110] According to the investigation undertaken by Y. Yadin, an Israelite woman had
the right to inherit and keep property, although this does not seem to be a general
view. Y. YADIN, «Expedition D − the Cave Letters», 235.

[111] m. Qid 1.1, see H. DANBY, *The Mishnah*, 321.

[112] m. Ned 9.5, see H. DANBY, *The Mishnah*, 276.

[113] m. Ket 7.6, and see H. DANBY, *The Mishnah*, 255, on loss of *ketubah* due to
violation of rabbinic law or tradition. M. Sot 4.3 says that a barren, sterile, or old
woman does not receive her *ketubah* upon divorce. See H. DANBY, *The Mishnah*,
297-298.

[114] See m. Ned 9.1, see H. DANBY, *The Mishnah*, 275.

[115] m. Ker 6.9, see H. DANBY 572-73.

[116] b. Yeb 62b, see I. EPSTEIN, *The Babylonian Talmud*, 419.

[117] m. Ket 5.5, H. DANBY, *The Mishnah*, 252; m. Git 7.6, H. DANBY, *The Mishnah*,
316.

[118] b. Ket 4b, 61a, see I. EPSTEIN, *The Babylonian Talmud*, 364-65.

although it was not the majority opinion. Normally we see that this commandment was required of men only[119].

A husband's duties were also equally extensive. It was the obligation of the husband to feed his wife[120], and take care of her material needs[121] such as clothing, redeeming her from captivity and providing her with shelter. A woman had the right to sexual pleasure[122]. According to the School of Hillel a man was not said to have been fulfilled Gen 1:28, until he had both a son and a daughter. The School of Shammai said that two sons would fulfill one's duty[123]. Rabbi Hisda's opinion is significant: «To me however daughters are dearer than sons»[124].

There were occasions when a woman could divorce her husband. R. Yaron gives evidence that even in Palestine a woman could occasionally divorce her husband[125], although a husband could divorce his wife even for a very small reason. According to the Mishnah, for reasons such as impotence, failure to consummate the marriage, his unpleasant occupation, his inability to provide for her or if they were separated for a long period of time, a woman could sue for divorce in the courts[126].

In spite of all the regulations concerning divorce, rabbis like Johannan and Eliezer constantly discourage divorce. R. Johannan interprets Mal 2.16 to mean that «the man who divorces his wife is hateful to God». According to R. Eliezer, the altar sheds tears over the one who divorces his wife[127].

Discouraging the practice of divorce, the Mishnah reports that for a man to divorce his wife was to dishonor her and the children, and to disgrace his own character[128]. Other than these rabbinical interpretations there were also legal impediments concerning the divorce of a

---

[119] m.Yeb 6.6, see H. DANBY, *The Mishnah*, 227; b. Yeb 65b, see I. EPSTEIN, *The Babylonian Talmud*, 436.

[120] m. Git 1.6, see H. DANBY, *The Mishnah*, 307-8.

[121] b. Ket 77a, 107a, see I. EPSTEIN, *The Babylonian Talmud*, 685-86.

[122] m. Ket 5.6, see H. DANBY, *The Mishnah*, 252.

[123] m.Yeb 6.6, see H. DANBY, *The Mishnah*, 227.

[124] b. Babba Bathra, 141a; See I. EPSTEIN, *The Babylonian Talmud*, 599-600.

[125] R. YARON, «Aramaic Marriage», 66-70.

[126] M. Ned 11.12 and M. Ket 5.5, 7.2-5 and 7.9-10, see H. DANBY, *The Mishnah*, 252, 254, 280.

[127] b. Git 90b, see I. EPSTEIN, *The Babylonian Talmud*, 439.

[128] m. Ned 9.9, see H. DANBY, *The Mishnah*, 277.

woman by her husband, which in a way protected women[129]. The Jewish law never allowed a husband to take the life of the wife even when she was an adulteress[130].

a) *Educational Status*

Concerning women's learning and the teaching of the Torah there are contradictory opinions in the rabbinical literature[131]. Some rabbis encouraged the minimal education of their daughters[132] while others rejected such a notion[133]. For some others women deserved no education[134], while their merit consisted in waiting for the husbands until they returned from the school of the Rabbis. Their education was limited to the learning of some domestic arts, because they were not capable of much more than this[135]. There were laws that taught that a woman should not be teaching her children[136], while in m. Sota 7.4 we are told that a woman was not expected to know the holy language[137]. Commenting on the women's right to study the Torah, R. Eliezer says, «If any man gives his daughter a knowledge of the law it is as though he taught her lechery»[138]. This view is confirmed by Sot 19a, which says, «Let the words of Torah be destroyed by fire rather than imparted to woman»[139]. Some Jewish scholars call it a minority opinion support

---

[129] A man whose wife had lost her mental capacity after they had been married was not allowed to divorce her, for it was feared that she could not ward off illicit advances. m. Yeb 14.1, see H. DANBY, *The Mishnah*, 240.

[130] See B. COHEN, «Concerning Divorce», 3-24.

[131] For a comprehensive review of the Halakhah and attitudes toward teaching women, and a strong orthodox advocacy of institutionalized Jewish education for girls, see RABBI TECHORESH, «Regarding the Education of Girls», 77-81. See also A. SILVER, «May Women», 74-85.

[132] m. Ned 4:3.

[133] m. Sot 3:4; H. DANBY, *The Mishnah*, 296.

[134] b. Ber 61a, see I. EPSTEIN, *The Babylonian Talmud, Zera'im,* I, 380-84.

[135] b. Ket 59b, see I. EPSTEIN, *The Babylonian Talmud, Nashim* III, 353.

[136] m. Kid 4.13 See H. DANBY, *The Mishnah*, 329.

[137] See H. DANBY, *The Mishnah*, 300.

[138] m. Sota 3.4, H. DANBY, *The Mishnah*, 296; According to H. FREEDMAN, R. Eliezer's statement probably refers to advanced Talmudic education only, because women had to have some instruction in the Torah to say their prayers properly. See H. FREEDMAN, «Nashim VIII», in I. EPSTEIN, ed., *Babylonian Talmud,* 141.1. The women had to recite *Tefillah,* the eighteen benedictions, and the table blessings. Against this background, it is unlikely that the women remained totally ignorant of the Law.

[139] A. COHEN, *Everyman's Talmud,* 189.

for which is found in the Mishnah in which Rabbi Azzai says, «A man ought to give his daughter a knowledge of the Law»[140]. There are also passages in the Mishnah which read that a man may «give his daughter knowledge of the Law» and «teach scripture» to the sons and daughters of others[141]. In the Babylonian Talmud Megillah 23a, women were qualified among the seven who read the Torah in the synagogue[142].

b) *Legal Status*

We get much information concerning the legal status of a minor girl from the Mishnah. A girl was considered to be minor till she passed from her father's house. Her legal position was extremely restricted with regard to inheritance as she was basically entitled only to maintenance and divorce. The Mishnah, despite having stated that a girl obtained independence at the age of twelve and half years, declares elsewhere that a daughter «continues within the control of the father until she enters into the control of the husband at marriage»[143].

It was the general opinion that the testimony borne by a woman in court bore little weight[144]. Some Jewish teachers accepted her testimony as valid, but others suspected it[145]. As regards the acceptance of the testimony of a woman, she was compared to the position of a Gentile slave. A woman's testimony could not be accepted because she was by nature a liar[146]. According to m. Yev 16.5, 7[147] and m. Ket 1.6[148] a woman's testimony concerning a death and her own virginity is to be accepted. The Mishnah in Ned 11.10 lists nine cases where a woman's vows are valid[149]. The Mishnah in Sot 9.8 lists a number cases when a

---

140 m. Sot 3.4, see H. DANBY, *The Mishnah*, 296.

141 m. Sot 3. 4, see H. DANBY, *The Mishnah*, 296; m. Ned 4.3, see H. DANBY, *The Mishnah*, 269.

142 Some modern scholars hold the view that women were familiar with the basic principles of the law (Prov 1:8; 6:20) and would have passed these on to their children but normally they were excluded from the technical and academic issues involved. P. MULLINS, «The Public, Secular Roles of Women», 107.

143 m. Ket 4.5.; See H. DANBY, *The Mishnah*, 250.

144 «An oath of testimony applies to men but not to women ...». m. Shevu 4.1, See H. DANBY, *The Mishnah*, 412; m. Yev 16.7, see H. DANBY, *The Mishnah*, 244-245.

145 m. Ned 11.10, see H. DANBY, *The Mishnah*, 280.

146 See J. JEREMIAS, *Jerusalem*, 372.

147 See H. DANBY, *The Mishnah*, 244.

148 H. DANBY, *The Mishnah*, 246.

149 H. DANBY, *The Mishnah*, 280.

woman's witness is equal to that of a man. Accordingly she could give a valid testimony[150], although she is not officially counted as a witness[151].

Josephus and Philo rejected the testimony borne by a woman. According to Josephus: «From women let no evidence be accepted because of the levity and temerity of their sex»[152].

4.2.2 Religious Status

The religious status that women enjoyed in Hellenistic Judaism could be understood in relationship with the four different roles they played in the Temple, Synagogue, at home and in the burial rituals.

a) *Women's Role in the Temple of Jerusalem*

Archeological, textual and inscriptional evidences suggest that within the temple precincts there existed a court of Gentiles, a court of women, a court of Israelites, a court of priests, the Holy Place and finally the Holy of Holies[153]. The women's access was limited to the court of women, and not to the court of Israelites to which men had access[154]. Maybe its purpose was to restrict women from active involvement in the temple rituals.

As regards their role, L. Archer notes that if women accompanied their men folk to the temple when the latter were fulfilling the command to appear before the Lord, then their role was one of a passive onlooker rather than an active participant, because they were not allowed to enter the inner precincts of the temple where the sacrifice was

---

[150] B. Witherington, listing evidence from Mishnah, suggests that «in practice her word was accepted even in some doubtful case». B. WITHERINGTON, *The women in the Ministry of Jesus,* 9; Jeremias on the other hand presents a contrary view that a woman's word was accepted only in rare cases. J. JEREMIAS, *Jerusalem,* 375.

[151] m. Sot 9.8, see H. DANBY, *The Mishnah,* 304; m. Sot 6.4, see H. DANBY, *The Mishnah,* 299-300.

[152] JOSEPHUS, *Jewish Antiquities,* IV: 219.

[153] For a full description of the temple precincts see JOSEPHUS, *The Jewish War,* V.

[154] Several authors hold the view that the temple of Jerusalem before 4 BC did not segregate women from men. According to Grossman and Corley the «Women's Court» in the Jerusalem Temple was an innovation of Herod's restoration. See K.E. CORLEY, «The Egalitarian Jesus», 291-315; S. GROSSMAN, «Women», 15-37.

In the so-called «women's court» women could have mixed freely with men. See S. GROSSMAN, «Women», 19; R.S. KRAEMER, *Her Share,* 95. T. ILAN, *Jewish Women,* 179-81.

conducted[155]. Commenting on women's access to the temple of Jerusalem Josephus writes:

> All who ever saw our Temple are aware of the general design of the building and the inviolable barriers which preserve its sanctity. It had four surrounding courts, each with its special statutory restrictions. The outer court was open to all, foreigners included; women during their impurity were alone refused admission. To the second court all Jews were admitted and, when uncontaminated by any defilement, their wives; to the third, male Jews, if clean and purified; to the fourth, the priests ... [156].

Only rarely were women permitted to enter the inner court. About this the Mishnah records:

> The rites of laying on of hands, waving, bringing near [the meal-offering], taking the handful and burning it, ... are performed by men but not by women, excepting in the meal-offerings of the suspected adulteress and of the female Nazirite, for which they themselves perform the act of waving[157].

According to m Sot 1:5, even for these exemptions women were not allowed to enter the inner area of the temple. The offering was made at the eastern Gate that lay against the Gate of Nicanor, the latter being the entrance that separated the court of women from the court of the Israelites.

Women were also disqualified from eating hallowed things in the Temple[158], from making the avowal at the offering of first fruits and mixing the ashes at the ceremony of the Red Heifer[159]. All these together prompt us to conclude that women did not have a major role to play in the rituals conducted in the temple of Jerusalem.

b) *Women's Role in the Synagogues*

Synagogues were the popular meeting places of Jewish communities throughout Judea, Galilee and the Diaspora. They were places of open and popular meetings in the Greco-Roman world. The primary function

---

[155] L.J. ARCHER, «The Role», 280.

[156] See JOSEPHUS, *The Life Against Apion*, I, 334-335

[157] Qid 1.8, H. DANBY, *The Mishnah*, 322. For details concerning the meal-offerings made at the temple, see Lev 1:3ff. For details see C.A. BARTON, «A Comparison», 79-89.

[158] m. Bik 4.3, see H. DANBY, *The Mishnah*, 98

[159] m. Bik 1.5, see H. DANBY, *The Mishnah*, 94.

of the synagogue was to serve as a place for the public reading of the Torah, and the Sabbath was the main day when people assembled to hear the Torah. The purpose of the Torah reading was more educational than devotional. The synagogue thus served as the main institution of the Jewish educational system[160].

As said earlier, the two post-exilic developments, that is, concentration upon ritual purity and the sharp differentiation between male-female social functions, resulted in women's non-obligation to the study of the Torah[161]. Naturally women had no prominent role to play in the synagogues.

Concerning women's participation in synagogue worship there is no consensus of opinions among scholars. Some of the recent studies have supported the thesis that there existed separate galleries for women in the synagogues, which urges to think that the women were present in the synagogue services. In the synagogues, according to E. Schürer, women were in a place different from men in their distinct galleries[162]. Avi-Yonah and Sukenik hold a similar view. Avi-Yonah, while writing on the excavations at Beth Alpha, a Galilean synagogue of basilica design says: «The remains furnish no evidence that would establish the existence of a second storey, but is reasonable to assume that there was one and that a women's gallery was built on top of the two colonnades and above the vestibule»[163].

The archaeologist Sukenik further affirms the notion of a separate women's gallery. According to him: «You may, however, confidently infer that the basilica was provided with a gallery for women worshippers, from the massive pillars at the north western corners of the colonnade»[164]. This view is further supported by the investigation undertaken by Brooten, who bases her thesis on evidence from nineteen Greek and Latin inscriptions that date from 27 BC to possibly as late as the sixth century AD. She, as we have seen before, suggests that in these inscriptions women were given titles such as «head of the synagogue», «leader», «mother of the synagogue», thus showing that women

---

[160] L.J. ARCHER, «The Role», 280.

[161] L.J. ARCHER, «The Role», 280.

[162] These galleries were erected for women at the feast of Tabernacles. A similar type of gallery is found in the third century synagogues also. But not in the synagogues prior to third century. According to Schürer, these galleries confirm a total separation of women from men. See E. SCHÜRER, *A History*, 75.

[163] M. AVI-YONAH, *Encyclopedia*, 187.

[164] E.L. SUKENIK, *The Ancient Synagogue*, 72.

played significant roles in the synagogues[165]. On the other hand R.S. Kraemer[166] holds the view that there is no real evidence that Jewish women were segregated from the men in the ancient synagogues.

Some of the rabbinic sayings convey their general attitude towards women and their roles in the synagogues. According to Hag 3a «If the men came to learn, the women came to hear...»[167]. Only men could form the quorum of ten, which was necessary for a service. If there were less than ten men, even though women were present, « ... they may not recite the *Shema‘* with its benedictions, nor may one go before the Ark, nor may they lift up their hands, nor may they read the prescribed portion of the law or the reading from the Prophets ...»[168]. The Talmud says that, «All are qualified to be among the seven [who read], even a minor and a woman, only the Sages said that woman should not read the Torah out of respect for the congregation»[169]. In the absence of a man, a woman could form the quorum of the three necessary for the saying of grace, but if a man was present «a hundred women are no better than two men»[170]. That is to say, although women were in theory eligible, it was not customary for them to obey the public call to read. [171] The rabbinic literature thus seems to preserve legally women's religious rights in theory, but in practice they were not accepted[172].

c) *Women's Role in the Home*

By and large women's religious roles and privileges were limited to those which they could participate at home, with the synagogues and even the cult being extensions of it[173]. Women's religious identity was marked by the observance of rituals associated with home, and which

---

165 In relation to the title 'head of the synagogue', Brooten uses three inscriptions, one from Smyrna, Ionia (around second century AD); another from Kastelli Kissamou, Grete (fourth to fifth century AD); and one from Myndos, Caria (fourth to fifth century AD). See D.M. SCHOLER, «Women», 881.

166 R.S. KRAEMER, *Her Share of the Blessings,* 126.

167 b. Hag 3a, see I. EPSTEIN, *The Babylonian Talmud,* 9.

168 b. Meg 4.3, see H. DANBY, *The Mishnah,* 206.

169 b. Meg 23:a, see I. EPSTEIN, *The Babylonian Talmud,* 140.

170 b. Ber 45b, see I. EPSTEIN, *The Babylonian Talmud,* 277.

171 Although women were not allowed to conduct any official service in synagogues, there are records of women making extempore prayers. Women were also permitted to say the eighteen benedictions and were expected to be present at the seven year reading of the law. See M.J. EVANS, *Woman in the Bible,* 35.

172 See I.J. PERITZ, «Woman in the Ancient Hebrew Cult», 115-119.

173 D.E. SAWYER, *Women,* 81.

instilled in children from their youngest years their own Jewish identity[174]. The rabbis assigned a certain degree of spiritual significance to a woman's presence and role at home,[175] evidence of which we find in the Midrash on Gen 2.18, b. Qid 31b and b. Yev 23a.

The presence of a wife at home was compared to the presence of joy, blessing, goodness and atonement[176]. Her remaining within the domestic seclusion of her family was compared to an atoning force not inferior to the altar[177].

GenR 47 reads that «her husband is adorned by her, but she is not adorned by her husband»[178]. Another indication of the rabbis' appreciation of a woman's potential spiritual influence is indicated by a Midrash which points out that if a man marries a wicked woman he will become wicked, but if a wicked man marries a pious woman, she will make him pious. «This proves that all depends on the woman»[179].

Despite the spiritual significance assigned to women at home, her religious role was limited. She normally carried out certain cultic activities conducted at home. Important among such activities were the cults associated with the birth of a child and the Passover celebration. The cultic activities at home, such as preparing the home for the annual Passover meal, cleaning the home thoroughly to ensure that no leaven existed in it so that the bread that is consumed at the meal is free from even any accidental action of leaven, and the matriarchal lighting of a lamp or candles, were carried out by women. Omission of any of these actions, it was taught, would cause the death of a woman in childbirth[180]. J.R. Wegner has brought out an interesting interpretation as to why these three prescriptions should have such fatal dangers associated with them. She associates this threat with the life of the husband. She states: «The three cultic duties listed here, like other biblical precepts, are primarily incumbent on men, but they happen to be the three rites

---

[174] See E. SCHÜRER, *A History*, III, 153.

[175] See B. WITHERINGTON, *Women in the Ministry of Jesus,* 6.

[176] «One who has no wife remains without good, and without a helper, and without joy, and without blessing, and without atonement». See B. WITHERINGTON, *Women in the Ministry of Jesus,* 6.

[177] B. WITHERINGTON, *Women in the Ministry of Jesus,* 6.

[178] B. WITHERINGTON, *Women in the Ministry of Jesus,* 6.

[179] GenR 17.7, see H. FREEDMAN, *Midrash* I, *Genesis* I, 138; L.J. SWIDLER, *Women in Judaism,* 214; B. WITHERINGTON, *Women in the Ministry of Jesus,* 6.

[180] According to the Mishnah, for three transgressions do women die in childbirth: for heedlessness of the laws of the menstruant, the Dough-offering, and the lighting of the [Sabbath] lamp (m. Shab 2.6). See D.E. SAWYER, *Women,* 81.

most often delegated to women ... A wife's neglect of these religious duties makes her husband a transgressor»[181]. She argues that actually the aim of the threat to the life of a wife in childbirth is to protect the husband's life. Therefore a woman's religious duties in the home do not necessarily show her highly esteemed position in Judaism. Rather they only remain instrumental in protecting men, the central characters of religion, from transgressions and impurity[182].

Women could not make up the number that was needed for the common grace or that was required for the slaughter of the Passover offering[183]. The prayers at home were usually led by men, and sons played more active roles than daughters[184].

d) *Women's Role in the Burial Rituals*

While women had no major roles to play in the Temple worship, synagogue or at home, they shared some specific roles in the burial rituals in Hellenistic Palestine, a practice that is found in the contemporary burial customs in Greece[185] as well as in Rome[186]. Perhaps the

---

[181] J.R. WEGNER, *Chattel or Person?*, 155.

[182] A similar attitude is emphasized in a comment found in the Talmud, ascribed to the rabbis of the early third century AD: «Rab said to R. Hiyya: Whereby do women earn merit? By making their children go to the synagogue to learn Scripture and their husbands to the Beth Hamidrash to learn Mishnah, and waiting for their husbands till they return from the Beth Hamidrash». b. Ber 17a. See I. EPSTEIN, *The Babylonian Talmud, Zera'im* I, *Berakoth*, 102.

[183] Ber 7.2, see H. DANBY, *The Mishnah*, 7.

[184] Pes 10.4, see H. DANBY, *The Mishnah*, 150.

[185] Women played important roles in the burial customs such as lamentation of the dead in the ancient Greece. They were normally assigned to wash and anoint the body, which was followed by a formal funeral procession to the gravesite in which the women mourners figured as prominent characters. The majority of participants in a funeral procession were women, who during the processions lamented aloud putting both their hands on their heads and tearing their hair as a sign of sorrow. They were usually family members, friends of the family or household family slaves, or professionals hired for the occasion. Again at the gravesite women performed various rites, such as calling the dead, accompanied by various offerings to the dead. These rites, especially calling the dead, cries and wailing, were thought to raise the spirit of the dead from the grave. See K.E. CORLEY, «Women», 182-183; M. ALEXIOU, *Ritual Lament in Greek Tradition*, 108-109.

[186] See A. RUSH, *Death*, 101-105.

According to Corley, catching the breath was so important to the bereaved that mothers even waited outside prisons hoping to give their sons this final kiss before their executions (See K.E. CORLEY, «Women», 187). There were certain customs

only privilege left to women in Hellenistic Palestine was that of mourning for the dead at funerals, an office common to women throughout the Near East[187]. Other than mourning for the dead, women were also involved in different activities associated with the dead and their burial[188].

Concerning the mourning rituals and burial practices of Greco-Roman Palestine, the first thing to say is that like men, women were also buried and mourned[189]. The Talmud assigned equal mourning periods to both: wife or husband, mother or father, sister or brother[190]. This equality is perhaps in accordance with the biblical commandment to honor one's father and mother (Exod 20:12).

It was taken for granted that normally men were allowed to prepare only the corpses of men while women were allowed to prepare corpses of either sex[191]. It was customary that prior to the burial the corpse was washed and anointed[192]; had its limbs straightened[193], eyes closed[194],

---

such as keeping a coin in the mouth of the dead, washing and anointing the dead, keeping a wreath on the head of the dead. See A. RUSH, *Death and Burial*, 92-137. The women or other relatives of the dead person normally carried out these rituals. It was customary that women began mourning immediately at the time of death, calling out to the dead. There was a belief that the wailing and calling out to the dead person would awake him if he was not really dead. Women had also prominent functions such as lamenting, beating their breast and stretching their arms towards the deceased as a sign of their grief for the dead. They were relatives of the dead or hired professional mourners. See A. RUSH, *Death and Burial*, 181.

[187] See MQ 3:8-9; m. Ket 4:4; Cf. Judg 11:40; 2Sam 14:2; 2Chr 35:25.

[188] 1Sam 28:7; Mark 16:1; Luke 23:55; 24:1.

[189] The mode of burial among the Jews was interment and not cremation. In ancient times corpses were simply laid to rest in caverns or in the earth without any coffin. With the Greco-Roman period came the custom of burying the dead in tombs hewn out of the living rock. It was a custom based upon the prescription of Gen 3:19, «you are dust, and to dust you shall return». The only exception to this would be when a person was burned to death by way of execution (see Lev 21:9, «When the daughter of a priest profanes herself through prostitution, she profanes her father; she shall be *burned* to death»). Cremation was normally reserved to criminals. See J.B. SEGAL, «Popular Religion», 1-22.

[190] m. Qid 20b

[191] See Semahot, 12:10. According to the Mishnah it was a requirement before burial that the corpse be washed (Shab 23:5).

[192] See Matt 26:12; Mark 14:8; 16:1; Luke 23:56; John 19:39-40; Josephus, *Jewish Antiquities*, XVII: 199; m. Shab 23.5, see H. DANBY, *The Mishnah*, 120.

[193] Naz, 9.3, see H. DANBY, *The Mishnah*, 292.

[194] Shab 23.5, see H. DANBY, *The Mishnah*, 120.

hair cut[195], mouth bound[196], and then it was dressed in a linen sheet enfolding the body from top to bottom[197] and was placed on the floor with a lighted candle close to the head[198]. The body was normally carried on a bier (see Luke 7:12-14) and it was customary to stop seven times on the route to the burial place for public lamentation and for praise of the dead to be made (*Ketuboth*, 2.10; *Oholoth*, 18.4). The outward signs of mourning were wailing (Gen 23:1-3; 50:10), rending of garments (Gen 37:33; 1Sam 4:12), wearing sackcloth (Gen 37:33-34; 2Sam 3:31), casting dust on the head (1Sam 4:12; 2Sam 13:19), refraining from washing and anointing (2Sam 12:20; 14:2), fasting (1Sam 31:13, 2Sam 1:11; 1Sam 31:13), hand clapping and beating the chest[199]. These mourning rituals continued unchanged in the Greco-Roman period, although with some minor changes[200].

Normally it was the male mourners who performed the formal religious rituals of death and burial in Hellenistic Palestine. But together with men, women also shared important rituals in the burial of the dead. While men conducted the official prayers, the formal and specific eulogies and benedictions, women were engaged in general and very vocal lamentation for the dead, which was an essential part of the burial and was mostly conducted by women, whether relatives of the deceased or professional mourners[201]. In spite of the manifold responsibilities which women shared in the funerary rites, they were not the important office bearers in the rituals. This was reserved to men. Commenting on this, Archer refers to two factors that draw our attention in this regard. First, although women were prominent at funerals, they

---

[195] Moed Qatan, 8b. See I. EPSTEIN, *The Babylonian Talmud, Mo'ed*, VIII, *Mo'ed Katan*, 42-43.

[196] Semahoth, 1.2.

[197] Matt 27:59; Mark 15:46; Luke 23:53; John 11:44; MQ, 8b, I. EPSTEIN, *The Babylonian Talmud, Mo'ed*, VIII, *Mo'ed Katan*, 42-43.

[198] Shab 151a, see I. EPSTEIN, *The Babylonian Talmud, Mo'ed* II, *Shabbath* II, 770-771; m. Ber 8.6, see H. DANBY, *The Mishnah*, 120; b. Ber 53a, I. EPSTEIN, *The Babylonian Talmud*, 319-322.

[199] L.J. Archer observes that the reason women were given the ritual of lamenting for the dead was because of the belief that women who performed these tasks were believed to be closer to the world of nature, and hence to the spirit realm and the possibility of demonic possession, than men. L. J. ARCHER, *Her Price*, 282.

[200] See I. EPSTEIN, *The Babylonian Talmud, Mo'ed* VIII, *Mo'ed Katan*, 140-43; 154-158; 177-81.

[201] b. Ket 46b, I. EPSTEIN, *The Babylonian Talmud*, Nashim III, *Ketuboth*, 266-69; See Judg 11:40; Jer 9:16.

this regard. First, although women were prominent at funerals, they were not responsible for the mourners' benediction or for the perform-ance of other religious duties designed to ensure the smooth passage of the dead. Secondly, those ritual areas of death in which women took an active part, belonged primarily to the shadowy region of popular super-stition and were not the concern of Judaism proper[202].

The investigation of the status of women in Hellenistic Judaism brings us to the conclusion that there exists a mixture of views and opinions concerning women. Some of these opinions help us to con-clude our discussion on the status of women in Hellenistic Judaism. Commenting on women's status in Hellenistic Judaism, M.J. Evans rightly summarizes the general rabbinic view of women as «half kindly, half oriental»[203]. Summarizing the social and religious status of women G.B. Caird writes: «For the subordinate status of women was accepted without question in Jewish, Greek, and Roman society»[204]. In the words of C.G. Montefiore: «Women, were, on the whole, regarded as inferior to men in mind, in function, and in status»[205]. According to J. Bonsirven, «Misogyny is another widespread characteristic in Is-rael»[206].

On the one hand rabbis described women as hard working, compas-sionate or intelligent[207], on the other hand they demonstrated that women were lazy, stupid, frivolous[208], vain with a tendency to the oc-cult,[209] seductive and the cause of unchastity[210].

The male literary sources of ancient Judaism present a fairly consis-tent pattern of a negative view towards women. We have examples from Josephus and Philo. Josephus, as a Jew, accepted the theoretical inferiority of women. As an historian he described a number of influen-tial women[211], but he insisted that women could not be witnesses and

---

[202] L.J. ARCHER, «The Role», 283.

[203] M.J. EVANS, Woman in the Bible, 33.

[204] G.B. CAIRD, «Paul and Women's Liberty», 269-281.

[205] C.G. MONTEFIORE – H. LOEWE, A Rabbinic Anthology, xix.

[206] J. BONSIRVEN, Palestinian Judaism, 100; Similar view is held by S. ZUCROW, Women, 74-84.

[207] b. Meg 14b, see I. EPSTEIN, The Babylonian Talmud, Mo'ed VIII, Megillah, 84-86.

[208] GenR 45; b. Qid 49b, 82b.

[209] Shab 33b, I. EPSTEIN, The Babylonian Talmud, Mo'ed I, Shabbath, 154-158; b. Ket 59b, I. EPSTEIN, The Babylonian Talmud, Nashim III, Kethuboth II, 352-355.

[210] See M. MCKEATING, «Jesus Ben Sira's Attitude», 85.

[211] JOSEPHUS, Jewish Antiquities, VII: 11.8; XI 3. 5; VII 9. 2.

were to be segregated from worship[212]. Similarly Philo saw women as inferior and therefore to be ruled by the father or husband.[213] He considered them as evil creatures[214] having traits of weakness,[215] because they were led by sensuality[216]. They were to stay at home, desiring a life of seclusion[217].

The book of Sirach, a proto-pharisaic work from about 180 BC, presents women both as good wishers and as problems. The text reads «better is the wickedness of man than a woman who does good: it is woman who brings shame and disgrace» (Sir 42:14). Throughout their lives, women's personal value to God was reckoned at roughly half that of men[218]. It was perhaps in the light of these facts that men each morning offered the following prayer of thanksgiving: «Blessed art thou, O Lord our God, king of the universe, who has not made me a woman»[219].

This literature reflects a social reality to some extent and sets a framework of societal expectations for the behavior and relationships of men and women[220]. Overall, the position of women in the Jewish religion, rituals and cults may well be summed up by the Mishnah's constant coupling of women with minors and slaves, and by a statement of Josephus that, in the eyes of the law, «... the woman ... is in all things inferior to the man»[221].

The present investigation supports neither an overly favorable view nor an overly unfavorable view concerning women. Instead, women in Hellenistic Judaism were neither totally free, nor did they occupy any

---

212 JOSEPHUS, *Jewish Antiquities,* V: 8.15.

213 PHILO, *In Flaccum,* 89; *De specialibus legibus* III: 169-71.

214 PHILO, *Hypothetica,* 11: 14-17.

215 PHILO, *De opificio mundi,* 151-52.

216 PHILO, *De opificio mundi,* 165.

217 PHILO, *De specialibus legibus,* III:169-77; *In Flaccum,* 89.

218 On this difference of valuation between men and women Philo writes, «the law laid down a scale of valuation in which no regard is paid to beauty or stature or anything of the kind, but all are assessed equally, the sole distinction being between men and women, and between children and adults». PHILO, *De specialibus legibus,* II: 32.

219 According to Archer, the use of this blessing may first have been authorized in the second century AD, either by R. Meir or Judah. Probably something of this sort was known to Paul when he wrote Gal 3:28. In this verse, maybe Paul is reacting to the prevalent opinions of his days that undervalued women. See L.J. ARCHER, «The Role», 287.

220 D.M. SCHOLER, «Women», 880.

221 JOSEPHUS, *The Life Against Apion,* II: 201.

socio-religious status equal to that of men. In general the dominant image of women in antiquity has been that of weaker beings in comparison to men. A woman's world consisted of the household, where she occupied herself with cooking, cleaning, spinning, and looking after children. Christianity was born into this complex and syncretistic world. It is into this cultural flux that Jesus comes with the Good News that propagated equality, inviting men and women to follow him. And it is precisely in this wide context of Hellenistic Judaism that Matthew composes his Gospel.

5. Women in Christian Antioch and in the Matthean Churches

Having arrived at some preliminary conclusions on the date, place and source of Matthew and having understood the social-religious status of women in Hellenistic Judaism in general, we now come to a close understanding of women in the Matthean community in particular, against the background of the first century Christian Churches in and around Antioch. For information and evidence on women's status in Christian Antioch we rely on texts from the Pauline letters and later evidence from Matthew itself. Like the previous section, here too, we start our discussion by presenting some of the more important research on the topic, although this was not an exhaustive study.

5.1 *Present Status of Research*

In the past three decades there emerged a number of studies, mostly feminist, on the role of women in the Gospel of Matthew. The research undertaken by authors J. Kopas, M.J. Selvidge, J.C. Anderson, A.C. Wire, A.J. Levine and E.M. Wainwright deserve special attention in this regard. Kopas surveys examples of women in the Gospel maintaining that «Matthew struggles to incorporate women moving from the periphery to greater involvement and from being victims and survivors to being disciples and leaders»[222]. Selvidge, in her redactional study, has examined Matthew's treatment of women taking into consideration women's situation in the background of the Matthean community[223]. Both Kopas and Selvidge utilize the text of the Gospel for theological

[222] J. KOPAS, «Jesus and Women in Matthew», 13-21.
[223] M.J. SELVIDGE, «Violence», 213-23.

insights and view Matthew as an ally for human rights and the dignity and authentic existence of women today[224].

Anderson's investigation of women in the Gospel of Matthew has exposed the androcentric perspectives within the Gospel, in which the role of women is couched in a «patriarchal, social, political, religious and economic» world view[225]. According to her, Mary and the other women of the Gospel of Matthew fulfil extraordinary roles while remaining in subordinate and auxiliary positions to men[226]. A similar conclusion is drawn by Wire who makes use of a different methodology, known as «macrosociological analysis». In her study, she explores «the meaning of gender in Matthew's Gospel». According to Wire, macrosociology can provide a basis for «evaluating how Matthew's gender construction is congruent and /or deviant within its social world»[227]. The study on women undertaken by Love has points of contact with that of Anderson and Wire. Like Wire, she makes use of macrosociology as a methodology. Unlike Wire, who examines gender roles in the scribal community, she investigates gender specific behavior in Matthew through a social analysis of the household[228]. Levine[229] and Wainwright[230] on the other hand describe the narrative role of women in Matthew.

Besides these researches based specifically on Matthew, there have also emerged many studies based on Mark and Luke. In recent years the women of the Synoptic Gospels have been the subject of numerous studies from those that determined their relative numeric presence in the Gospel[231] to those studying their relative role in a Gospel. The studies undertaken by E. S. Malbon[232], M.A. Tolbert[233], J. Dewey[234] and H. Kinukawa[235] concentrate on the narrative roles of women in Mark. The

---

224 M.A. TOLBERT, «Introduction», 113-126.

225 J.C. ANDERSON, «Matthew: Gender and Reading», 3-27; ID., «Mary's Difference», 183-202.

226 J.C. ANDERSON, «Matthew: Gender and Reading», 3-27.

227 A.C. WIRE, ed., «Gender Role in Scribal Community», 87-121.

228 S.L. LOVE, «The Household», 21-31.

229 A.J. LEVINE, «Matthew», 252-262.

230 E.M. WAINWRIGHT, *Towards a Feminist Critical Reading*

231 L.J. SWIDLER, *Biblical Affirmations of Women*.

232 E.S. MALBON, «Fallible Followers», 29-48.

233 M.A. TOLBERT, «Mark», 263-274.

234 J. DEWEY, «From Storytelling to Written Text», 71-78.

235 H. KINUKAWA, *Women and Jesus in Mark*.

research undertaken by M.R. D'Angelo[236], T.K. Seim[237] and B.E. Reid[238] speak of the narrative roles of women in Luke

5.2 *The Economic, Social and Religious Background of First Century Antioch*

A close scrutiny of the social-economic-religious setting of first century Antioch suggests to us that it tended towards egalitarianism, thus supporting the elevation of women's status in society. Different elements such as the emergence of the «collegial household», pagan religious practices and the Gnostic influence seem to have inspired Matthew towards the positive portrayal of women in the Gospel.

5.2.1 Economic Background

Syria, being the most strategic province for Rome in the East and a center of trade and industry, had a two-fold importance in the first century AD. Syria, together with Palestine remained the most important eastern corridor for trade with the Mediterranean countries[239]. Now, Antioch being the capital of Syria and being made the focus of the Roman empire by Pompey in 64 BC, was also a center for the caravan trade, and it vied with Rome along with the «capitals of the richest and the most prosperous provinces»[240].

At least in comparison to Mark, we can assume that the Gospel of Matthew was addressed to an urbanized community. This assumption is supported by two examples such as Matthew's use of the word πόλις, «city»[241] and words such as ἀργύριον «silver», χρυσίον «gold» and τάλαντον «talent»[242]. This refers to the prosperous background of Matthew. Commenting on this M.H. Croby states: «Accordingly, in the light of the preceding there is a further reason to postulate that real readers of Matthew's Gospel lived in or near a city, such as Antioch of

---

[236] M.R. D'ANGELO, «Women in Luke-Acts», 441-461.

[237] T.K. SEIM, *The Double Message.*

[238] B.E. REID, *Choosing the Better Part?.*

[239] See M.H. CROSBY, *The House of Disciples,* 37.

[240] M.H. CROSBY, *The House of Disciples,* 39-40.

[241] Mark uses the word πόλις (city) eight times, and κώμη (village) seven times. Matthew on the other hand uses the κώμη (village) four times and πόλις (city) at least 26 times.

[242] For a discussion of Leviticus on the monetary value upon persons dedicated to Yahweh see P. TRIBLE, «Women in the OT», 963-966.

Syria, and it also seems that they were prosperous and in no sense materially disadvantaged»[243]. We think that the above Matthean references may only imply that he writes about something that could be referred to a city or to prosperity, and not that the readers necessarily are prosperous or in a city. However, when with these references Matthew addressed himself to a situation, he was at least addressing a section of people who were prosperous and lived in a city.

5.2.2 Social-Religious Background

As we have seen above, the dominating household system in the Greco-Roman settings of the first century in general was patriarchal by nature. We have also made note of some of the voluntary associations that existed along with the patriarchal household, and which posed a threat to the patriarchal social system. First century Antioch was not an exception. We can study the social system of first century Antioch under two titles: patriarchal household and collegial household.

a) *Patriarchal Household*

The *paterfamilias*[244] had ultimate authority in the patriarchal household in which «the family» was defined not primarily by kinship, but by relations of dependence and subordination[245]. Commenting on this, W.A. Meeks states: «The head of a substantial household was thus responsible for—and expected a degree of obedience from—not only his immediate family but also his slaves, former slaves who were now clients, hired laborers and sometimes business associates and tenants»[246]. The *paterfamilias* was divided principally into three elements: *potestas* (power over the children, grandchildren, slaves); *dominium* (power over possessions); *manus* (power over the wife and sons' wives)[247].

According to M.H. Crosby there existed two types of legal marriage in Roman law: marriage in *manu* and marriage in *sine manu*. Marriage in *manu* transferred the father's *patria potestas* over the woman into the hands of the husband. In this case the woman had no distinct legal posi-

---

243 M. H. CROSBY, *The House of Disciples*, 41.
244 By *paterfamilias* we do not mean the biological father, but the authority over the household
245 See P. TRIBLE, «Women in the OT», 963-966.
246 See W.A. MEEKS, *The First Urban Christians*, 30.
247 See K. POLANYI, *The Great Transformation*, 19.

tion, but was like a daughter[248]. According to marriage in *sine manu*, the wife was not subject to any of her husband's *patria potestas*. Instead she was technically under the authority of her father. Upon his death, she could seek formal emancipation to become a person *sui iuris*, legally competent to conduct her affairs[249]. Naturally in this case women enjoyed more freedom. Their growing economic power as a matter of fact brought them legal and household independence[250]. This stood as a potential threat to the city and the empire. The basic household division remained. Generally speaking men worked outside while the woman worked inside[251].

b) *Collegial Household*

The collegial household model or associations of brotherhoods was a different emerging social system. Greeks called it *koina*, while the Romans called it *collegia*. According to Crosby, these associations were formed for social and economic purposes, such as eating and drinking and burying the dead. Such organizations had an egalitarian nature in comparison to the patriarchal household.

Archeological evidence suggests that religion occupied the central position in these organizations. There existed principally two types of worship among these collegial households: the worship of Dionysius and the worship of the goddess Isis. Both these religious cults, especially the cult of Isis, stood as a threat to the existing patriarchal system with its household mixture of slaves and free persons, women and men, blacks and whites.

According to R.E. Witt, the cult of Isis was an international religion that subverted proper distinctions between men and women[252]. The cult of Isis as well as the cult of Dionysius was thus *collegial* by nature. They functioned in a more egalitarian form than the patriarchal mode of household, especially in their treatment of women[253].

---

[248] M.H. CROSBY, *The House of Disciples*, 27.
[249] See D. HERLIHY, *Medieval Households*, 8-9.
[250] M.H. CROSBY, *The House of Disciples*, 27.
[251] See E.M. TETLOW, *Women and Ministry*, 23; M.H. CROSBY, *The House of Disciples*, 27.
[252] R.E. WITT, *Isis-Hellas*, 62.
[253] See J.H. ELLIOT, *A Home for the Homeless*, 180.

c) *Christian House Churches and Women*

The dispersion of Christians from Jerusalem started with the martyrdom of Stephen (Acts 11:19). As the text shows, the Christians in Antioch begin to be composed of Jews and Greeks[254].

Scholars generally accept that the Church in the first two centuries consisted of «house churches»[255], which were «egalitarian» and «collegial»[256] in nature. Christian house churches by nature paralleled «collegial households».

Both the house churches and collegial households, according to E.M. Wainwright, J.E. Stambaugh and D.L. Balch, and K.H. Rudolf, afforded greater opportunities for leadership and participation to all, and especially to women and slaves[257].

Writing on the house churches in the early Christian centuries, R. Aguirre states:

> In the house church people of many diverse situations and social strata participated. It appears that they developed a model which did not normally take place in Graeco-Roman religious settings. They intended to live the Christian spirit in the interior of these communities by promoting a new

---

[254] According to Hadrill, besides the Jews and Pagans, there existed also Gnostics. He comments: «The network of interconnected pagan cults in Syria had grown from the early Semitic conception of *ba'al* into more clearly-defined pantheons of local deities, who in turn had to a considerable extent been overlaid first by the Hellenistic pantheon introduced by Alexander the Great, and then again by the Roman pantheon. Judaism was undergoing a process of remolding through the latter half of the first century into a strongly flexible religion more suited to the changed conditions of its existence in the Roman Empire. Gnosticism was at this early period in its infancy ...» D.S. WALLACE-HADRILL, *Christian Antioch*, 14.

In this process of remolding and evolution, these religious sects, as we have already mentioned before, assigned places of importance women. Matthew's interest in women in the Gospel makes sense in this social-religious background of first century Christian Antioch.

[255] E. SCHÜSSLER FIORENZA, *In Memory of Her*, 175-84; A.J. MALHERBE, *Social Aspects of Early Christianity*, 60-91; W.A. MEEKS, *First Urban Christians*, 75-77; J.E. STAMBAUGH – D.L. BALCH, *The New Testament*, 138-140; G. DOWNEY, *A History of Antioch in Syria*, 277; E.M. WAINWRIGHT, *Towards a Feminist Critical Reading*, 341.

[256] E.M. WAINWRIGHT, *Towards a Feminist Critical Reading*, 341; E. SCHÜSSLER FIORENZA, *In Memory of Her*, 180, 183-184; W.A. MEEKS, *First Urban Christians*, 76; M. H. CROSBY, *House of Disciples*, 29-31.

[257] E.M WAINWRIGHT, *Towards a Feminist Critical Reading*, 342; J.E. STAMBAUGH – D.L. BALCH, *The New Testament in Its Social Environment*, 124 -26; See K.H. RUDOLF, *Gnosis*, 211-14.

model of human relations and a very unique kind of fraternity among the members. This interclass movement created something authentically new. It could be historically innovative due to genuine faith[258].

Various studies on the early Christian house churches show that they were not a culturally well-adapted, monolithic group, but rather were an egalitarian, counter cultural[259] and multifaceted movement[260]. There was a great thrust towards equality in these house churches. Membership in this egalitarian movement was not defined by gender roles, but by commitment to Christ. Women were no longer marginal figures here, but exercised responsible leadership[261]. Early Christians understood themselves as freed by the Spirit to a new life in Jesus[262]. That is to say there is no more any distinction between Jew and Gentile, free person and slave, male and female, but all are united in Christ Jesus (Gal 3:28).

Over against the existing patriarchal as well as the androcentric view, Christians understood themselves to be a new community in which all members shared equally in the freedom of the children of God. This shows the relationship that existed within the members of the community. The existing patriarchal relationships marked by subordination and segregation was slowly replaced by the vision of the community where people lived in love and service to one another. In this egalitarian system, the marginalized of the patriarchal society shared equal status, evidence of which is found in the Pauline corpus.

d) *Egalitarianism in the Pauline Corpus*

The Pauline corpus contains elements that depict women as active in the missionary works of the early Christian movement. Women were among the owners of the houses in which early Christians met[263], and their role as patrons may well have imposed upon them responsibilities as church leaders (Act 12:12; Rom 16:3-5; 1Cor 16:19; Col 4:15)[264].

---

258 R. AGUIRRE, «La casa», 44.

259 For examples of counter-cultural elements in the Synoptic Gospels, especially in the healing stories see J. DEWEY, «Jesus' Healing of Women, 122-131.

260 See J.G. GAGER, *Kingdom and Community;* G. THEISSEN, «Soziale Schichtung», 232-272; R. SCROGGS, «The Earliest Christian Communities», 1-23.

261 See E. SCHÜSSLER FIORENZA, «Word, Spirit and Power», 31.

262 See W.A. MEEKS, «The Image of Androgyne», 165-208; H.D. BETZ, «Spirit, Freedom and Law», 145-60; M. BOUTTIER, «Complexio Oppositorum», 1-19.

263 See F.M. GILLMANN, ed., *Women Who Knew Paul*, 29-42.

264 E.A. CLARK, «Women», 1281-83.

The Christians assembled themselves in house churches for the celebration of the Eucharist (Act 2:46; 20:7) and the assembly was usually called the «house of God» (1Tim 3:15; see Heb 10:21) or «temple» (2Thess 2:4; Eph 2:21) because of the presence of the Spirit of God in them[265]. Women mingled freely and publicly with men in the Christian services, otherwise unheard of in the ancient world[266]. Women often exercised a certain degree of influence in these house churches and in the gatherings conducted in it[267]. It is interesting to note that nine of the twenty-six persons Paul greets in Rom 16 are women. Further Paul speaks of missionary co-workers, and the texts do not suggest that they were subordinate to Paul, neither were they dependent on Paul–rather they were equal to him. Paul himself says that women have worked with him (Phil 4:3). One prominent co-worker of Paul, Prisca[268] together with her husband Aquila, like Barnabas or Apollos, worked independently of Paul[269].

Some women like Damaris (Acts 17:34), Lois and Eunice (2Tim 1:5) were remembered for their faith[270]. In Rom 16:1 we find Phoebe, a woman, who holds an important title διάκονος[271]. Commenting on the title διάκονος assigned to women H. Lietzmann says: «Even at that time there had long been women deacons in the Christian church who, when their sex made them specially suitable, came forward and gave signal help in caring for the poor and sick, and at the baptism of

---

[265] B. GÄRTNER, *The Temple;* R.J. MCKELVEY, *The New Temple;* See E. SCHÜSSLER FIORENZA, «Word, Spirit and Power», 32.

[266] See J.K. MCNAMARA, *Sisters in Arms,* 13; M.T. MALONE, *Women & Christianity,* 68-69.

[267] In Acts 12:12 we find a reference to a prayer meeting conducted in the house of Mary, the mother of John Mark, one of Paul's companions. Paul greets Apphia, «our sister», who was a leader of a house church in Colossae (Phil 2). The foundation of the Church at Philippi is realized because of the assistance of a converted business-woman, Lydia, from Thyatira (Acts 16:14-15, 40). In Col 4:15, we find reference to Nympha of Laodicea and the «church in her house». On two occasions Paul mentions the missionary couple Prisca (Priscilla) and Aquila and the church in their house» (1Cor 16:19; Rom 16:3-5). See M.T. MALONE, *Women & Christianity,* 69; L. FUCHS, *We Were There,* 111-17.

[268] See A. HARNACK, «Probabilia», 16-41.

[269] M.T. MALONE, *Women & Christianity,* 64-86.

[270] See M. GILLMANN, ed., *Women Who Knew Paul,* 21-28.

[271] M. GILLMANN, ed., *Women Who Knew Paul,* 69-70.

women»[272]. Phoebe also is given one more title, προστάτις, which is usually translated as «helper» or «patroness» (Rom 16:2)[273]. Commenting on the title προστάτις assigned to Phoebe, E. Schüssler Fiorenza says that she was a person with authority and had a designated role of leadership and teaching in the community of Cenchreae[274].

Paul calls three women, namely, Euodia, Syntyche, and Prisca, as his συνεργοί, «fellow-workers» (Phil 4:3; Rom 16:3)[275]. Paul never describes them as subordinate to him. But four male-fellow workers, namely, Erastus, Timothy, Titus and and Tychicus (Acts 19:22; 2Cor 8:6, 12:18; Eph 6:21) are described as subordinate to Paul, serving him or being subject to the instructions of Paul[276].

In spite of the fact that the Pauline corpus promotes egalitarianism there are passages in which Paul seems to restrict women's ministry (1Cor 11:2-16 and 1Cor. 14:33b-36)[277]. In fact some scholars dispute on the contention that Paul himself initiated this trend of subordinating the role of women[278]. There are authors who think that such subordination was the result of a particular situation[279]. However a clear look into the Pauline corpus shows that Paul who upheld the distinction of sex

---

[272] H. LIETZMANN, *The History,* 146. Although Lietzmann notes that Phoebe's ministry is limited to the «ministry of women» the text does not suggest it. For a similar interpretation see also E.A. JUDGE, «St. Paul and Classical Society», 28.

[273] The verb προσδέχομαι as well as the substantive προστάτις contain a «two-fold sense of leadership and care». See B. REICKE, «προΐστημι», 703. The exact status of Phoebe, called by Paul a διάκονος («deacon» or «servant») of the Church at Cenchreae and a προστάτις («patroness» or «supporter») «of many and of myself as well» (Rom 16:1-2) has been much debated. See E.A. CLARK, «Women», 1281-1283.

[274] See E. SCHÜSSLER FIORENZA, «Word, Spirit and Power», 36; M. BOUCHER, «Women and Priestly Ministry», 608-613.

[275] Such women include Phoebe (Rom 16:2), the mother of Rufus (16:13), Prisca (Act 18:2; Rom 16:3; 1Cor 16:19; 2Tim 4:19), Nympha (Col 4:15) and Lydia (Acts 16:14-15). See F. M. GILLMANN, *Women Who Knew Paul,* 71-90.

[276] See E.E. ELLIS, «Paul and His Co-Workers», 437-452.

[277] See C.S. KEENER, «Man and Woman», 683-692; S. LÖSCH, «Christliche Frauen in Korinth» 216-261; G.H. GILBERT, «Women in the Churches of Paul», 38-47; M.D. HOOKER, «Authority on Her Head», 410-416; G.B. GAIRD, «Paul and Women's Liberty», 268-281; W.J. MARTIN, «1Corinthians 11:2-16», 231-241; J.B. HARLEY, «Did Paul Require Veils», 190-220; A. JAUBERT, «Le voile», 422-430; J. GALOT, *Mission,* 123.

[278] E.A. JUDGE, «St. Paul and Classical Society», 28.

[279] E. SCHÜSSLER FIORENZA, «Word, Spirit and Power», 37; D. DIBELIUS – H. CONZELMANN, *The Pastoral Epistles,* 65; R.J. KARRIS, «The Background», 459-464.

never upheld the discrimination of it, but rather affirmed the equal dignity of all.

The above given indications from the Pauline corpus concerning the status of women in the primitive Christian communities suggest that women were among the prominent and leading missionaries in the primitive Christian communities. Women played important roles in the early Christian communities, and their ministry was not limited to gender specific functions in society. Like men, women too shared important roles in the communities[280]. They were remembered for their faith; they were considered household heads and co-workers with Paul[281].

6. Conclusion

Our intention in this chapter was to comprehend the social, religious and cultural status of women in the Matthean settings, with special reference to Hellenistic Judaism and first century house churches. Although women enjoyed a certain degree of social and religious freedom in Hellenistic settings, as a whole they were considered inferior to men, evidence of which we find in the OT as well as inter-testamental literature. Unlike the social-religious inferiority that women suffered in the Greco-Roman settings in general and Hellenistic Judaism in particular, Jesus, and the early Christian documents, assigned to women a status equal to that of men. The fact that women enjoyed freedom and equality in the first century Christian Churches, support of which we find in the Pauline corpus, speaks of the newness of the kingdom of God that Jesus preached. Against the patriarchal and androcentric background of Matthew, which normally relegated women to a status inferior to men, his teaching about gender equality becomes significant.

---

[280] See S.L. LOVE, «Women's Roles», 50-59.
[281] M. GILLMANN, *Women Who Knew Paul*, 71-90.

CHAPTER II

Women in the Structure and Strategy of Matthew

1. Introduction

We begin the discussion with an illustration of all the verses that concern women in Matthew, and then follow with an exegesis of five selected passages in which women play significant roles: a) women in the genealogy of Jesus (Matt 1:1-17); b) Jesus' healing of Peter's mother-in-law (8:14-17); c) Jesus' healing of the woman with a hemorrhage (9:20-22); d) the Canaanite woman (Matt 15:28), and e) the woman who anoints Jesus (26:6-13). Among these five passages we give more attention to Matthew's depiction of women in the genealogy where the Evangelist proposes a strategic theme as well as a strategic scheme, which he follows from the beginning to the end of the Gospel.

2. Verses Concerning Women in Matthew

Matthew's portrayal of women in the Gospel, as suggested by J.C. Anderson, can roughly be enumerated and arranged under four titles: 1) women in the direct narrative comments; 2) women as imagery; 3) women in Jesus' teaching and 4) women as characters[1].

2.1 *Women in the Direct Narrative Comments*

There are eight occasions in which Matthew mentions women in direct narrative comments: Genealogy (Tamar, Matt 1:3; Ruth, 1:5;

---

[1] J.C. ANDERSON, «Matthew: Gender and Reading», 3-27.

Rahab, 1:5; Bathsheba 1:6; Mary 1:16); besides women and children (14:21; 15:38) and Pilate's wife (27:19).

2.2 *Women as Imagery*

In Matthew we find women used as important images, e.g.: Rachel as image of Israel (2:18); the woman with leaven as an image of God (13:33); daughter of Zion (21:5) and Jerusalem as mother (23:37).

2.3 *Women in Jesus' Teaching*

Women-related themes form part of the important teachings of Jesus in Matthew, such as: women looked at lustfully (5:27-30); divorced wife (5:31-32; 19:3-9); daughters and daughters-in-law against mothers and mothers-in-law (10:21, 35-39); queen of the South (12:42); family (12:46-50); woman and leaven (13:33); honoring mother and father (15:1-9; 19:19); wife (and husband and children) sold to pay off debt (18:25); mothers and sisters left for the sake of Jesus' name (19:29); prostitutes (21:31-32); woman married to seven brothers in succession (22:23-33); Jerusalem, hen brood (23:37-39); birth pangs of new age (24:8); women nursing or at the end of the age (24:19); two women grinding meal (24:41); ten bridesmaids (25:1-13).

2.4 *Women as Characters*

On several occasions in Matthew we find women presented as important characters closely related to Jesus, e.g: Mary, the mother of Jesus (1:18-2:23); mother and brothers of Jesus (12:46-50); Mary, brothers and sisters (13:53-58); Peter's mother-in-law (8:14-17); the ruler's daughter (9:18-19, 23-26); the woman with a hemorrhage (9:20-22); Herodias and daughter (14:1-12); the women fed by Jesus (14:21; 15:38); Canaanite woman (15:21-28); mother of the sons of Zebedee (20:20; 27:56); the woman who anoints Jesus (26:6-13); Pilate's wife (27:19); two servant girls who accuse Peter (26:69-72); the women at the cross and tomb (27:55-56, 61; 28:1-10).

At first glance it seems that Matthew, who mostly copies and abbreviates Markan accounts of women, is not interested in the theme of women and their following of Jesus. E.M. Tetlow justifies Matthew's disinterestedness as emerging «from within the traditions of rabbinic Judaism, which at that time excluded women from rabbinic schooling»[2]. A closer look at the Gospel, however, will suggest the Evangelist's continued and consistently positive portrayal of women[3].

We tend to think that in Matthew there is a gradual emergence of women from the domestic sphere—a realm to which they were often set apart—to the public arena of following Jesus as his disciple. We begin the survey analyzing the Matthean rationale for the inclusion of women in the Messianic ancestry, which will be followed by a chronological treatment of the five strategic passages in the Gospel.

3. Women in the Genealogy of Jesus (Matt 1:1-17)

Among the Evangelists, only Matthew and Luke seem to have known the genealogy[4] of Jesus. Matthew alone begins the Gospel with a genealogy (1:1-17), while Luke (3:23-38) introduces it after Jesus' baptism and just before the public ministry of Jesus[5]. Unlike Luke, Matthew

---

[2] E.M. TETLOW, *Women and Ministry*, 98-99.

[3] See G.R. OBSORNE, «Women in the Ministry of Jesus», 272.

[4] Commonly used Hebrew equivalent for the English word «genealogy» is תּוֹלְדֹת. For details see R.R. WILSON, «Genealogy, Genealogies», 930.

The Greek substantive that represents the word «genealogy» is γενεαλογία. In the NT it is found twice only (1Tim 1:4; Titus 3:9). See V. HASLER, «γενεαλογία», 242.

A frequently used word in the Gospels is γενέσις or γενέσεως meaning «source», «origin», «beginning», «descent», «procreation» or «existence». It is found four times in the NT («birth», Matt 1:18; Luke 1:14; «genealogy», Matt 1:1; «source», Jam 1:23; 3:6). See A. KRETZER, «γένεσις, εως», 242-243.

Genealogies were often treated as mere list of ancestors, without much significance added to them. In spite of their monotonous style and content, the genealogies were included in the biblical books for a good reason, to give people a sense of rootedness in the biblical world. This was especially important for the ancient Jews who had been uprooted by the Babylonian exile.

At this time genealogies played an important role in establishing one's identity, both national as well as religious, thus linking a person to his roots in the past and at the same time expressing his identity in the present. J.J. McDERMOTT, «Multipurpose Genealogies», 382.

Genealogy reflects the identity, status and collective personality or the individuality of a person, and provides his family story. It had significant roles in the OT. OT genealogy, according to B.M. Nolan, serves three main purposes; a) Identification; b) Legitimation and c) Organization. See B.M. NOLAN, *The Royal Son of God*, 26-27.

[5] Matthew traces the Messianic ancestry back to Abraham and presents Jesus as the fulfillment of God's promise to Abraham. Luke, on the other hand, traces Jesus' ancestry back to Adam and God. His placing of the genealogy just after the baptism and before the public ministry of Jesus, interprets the baptism of Jesus as revealing the Son of the Most High whom God appointed as the Savior of the world from the beginning of humanity. See *EDNT* I, 242.

inserts a list of female characters in Jesus' ancestral story. Why he did this continues to be a basic question intriguing Matthean scholars[6].

3.1 *Compositional Features (Matt 1:1-17)*

1:1 Βίβλος γενέσεως   Ἰησοῦ Χριστοῦ   υἱοῦ Δαυὶδ υἱοῦ Ἀβραάμ.

2 Ἀβραὰμ   ἐγέννησεν   τὸν Ἰσαάκ,
  Ἰσαὰκ   δὲ   ἐγέννησεν   τὸν Ἰακώβ,
  Ἰακὼβ   δὲ   ἐγέννησεν   τὸν Ἰούδαν καὶ τοὺς ἀδελφοὺς αὐτοῦ,
3 Ἰούδας   δὲ   ἐγέννησεν   τὸν Φάρες καὶ τὸν Ζάρα ἐκ τῆς Θαμάρ,
  Φάρες   δὲ   ἐγέννησεν   τὸν Ἐσρώμ,
  Ἐσρὼμ   δὲ   ἐγέννησεν   τὸν Ἀράμ,
4 Ἀρὰμ   δὲ   ἐγέννησεν   τὸν Ἀμιναδάβ,
  Ἀμιναδὰβ   δὲ   ἐγέννησεν   τὸν Ναασσών,
  Ναασσὼν   δὲ   ἐγέννησεν   τὸν Σαλμών,
5 Σαλμὼν   δὲ   ἐγέννησεν   τὸν Βόες ἐκ τῆς Ῥαχάβ,
  Βόες   δὲ   ἐγέννησεν   τὸν Ἰωβὴδ ἐκ τῆς Ῥούθ,
  Ἰωβὴδ   δὲ   ἐγέννησεν   τὸν Ἰεσσαί,
6 Ἰεσσαὶ   δὲ   ἐγέννησεν   τὸν Δαυὶδ τὸν βασιλέα.
  Δαυὶδ   δὲ   ἐγέννησεν   τὸν Σολομῶνα ἐκ τῆς τοῦ Οὐρίου
7 Σολομὼν   δὲ   ἐγέννησεν   τὸν Ῥοβοάμ,
  Ῥοβοὰμ   δὲ   ἐγέννησεν   τὸν Ἀβιά,
  Ἀβιὰ   δὲ   ἐγέννησεν   τὸν Ἀσάφ,
8 Ἀσὰφ   δὲ   ἐγέννησεν   τὸν Ἰωσαφάτ,
  Ἰωσαφὰτ   δὲ   ἐγέννησεν   τὸν Ἰωράμ,
  Ἰωρὰμ   δὲ   ἐγέννησεν   τὸν Ὀζίαν,
9 Ὀζίας   δὲ   ἐγέννησεν   τὸν Ἰωαθάμ,
  Ἰωαθὰμ   δὲ   ἐγέννησεν   τὸν Ἀχάζ,
  Ἀχὰζ   δὲ   ἐγέννησεν   τὸν Ἐζεκίαν,
10 Ἐζεκίας   δὲ   ἐγέννησεν   τὸν Μανασσῆ,
   Μανασσῆς δὲ   ἐγέννησεν   τὸν Ἀμώς,
   Ἀμὼς   δὲ   ἐγέννησεν   τὸν Ἰωσίαν,
11 Ἰωσίας   δὲ   ἐγέννησεν   τὸν Ἰεχονίαν καὶ τοὺς ἀδελφοὺς αὐτοῦ
                                     ἐπὶ τῆς μετοικεσίας Βαβυλῶνος.
12 Μετὰ   δὲ   τὴν μετοικεσίαν Βαβυλῶνος
   Ἰεχονίας   ἐγέννησεν   τὸν Σαλαθιήλ,
   Σαλαθιὴλ   δὲ   ἐγέννησεν   τὸν Ζοροβαβέλ,
13 Ζοροβαβὲλ δὲ   ἐγέννησεν   τὸν Ἀβιούδ,
   Ἀβιοὺδ   δὲ   ἐγέννησεν   τὸν Ἐλιακίμ,
   Ἐλιακὶμ   δὲ   ἐγέννησεν   τὸν Ἀζώρ,
14 Ἀζὼρ   δὲ   ἐγέννησεν   τὸν Σαδώκ,

---

6 See R.E. BROWN, *Birth,* 66-84; D.R. BAUER, «The Literary Function», 461-463; J. GNILKA, *Das Matthäusevangelium,* II, 1-13; W.D. DAVIES-D.C. ALLISON, *The Gospel according to St. Matthew,* I, 170-72; E.D. FREED, «The Women in Matthew's Genealogy», 3-19; M.D. JOHNSON, *The Purpose,* 152-179. J.P. HEIL, «Narrative Roles», 538-545.

Σαδὼκ   δὲ   ἐγέννησεν   τὸν Ἀχίμ,
Ἀχὶμ   δὲ   ἐγέννησεν   τὸν Ἐλιούδ,
15 Ἐλιοὺδ   δὲ   ἐγέννησεν   τὸν Ἐλεάζαρ,
Ἐλεάζαρ   δὲ   ἐγέννησεν   τὸν Ματθάν,
Ματθὰν   δὲ   ἐγέννησεν   τὸν Ἰακώβ,
16 Ἰακὼβ   δὲ   ἐγέννησεν   τὸν Ἰωσὴφ τὸν ἄνδρα Μαρίας, ἐξ ἧς ἐγεννήθη
Ἰησοῦς ὁ λεγόμενος Χριστός.

17 Πᾶσαι οὖν αἱ γενεαὶ
ἀπὸ Ἀβραὰμ   ἕως Δαυὶδ γενεαὶ δεκατέσσαρες,
καὶ ἀπὸ Δαυὶδ   ἕως τῆς μετοικεσίας Βαβυλῶνος γενεαὶ δεκατέσσαρες,
καὶ ἀπὸ τῆς μετοικεσίας Βαβυλῶνος ἕως τοῦ Χριστοῦ γενεαὶ δεκατέσσαρες.

The structural presentation of the text highlights «three blocks of fourteen generations» (1:2-6a; 6b-11; 12-16), each designating a part of salvation history[7], framed within an introduction (1:1) and a conclusion (1:17), which by way of a chiastic inclusion summarizes Jesus' ancestral history and at the same time demarcate the pericope[8]. We start the analysis with the introduction and conclusion that summarize the genealogy. This will be followed by the genealogy itself.

3.1.1 Introduction (1:1) and Conclusion (1:17)

The introduction and conclusion could be structured as below:

v. 1Βίβλος *γενέσεως*[9] Ἰησοῦ Χριστοῦ υἱοῦ Δαυὶδ υἱοῦ Ἀβραάμ.

v. 17 Πᾶσαι οὖν αἱ *γενεαὶ*
ἀπὸ Ἀβραὰμ ἕως Δαυὶδ
γενεαὶ δεκατέσσαρες,
καὶ ἀπὸ Δαυὶδ ἕως τῆς μετοικεσίας Βαβυλῶνος   γενεαὶ δεκατέσσαρες,
καὶ ἀπὸ τῆς μετοικεσίας Βαβυλῶνος ἕως τοῦ Χριστοῦ γενεαὶ δεκατέσσαρες.

---

7 1) From Abraham to the climax of kingship in the person of David (1:2-6a); 2) from David to the loss of the kingship during the Babylonian exile (6b-11); 3) from the Babylonian exile to the birth of Jesus, the Messiah (12-16). See L. RODGER, «The Infancy Stories», 62.

8 A. Vögtel has pointed out three main structural elements in the Matthean genealogy of Jesus: a) the superscription (v. 1), b) the genealogy (vv. 2-16), and c) a commentary to the whole genealogy. A. VÖGTEL, «Die Genealogie», 240.

9 The literal translation of the phrase βίβλος γενέσεως, as is noted by R.E. Brown, would be «the book of the genesis» or «book of genealogy». The translation, «birth record» would be in tune with the translation of the word as «birth» in 1:18 and thus connecting 1-17 with 18-25 as intended by Matthew. See R.E. BROWN, *The Birth,* 58.

The introductory sentence (1:1), which functions both as an introduction to the genealogy as well as to the whole Gospel, is composed of eight words. The content of this sentence is expressed in the concluding summary statement (1:17), as well as in the genealogy (vv. 2-16). Similarly the concluding statement (1:17) gives a summary of the whole ancestral history and further highlights the structure of the Matthean genealogy.

These two «meta-narrative sentences»[10] (1:1 and 1:17) by way of inclusion mark the delimitation of the text (1:1-17)[11] and give a structural unity to the text. Taken together they form the following chiastic trio which highlights three important figures: Christ, David and Abraham:

v. 1	Introduction	*Christ*	**David**	Abraham
v. 17	Conclusion	Abraham	**David**	*Christ*

The key figures and the pivotal characters «Abraham», «David» and «Jesus» are presented in reverse order (1:1; 1:17). Thus Jesus is the son of Abraham[12] and the son of David[13]. David is presented as the central figure.

Further, the conjunction οὖν and the threefold repetition of the phrase «fourteen generations», together with the three pivotal characters, «Christ, David, Abraham», indicate that verse 17, together with giving a logical conclusion[14], provides also a summary as well as a commentary to the genealogy of Jesus.

---

[10] A. VÖGTEL, «Die Genealogie», 240; F. SCHNEIDER, «Die Frauen», 194.

[11] According to K. Stendahl Matt 1:1 and 1:17 form a redactional framework, and vv. 18-25 a midrashic, redactional footnote. See K. STENDAHL, «Quis et Unde»?, 69−80.

[12] Although some regard «son of Abraham» as a Messianic title, it is the «son of David title» that performs the Messianic function here (1:20; 9:27; 12:23; 15:22; 20:30-31; 21:9, 15). For «son of Abraham» as a Messianic title, see A.W. ARGYLE, *The Gospel according to Matthew*, 25; C.H. GORDON, *The Common Background*, 143.

[13] Jesus is the «son of David». This title refers to Jesus as the rightful heir to Israel's throne (Jer 23:5; 33:15). See J.A. FITZMYER, *Essays*, 113-126; E.W. GEORGE NICKELSBURG, *Jewish Literature* , 304.

[14] M.D. JOHNSON, *The Purpose*, 189.

3.1.2 The Genealogy (1:2-16)

Presented within the redactional frame of an introduction (1:1) and conclusion (1:17), the genealogy, structured under «three blocks of fourteen generations»[15], highlights the names of forty-two Messianic ancestors, and four ancestresses (Tamar, 1:3; Rahab, 1:5a; Ruth, 1:5b and the wife of Uriah, 1:6b, and Jesus' mother (Mary, 1:16).

What surprises us in the Matthean genealogy are some elements that do not smoothly fit into this traditional genealogical pattern. We call such elements «pattern breaks»[16]. What calls for special mention is the names of five women in the genealogy. Matthew follows a unique pattern in introducing these female characters. A discussion of the traditional genealogical pattern will help us understand the distinct pattern that Matthew follows in order to speak of the women in the genealogy.

a) *Traditional Genealogical Pattern*

The standard genealogical formula that Matthew follows, like any other writer of genealogy, is «A (a man) + ἐγέννησεν + τόν B (a man)», which represents a male ancestor who is coupled together with the verb ἐγέννησεν and which he uses thirty-nine times in the genealogy. Here, in Matthew, the subject of the verb ἐγέννησεν is a male character:

---

[15] Many see an allusion to David in the number of generations Matthew enumerates in three sets of fourteen names; «fourteen» is the total numerical value of the three Hebrew letters of David's name in Hebrew. R.P. MARTIN, «Approaches to New Testament Exegesis», 246; A.W. ARGYLE, *The Gospel according to Matthew,* 24; J. P. MEIER, *Matthew,* 4; R.H. GUNDRY, *Matthew,* 13, 19; S.T. LACHS, *A Rabbinic Commentary,* 3. We think that the numerical allusion here is apparently doubtful. The name of David is also differently spelled in the Bible. The numerical value of this is then 24. Perhaps it is for ease of memorization that Matthew chose this number. Further the numbers three, four, seven and fourteen are symbolic numbers in Matthew.

The striking conflict between the genealogies in Matthew and Luke have always been problematic for NT commentators. Scholars have offered various proposals to answer the discrepancy. According to Luther, Matthew offers Joseph's ancestry, whereas Luke gives Mary's. Modern scholars frequently argue that Matthew provides the legal line of royal inheritance. For a summary view of the modern scholars on this see M.D. JOHNSON, *The Purpose,* 142.

[16] Various words have been suggested to designate this phenomenon: D.R. Bauer calls it «interruptions». D.R. BAUER, «The Literary Function», 458; C.T. Davis calls it «a break in the rhythm». See C.T. DAVIS, «The Fulfillment of Creation», 522. By the use of the phrase «pattern break» what I mean here is an expression that is different from the normal pattern.

^{2} Ἀβραὰμ		ἐγέννησεν τὸν Ἰσαάκ,
Ἰσαὰκ	δὲ	ἐγέννησεν τὸν Ἰακώβ,
Ἰακὼβ	δὲ	ἐγέννησεν τὸν Ἰούδαν

This model pattern follows a clear rhythm: the name of the «genitor» (ἀβραάμ, ἰσαάκ, ἰακώβ), the verb ἐγέννησεν, followed by the name of the «genitus» (Ἰσαάκ, Ἰακώβ, Ἰούδαν).

Every clause here forms a unit, which is constructed as «Α ἐγέννησεν Β, Β ἐγέννησεν C» and so on[17]. This stereotyped traditional pattern runs to the end of the genealogical list in 16b where the form of the verb changes from active ἐγέννησεν to passive ἐγεννήθη.

Significant to our investigation at this point are some of the outstanding compositional features in the Matthean genealogy of Jesus which do not otherwise fit into the traditional male ancestral pattern.

b) *Female Pattern Shift*

There are two categories of female pattern breaks. The first category concerns four OT women, whom Matthew pictures as foremothers of Jesus. The second category concerns Mary, the mother of Jesus.

+ The Foremothers of Jesus (1:3a, 5:a, 5b; 6b)

The first break in the traditional pattern concerns the four OT women in the ancestral list: Tamar (1:3a), Rahab (1:5a), Ruth (1:5b) and the wife of Uriah (1:6b). When it concerns these women, Matthew follows a unique and identical structural pattern:

1:3a	Ἰούδας	δὲ ἐγέννησεν	τὸν Φάρες καὶ τὸν Ζάρα	ἐκ τῆς	Θαμάρ
1:5a	Σαλμὼν	δὲ ἐγέννησεν	τὸν Βόες	ἐκ τῆς	Ῥαχάβ,
b	Βόες	δὲ ἐγέννησεν	τὸν Ἰωβὴδ	ἐκ τῆς	Ῥούθ,
1:6b	Δαυὶδ	δὲ ἐγέννησεν	τὸν Σολομῶνα	ἐκ τῆς	τοῦ Οὐρίου,

Compared to the traditional patriarchal pattern, this is an entirely new pattern because it breaks the normal rhythm in the otherwise male dominated ancestral history of Jesus, and stands apart in the structure of Matt 1:1-17.

The outstanding feature in these extensions is the identical formula «ἐκ τῆς + a woman» used in every segment, although the last extension (1:6b) has a peculiar structure. Further the matriarchal pattern high-

---

[17] R.E. BROWN, *The Birth*, 68.

lights some fixed elements such as the particle δέ, the principal verb ἐγέννησεν and the position of the subjects and the objects.

The phrase ἐκ τῆς τοῦ Οὐρίου, (1:6b) has three genitives, the first being τῆς and the second and third τοῦ Οὐρίου. The phrase is normally translated «by the wife of Uriah»[18]. Unlike the male ancestors, the «ancestresses» are not the subjects of the verb γεννάω but they are connected to the verb γεννάω with the preposition ἐκ.

+ Mary, the Mother of Jesus

In order to introduce Mary, Matthew follows a unique style, which has the following structure:[19]

```
16 Ἰακὼβ    δὲ   ἐγέννησεν   τὸν Ἰωσὴφ
                             τὸν ἄνδρα                 Μαρίας,
           ἐξ ἧς ἐγεννήθη    Ἰησοῦς ὁ λεγόμενος        Χριστός.
```

This verse portrays an unusual structure, different both from the patriarchal as well as from the matriarchal patterns we came across above. It is different from the first pattern. If Matthew had followed the patriarchal pattern, the text would be as below:

```
Ἰακὼβ    δὲ   ἐγέννησεν      τὸν Ἰωσὴφ
Ἰωσὴφ    δὲ   ἐγέννησεν τὸν   Ἰησοῦν τὸν λεγόμενος Χριστό;
```

It is also different from the second pattern. If Matthew had followed the matriarchal pattern he would have written as below:

```
Ἰακὼβ  δὲ ἐγέννησεν τὸν Ἰωσὴφ
Ἰωσὴφ  δὲ ἐγέννησεν τὸν Ἰησοῦν τὸν λεγόμενος Χριστός ἐκ τῆς Μαρίας
```

Now the most important element in this pattern break is the change of the verbal form from ἐγέννησεν (active) to the passive ἐγεννήθη (aorist passive).

By way of a double pattern break, Matthew seems to indicate already at the outset of the Gospel the special role the women play in the ancestry of Jesus. A question that is normally raised is the Matthean rationale for the incorporation of the OT women in the genealogy. An answer to

---

[18] Matthew does not use the name Bathsheba, but identifies the woman «as the wife of Uriah».

[19] The genealogy of Jesus reaches its climax with the appearance of Mary, the fifth and the final woman in the ancestral list. The dramatic break in the pattern indicates the importance of Mary in the genealogy, a role that surpasses that of the other four biblical women. See D.R. BAUER, «The Literary Function», 461-463.

this question necessarily demands knowledge of the roles they played in biblical as well as extra-biblical literature.

3.2 Biblical and Extra Biblical Evidence

3.2.1 Tamar

The word תָּמָר, literally «palm tree»[20], in the Hebrew Bible it occurs in Gen 38; Ruth 4:12; 1Chr 2:4, and in the NT it is seen in Matt 1:2. Matthew's extension ἐκ τῆς Θαμάρ seems to be based on 1Chr 2:4.

a) Biblical Evidence

The story of Tamar and Judah in the Joseph cycle (Gen 38) has been of scholarly interest in recent years[21]. Gen 38 gives the story of Tamar who was married to Er, Judah's first son by the Canaanite daughter of Shua. Two other sons of Judah were Onan and Shelah. Er was slaughtered by Yahweh as he was wicked in the sight of Yahweh, and then Tamar was given as wife to his brother Onan so that he might beget children for his dead brother, according to the levirate custom[22]. As Onan refused to fulfill his duty of begetting children for his brother and thus violated the law, Yahweh slew him (Gen 38:10). Now Judah, on the assumption that the death of his sons was because of Tamar, asked her to remain a widow in her father's house till his last son Shelah grew up, for he feared that Shelah would also have the same fate as his two other sons if he was married to Tamar. Meanwhile Judah's wife dies. On his way up to Timnah to his sheepshearers, Tamar is spotted by Judah and thinking that she is a prostitute, asks to have relations with her with a pledge to «send her a kid from the flock». At the request of Tamar, as a sign of his pledge he leaves his signet, his cord, and his staff that was in his hand. When the time came that Tamar was found to be pregnant and news reached Judah, he on hearing the news wanted to kill Tamar charging her with adultery. But Tamar battled her father-in-

---

[20] A.J. LEVINE, «Tamar», 161-163.

[21] See J. GOLDIN, «The Youngest Son», 27-44; R. ALTER, «A Literary Approach to the Bible», 70-77. For a structural presentation of the story of Tamar see G.W. COATS, «Widow's Rights», 461-466.

[22] According to the levirate custom, if a man who lived with his brothers in his father's family left his widow childless, his brothers had the responsibility for producing a male heir (Deut 25:5-10). The purpose of this custom was to keep the name of the dead husband for future generation.

law using the evidence he had left behind when he had relations with her. Judah then admits that he had relations with her. Tamar gives birth to twin children called Perez and Zerah.

Tamar is pictured as a widow fighting for her rights within the family of her dead husband. Although she faced a death sentence, she is finally presented as more righteous than Judah himself (Gen 38:26). The surprising aspect of this story is the positive presentation of Tamar[23] in contrast to Judah and his sons[24]. What is noteworthy is the role Tamar played in «the history of Israel», a role that gives continuity to it, a history which would otherwise have terminated unrealized with Judah.

Tamar is presented as a victim of injustice, deprived of her right to marry the brother of her dead husband and thus to bear children[25] who would continue the lineage of her husband, according to the levirate custom. Although she seems to be presented under a cloud of doubt and immorality, she finally wins the battle and stands as a symbol of victory to continue the lineage of Israelite history. Thus the least in the hands of Yahweh is made great by Him and helps the history of Israel to reach its goal as destined by God. Thus what is manifested is the providence of God in shaping the history of Israel, continuing the line of Judah[26].

b) *Extra-biblical Evidence*

Important Jewish traditions that give Tamar prominence are the *Book of Jubilees* (*Jub* 41:1), *The Testament of Twelve Patriarchs* (*T. Jud*

---

[23] J. EMERTON, «Judah and Tamar», 403-415.

[24] Different theories have been proposed to explain this surprising contrast. O. Eissfeldt believes that it reveals the point of view of the L source, which favors the nomadic ideal and is opposed to settlement in Canaan. Accordingly Judah was at fault in leaving his brothers and settling down, and it is no wonder he ran into trouble. O. EISSFELDT, *Hexateuch-Synopse* 26-27; O. EISSFELDT, *Einleitung,* 28; J. EMERTON, «Judah and Tamar», 403-415.

R.H. PFEIFFER ascribes Gen 38 to the S source which keeps a hostile attitude towards Judah and the other Leah tribes. See R.H. PFEIFFER, «A Non-Israelite Source», 70-72; ID., *Introduction to the Old Testament.*

Both these theories are refuted by J. A. Emerton, who questions the very existence of the S and L sources. See J.A. EMERTON, «An Examination», 338-361.

[25] This is to be understood against the sociological background of OT women. Sterility was considered a curse of God. The stories of Sarah, Rebecca, and Rachel are some of the examples of this. Bearing children was also significant from an economic point of view. A widow had to depend on her children for her daily sustenance.

[26] G. VON RAD, *Genesis,* 348.

10:1, 6; 12:1-10; 13:3) and the writings of Philo (*Quod Deus* 29.36-137; *Cong.* 23.124-126; *Mut.* 23.134-136; *Virt.* 40.220-222; *De Fuga* 27.149-156). These traditions portray Tamar positively.

Jewish traditions unanimously place the narrative on Tamar in high esteem as providential. They draw from it a profound meaning in the designs of God and the providential manner with which God acts in history. We have tradition on Tamar especially in the *Jub* 41:1 and *T. Jud* 10:1, in which a large share of the responsibility is attributed not to Tamar but to the Canaanite wife of Judah who refused to allow Shelah to marry Tamar according to the levirate law. *T. Jud* 12:2 justifies Tamar's action as in accord with the customs of her people, that is to say «... that she who was about to marry should sit in fornication seven days by the gate». Together with Ruth 4:12, that mentions Tamar favorably, the *Book of Jubilees* and *The Testament of Twelve Patriarchs* project her without guilt.

In one of the Jewish interpretations of Tamar's story, after Judah has recognized the three pledges as his own and declared Tamar innocent, a divine voice comes down from heaven and says: «You are both innocent, the matter came about from before me»[27].

Later rabbinical sources present Tamar's action as inspired by divine initiative.[28] She was honored as the ancestress of kings and prophets. Compared with Zimri, Tamar's action is seen as a source of blessing[29].

Philo, commenting on Gen 38, in *De Congressu Eruditionis Gratia* 124-126, projects θάμαρ «a type of virtue and even chastity»[30] while in *De Virtutibus* 220-222 she is described as «a woman from Syria Palestine who had been bred up in her own native city, which was devoted to the worship of many gods. But, when she, emerging, as it were, out of profound darkness was able to see a light beam of truth ... But even though she was a foreigner still she was nevertheless a freeborn woman, and born also of freeborn parents of no insignificant importance ...»[31].

---

[27] The quotation is as cited in Wainwright, *Towards a Feminist Critical Reading,* 163; see also H.N. HENDRICKX, *The Infancy Narratives,* 25.

[28] Gen R. 85 (787). See M.D. JOHNSON, *The Purpose,* 160.

[29] «Tamar committed adultery, and Zimri also committed adultery. Tamar committed adultery and kings and prophets descended from her; Zimri committed adultery and through him many ten thousands of Israel fell» (b. Hor 10 *b* 74).

[30] See M.D. JOHNSON, *The Purpose,* 159.

[31] Cited from M.D. JOHNSON, *The Purpose,* 160.

3.2.2 Rahab[32]

The Hebrew name רָחָב, from the root רחב, means «to be wide», «to enlarge». Possibly it is a shortened form of a theophoric name meaning, «God has changed»[33].

a) *Biblical Evidence*

Rahab, an inhabitant of Jericho, identified as a harlot, helps the spies of Joshua to search out Jericho, and the spies in turn promise to protect her and her family during the conquest. Rahab's co-operation with the spies eases Israel's entry into the Promised Land, thus realizing Yahweh's promise. Concerning Rahab, Matthew seems to have drawn inspiration from Josh 2:1-21 and 6:2, 17, 23, 25.

b) *Extra-biblical Evidence*

While there is no mention of Rahab in the Apocrypha, Pseudepigrapha nor Philo, Josephus presents Rahab in a favorable manner. She is presented as «an inn keeper», not once is she mentioned as a harlot:

> But When Rahab ('Ραάβη) learnt of their approach, being then engaged in drying some bundles of flax upon the roof, she concealed the spies there in, and told the kings' messengers that some unknown strangers had shortly before sundown supped with her and gone their way[34].

According to a Midrashic discussion of 1Chr 4:21-23, Rahab was rewarded for her bravery by being saved together with her family from

---

[32] Concerning the identity of Rahab there exists a scholarly dispute. The name that Matthew uses is 'Ραχάβ a name that is never documented anywhere else in the Greek LXX, or in the writings of the second century Fathers. The Septuagintal form and that found in the patristic tradition is 'Ραάβ. *First Clement* 12:1, 3; see J.D. QUINN, «Is RAXAB», 224-228. For some basic studies on Rahab see M.D. COOGAN, *Rahab*, 642.

Josephus uses the name Ραάβη (*Jewish Antiquities* V: 8, 9, 11, 15, 26, 30). The Hebrew (MT) rendering of the word is רָחָב.

Now, the dispute concerns the source for the Matthean use of 'Ραχάβ which is otherwise not attached to any tradition. J.D. Quinn proposes three suggestions for this: a) that it is the creation of the author; b) that the author transliterated it directly from a Hebrew Document which named *rhb* as the mother of *b'z*; c) that the author of the first Gospel borrowed the name from a Greek document which used the name Rahab. See J.D. QUINN, «Is RAXAB», 226.

[33] T. FRYMER-KENSKY, «Rahab», 140-141.

[34] F. JOSEPHUS, *Jewish Antiquities*, V: 9.

the destruction of Jericho[35]. A first century midrashic exegesis mentions that by becoming the ancestress of several prophets, Rahab was rewarded[36].

3.2.3 Ruth[37]

The Hebrew word רוּת means «satiation», «refreshment»[38]. In the Hebrew Bible the proper name רוּת appears in the Book of Ruth, and in the NT in Matt 1:5. Here the name designates the daughter-in-law of Naomi, wife of Boaz and the grandmother of David.

a) *Biblical Evidence*

The third ancestress in the Matthean list is Ruth, a Moabitess, Gentile and widow (Ruth 1:4; 2:1, 6) who perpetuates the name Elimelech by marrying Boaz and bearing him a son.

Ruth is presented as a childless young widow who uses different means to justify her position in the dead husband's family. In spite of her mother-in-law Naomi's attempt to send her back to her own people, she stays back with Naomi and eventually marries the patriarchal kinsman, Boaz[39], who belongs to the extended family of Elimelech. To them is born Obed, who continues the family line to become the progenitor of David. Ruth is thus presented as an important link in the ancestral history.

---

[35] See M.D. JOHNSON, *The Purpose,* 163.

[36] See Sifre on *Numbers,* 78; *Ruth Rabbah* 2:1 (25). According to Johnson, these two references give clues as to why Matthew alone, among all Jewish or Christian sources of biblical and Talmudic times, connects Rahab to the tribe of Judah and the ancestry of David. See M.D. JOHNSON, *The Purpose,* 165.

[37] The Book of Ruth tells the story of Naomi and Ruth, which is a tale of human kindness and devotion that transcends the boundaries of self-interest and other concerns. In our investigation we concentrate on Ruth as an ancestress in the genealogical tree of Jesus, who keeps the lines of generation united. The book of Ruth has been a subject of consideration in Old Testament scholarship, and it has a place of importance for its social, political, religious and aesthetic values in the history of Israel. See D.R.G. BEATTIE, «The Book of Ruth», 251-267; A. BERTMAN, «Symmetrical Design», 165-168; A. BRENNER, «Naomi and Ruth», 385-397; R. GORDIS «Love», 241-264; R.M. HALS, *The Theology of the Book of Ruth;* E.H. MERRIL, «The Book of Ruth», 130-141; O. LORETZ, «The Theme of Ruth Story», 391-99.

[38] P. TRIBLE, «Ruth», 146-147.

[39] Some scholars have pointed out that Naomi and Ruth belong together, and cannot be separated» and that «the one would be nothing without the other». See O. EISSFELDT, *The Old Testament,* 481-482.

b) *Extra-biblical Evidence*

Rabbinic literature holds Ruth in high esteem. The story of Ruth impressed the rabbis because of the surprising generosity with which she decides to follow her mother-in-law to a foreign country. Following her mother-in-law meant inserting herself in the Hebrew people, which the Talmud speaks of as «determined by God»[40]. It was God's own design to bring her to a new place and thus make it possible for her to meet Boaz[41]. According to *bHorayoth* 10b, Ruth was the granddaughter of Eglon. As an ancestor of Ruth, Eglon also receives a favorable mention[42].

3.2.4 The Wife of Uriah

The wife of Uriah is identified as «Bathsheba»[43]. The word Bathsheba, probably, signifies «daughter of Sheba» or daughter of «abundance». It derives from the Hebrew root *bat* (daughter) and *seba* («Sheba» or «abundance» (2Sam 11-12; 1Kgs 1-2; 1Chr 3:5; Psa 51).

a) *Biblical Evidence*

The fourth and last OT woman in the Messianic genealogy according to Matthew is Bathsheba (1Chr 3:5), the daughter of Eliam and the former wife of Uriah the Hittite. She later became the wife of David (reigned c. 1005-965) and the mother of Solomon (reigned c. 968-928 BC).

The story about Bathsheba is to be found in 2Sam 11-12 and 1Kgs 1-2, which describe at length the events concerning David's conduct with Bathsheba and his effort to cover up his sin. The David-Bathsheba narrative (2Sam 11-12) portrays David as culpable of misconduct while it makes no comment about Bathsheba's participation in the event except that «she came to him».

---

[40] See *BabaBatra* 91b.

[41] See the midrashic commentary to *Ruth* 4.14 in A. WÜNSCHE, *Midrash Ruth Rabba*, 39-42, 57.

[42] See M.D. JOHNSON, *The Purpose*, 166.

[43] This title, according to A. J. Levine, anticipates two Matthean themes: Uriah, a Hittite, foreshadows the entry of the Gentiles into the church; Bathsheba commits adultery with David and thereby foreshadows Jesus' unexpected conception (A.J. LEVINE, «Matt 9:20-22», 407). It is true that Matthew believes in the entry of the Gentiles into the Church (28:16-20). It is also true that he believes in the unusual conception of Jesus. But it is difficult to see how they are linked to the title Bathsheba.

b) *Extra-biblical Traditions*

Bathsheba has a prominent place in the Jewish world because of her relation to David[44]. Rabbinical traditions contain several allusions to the David and Bathsheba incidents[45]. The Midrash reads: «It is revealed and known to thee that Bath-sheba was held ready for me from the six days of creation, yet she was given to me for sorrow» (*Midrash Psalms* 3:5). On David's conduct the Damascus Documents of Qumran Literature (CD V:1-5) says:

> And the ones who went into the ark, Gen 7:9 «went in two by two into the ark». And about the Prince it is written: 2Deut 17:17 «He should not multiply wives to himself». However, David had not read the sealed book of the law which was in the ark, for it had not been opened in Israel since the day of the death of Eleazar and of Jehoshua, and Joshua and the elders who worshipped Ashtaroth had hidden the public (copy) until Zadok's entry into office. And David's deeds were praised, except for Uriah's blood[46].

By way of summarizing this discussion on these four OT women, we conclude with the observation that both the biblical as well as the extra-biblical traditions hailed them as co-operating with the divine plan for the realization of the messianic birth[47]. We are inclined to believe that Matthew's incorporation of these women in the ancestral list was with a special purpose, which becomes more intelligible by comparing their mention with the various male-pattern breaks in the genealogy.

3.3 *Interpretation*

In interpreting Matt 1:1-17, we will first critically analyze some of the contemporary scholarly opinions on the Matthean rationale for the

---

[44] M.D. JOHNSON, *The Purpose*, 159.

[45] The most important among them are *Qiddushin* 43a, *Midrash Samuel* 25:2, *Taanith* 2:10; *Midrash Psalms* 3:3; 3:5; 4:2; *Shabbath* 55b: *Numbers Rabbah* 11:3; *Numbers Rabbah* 10:4; *Leveticus Rabbah* 12:5.

[46] F.G. MARTINEZ, *The Dead Sea Scrolls*, 36.

[47] Analysis of the Matthean genealogical structure and both the biblical as well as the extra-biblical background to the genealogy reveal its Midrashic character (M.D. JOHNSON, *The Purpose*, 209) which explains Matthew's insertion of four women in the Messianic ancestry. The Matthean genealogy is not to be understood as a mere compilation of names from history for preaching or catechesis, but it is to be understood as Matthew making use of various elements from his own time in a creative manner to bring out the message of the Messiah to his community.

inclusion of the women in the genealogy. We will then see it against the background of the discipleship theme in Matthew.

3.3.1 A Critical Appraisal of the Contemporary Interpretation

R.E. Brown offers a threefold summarized view of the contemporary scholarly interpretation on the presence of the women in the Matthean genealogy. The first interpretation is based on the «sinful status» of these women; the second interpretation is based on the «Gentile status» of these women, and the third interpretation is based on their irregular sexual union with their partners[48].

a) *Women and their Sinful Status*

The first interpretation rests on the women's sinful status. Scholars who hold this interpretation argue that the women's inclusion in the family tree of Jesus indicates Matthew's concern to show Jesus as the Savior of sinners, men as well as women[49]. On this R.E. Brown observes: «... the four OT women were regarded as sinners and their inclusion foreshadowed for Matthew's readers the role of Jesus as the Savior of sinful men»[50]. These women's inclusion in the genealogy means that they are included in salvation (Matt 1:21). Thus already at the very outset of the Gospel, Matthew intends to present Jesus as the Savior of sinners. God's purpose is achieved despite human failure[51]. Scholars A. Plummer[52], E. Lohmeyer[53], D. Heffern[54], T. H. Robinson[55], H. Milton[56], and F. Rienecker[57] support this interpretation.

This interpretation has received widespread criticism. For, neither the biblical nor the extra-biblical traditions treat all these women as sinners[58]. Rather, some traditions even portray them as models of faith and

---

[48] R.E. BROWN, *The Birth*, 71-74.

[49] See L. RODGER, «The Infancy Stories», 63.

[50] R.E. BROWN, *The Birth*, 71; D. HEFFERN, «The Four Women», 68-81.

[51] See C. BLOMBERG, «The Liberation of Illegitimacy», 145; R.E. BROWN, *The Birth*, 71; N. CASALINI, *Libro*, 63.

[52] A. PLUMMER, *An Exegetical Commentary*, 2-3.

[53] E. LOHMEYER, *Das Evangelium des Matthäus*, 5.

[54] D. HEFFERN, «The Four Women», 77-78.

[55] T.H. ROBINSON, *The Gospel of Matthew*, 3.

[56] H. MILTON, «The Structure», 176.

[57] F. RIENECKER, *Das Evangelium des Matthäus*, 15.

[58] M. -J. LAGRANGE, *Evangile selon saint Matthieu* I, 1; F.W. BEARE, *The Gospel according to Matthew*.

virtue. For example, there is no instance where Ruth is presented as a sinful woman, instead she is praised (Ruth 3:10)[59]. If, on the one hand, Rahab is presented as a harlot, on the other hand, she is portrayed as a heroine for Israel and a model of faith (Josh 2:1-24; see Heb 11:31). Similarly while Uriah's wife is pictured as an adulteress, what the story emphasizes more is the displeasure of the Lord with David (2Sam 11-12)[60]. Hence this interpretation of Matthew's inclusion of women in the genealogy is not convincing.

b) *Women and their Gentile Status*

The second interpretation rests on the Gentile status of the women[61]. The scholars who support this interpretation hold the view that Matthew inserts these women in the genealogy of Jesus as a symbol of the inclusion of the Gentiles in the salvation that God offers in Jesus[62]. Summarizing this opinion Brown writes: «…the women were regarded as foreigners and were included by Matthew to show that Jesus, the Jewish Messiah, was related by ancestry to the gentiles»[63]. The Matthean scholars Gundry[64], Plummer[65], Sabourin[66] and Lohmeyer[67] have supported this interpretation. This view is also challenged. We have no substantial evidence that supports the Gentile status of all these women[68].

c) *The Virgin Birth of Jesus Explained*

While the first two explanations rest on the OT women's «contrast» to Mary, this third explanation rests on their «correspondence» with her. This interpretation proposes a link between the four women and Mary. This, according to M.D. Johnson, explains «the contention that Matthew, by including the four women, is consciously refuting or miti-

---

[59] See S. NIDITCH, «The Wronged Woman Righted», 147; M.D. JOHNSON, *The Purpose,* 159-75; A. PAUL, *L'Evangile,* 31-35.

[60] E.M. WAINWRIGHT, *Towards a Feminist Critical Reading,* 65.

[61] U. LUZ, *Das Evangelium nach Matthäus,* I, 93-95.

[62] L. RODGER, «The Infancy Stories», 62.

[63] R.E. BROWN, *The Birth,* 72.

[64] R. H. GUNDRY, *Matthew,* 14-15.

[65] A. PLUMMER, *Matthew,* 2.

[66] L. SABOURIN, *L'Evangile selon saint Matthieu,* 19.

[67] E. LOHMEYER, *Das Evangelium des Matthäus,* 5.

[68] D.H. HAGNER, *Matthew 1-13,* 10.

gating attacks on the legitimacy of Jesus' birth by pointing to blemishes in the biblical pedigree of David and the Davidic kings themselves»[69]. This view is supported by T. Zahn[70], J. Weiss[71], A. McNeil[72], R. Leaney[73], C.J.G. Monterfiore[74], F.W. Beare[75], and J. Schaberg[76]. The structure that we propose to the Matthean genealogy of Jesus supports this interpretation. According to the proposed structure, a pattern shift, (ἐγέννησεν .... ἐκ τῆς + woman, 1:3, 5-6) was necessary in order to introduce the OT women.

This pattern shift prepared for the introduction of Mary whom Matthew introduces using an entirely unique style (ἐξ ἧς ἐγεννήθη, 1:16). Matthew does it in a symbolic way, by shifting the verbal pattern from «"male"+ ἐγέννησεν τὸν + ἐκ τῆς + "woman's name"» to Μαρίας (female) + ἐξ ἧς ἐγεννήθη Ἰησοῦς ὁ λεγόμενος Χριστός.

The inclusion of the OT women becomes background material to help readers accept the forthcoming virginal birth (1:18-25). As God vindicated these women of the Old Testament, he would also vindicate Mary[77]. Having prepared the whole background to the birth of Jesus in the genealogy, Matthew's birth story of Jesus (1:18-25) begins to offer a more complete explanation, that is to say, how Jesus is conceived ἐκ πνεύματος ἁγίου (1:18, 20). Thus Jesus is both the Son of God and of Davidic origin. Therefore, the inclusion of women in the genealogy is important as it highlights the identity of Jesus.

3.3.2 Genealogy and the Discipleship Theme

Having analyzed Matt 1:1-17, and having presented three generally proposed interpretations of the Matthean inclusion of the women in the

---

[69] M.D. JOHNSON, The Purpose, 158.

[70] T. ZAHN, Das Evangelium des Matthäus, 64.

[71] J. WEISS, Die Schriften des NT, 234.

[72] A. McNEIL, The Gospel according to St. Matthew, 5.

[73] R. LEANEY, «The Birth Narratives», 165.

[74] C.J.G. MONTEFIORE, The Synoptic Gospels, 4.

[75] F.W. BEARE, The earliest Records, 30.

[76] J. SCHABERG, The Illegitimacy of Jesus, 20-34.

[77] See R.E. BROWN, The Birth, 71-74; K. STENDAHL, «Quis et Unde»?, 74; E. STAUFFER, Jesus and His Story, 17; R.V.G. TASKER, The Gospel according to St. Matthew, 32; M. SMITH, Jesus the Magician, 26, 66-67; S.S. LAWS, A Commentary on the Epistle of James, 137; D.J. HARRINGTON, Matthew, 13-14; R.A. EDWARDS, Matthew's Story of Jesus, 11; E.D. FREED, «The Women», 3-19: G.L. BLOMBERG, Matthew, 55-56.

genealogy, let us now see if it is related to the discipleship theme in the Gospel. We do it by analyzing different elements that we have high-lighted in the above discussion.

a) *Abrahamic Origin of Jesus*

The first important element is the title «son of Abraham»[78], a title that traces Jesus' origin back to Abraham, the first in the succession of names of generations that lead up to Jesus Christ. It is clear that Matthew is interested in the Abrahamic origin of Jesus. Abraham is an eschatological figure, connected to salvation stretching beyond Jewish confines[79]. Thus Abraham remains a symbol of universal blessing, through whom all the nations will be blessed[80]. Abraham is the bearer of God's promise, which is carried on to the succeeding generations, exemplified by Isaac and Jacob (Matt 1:2). This pattern is expected to be continued till the realization of God's promise in the future. The beneficiaries of God's promise in each case are always all the nations of the earth.

Now when Matthew calls Jesus «υἱοῦ 'Αβραάμ», he wants to evoke the idea of God's promise to Israel, and thus the blessing of all the na-tions. Jesus' identity as the Son of Abraham therefore means that Jesus is the one who will realize God's promise of the blessings for all the nations.

In Jesus, the climax of Israel's history, God blesses all the nations. Thus the title υἱοῦ 'Αβραάμ links Jesus to his coming ministry which culminates in his commission to the apostles to make disciples of all nations (28:19)[81].

---

[78] This title does not occur anywhere else in Matthew. But the name Abraham is found three times in the genealogy (Matt 1:1, 2, 17). Elsewhere in Matthew it occurs in 3:9; 8:11; 22:32.

[79] Especially important is the occurrence of the name Abraham in Matthew. In Matt 3:9, John the Baptist challenges the false security of the Jewish leaders as sons of Abraham. God's power to bring forth progeny from Abraham out of the stones is stressed here. The use of the word τέκνα (posterity, children), instead of υἱος, perhaps refers to a wider meaning. See G. SCHNEIDER, «τέκνον», 818.

[80] Abraham is the bearer of God's promise (Gen 18:18; 22:18; 26:4; 28:14). The content of God's promise is blessing, the beneficiary of which is universal, «all the tribes of the earth», (12:3b) and which will be effected through Abraham.

[81] See G. TISERA, *Universalism*, 39.

b) *The Davidic Ancestry of Jesus*

The second important element is the title υἱοῦ Δαυίδ («son of David») applied to Jesus. The Evangelist's intention is to show that the origin of Jesus is from the Davidic line. The title υἱοῦ Δαυίδ, applied to Jesus, reveals both the identity and mission of Jesus, anticipating one of the major themes of the Gospel. Jesus is the Son of David who brings salvation to Israel in a special way by his performing mighty acts. In this manner, identifying Jesus as «son of David», Matthew anticipates his coming ministry. Jesus assumes a Messianic function[82].

c) *Four OT Women and the Discipleship Theme*

Matthew's mention of Tamar, Rahab, Ruth and the wife of Uriah is in conformity with the Abrahamic and the Davidic lineage of Jesus. At this point of our discussion Matthew does not seem to have any explicit intention of associating the OT women with the theme of discipleship in the Gospel. We find no discipleship vocabulary to establish it. The Evangelist's direct intention seems to highlight the role of women in the ancestry of Jesus. God chooses these women as important links that give continuity to the ancestry. Being sinners or pagans, under divine providence, they enter into a new «way of life». They become important vehicles of the Messianic ancestry. In this sense we see that a remote discipleship theme is perhaps contained in Matthew's presentation of the women in the genealogy.

d) *Mary and the Discipleship Theme in Matthew*

We have already seen the important structural position that Mary occupies in the genealogy of Jesus. The peculiar way Matthew introduces her, projects the vision of the author who prepares the way for her through a matriarchal pattern break (1:2, 5-6). Various scholars have tried to interpret it in terms of discipleship in the Gospel. For example, John de Stagé calls Mary a disciple because «the mother of Jesus was her son's disciple»[83]. This author states it, but does not show it in the Gospel. Similarly, P.J. Bearsley states that in Mary Matthew offers us the paradigm for our own discipleship[84]. We are of the opinion that the peculiar way that Matthew introduces Mary, the mother of Jesus, shows

---

82 G. TISERA, *Universalism*, 19.
83 J.D. STAGÉ, *Mary and the Christian Gospel*, 57.
84 P.J. BEARSLEY, «Mary the Perfect Disciple», 469.

the importance she is given in the Gospel of Matthew in general, and in the genealogy in particular. At this point of our research we find no clear indication of Mary as a disciple of Jesus. Matthew does not speak of her discipleship here. However, because she made herself available to the divine plan, and because «it was of her» (1:16) that Jesus is born, we can perhaps say that a discipleship theme is also present here.

In short, Matthew is the only Evangelist who begins the Gospel with the genealogy of Jesus. Among the various features that are highlighted in the narrative, one that calls for our special attention is the presence of the women in the genealogy: Tamar, Rahab, Ruth, the Wife of Uriah and Mary. We are not sure of Matthew's intention in incorporating these women in the genealogy. Certainly it is an intentional act.

None of the above interpretations are left unchallenged. Whatever be the intention of the author, one message that we get from the text is that God has made use of these women as important and unavoidable links in the ancestry of Jesus. Without these female characters, the ancestry of Jesus would remain broken. Matthew's portrayal of the women in the genealogy gives us an indication of the special role women will play in the Gospel narratives.

4. Jesus and Peter's Mother-in-law (Matt 8:14-15)

We now discuss Matt 8:14-15 in which the Evangelist speaks of Jesus' healing of a woman. She has no name. But she is identified in relation to Peter: she is the mother-in-law of Peter. There is no dialogue in this passage[85]. It is the first healing story of a woman in the Gospel[86], and the third of ten «miracles» described in Matt 8-9. The whole story is centered on Jesus and the sick woman whom he heals[87]. Matthew describes that Jesus saw (εἶδον) the woman lying sick with a fever[88]. Jesus touches and heals her[89]. As a result «she rose and began to serve him» (καί ἠγέρθη καὶ διηκόνει αὐτῷ).

---

[85] The text focuses on the healing itself rather than on a dialogue about it. See D. PATTE, *The Gospel according to Matthew*, 116.

[86] See E. HAENCHEN, *Der Weg Jesu*, 89.

[87] See S. GRASSO, *Il Vangelo di Matteo*, 231; R.H. GUNDRY, *Matthew*, 148; A. STOCK, *The Method and Message of Matthew*, 135.

[88] That the woman lies with a fever means that she is not able to be active any more in the domestic sphere, which in the ancient Mediterranean world was the sphere proper to a woman. See J.J. PILCH, *Healing in the New Testament*, 79.

[89] On Jesus' healing of the woman see A. FUCHS, «Entwicklungsgeschichtliche Studie», 21-76; H.M. KELLER, *Jesus und die Frauen*, 106-110. P. BONNARD,

4.1 Compositional Features

Matt 8:14-15, a structurally concise and unique pericope devoid of unnecessary details[90], illustrates the Matthean precision and rhetoric[91]. On the structure of vv. 14-15 D. Hill states that these «may be evidence of a Christian rabbinic mind in action, making a narrative easily remembered for the community»[92]. This short pericope portrays a striking chiasmus[93]:

Introduction: [14] Καὶ ἐλθὼν ὁ Ἰησοῦς εἰς τὴν οἰκίαν Πέτρου
    a εἶδεν τὴν πενθερὰν αὐτοῦ
      b βεβλημένην
        c καὶ πυρέσσουσαν·
          d [15] καὶ ἥψατο τῆς χειρὸς αὐτῆς,
        c' καὶ ἀφῆκεν αὐτὴν ὁ πυρετός,
      b' καὶ ἠγέρθη
    a' καὶ διηκόνει αὐτῷ.

The minimalist Matthean miracle story directs attention both to the person and to the power of Jesus. The chiastic structure emphasizes it. Matthew's tightening up the little story makes of it a pure Jesus story. There is no mention of the disciples here. No request is made of Jesus. Jesus, who comes to the house and sees the woman, touches and heals her on his own initiative. As a result the fever left her, she got up, and served him. The central figure is Jesus himself.

Similar to different pattern breaks introduced in the genealogy, this pericope also contains certain pattern shifts that make the sick woman

---

L'évangile selon Saint Matthieu, 182; F.W. BEARE, *The Gospel according to Matthew*, 211; R.H. GUNDRY, *Matthew*, 148; H.N. HENDRICKX, *The Miracle Stories*, 75.

[90] Matthew's dependence on and abbreviation of Mark 1:29-31 is clear. Various changes deserve special mention. First, Matthew omits the opening Markan introduction Καὶ εὐθὺς ἐκ τῆς συναγωγῆς ἐξελθόντες («immediately coming from the synagogue»). The second alteration concerns Matthew's substitution of the name Πέτρου for the Markan Σίμωνος, at the same time omitting the names of Andrew, James and John who accompanied them. Third, Matthew employs the demonstrative pronoun αὐτῷ («him») instead of Mark's αὐτοῖς («them»), lending therefore a distinct Christological aspect to the story. See E.M. WAINWRIGHT, *Towards a Feminist Critical Reading*, 183-187.

[91] See H.J. HELD, «Matthew as Interpreter», 167; A.C. WIRE, «The Structure», 83-113.

[92] D. HILL, *The Gospel of Matthew*, 160.

[93] See D.H. HAGNER, *Matthew 1-13*, 209; H.N. HENDRICKX, *The Miracle Stories*, 75.

important in the narrative and which help us to understand the meaning of the text. Normally in any healing story it is the penitent or someone on his/her behalf that takes the initiative to come to Jesus and make a request for healing. We have two examples: the leper's request to Jesus for healing (Matt 8:2) and the centurion's request to heal his servant (8:8):

«Lord, if you will, you can make me clean» (8:2).
«Lord... only say the word, and my servant will be healed» (8:8).

Both the leper (8:2) as well as the centurion (8:8) make a request to Jesus. In comparison to these characters, Peter's mother-in-law is passive; neither she nor anyone else on her behalf takes the initiative or makes a request to Jesus for healing. On the contrary Jesus takes the initiative of approaching her, touching and healing her[94]. This indicates a pattern break. It is confirmed by Jesus' silence throughout this healing event, a silence which is exceptional in such stories[95].

4.2 Interpretation: Peter's Mother-in-Law as a Model of Service

Various interpretations are given to Jesus' healing of Peter's mother-in-law, and her response to Jesus. Some scholars call it a vocation story. One argument that they suggest is its structural similarity to the call of Matthew in Matt 9:9. Citing Boismard, E.M. Wainwright proposes the following structural comparison between these two passages[96]:

Compositional Motifs	Matt 8:14-15	Matt 9:9
Introduction Coming of the Caller	Καὶ ἐλθὼν ὁ Ἰησοῦς εἰς τὴν οἰκίαν Πέτρου εἶδεν τὴν πενθερὰν αὐτοῦ	Καὶ παράγων ὁ Ἰησοῦς ἐκεῖθεν εἶδεν ἄνθρωπον ... Μαθθαῖον
Sees one to be called	βεβλημένην καὶ πῦ ρέσσουσαν·	καθήμενον ἐπὶ τὸ τελώνιον,

---

[94] «Touching» in Matthew is for the purpose of healing. Jesus touches the leper and heals him (8:3). Here too Jesus continues to heal by physical contact. See D. PATTE, *The Gospel according to Matthew*, 116.

[95] In Mark and Luke too Jesus doesn't speak to the woman. But in Luke we are told that Jesus «stood over her and rebuked the fever, and it left her» (Luke 4:39). See F.W. BEARE, *The Gospel according to Matthew*, 210.

[96] E.M. WAINWRIGHT, *Towards a Feminist Critical Reading*, 181.

Exposition Description of the One to be called	καὶ ἥψατο τῆς χειρὸς αὐτῆς, καὶ ἀφῆκεν αὐτὴν ὁ πυρετός,	καὶ λέγει αὐτῷ, ᾽Ακολούθει μοι.
Middle Call-word or ac- tion	καὶ ἠγέρθη καὶ διηκόνει αὐτῷ.	καὶ ἀναστὰς ἠκολούθησεν αὐτῷ.
Conclusion Response to Call		

Wainwright argues that the story of Peter's mother-in-law is clearly a vocation story. She holds:

> The earliest memory, therefore, that influenced the Matthean community was the vocation of a woman, as it was this memory that was preserved by the community during the course of the story's development. It is difficult to establish whether the healing motif belonged to the story in its origin or whether it was inserted later under the influence of the story as preserved in the Markan and Lukan traditions. The most likely possibility seems to be it belonged to the origin of the story, and that the Matthean community has maintained its two-fold aspect: vocation and healing[97].

According to Boismard, the vocation story-type used in Matt 8:14-15; 9:9 and the calling of the first four disciples (Mark 1:16-20; Matt 4:18-22) had their origin in one of the earliest written collections of the Gospel traditions[98]. F. Martin maintains a similar position[99]. R. Pesch also notes elements of the vocation story in the pericope[100]. Commenting on Matt 8:14-15, D. Patte states:

> Furthermore, that she is presented as the mother-in-law of Peter, a disciple, suggests that by serving Jesus and acknowledging his authority over her she adopts the attitude of a disciple. This connotation is barely marked and should not be taken into consideration if Matthew did not introduce the theme of discipleship in the following verses (8:18-22). Then too one wonders whether this third type of healing initiated by Jesus—without request from anyone and thus without expression of prior faith on the part of the patient—is not comparable to discipleship (cf. 4:18-22; 9:9); they too are

---

[97] E.M. WAINWRIGHT, *Towards a Feminist Critical Reading*, 182.
[98] M.É. BOISMARD, *Synopse*, 97.
[99] F. MARTIN, *Encounter Story*, 62.
[100] R. PESCH, «Die Heilung», 166.

fully initiated by Jesus. But would this mean that a call to discipleship is to be viewed as comparable to healing? This suggestion, perhaps now far-fetched, is to be confirmed and specified in 9:9-13[101].

D.A. Hagner holds the opinion that the grateful woman's response in service becomes a model for the Christian readers of Matthew. This woman ministered to Jesus in grateful response to what he had done for her. Hagner calls it a fundamental aspect of discipleship[102].

C.S. Keener concludes: «This structure may make emphatic the model for discipleship: after Jesus transforms a person, the person serves him»[103].

It is true that there is some structural resemblance between Matt 8:14-15 (Jesus' healing of Peter's mother-in-law) and Matt 9:9 (Call of Matthew). In our opinion the structural similarity alone is not enough to call 8:14-15 a vocation story. Other than a structural similarity we find nothing that suggests it to be a vocation story. There is no call from Jesus to follow him. We have no evidence that this woman later followed Jesus. Nowhere in the Gospel is she labeled a disciple of Jesus.

However, along with D. Patte and D.A. Hagner, we find certain discipleship elements in the story. The account of Jesus' healing of Peter's mother-in-law ends with the note that, healed by the touch of Jesus, the woman «rose up» (ἠγέρθη) and «served him» (διηκόνει αὐτῷ). The aorist passive form ἠγέρθη has both an active («she rose up»,) as well as a passive sense («she was raised up»)[104]. Here Matthew uses this verb in an active sense to speak of the woman's rising up. The healed woman is described as having got up and «served him» (διηκόνει αὐτῷ). Her action indicates that she is really healed by Jesus. The word διακονέω may refer to service in general as well as service to Jesus in particular (Matt 4:11; 27:55)[105]. In Matthew we find this verb used mainly in reference to the mission and ministry of Jesus (20:28; 25:44). Matthew's Gospel emphasizes service, not necessarily to Jesus, as a discipleship element. It is clear that every service need not be related to discipleship

---

[101] D. PATTE, *The Gospel according to Matthew*, 116.

[102] D.A. HAGNER, *Matthew 1-14*, 208-289.

[103] C.S. KEENER, *Matthew*, 271.

[104] The verb ἐγείρω here refers to the effect of the total healing (Matt 9:5, 6, 7). Besides this meaning of getting up it refers also to a 'passage' from death to life. Later the verb becomes a technical word that refers to the resurrection of Jesus (28:6, 7). See S. GRASSO, *Il Vangelo di Matteo*, 259; R.H. GUNDRY, *Matthew*, 148.

[105] See S. GRASSO, *Il Vangelo di Matteo*, 230-31; L.L. MORRIS, *The Gospel According to Matthew*, 197; G.S. TWELFTREE, *Jesus the Miracle Worker*, 110-111.

of Jesus. In this context, the service that the mother-in-law of Peter extended to Jesus can point either to her service in gratitude for Jesus' healing her or merely as a gesture of hospitality towards him[106]. In describing this woman as serving Jesus, Matthew introduces her to his readers as a model of service. Although we cannot call this healing story a discipleship story, certainly we see some discipleship implications contained in it.

5. Jesus and the Woman with a Hemorrhage (Matt 9:20-22)

Having studied the miracle story that presents a woman as a model for service in Matthew (8:14-15), we now discuss another miracle story in which Matthew presents a woman with a hemorrhage, whom the Matthean Jesus praises for her great faith[107].

5.1 *Compositional Features*

It is generally believed that Matthew took this passage over from Mark, which he abbreviated to suit to his purpose. Of all the miracle accounts this is the one that Matthew shortened most. In comparison to Mark and Luke, all vivid scenes and expansive motives are eliminated. Matthew, like Mark and Luke, places this healing story (9:20-22) within the framework of the raising of the ruler's daughter (vv. 18-19 and 23-26)[108]. Some scholars have indicated an intrusion of a new story[109], which is signaled by Matthew's use of the phrase καί ἰδού, «and look»[110]. We think that it is an intercalation, which means the sandwiching of one unit in the middle of another. Whether the intercalation is due to Mark[111] or due to pre-Markan tradition[112] is not clear.

---

106 See G.S. TWELFTREE, *Jesus the Miracle Worker*, 110.

107 See V.K. ROBBINS, «The Woman», 502-515; M.J. SELVIDGE, «Mark 5:25-34», 619-623.

108 See D.C. ALLISON, *Matthew*, II, 123-24; V.K. ROBBINS, «The Woman who touched Jesus' Garment», 502-515; R.H. GUNDRY, *Matthew*, 173-175; E.M. WAINWRIGHT, *Towards a Feminist Critical Reading*, 191-215.

109 D.A. HAGNER, *Matthew 1-13*, 248; L.L. MORRIS, *The Gospel according to Matthew*, 230-231; R.H. SMITH, *Matthew*, 143; D. PATTE, *The Gospel according to Matthew*, 132.

110 Matthew uses ἰδού throughout the narrative in order to draw attention to different characters and events. For a list of sixty-two occurrences of it in Matthew in comparison to seven in Mark see R. MORGENTHALER, *Statistik*, 106.

111 H. SCHÜRMANN, *Das Lukasevangelium* I, 492; J. GNILKA, *Markus* I, 210.

112 See M. DIBELIUS, *From Tradition to Gospel*, 72.

Those who suggest a Markan priority usually consider intercalation to be a special Markan technique of composition[113]: We see a «healing» within a raising[114]:

Ruler's request to raise his daughter (9:18-19)
    Healing of a woman with a hemorrhage (9:20-22)
Raising of the ruler's daughter (9:23-26)

Our focus is on the central scene, which is on Jesus' healing of the woman with a hemorrhage (9:20-22). It contains four elements that are presented in a consecutive and progressive manner: a) the initiative of the woman (v. 20); b) the reasoning of the woman's approach to Jesus (v. 21); c) the pronouncement of Jesus (22), and finally d) Jesus' healing of the woman (v. 22b). This scene stands out because of the catchword σῴζω («to save») used three times in this passage.

Interrupting Jesus' journey to raise the dead girl (9:18-19, 23-26), the sick woman touches the fringe of Jesus' garment from behind, in the hope of gaining a cure. Jesus turns and sees the woman, and states, «Take heart, daughter; your faith has saved you» (v. 22). The conjoined healing thus involves the woman's touching Jesus, Jesus' calling her «daughter» and the woman's faith in Jesus' power[115]. The emphasis falls on the woman's faith[116].

Similar to the previous passage, the woman in this episode has neither a name nor any identity of her own. She approaches Jesus from behind and touches the fringe of his garment[117] telling herself: «If I only touch his garment, I will be healed» (9:21)[118].

---

[113] See J.R. DONAHUE, *Are You Christ,* 42, 58-63.

[114] A. STOCK, *The Method and Message of Matthew,* 153-54.

[115] A.J. LEVINE, «Matt 9:20-22», 408.

[116] See P. TRUMMER, *Blutende Frau,* 87-89, 109-17; H. FRANKMÖLLE, *Matthäus Kommentar,* I, 320; W.D. DAVIES – D.C. ALLISON, *Matthew,* II, 127.

[117] Seizing the edge of someone's robe was a gesture of fervent entreaty in biblical tradition (1Sam 15:27). See M. HUTTER, «Ein altorientalischer Bittgestus», 133-135; See KEENER, *Matthew,* 303. See also R.H. GUNDRY, *Matthew,* 173; L.L. MORRIS, *The Gospel According to Matthew,* 229; W. HENDRICKSEN, *The Gospel of Matthew,* 431.

[118] The idea of being healed even through the garments a holy person wore was not very unusual in the time of Jesus. For a discussion see D.A. HAGNER, *Matthew 1-13,* 249; M. COHEN, «The Tallit», 3-15; L.L. MORRIS, *The Gospel according to Matthew,* 229; W.F. ALBRIGHT – C.S. MANN, *Matthew,* 111.

5.1.1 Pattern Break

According to Lev 15:25, a woman who has a discharge of blood for many days and not at the time of her impurity is unclean. Through physical contact, she could make others too unclean transmitting ritual uncleanness (see Lev 15:19-24). Matt 9:20-22 seems to offer a contrast. The woman with an issue is presented in a wholly positive light. There is no description that her touch effects indignation. Neither does any of the onlookers whisper that Jesus has come into contact with an unclean woman. It is something new to the reader. For the first time Matthew presents an unclean woman seeking grace from Jesus[119]. The woman touches Jesus. Instead of the uncleanness passing from the woman to Jesus, healing power flows from Jesus to the women. So there is a contrast, a pattern shift[120].

5.1.2 A Male-Female Comparison

Because of being inserted within the story of the healing of the ruler's daughter, the woman's situation, handicapped by a permanent state of uncleanness, may be compared and contrasted with that of the male ruler.

The ruler is described to be kneeling down in front of Jesus (προσεκύνει αὐτῷ), while the woman is said to have approached Jesus from behind (προσελθοῦσα ὄπισθεν). In comparison to the ruler, the woman is timid either because of her sex or because of her illness that keeps her unclean and therefore untouchable (Lev 15:25). In contrast to the ruler who is wealthy and powerful, the woman is sick and socially as well as religiously marginalized[121].

The woman's faith in Jesus saves her: Θάρσει, θύγατερ· ἡ πίστις σου σέσωκέν σε (9:22). By healing her Jesus responds to her faith: Θάρσει, θύγατερ ἡ πίστις σου σέσωκέν σε (9:22). Here the woman is addressed

---

119 A. J. LEVINE, «Matt 9:20-22», 408-409.

120 See W.D. DAVIES – D. C. ALLISON, *Matthew* II, 127.

121 Her flow of blood made her ritually unclean and therefore defiling to others (see Lev 15:19-33; *m. Toharot* 5:8). The woman's disability was not only a physical malady, but one that had significant social implications. Her uncleanness kept her dissociated from society and cut off from the ceremonial observances of the community. See L.L. MORRIS, *The Gospel according to Matthew*, 229; G.S. KEENER, *Matthew*, 193. According to Albright and Mann, the extension of the taboo of ritual uncleanness arose from a desire to avoid infection or contagion. W.F. ALBRIGHT – C.S. MANN, *Matthew*, 111.

tenderly θύγατερ, «daughter» (9:22)[122], which is analogous to τέκνον, «son» (9:2). This shows that both men and women believe in Jesus and witness to the Kingdom of God and are addressed as «sons» and «daughters».

Matthew seems to contrast, though indirectly, the woman's faith to the faith of the disciples. According to Matthew the woman's faith even exceeds the faith of the disciples. If on the one hand, Jesus accuses the disciples of little faith, on the other hand he praises the faith of the woman:

ὀλιγόπιστοι, «men of little faith» (8:26).

ἡ πίστις σου σέσωκέν σε, «your faith has saved you» (9:22).

5.2 Interpretation: The Hemorrhaging Woman as a Model of Faith

Several interpretations are given to the passage on Jesus' healing of a woman with a hemorrhage (9:20-22). We single out four scholars who interpret this story making use of different approaches. They are H.J. Held[123], G. Theissen[124], K. Burke[125] and V.K. Robbins[126].

Using *Redaktionsgeschichte*, H.J. Held has observed Matthew's creation of a conversation in the center of the story[127]. According to him the woman here exhibits «active» believing with «a movement of the will»[128] which presses her towards Jesus. Through the catchwords πίστις («faith») and σῴζω («save»), and through the woman's action, Matthew establishes a rule for the early Church: «confidence in the helpful kindness brings help to pass and no faith is put to shame and destroyed»[129]. «Of the details of Mark's presentation of the story only the behavior of the woman towards Jesus remains, what she did and what she thought (Mt 9.20b and 21)—the things by which her faith becomes known»[130].

G. Theissen, using *Kompositionsgeschichte* and motif analysis as a means of discussing social function, expanded Held's analysis of the

---

122 This is the only time Jesus addresses a woman as «daughter».
123 H.J. HELD, «Matthew as Interpreter», 165-299.
124 G. THEISSEN, *The Miracle Stories*.
125 K. BURKE, *Counter-Statement*, 124.
126 V.K. ROBBINS, «The Woman Who Touched Jesus' Garment», 502-515.
127 H.J. HELD, «Matthew», 216, 235.
128 H.J. HELD, «Matthew», 200-201.
129 H.J. HELD, «Matthew», 281-283.
130 H.J. HELD, «Matthew», 281-283.

Matthean version. According to Theissen, Jesus' direct knowledge of the woman's thought allows him to assert that her faith has made her well. The dynamics of the woman's approach to Jesus are like those which accompany a person's approach to God. He interprets the woman's action as a petition based on faith[131].

K. Burke has studied the Matthean version of the story making use of the social-rhetorical approach. According to him the Matthean version of the story features a form of repetition which creates «a logical progressive form»[132]. As a result of the logic, the expectations raised by the text are fulfilled in the narrative sequence. He highlights two repetitions. The first instance of repetition is found when the woman presents her motive through speech which repeats the action in the narration: she *touched* the fringe of his garment, for she said to herself «If I only *touch his garment*, I shall be made well». The second instance of repetition occurs when Jesus repeats the woman's thought:

The woman: «I shall be made well» (v. 21)
Jesus: «Your faith has made you well» (v. 22)

Through a chain-link repetition the words are connected[133]. V.K. Robbins has approached the text from a rhetorical point of view[134]. He interprets this miracle story in terms of Matthew's interest in communicating to «all nations» (Matt 28:19-20). According to him, when the woman thinks to herself, «If I only touch his garment, I shall be made well» the reader might wonder about her motivation. Is it simplemindedness, boldness, faith, hope, courage or despair? Jesus, by naming faith as her impulse, and by affirming that her faith has saved her, not only clarifies her action, but also reveals the tacit reasoning imbedded in the narrative:

Major premise: An act of faith is able to make a person well.
Minor premise: Touching Jesus' garment was an act of faith.
Conclusion: Therefore, the woman was made well[135].

The theme of faith is the explicit factor that causes healing and an explicit condition for miracles. Confidence in the helpful kindness of

---

131 G. THEISSEN, *The Miracle Stories*, 134, 138.
132 Logical progression has «the form of a perfectly conducted argument, advancing step by step».
133 K. BURKE, *Counter-Statement*, 124.
134 V.K. ROBBINS, «The Woman», 506-507.
135 V.K. ROBBINS, «The Woman», 506-507.

Jesus is what counts. The Matthean miracle story in 9:20-22 highlights that this woman has an unlimited trust in Jesus. She hopes to be healed by touching his garment: «If I only touch his garment, I shall be made well».

Along with these scholars, we too think that the redactional and the compositional features of the story suggest Matthew's rhetoric of presenting the hemorrhaging woman as a model of faith. In the Matthean redaction of the story of the hemorrhaging woman the whole attention remains mainly on what the woman thinks and Jesus' knowledge of her thinking. Matthew highlights this by avoiding several details that are found in Mark. Similarly, the compositional features emphasize the faith of the woman. The assertion that the healing did indeed take place certifies that healing and saving follow from faith in Jesus (see 8:13; 15:28; 17:18). The threefold use of the verb σῴζω indicates not only physical healing, but also a spiritual healing that refers to the totality of salvation (1:21)[136]. Jesus heals this woman on the basis of her faith. Importantly, Matthew places this woman as a model of true faith in Jesus, a model for his readers to follow.

6. **Jesus and the Canaanite Woman (Matt 15:21-28)**

This episode takes place in the province of «Tyre and Sidon»[137]. According to Matthew, a Canaanite[138] woman solicits Jesus' healing pow-

---

[136] See S. GRASSO, *Il Vangelo di Matteo,* 258; L.L. MORRIS, *The Gospel according to Matthew,* 230.

[137] The Synoptic Gospels use the names Tyre and Sidon always together (Matt 11:21-22; Mark 3:8; 7:31; Luke 6:17; 10:13-14). This stereotyped pairing of the cities conforms to the language of the OT and makes them typical of the whole world of the Gentiles. What is important to Matthew is the Gentile nature of these two cities. See R.H. GUNDRY, *Matthew,* 310; See S. GRASSO, *Il vangelo di Matteo,* 392; See D.J. HARRINGTON, *Matthew,* 437; W. HENDRIKSEN, *The Gospel of Matthew,* 621.

[138] Mark identifies her as Greek, Syrophoenician by birth, while Matthew calls her a Canaanite. The Aramaic word כְּנַעֲנִיתָא designated either Canaanite or Phoenician. D. DALMAN, *Aramäisch-neuhebräisches Handwörterbuch,* 202. See also G. SCHWARZ, «ΣΥΡΟΦΟΙΝΙΚΙΣΣΑ-ΧΑΝΑΝΑΙΑ», 626-628.

The word Χαναναῖος is found only in the NT. It denotes «belonging to the land and people of Canaan, Canaanite» (BAGD). *AB* renders «Phoenician» and points out that «the native name» of a Phoenician «was in the Greek *Chananaios*». In this sense, the people could be called either Canaanite or Phoenician (see L.L. MORRIS, *The Gospel according to Matthew,* 401). The adjective Canaanite to readers of Hebrew Scriptures meant everything that is dangerous to the faith of Israel (see F.D. BRUNER, *Matthew,*

ers on behalf of her demon-possessed daughter[139]. First Jesus ignores her, then he rebuffs her insisting that his mission is limited to the «lost sheep of the house of Israel» (Matt 15:24), and finally he seems to insult her by stating: «It is not fair to take the children's bread and throw it to the dogs» (15:26). But due to her persistent faith, Jesus finally concedes to her request to heal her daughter.

A number of recent studies highlight the significant role of the Canaanite woman in this pericope[140]. As in the previous passages, here too we look into the compositional features such as pattern breaks, male and female parallelism and scriptural evidence for an understanding of the text.

6.1 Compositional Features

The pericope has a threefold structure: exposition (vv. 21-23a); Jesus' teaching of the disciples (vv. 23b-24); Jesus and the woman, and the healing (vv. 25-28). As is observed by J. Gnilka, it is dialogical by nature, which he calls Lehrgespräch[141]. Accordingly, the woman speaks three times (Matt 15:22, 25, 27); Jesus speaks three times (vv. 24, 26, 28) and the disciples speak once (v. 23). Thus there is a sense of motion that leads to the final statement in v. 28 in which Jesus praises the woman for her strong faith[142].

6.1.1 Pattern Shift

In 9:21, the readers were merely given an insight into the woman's thoughts as she said to herself: «If I only touch his garment, I shall be saved». In the story of the Canaanite woman (15:21-28), for the first time in the narrative a woman has been given a speech. A woman comes to Jesus and speaks to him face to face. In his presentation of

---

551). Canaanites were identified as the bitter enemies of Israel. C.S. KEENER, Matthew, 414; W. HENDRIKSEN, The Gospel of Matthew, 237.

[139] On demon possession see W. HENDRIKSEN, The Gospel of Matthew, 436-437; E. LOHMEYER, Das Evangelium des Matthäus, 252.

[140] G.R. O'DAY, «Surprised by Faith», 294; E. SCHÜSSLER FIORENZA, But She Said, 11-14, 96-101; A. J. LEVINE, The Social and Ethnic Dimensions, 131-164; E.M. WAINWRIGHT, Towards a Feminist Critical Reading, 102, 217-247; ID., Shall We Look for Another, 84-100.

[141] J. GNILKA, Das Matthäusevangelium, II, 30; See also S.H. RINGE, «A Gentile Woman's Story», 65-72; S. GRASSO, Il vangelo di Matteo, 391.

[142] See E.M. WAINWRIGHT, Towards a Feminist Critical Reading, 102-103.

women in relation to Jesus, Matthew seems to advance a step forward[143]. This, therefore, refers to a pattern break.

6.1.2 Male-Female Parallelism

Like any other healing pericope, here too Matthew juxtaposes the «female character» with different male and female characters both within and outside the passage[144]. The Canaanite woman can be compared to the centurion (Matt 8:5-13), the woman with a hemorrhage (Matt 9:20-22), the Jewish blind men (Matt 9:27-31; 20:29-34) and finally the apostles themselves (Matt 15:32-39). First, the woman may be compared to the centurion who requests Jesus to heal his servant (8:5-

---

[143] See J. JEREMIAS, *Jerusalem*, 359-360.

[144] Scholar E.M. Wainwright and J.C. Anderson show a tendency to overemphasize the Canaanite woman from a structural point of view. According to E.M. Wainwright, the episode together with the discussion regarding the tradition of the Elders with which it is linked form the central point around which a chiasm is structured:
The Feeding of 5000 (14:13-21)
    +a disciple's little faith (14:28-33)
Jesus heals many (14:34-36)
                The Tradition of the Elders (15:1-20)
                The Canaanite Woman (15:21-28
Jesus heals many (15:29-31)
The feeding of 4000 (15:32-39)
    +the disciples' little faith (16:5-12). See E.M. WAINWRIGHT, *Towards a Feminist Critical Reading*, 100.
The structural significance of the Canaanite woman has further been presented by J.C. Anderson. She extends the structure and points out to a fulcrum of a chiastic pattern of nearly identical Matthean doublets. She also locates the story of the Canaanite woman at the center of a chiastic structure:
A Two Blind Men (9:27-31)
    B Sign of Jonah (12:38-42)
        C Feeding of 5000 (14:13-21)
            D Canaanite Woman (15:22-28)
        C' Feeding of 5000 (15:30-38)
    B' Sign of Jonah (16:1-4)
A' Two Blind Men (20:29-34). See J.C. ANDERSON, «Matthew: Gender and Reading», 3-27.
We see some kind of forced exegesis here. Both these authors seem to put just what they want. Such a structural proposal seems to leave out important scenes on the disciples and Peter (14:22-33) or the teaching of Jesus (15:1-20). So many chapters are left out of this consideration, that it hardly seems to be a complete structure.

13)[145]. Both the stories consist of a healing from a distance in which the healed are Gentiles' dependents: a servant boy of the centurion and the daughter of the Canaanite woman[146]. The short notice at the end of the pericope that the daughter was healed (ἰάθη) from that hour (15:28) exactly parallels the conclusion of the story of the healing of the centurion's son in 8:13[147]:

καὶ ἰάθη　　ὁ παῖς [αὐτοῦ]　ἐν τῇ ὥρᾳ ἐκείνῃ (Matt 8:13)
καὶ ἰάθη　　ἡ θυγάτηρ αὐτῆς ἀπὸ τῆς ὥρας ἐκείνης (Matt 15:28)

Second, the Canaanite woman episode may be compared to the episodes on the blind men as they follow a similar pattern: crying for help (Matt 9:27; 15:22; 20:30); the blind men are asked to be silent, while the woman is not given an answer first (20:31; 15:23); renewed request, questioning by Jesus, and healing on the basis of faith (9:29; 15:25; 20:34). The woman and the blind men make similar requests to Jesus:

... κράζοντες καὶ λέγοντες, Ἐλέησον ἡμᾶς, υἱὸς Δαυίδ (Matt 9:27)
... ἔκραξαν　　λέγοντες, Ἐλέησον ἡμᾶς, [κύριε], υἱὸς Δαυίδ (Matt 20:30)
... ἔκραζεν　　λέγουσα, Ἐλέησόν με,　κύριε　υἱὸς Δαυίδ· ...(Matt 15:22)

In comparison to the blind men, the Canaanite woman is faced with a double objection. The blind men are asked to be quiet by the crowd alone (ὁ δὲ ὄχλος ἐπετίμησεν αὐτοῖς ἵνα σιωπήσωσιν, 20:31), whereas the Canaanite woman has to overcome objections from the disciples (Ἀπόλυσον αὐτήν, ὅτι κράζει ὄπισθεν ἡμῶν, 15:23) as well as from Jesus himself (Οὐκ ἀπεστάλην εἰ μὴ εἰς τὰ πρόβατα τὰ ἀπολωλότα οἴκου Ἰσραήλ, 15:24). All are healed (9:29; 15:28; 20:34). But Jesus praises only the woman for her faith (... Ὦ γύναι, μεγάλη σου ἡ πίστις· γενηθήτω σοι ὡς θέλεις. καὶ ἰάθη ἡ θυγάτηρ αὐτῆς ἀπὸ τῆς ὥρας ἐκείνης, Matt 15:28).

Thirdly, the Canaanite woman episode may be compared to the episode of the healing of the woman with the hemorrhage in 9:18-26. If the woman in 9:20 is identified by her sickness (αἱμορροοῦσα), the sec-

---

145 D.J. VERSUPT, «The Faith of the Reader», 17; D.A. HAGNER, *Matthew 14-28*, 439; S.H. RINGE, «A Gentile Woman's Story», 65-72; J.D.M. DERRET, «Law in the New Testament, 161-186; S. GRASSO, *Il vangelo di Matteo*, 395; R.E. BROWN, *An Introduction to the New Testament*, 188.

146 E.M. WAINWRIGHT, *Feminist Interpretation of the Bible*, 67.

147 The only differences being ὁ παῖς αὐτοῦ and the use of ἐν with the dative rather than ἀπό with the genitive, «in that hour» for «from that hour».

ond woman (15:22) is identified by her geographical origin. But what makes them similar is their marginalized position in the society.

Fourthly, the Canaanite woman functions as a foil for the lack of faith and understanding of the disciples in general and of Peter in particular. The woman's crying out to Jesus could be compared to Peter's crying out but with a difference. The woman cries out in supplication, whereas Peter cries out in fear (14:30):

... ἔκραξεν λέγων, κύριε, σῶσόν με (Matt 14:30)
... ἔκραζεν λέγουσα, ᾿ελέησόν με, ... (Matt 15:22)

On the one side Jesus praises the great faith of the woman (15:28), while on the other side he reprimands Peter's little faith (14:31)[148]:

... ῏Ω γύναι, μεγάλη σου ἡ πίστις (Matt 15:28).
... ᾿Ολιγόπιστε, εἰς τί ἐδίστασας (Matt 14:31).

6.2 Interpretation: The Canaanite Woman as a Model of Faith

The Canaanite woman episode is traditionally explained as a «faith test episode»[149], an episode often explained in terms of the Gentile mission of Jesus, thus referring to the theme of universalism in the Gospel[150].

H. J. Held opines that «In Matthew the whole narrative is directed towards this last sentence (i.e. «your faith is great; be it as you wish») which has a majestic note about it ... In Matthew only the fact and power of faith are expressed»[151].

---

[148] See S. GRASSO, Il vangelo di Matteo, 392.

[149] W. HENDRIKSEN, The Gospel according to Matthew, 622; L.L. MORRIS, The Gospel according to Mattthew, 401; R.H. GUNDRY, Matthew, 312; F.W. BEARE, The Gospel according to Matthew, 340-41; J.P. MEIER, «Matthew 15:21-28», 399; D.J. VERSUPT, «The Faith of the Reader», 17; K.M. WOSCHITZ, «Erzählter Glaube», 319-332.

[150] G.T. MONTAGUE, Companion God, 175; A. STOCK, The Method and Message of Matthew, 258; F.W. BEARE, The Gospel according Matthew, 342; J.P. MEIER, «Matthew 15:21-28», 399; A. J. SALDARINI, Matthew's Christian-Jewish Community, 74; D.A. HAGNER, Matthew 14-28, 438-443; T. A. BURKILL, «The Historical Development», 161-177; S. H. RINGE, «A Gentile Woman's Story», 71; G.THEISSEN, «Lokal und Sozialkolorit», 202; J.D.M. DERRET, «Law in the New Testament», 161-186; S. GRASSO, Il vangelo di Matteo, 392; G. R. OBSORNE, «Women in the Ministry of Jesus», 259-291.

[151] H.J. HELD, Matthew as Interpreter, 199. See also pages 239-241, 275-296.

A. Stock states:

> Faith is the theme of this pericope. It indicates to the community what faith
> means and what «scope» it has. Thereby the theme «the Church and Is-
> rael», which was being discussed in the community, is addressed, culminat-
> ing in the theme «Israel's Election-Salvation for all»[152].

While accepting the traditional interpretation of the faith model different elements that we discussed in this section suggest some discipleship
elements in our passage. Some of the redactional as well as compositional elements such as Matthew's identification of the woman as a
«Canaanite» and his favorable presentation of this woman in comparison to different male characters such as the centurion, the blind men
and the disciples themselves in the Gospel, give the pericope a discipleship nuance.

The Matthean mention of the word «Canaanite» indicates a biographic identity. This biographic note is important as it has inevitable
associations with the pagan inhabitants of Palestine displaced by the
Jews and thus contrasts the woman all the more with the people of
God[153].

Matthew's identification of the woman as a Canaanite is in tune with
the Abrahamic origin of Jesus. When Jesus heals this Canaanite
woman, God through Jesus fulfills His promise made to Abraham: in
Abraham all nations will be blessed (Gen 12).

Matthew's presentation of the Canaanite woman is in tune with the
Davidic lineage emphasized in the genealogy[154]. When the woman addresses Jesus as the «Son of David», Matthew is once again reaffirming
the Davidic lineage of Jesus. He portrays Jesus as acting in his capacity
as the Son of David and hence fulfilling in his ministry the end-time
expectations associated with David (21:9, 15)[155]. Just as the title «son
of Abraham characterizes Jesus as the one in whom the Gentiles will
find blessing, so the title «son of David» characterizes Jesus as the one
in whom Israel will find blessing[156]. Those who are directly or indi-

---

[152] A. STOCK, *The Method and Message of Matthew,* 258.

[153] See D.A. HAGNER, *Matthew 14-28,* 441; F.W. BEARE, *The Gospel according to
Matthew,* 341.

[154] E.M. WAINWRIGHT, *Shall We Look for Another,* 91.

[155] E.M. WAINWRIGHT, *Shall We Look for Another,* 150.

[156] A. STOCK, *The Method and Message of Matthew,* 256.

rectly linked to the ministry of Jesus are people who count for nothing in Israel's society: the poor, the sick, Gentiles and women.

The Canaanite woman's addressing of Jesus as κύριε υἱὸς Δαυίδ is significant. Such an addressing gives indication of her recognition of Jesus as the Messiah for whom the Israel was waiting[157]. Noteworthy is the fact that only later do his own disciples recognize Jesus as the Messiah when Peter confesses him thus in the region of Caesarea Philippi (Matt 16:16)[158].

Jesus' delay in responding favorably to the woman and in healing her daughter reminds us of many instances in the OT and the NT in which requests are not immediately granted. We have evidence from the story of Abraham (Gen 21:1-5) and from Psalm 22:2 in the OT; from the raising of Jairus' daughter (Mark 5:35), and from the blind men (Matt 9:27, 28) in the NT[159]. In all these instances there was a faith test[160]. Similarly Jesus' delay in heeding the request of the woman was probably to test her faith[161].

Again, as in the case of the healing of the centurion's son (8:5-13), it anticipates the ultimate goal of the mission of Christ, which is to bring blessing to humankind universally[162], a mission that becomes progressively clear later in the Gospel (24:14; 28:19). The mission of Jesus, as well as that of the disciples, which was originally designed for Israel, gets widened and slowly spreads to all nations. What determines God's blessing is not Jewishness, but receptive faith[163]. In the Canaanite woman Matthew offers his readers a model to follow, a model of faith that even at times excels the faith of the apostles themselves.

---

[157] S. GRASSO, Il vangelo di Matteo, 393.

[158] F.W. BEARE, The Gospel according to Matthew, 341.

[159] Abraham and Sarah had to wait a long time before they finally received Isaac (Gen 21:1-5). In Psalm 22:2 we see the author expressing his dismay because God did not immediately answer his prayers. Jesus arrives at the home of Jairus too late (Mark 5:35). A similar divine delay is seen in Jesus' raising of Lazarus: «So when he [Jesus] heard that he [Lazarus] was ill, he then remained two days in the place where he was» (John 11:6). In all these instances faith is an unavoidable factor.

[160] «… he (Abraham) grew strong in faith» (Rom 4:20); Jesus tells Jairus, «Fear not, only believe» (Mark 5:36); in connection with the raising of Lazarus Jesus tells the disciples, «For your sake, I am glad I was not there, so that you may believe» (John 11:15).

[161] W. HENDRIKSEN, The Gospel of Matthew, 624.

[162] D.A. HAGNER, Matthew 14-28, 443.

[163] D.A. HAGNER, Matthew 14-28, 441; G. T. MONTAGUE, Companion God, 175.

7. Jesus and the Woman at Bethany (Matt 26:6-13)

Having understood the Canaanite woman episode in the preceding section, we will now study the passage on the woman who anoints Jesus at Bethany. If Matt 26:3-5 illustrates one response to Jesus' mission, namely opposition from the chief priests, scribes and elders of the people, a theme continued in 26:14-17, Matt 26:6-13 contains two more different responses to Jesus: the woman's anointing of Jesus, and the disciples misunderstanding of her act.

7.1 *Compositional Features*

Like the previous pericopes on women, Matt 26:6-13 is also a concise and clearly well-structured pericope presented within a frame that includes an introduction (26:6) and conclusion (26:13), and has the following structure:

Introduction (26:6)
Woman's Action (26:7)
Disciples' Reaction (26:8-9)
Jesus' Reaction (26:10-12)
Conclusion (26:13)

7.1.1 Introduction

The introduction of the pericope first of all provides the setting of the event, which has moved from the courtyard or palace of the high priest at Jerusalem to the residence of Simon the leper[164] at Bethany[165] on the outskirts of Jerusalem[166].

7.1.2 The Woman's Action (26:7)

Having set the arena of the event, Matthew introduces an unnamed woman[167] who approaches Jesus and anoints him: προσῆλθεν αὐτῷ ...

---

[164] Simon the leper appears only here and in the parallel in Mark 14:3. Whether he is the same person healed by Jesus is disputed. D. A. HAGNER, *Matthew 14-28*, 757; DAVIES and ALLISON, *Matthew* III, 443.

[165] J. GNILKA, *Das Matthäusevangelium*, 386.

[166] W.D. DAVIES – D.C. ALLISON, *Matthew* III, 443.

[167] That Matthew does not identify the woman has been variously interpreted. Commenting on this V. Taylor writes, «The absence of the name is usual in a story in which the emphasis lies on the words of Jesus, but it is strange in view of the proph-

καὶ κατέχεεν ἐπὶ τῆς κεφαλῆς αὐτοῦ ἀνακειμένου[168]. We learn nothing of this woman save her action[169] by which she honors Jesus. In our text, however, she is not a supplicant coming to make a request of Jesus but rather one who comes to anoint the head of Jesus[170], an act that suggests Jesus' messianic status: Jesus is the anointed one.

7.1.3 The Disciples' Protest (26:8)

The woman's action is immediately followed by the disciples' indignant[171] protest. Through this Matthew probably wants to draw attention to the disciples' failure to grasp the significance of the woman's act[172]. The disciples' protest against the woman's action perhaps foreshadows what is to come: whereas the male disciples flee (26:56), the faithful women follow Jesus to the cross and tomb (27:55, 61; 28:1).

The woman is juxtaposed to the disciples of Jesus. By anointing Jesus' head, the woman expresses her hospitality and love towards Jesus. Her action is in harmony with the death and burial of Jesus. In contrast to the woman, the disciples seem to have a different attitude. They misunderstand her act of anointing Jesus' head when they say: «why this waste?» Their misunderstanding is further emphasized by their reasoning: «For this ointment might have been sold for a large sum and

---

ecy that her deed will be remembered». V. TAYLOR, *Gospel according to St. Mark*, 530.

Thiemann sees a Matthean discipleship motif in it. That is to say, the unnamed woman broadens the category «disciples» beyond the Twelve (see R.F. THIEMANN, «The Unnamed Woman at Bethany», 179-188). Against this view, we think that based on this pericope alone, one cannot make such an assertion. There are previous indications in Matthew that the category of «disciples» is wider than the Twelve. We will study this point in detail in the third and fourth chapters of this work.

[168] Anointing was often a striking gesture of hospitality (Psa 23:5; 133:2; 141:5; Luke 7:46).

[169] Luke describes her as a sinner (Luke 7:37)

[170] For a brief historical survey on the linguistic background to κατέχεεν ἐπὶ τῆς κεφαλῆς see E.M. WAINWRIGHT, *Towards a Feminist Critical Reading*, 126-127, who narrates the significance of the phrase under three headings: its significance in the Septuagint, rabbinic literature and Christian scriptures.

[171] The word ἀγανακτέω («indignant») is used earlier in 20:24 and 21:15. See D.A. HAGNER, *Matthew 14-28*, 757; R.H. GUNDRY, *Matthew*, 520.

[172] Because prophets anointed the heads of kings (2Kgs 9:6) some scholars suspect that Matthew and Mark intended a Messianic anointing alongside Jesus' emphasis on an anointing for burial. See M. DIBELIUS, *Jesus*, 96; M.D. HOOKER, *The Message of Mark*, 98.

given to the poor». Perhaps, Matthew intends to show that the disciples fail to catch the christocentric nuance of this anointing[173].

Similarly the woman's action of anointing the head of Jesus, stands in sharp contrast to the chief priests and the elders who plot to kill Jesus (26:3-4). In a similar manner the disciples who doubt the significance of the woman's actions stand in opposition to her.

The woman's action of pouring the ointment (v.7) is opposite to the hypothetical action of the disciples who would prefer to sell the ointment for a large sum of money in favor of the poor (v. 9). The woman's action is exclusively centered on Jesus, while the disciples' hypothetical action is centered on the needs of the poor. For the woman the ointment is her gift to Jesus, a gesture of hospitality, devoid of any price. But for the disciples it is an expensive «item», and therefore they view it for its monetary benefits, which is emphatically re-asserted when Judas, one of the Twelve, betrays Jesus for money.

7.1.4 Jesus' Reaction (Matt 26:10-12)

Jesus who defends, justifies and interprets the woman's action[174] stands in contrast to the disciples who accuse her[175]. Jesus comments her action as a good work done to him: ἔργον γὰρ καλὸν ἠργάσατο εἰς ἐμέ (26:10). Jesus values her act as a good work and justifies it telling the disciples that the poor they will have always, but not he. He interprets the woman's action in reference to his own burial. Jesus' response contains his respect for this woman, more highly than any of the male disciples of Jesus[176].

7.1.5 Conclusion (26:13)

The conclusion is comprised of Jesus' solemn affirmation (ἀμὴν λέγω ὑμῖν, «Truly I say to you»), that the act of this woman will become part of the Gospel tradition and will be told (λαληθήσεται) wherever the Gospel is preached. Her act would therefore be preserved as part of the passion tradition relating to Jesus' burial recounted «in the whole world» (26:13), which means wherever the Gospel will be preached. Jesus commends her action very highly.

---

173 J.C. FENTON, *Saint Matthew*, 412.
174 K. STOCK, *Il Racconto della passione*, 40-41.
175 D. PATTE, *The Gospel according to Matthew*, 359.
176 C.S. KEENER, *Matthew*, 618.

7.2 *Interpretation: The Anointing Woman as a Model of Service*

The passage under our investigation (26:6-13) illustrates two different responses: service—as evidenced in the unnamed woman, and misunderstanding—as evidenced in the male disciples of Jesus[177].

The significance of the woman's anointing of Jesus' head has been variously interpreted. We will first enumerate some important views of the NT scholars. C.H. Dodd holds the opinion that «the idea of an anointing, as of a king or priest, which is also an embalming of the dead» means that Jesus is the «messianic king whose throne is a cross»[178]. J.C. Fenton interprets the woman's act in terms of her understanding of Jesus' person over against the disciples' misunderstanding.[179] On the woman's anointing in the John's version (12:1-8) C.K. Barret says that the anointing is «a means of expressing the royal dignity of Jesus in preparation for his triumphal entry into Jerusalem»[180].

A. Stock holds that

> Since it is the disciples who object to the woman's action, in Matthew's thought the account is a discipleship rule. The community must learn that while the service of the poor is right, necessary, and obligatory, its place in the scale of value changes when other concerns (here: the death of the Messiah) are involved. Good works are in place in any time, but the service of Jesus has its unique Kairos, never to be repeated. And not only the woman's deed is raised to the level of a guiding norm; the woman herself enters New Testament tradition because she merited by her act of love to be offered to later Christians as an example proposed for imitation[181].

According to J.P. Heil, the merit of the woman's good act «surpasses that of almsgiving since it demonstrates a personal commitment of love for the specific person of Jesus at a time of urgent need rather than an impersonal giving to the general group of the poor always in need (26:11)»[182].

---

[177] W.D. DAVIES – D.C. ALLISON, *Matthew* III, 448; E.M. WAINWRIGHT, *Towards a Feminist Critical Reading,* 129-137.

[178] C.H. DODD, *Historical Tradition,* 173; See also W. CARTER, *Matthew and the Margins,* 503.

[179] J.C. FENTON, *Saint Matthew,* 412.

[180] C.K. BARRET, *The Gospel according to St. John,* 409.

[181] A. STOCK, *The Method and Message of Matthew,* 394.

[182] J.P. HEIL, *The Death and Resurrection of Jesus,* 26.

Having considered some of the scholarly opinions, let us now state our observation. We have no evidence in the Gospel that affirms the women's comprehension of the messianic implication of her action (Fenton). We do not know if Matthew alludes to Jesus' dignity as the Messiah, «the anointed king» here (Dodd, Barret). We do not even know if this woman heard the passion predictions. We doubt if she could have understood her action as a preparation for Jesus' burial. There is no evidence for this in the Gospel. Her act of anointing could probably be understood as a simple act of hospitality[183], love[184] and honor for Jesus[185]. Such an interpretation is the most fitting after 25:31-46, which attributes profound meaning to the modest deeds of kindness. Jesus interprets this woman's act as a preparation for his own burial[186]. Matthew's portrayal of the positive act of the woman and the disciples' indignant protest foreshadow what is to come: whereas the male disciples struggle to be loyal (26:14-16, 20-25, 33-35, 40-43, 47-52, 56, 69-75), the women remain faithful to Jesus, and follow him to the cross and to his tomb (27:55-61; 28:1-10)[187].

8. Conclusion

Our discussion of the women in Matthew, especially in reference to the five selected passages in the Gospel, brings us to the conclusion that women play significant roles in this Gospel. By incorporating four OT women in the genealogy (Tamar, 1:3; Rahab, 1:5; Ruth, 1:5; the wife of Uriah, 1:6), Matthew prepares the way for the introduction of Mary, who plays a significant role in the infancy narratives, although Joseph is the main actor (1:18-25). The Matthean Jesus advocates respect and dignity for women when he forbids lust (5:27, 28), forbids divorce (5:31-32; 19:3-9), heals women such as Peter's mother-in-law (8:14-15), the daughter of a ruler (9:18-19, 23-26), a woman with a hemorrhage (9:20-22), and the daughter of a Canaanite woman (15:21-28).

---

183 J.P. HEIL, *The Death and Resurrection of Jesus*, 26.

184 W.D. DAVIES – D.C. ALLISON, *Matthew* III, 448; D. SENIOR, *The Passion of Jesus*, 54.

185 A. STOCK, *The Method and Message of Matthew*, 393

186 A. STOCK, *The Method and Message of Matthew*, 393. See also T. W. BEVAN, «The Four Anointings», 137-139; S. GRASSO, *Matteo*, 602-604; A. STOCK, *Method and Message of Matthew*, 392-394.

187 S. GRASSO, *Matteo*, 604; D. PATTE, *The Gospel according to Matthew*, 359.

Jesus commends the faith of women (9:22; 15:21-28). It is a woman who anoints Jesus, anticipating the preparation for burial (26:6-13).

Up to this point of our research on women in the narratives of Matthew, we find no substantial evidence in the Gospel that states any woman as a disciple of Jesus. There is no description of Jesus' call of a woman to follow him. There is neither any evidence of a woman having «followed» Jesus. However, Matthew portrays several women whose activities contain certain discipleship implications when the Evangelist presents some women as the models of service, love and faith.

CHAPTER III

The Death of Jesus and the Women's Role (Matt 27:51b-56)

1. Introduction

In this chapter we discuss Matt 27:51b-56, in which Matthew speaks of various divine and human responses to the death of Jesus. We begin our study with a discussion on the various textual as well as grammatical problems, which will be followed by a close reading of the text in which we will discuss the various vocabulary items with special reference to those which help us to understand the discipleship theme in the Gospel. This will be followed by the compositional features of the text and its biblical background, all of which will contribute to the interpretation of the text.

2. The Text

^{51b} καὶ ἡ γῆ ἐσείσθη καὶ αἱ πέτραι ἐσχίσθησαν, ^{52} καὶ τὰ μνημεῖα ἀνεῴχθησαν καὶ πολλὰ σώματα τῶν κεκοιμημένων ἁγίων ἠγέρθησαν, ^{53} καὶ ἐξελθόντες ἐκ τῶν μνημείων μετὰ τὴν ἔγερσιν αὐτοῦ εἰσῆλθον εἰς τὴν ἁγίαν πόλιν καὶ ἐνεφανίσθησαν πολλοῖς. ^{54} Ὁ δὲ ἑκατόνταρχος καὶ οἱ μετ' αὐτοῦ τηροῦντες τὸν Ἰησοῦν ἰδόντες τὸν σεισμὸν καὶ τὰ γενόμενα ἐφοβήθησαν σφόδρα, λέγοντες, Ἀληθῶς θεοῦ υἱὸς ἦν οὗτος. ^{55} Ἦσαν δὲ ἐκεῖ γυναῖκες πολλαὶ ἀπὸ μακρόθεν θεωροῦσαι, αἵτινες ἠκολούθησαν τῷ Ἰησοῦ ἀπὸ τῆς Γαλιλαίας διακονοῦσαι αὐτῷ· ^{56} ἐν αἷς ἦν Μαρία ἡ Μαγδαληνὴ καὶ Μαρία ἡ τοῦ Ἰακώβου καὶ Ἰωσὴφ μήτηρ καὶ ἡ μήτηρ τῶν υἱῶν Ζεβεδαίου.

3. Textual and Grammatical Problems

In trying to understand well Matt 27:51b-56, we meet with two problems, one textual and the other grammatical. The first problem concerns the translation of the phrase θεοῦ υἱὸς (Matt 27:54c). The second problem concerns the variant reading found in 27:56. Solving these two problems will help us to gain the proper meaning of the text. So we will now address them.

3.1 *The Translation of θεοῦ υἱὸς (Matt 27:54)*

The first problem concerns the translation of the phrase θεοῦ υἱὸς. Shall we translate it with the definite article to mean, «the Son of God» or with an indefinite article to mean, «a son of God»[1]?

NT scholars have interpreted the phrase θεοῦ υἱὸς in Matt 27:54 in two different ways. E.P. Gould understands θεοῦ υἱὸς as «*a* son of God», and thus views Jesus as a hero after the heathen conception[2]. One of the important arguments in support of this view is that the phrase θεοῦ υἱός is anarthrous[3]. In 27:54 we have an example of an anarthrous predicate preceding the verb. Being indefinite, the minimal expression «*a* son of God», signifies nothing other than a rank shared by other human beings. R.G. Bratcher, E.C. Colwell, A. Stock, D. Patte, F.W. Beare, W.D. Davies and D.C. Allison on the other hand adopt θεοῦ υἱὸς as «the Son of God», in the Christian sense[4].

Along with R.G. Bratcher and E.C. Colwell, we translate θεοῦ υἱὸς as «the Son of God», in the Christian sense. Because, even if the defi-

---

[1] For various translations see B.M. NEWMAN – P.C. STINE, *A Translator's Handbook,* 893-894.

[2] E.P. GOULD, *Critical and Exegetical Commentary,* 295.

[3] «Anarthrous» means that which does not have a definite article before the noun and «arthrous» means that which has a definite article before the noun.

[4] See R.G. BRATCHER, «A Note on υἱὸς θεου», 27-28. Bratcher supports this position partly by referring to Colwell's principle, which he accepts without doubting the qualitative meaning of this type of clause. See E.C. COLWELL, «A Definite Rule», 12-21; A. STOCK, *The Method and Message,* 429-430; D. PATTE, *The Gospel according to Matthew,* 390; F.W. BEARE, *The Gospel according to Matthew,* 536-537; W.D. DAVIES – D.C. ALLISON, *Matthew,* 636; J.P. MEIER, *The vision of Matthew,* 205; J. GNILKA, *Das Matthäusevangelium,* II, 478; L.L. MORRIS, *The Gospel According to Matthew,* 726; A. PLUMMER, *Matthew,* 405; R. FABRIS, *Matteo,* 556; L. SABOURIN, *The Gospel according to St Matthew,* 920; P.S. MINEAR, «The Uniqueness of the Death», 55-59.

nite article is absent, the expression already carries a definiteness as can be observed in other instances like Matt 4:3-6; 14:33; 27: 40. 43[5].

3.2 *The Variant Readings in 27:56b*

The second problem, which is textual, concerns the variant readings in 27:56b. The text reads Μαρία ἡ Μαγδαληνὴ καὶ Μαρίαμ ἡ τοῦ Ἰακώβου καὶ Ἰωσὴφ μήτηρ καὶ ἡ μήτηρ τῶν υἱῶν Ζεβεδαίου (א² D* L W Θ *pc* lat sy^s.hmg sa^mss mae bo). Four variant readings are found:

1) Μαρίαμ ἡ Μαγδαληνὴ καὶ Μαρίαμ ἡ τοῦ Ἰακώβου (C (L) Δ Θ *f^1.13 pc* sa(^mss).
2) Μαρίαμ ἡ Μαγδαληνὴ καὶ Μαρία ἡ τοῦ Ἰακώβου καὶ Ἰωση (Ἰωσητος) (A B C D^c f^1.13 33 sy^(p).h sa^mss, Eus).
3) η Μαρια η Ἰωσηφ και η Μαρια η (א*).
4) Ἰωσηφ και η μητηρ (*it*).

The first variant reads twice Μαρίαμ (instead of Μαρία). The second variant substitutes Ἰωσὴφ with Ἰωση (Ἰωσητος). The third variant alters the syntax with the additions of η Μαρια η Ἰωσφ και η Μαρια η in-between Μαρία ἡ τοῦ Ἰακώβου και and ἡ μήτηρ τῶν υἱῶν Ζεβεδαίου of the main text. The fourth variant replaces καὶ Ἰωσηφ μητηρ και ἡ μήτηρ with Ἰωσηφ και η μητηρ.

The dates of the manuscripts in support of these variants are comparatively recent. The variants with the two Μαρίαμ, «with Ἰωση» and that proposed by our text, have a good geographical spread. In these three, the spreading began from the Alexandrian block and gradually became diffused into the West and the Byzantine.

Based on external evidence, there is no clear criterion to support the preference of our text over its alternative readings. Apart from «the conclusive variant», all have some level of contact with the Alexandrian block in the fourth century, thereby sharing almost the same characteristics and weight.

In the variants with the two Μαρίαμ, what we seem to have is a scribal omission of materials deemed to be superfluous. To him, that

---

[5] This type of clause is found more often in the Gospel of John (1:1. 12. 14. 49; 2:9; 3:4. 6). See P.B. HARNER, «Qualitative Anarthrous Predicate Nouns», 75-87; See W.D. DAVIES – D.C. ALLISON, *Matthew*, 636; D.A. HAGNER, *Matthew 14-28*, 350-353; E.C. COLWELL, «A Definite Rule», 12-21; C.F.D. MOULE, *An Idiom-Book*, 115.

Maria who is the mother of James is the same as the one identified later in our text as the mother of Joseph and of the sons of Zebedee.

The substitution of Ἰωσήφ with Ἰωσή (Ἰωσητος) by the second variant must have been a scribal attempt to present a more common word. That «variant with alteration» is expletive as through it the scribe fills up the gap left out in the main text. In this way he presents a reading smoother than that of the original text. «The conclusive variant» is also another example of a scribal effort to attain a smooth text. There he rearranges what he considers a less refined text with a more elegant syntax. Based on the fact that the text as it appears in our pericope is the most difficult and the least elegant, we consider it most probably the original and therefore retain it for the purpose of this work.

4. Compositional Features

Matthew 51b-56[6] is composed of two parts: a) the divine reaction to the death of Jesus (51b-53) and b) the human response to the death of Jesus (54-56).

---

[6] A good majority of the Matthean scholars support the view that the presence of the phrase καὶ ἰδοὺ in v. 51a, marks the beginning of a new scene, and therefore has to be treated together with v. 51b. Such an argument is well in harmony with many other Matthean usage of the phrase καὶ ἰδοὺ in Matthew.

While respecting the opinions held by the majority of the Matthean scholars, we, along with R. Meynet and D.C. Allison, follow a different structural presentation as it helps us to describe the various male and female characters in the narrative. Such a position helps us to explain better the discipleship of the women in the Gospel. We have two reasons that support our argument:

First, from a biblical rhetorical point of view it can be argued that 27:51a refers back to 27:40, in which the bystanders were challenging the crucified Jesus: Ὁ καταλύων τὸν ναὸν καὶ ἐν τρισὶν ἡμέραις οἰκοδομῶν, σῶσον σεαυτόν, εἰ υἱὸς εἶ τοῦ θεοῦ, [καὶ] κατάβηθι ἀπὸ τοῦ σταυροῦ. In v. 51a we read that the curtain of the temple was broken into two: Καὶ ἰδοὺ τὸ καταπέτασμα τοῦ ναοῦ ἐσχίσθη ἀπ' ἄνωθεν ἕως κάτω εἰς δύο. The breaking of the temple veil, symbolically indicates the destruction of the temple itself. What the bystanders ask of Jesus is dramatically realized in v. 51a. Hence, we think that v. 51a goes along with the preceding passage. See R. MEYNET, Jésus passe, 289.

Second, Matthew's incorporation of the special material (51b-53) seems to parallel similar material in vv. 28:3. Thus, although one is initially inclined to attribute the use of σχίζω (in the passive) in v. 51b to the influence of 51a, the extra-Matthean parallels call for caution. The splitting of the rocks appears to have been a traditional motif and could have been tied, along with notice on an earthquake, to a story of resurrection in Matthew. See D.C. ALLISON, The End, 41.

4.1 Part one: The Divine Reaction to the Death of Jesus (Matt 27:51b-53)

The first part is composed of two pieces: 51b-52a and 52b-53.

4.1.1 Piece One: God's Reaction in the Natural World (27:51b-52a)

[51b] καὶ ἡ   γῆ   ἐσείσθη
      καὶ αἱ   πέτραι   ἐσχίσθησαν,
[52] καὶ τὰ   μνημεῖα   ἀνεῴχθησαν

Piece one is a *trimember* segment, each part having an identical structure. Every member begins with a conjunction, and is followed by an article, a substantive, and the aorist passive form of the verb. All the substantives in this piece (γῆ, πέτραι and μνημεῖα) are complementary to each other, because they belong to the same category of words. Similarly all the three verbs (ἐσείσθη, ἐσχίσθησαν and ἀνεῴχθησαν) have an identical grammatical form called the *aorist passive*. This piece has a paratactic structure because one action causes the other. The shaking of the earth leads to the splitting of the rocks, and the splitting of the rocks in turn causes the opening of the tombs.

4.1.2 Piece Two: God Reacts by Raising the Dead (27:52b-53)

A [52b] *καὶ πολλὰ σώματα τῶν κεκοιμημένων ἁγίων ἠγέρθησαν,*
    B [53] *καὶ ἐξελθόντες* ἐκ τῶν μνημείων

            C μετὰ τὴν ἔγερσιν αὐτου

        B' *εἰσῆλθον* εἰς τὴν ἁγίαν πόλιν
A' *καὶ ἐνεφανίσθησαν* πολλοῖς.

Matt 27:51b-53 is concentrically structured around the phrase μετὰ τὴν ἔγερσιν αὐτοῦ. It has an AB /C/ B'A' structure. Different members in this piece correspond to each other. The word ἠγέρθησαν, in A parallels ἐνεφανίσθησαν in A'. The compound verb ἐξελθόντες (aorist active nominative plural participle of ἐξέρχομαι) in B parallels εἰσῆλθον (indicative aorist active of εἰσέρχομαι) in B'. The phrase ἐκ τῶν μνημείων, «out of the tombs», in B corresponds to εἰς τὴν ἁγίαν πόλιν, «into the Holy City», in B'. Different actions such as the resurrection of

---

For further points that support such a structural presentation, see pages 180-184 that highlight the interrelationship between Matt 27:51a-61 and 28:1-10.

the saints, their coming out of the tombs, their entry into the Holy City, and their appearance to many, are centered around the phrase μετὰ τὴν ἔγερσιν αὐτοῦ.

4.2 *Part Two: Human Reaction to the Death of Jesus (Matt 27:54-56)*

The second part is composed of two pieces: the male and female reaction to the death of Jesus (vv. 54-55), and the names of the women who had followed Jesus watching from a distance (v. 56).

4.2.1 Piece One: Male and Female Reactions to the Death of Jesus (27: 54-55)

A ⁵⁴ Ὁ δὲ ἑκατόνταρχος καὶ οἱ μετ' αὐτοῦ <u>τηροῦντες τὸν Ἰησοῦν</u>
   B <u>ἰδόντες</u> τὸν σεισμὸν καὶ τὰ γενόμενα

        C ἐφοβήθησαν σφόδρα, λέγοντες, Ἀληθῶς θεοῦ υἱὸς ἦν οὗτος.

   B' ⁵⁵ Ἦσαν δὲ ἐκεῖ γυναῖκες πολλαὶ   ἀπὸ μακρόθεν   θεωροῦσαι,
A' αἵτινες <u>ἠκολούθησαν τῷ Ἰησοῦ</u> ἀπὸ τῆς Γαλιλαίας <u>διακονοῦσαι αὐτῷ.</u>

Vv. 54-55 is a concentrically arranged piece (AB /C/ B'A') which places the confession of the centurion and the men with him (Ἀληθῶς θεοῦ υἱὸς ἦν οὗτος) at the central position. The confession of the true identity of Jesus is bracketed by two groups of persons: a) the centurion and the men with him guarding Jesus on the one side (AB) and b) the women who followed Jesus from Galilee (B'A') watching Jesus from a distance, on the other side[7]. Although such a structural presentation may look a bit artificial, and less profound, it certainly helps one to identify and differentiate various male female characters in the scene, and their response to the death of Jesus.

The particle δε[8] in v. 54 shifts the scene from the divine reaction to the human reaction. Matthew uses the same particle in v. 55 in order to shift the scene from the male characters to the female characters. Both groups witness the extraordinary events that followed the death of Jesus.

---

[7] R. MEYNET, *Jésus passe*, 291.

[8] The connective δέ is normally used to show continuation of a narrative, examples of which we come across both in the Classical as well as the Hellenistic period of Greek literature. See M.E. THRALL, *Greek Particles*, 51.

The ἑκατόνταρχος καὶ οἱ μετ᾿ αὐτοῦ in v. 54 balances γυναῖκες πολλαί in v. 55. Similarly their actions correspond to each other. The centurion and the men are identified as «guarding Jesus» (τηροῦντες τὸν Ἰησοῦν). They are parallel to γυναῖκες πολλαί, «many women», who are identified as ἠκολούθησαν τῷ Ἰησοῦ ἀπὸ τῆς Γαλιλαίας διὰ κονοῦσαι αὐτῷ, «followed Jesus from Galilee, serving him» (v. 55). Similarly the soldiers' action of «seeing» (ἰδόντες) parallels the women's action of «watching» (θεωροῦσαι), both of which make them witnesses to the events that followed the death of Jesus.

4.2.2 Piece Two: The Identity of the Women (27:56)

ἐν αἷς ἦν   Μαρία ἡ Μαγδαληνὴ
καὶ   Μαρία ἡ τοῦ Ἰακώβου καὶ Ἰωσὴφ μήτηρ
καὶ   ἡ μήτηρ τῶν υἱῶν Ζεβεδαίου.

Piece two (v. 56) is a tri-member single segment, which lists the names of the women who followed Jesus from Galilee, ministering to Jesus. Placing similar prepositional phrases at the beginning of v. 56 (ἐν αἷς ἦν) and v. 55 (ησαν δὲ ἐκεῖ) Matthew links these verses.

4.3 *The Passage Taken Together (Matt 27:51b-56)*

If the whole passage is taken together it has the following structure:

51b   καὶ ἡ γῆ   *ἐσείσθη*
      καὶ αἱ πέτραι   ἐσχίσθησαν,
52   καὶ τὰ *μνημεῖα*   ἀνεῴχθησαν

      καὶ πολλὰ σώματα τῶν κεκοιμημένων ἁγίων ἠγέρθησαν,
            53 καὶ ἐξελθόντες   ἐκ τῶν *μνημείων*
                              μετὰ τὴν *ἔγερσιν* αὐτοῦ
                              εἰσῆλθον εἰς τὴν ἁγίαν πόλιν
      καὶ ἐνεφανίσθησαν πολλοῖς.

+ 54 Ὁ δὲ ἑκατόνταρχος   καὶ οἱ μετ᾿ αὐτοῦ *τηροῦντες τὸν Ἰησοῦν*
   = ἰδόντες τὸν *σεισμὸν* καὶ τὰ *γενόμεν*

   # ἐφοβήθησαν σφόδρα, λέγοντες, Ἀληθῶς θεοῦ υἱὸς ἦν οὗτος.

   = 55 Ἦσαν δὲ ἐκεῖ γυναῖκες πολλαὶ ἀπὸ μακρόθεν   θεωροῦσαι,
+ αἵτινες ἠκολούθησαν τῷ Ἰησοῦ ἀπὸ τῆς Γαλιλαίας διακονοῦσαι αὐτῷ·

----

56   ἐν αἷς ἦν Μαρία ἡ Μαγδαληνὴ
     καὶ Μαρία ἡ τοῦ Ἰακώβου καὶ Ἰωσὴφ μήτηρ
     καὶ ἡ μήτηρ τῶν υἱῶν Ζεβεδαίου.

Matt 51b-56 is composed of two parts. The first part (27:51b-53) speaks of the divine reaction to the death of Jesus and the second part (27:54-56) speaks of the human reaction to the death of Jesus. Both the parts are closely joined using similar vocabulary: ἐσείσθη (v. 51b) and σεισμός (v. 54); πολλὰ (vv. 52b. 53e. 55a).

5. Etymological Analysis

In order to express the concept of discipleship, Matthew makes use of several vocabulary items, important among them being καλέω (ἐκάλεσεν αὐτούς, «he called them», 4:21), δεῦτε ὀπίσω μου («come after me», 4:19), ἀκολουθέω (ἀκολούθει μοι, «follow me», 9:9; ἀκολουθεῖ ὀπίσω μου, «follow after me», 10:38; ἀκολουθείτω μοι, «follow me», 16:24; 8:22) ὀπίσω μου ἐλθεῖν (come after me, 16:24) and διακονέω (27:55).

Two discipleship vocabulary items in our text deserve special mention: a) ἠκολούθησαν τῷ Ἰησοῦ ἀπὸ τῆς Γαλιλαίας; b) διακονοῦσαι αὐτῷ.

5.1   ἠκολούθησαν τῷ Ἰησοῦ ἀπὸ τῆς Γαλιλαίας

As we have said elsewhere, a call from Jesus and a literal following behind Jesus marked two significant characteristics of the discipleship of Jesus. One important word that Matthew uses in order to refer to both a call of Jesus as well as a response to the call is ἀκολουθέω («to follow»). The NT uses this word as one of the technical words designating the discipleship of Jesus.

The word that expresses the concept of following in the Hebrew Bible is the verb הָלַךְ, to which the Greek ἀκολουθέω corresponds, and it means «to walk». The verb הָלַךְ, when it is paired with אַחֲרֵי, «behind», in a general sense means «to go after» or «follow» someone (Gen 24:5). In an ordinary sense, the root הָלַךְ is used to express a spatial movement (a warrior following his leader, Judg 9:4. 9; a wife following her husband, Hos 2:5, 7; a bride following her bridegroom, Jer 2:2, and a disciple following his master, 1Kgs 19:19-21). In a metaphorical sense, the verb הָלַךְ means «grow», «increase» or «progress» (Gen

26:13; Exod 19:19; Judg 4:24; Jonah 1:11, 13; Esth 9:4)[9]. In a theological sense, especially in the books of Hosea, (1:2; 2:7) Jeremiah (2:5, 8,
23, 25) and Deuteronomy (6:14; 8:19; 11:28), the verb הָלַךְ is comple-
mented by the adverb אַחֲרֵי (הָלַךְ אַחֲרֵי) to mean apostasy into Baalism[10].

In the LXX the verb ἀκολουθέω occurs thirteen times (Num 22:20;
Ruth 1:14; 1Sam 25:42; 1Kgs 19:20; Jdt 2:3; 5:7; 12:2; 15:13; 2Macc
8:36; Sir 1:2; Hos 2:7; Isa 45:14; Ezek 29:16). In most instances in the
LXX, the verb has a secular sense of following a person spatially (Num
22:20; Ruth 1:14; Jdt 15:13). On one occasion it is used in the sense of
«following» other gods (Jdt 5:7), while in 2Macc 8:36 it is employed in
the sense of «following» or «obeying» the law of God.

There are 90 occurrences of the verb ἀκολουθέω[11] in the NT, of
which 79 are found in the Gospels[12] and 11 outside the Gospels[13]. The
NT in general understands this verb almost exclusively in terms of following Jesus. Seventy-three out of ninety occurrences refer to discipleship[14]. The subject of ἀκολουθέω are normally persons (Matt 8:10;
Mark 3:7; Luke 9:49)[15] and the object of this verb is similarly «a per-

---

[9] HELFMEYER, «הָלַךְ», 392.

[10] G. KITTEL, «ἀκολουθέω», 211.

[11] The verb «ἀκολουθέω is used almost always with the dative of the person. Very
rarely is it used with ὀπίσω followed by the genitive of the person (Matt 10:38, Mark
8:34). Other than the simple form ἀκολουθέω, there exist different compound forms of
this verb in the NT: ἐξακολουθέω («follow» in a figurative sense: 2Pt 1:16; 2:2, 15);
ἐπακολουθέω (literally «pursue» every good work, 1Tim 5:10; «imitate» or «follow»
the footsteps of Christ, 1Pt 2:21); παρακολουθέω («go along», «accompany», Mark
16:17; «investigate» a thing, Luke 1:3; «concentrate» or «follow» faithfully, 1Tim
4:6, 2Tim 3:10); συνακολουθέω («accompany», Luke 23:49). See G. SCHNEIDER,
«ἀκολουθέω», 52. G. KITTEL, «ἀκολουθέω», 215.

[12] 25 in Matthew, 18 in Mark, 17 in Luke and 19 in John.

[13] Four times in Acts, six times in Revelation and once in 1Corinthians.

[14] Outside the Gospels it is used only once in reference to following Jesus, and that
too in a figurative sense (Rev 14:4). We note at least six occurrences where the verb
refers to something other than discipleship: John said to him «... we forbade him,
because he was not *following* us» (ἠκολούθει ἡμῖν, Mark 9:38). «And he sent two of
his disciples, and said to them, go into the city, and a man carrying a jar of water will
meet you; *follow him* (ἀκολουθήσατε αὐτῷ, Mark 14:13; see Luke 22:10); «And Jesus
rose and *followed him* (ἠκολούθησεν αὐτῷ, Matt 9:19); «... they *followed her* suppos-
ing that she was going to the tomb to weep there» (John 11:31); «... then Simon Peter
came *following* him» (ἀκολουθῶν αὐτῷ, John 20:6).

[15] The only exception that is found is Rev 14:13: «And I heard a voice from
heaven saying, "Write this: Blessed are the dead who die in the Lord henceforth".
"Blessed indeed", says the Spirit, "that they may rest from their labors, for their deeds
follow them!"».

son» or «a group of persons». The Gospels normally present Jesus as the object of the verb ἀκολουθέω.

The imperative ἀκολουθεῖ is always used by Jesus himself to invite people to be his disciples (Matt 8:22; 9:9; 19:21; 10:38) and when the response of an individual is in accordance to this call of Jesus, it clearly signifies discipleship.

5.1.1 Use of ἀκολουθέω in the Gospel According to Matthew

Among the Synoptic writers, Matthew has the most frequent use of the verb ἀκολουθέω (25 times)[16]. Seven of them denote Jesus' action. In three instances it is a direct invitation by Jesus to follow him ('ακολούθει μοι, «follow me», Matt 8:22; 9:9; 19:21). Once it shows Jesus' action of following a ruler (ἄρχων, 9:19), six occurrences denote different persons following Jesus (Matt 4:20; 4:22; 8:23; 9:9; 19:27; 26:58)[17]. In eight instances the verb refers to the crowds' action of following Jesus (Matt 4:25; 8:1; 8:10; 12:15; 14:13; 19:2; 20:29; 21:9) and twice it shows two blind men following Jesus (Matt 9:27; 20:34) and once a scribe (Matt 8:19). In one instance, it describes the women who had followed Jesus from Galilee to Jerusalem (27:55).

With this general understanding of the verb, we will now try to understand the discipleship nuance of this verb in the Gospel of Matthew. For this purpose we single out four passages: a) Jesus' call of the first disciples (4:18-22); b) an eager scribe and a reluctant disciple (8:18-22); c) Jesus' call of Matthew (9:9-13), and finally d) the taking of the cross and following (10:37-38). This discussion will help us to explain the use of this verb in Matt 27:55, which speaks of the women's following of Jesus.

5.1.2 The Use of ἀκολουθέω in Matt 4:18-22

This pericope describes the calling of four fishermen to become Jesus' disciples. They are Simon Peter and his brother Andrew, and James and his brother John[18]. It is preceded by a summary statement of

---

[16] Mark contains 18 occurrences of the verb ἀκολουθέω. Matthew takes 12 out of Mark while omitting six Markan usage (Mark 2:15; 6:1; 8:34; 9:38; 10:32 and 14:13). See G. SCHNEIDER, «ἀκολουθέω», 51.

[17] In order to describe a person's action of following Jesus, Matthew often uses the indicative aorist active ἠκολούθησαν.

[18] The Lake of Galilee is the geographical background of this call passage. Galilee is the center of Jesus' activity and has an important place in Matthew as it is closely

Jesus' message, which also functions as an adequate summary of his call to Israel to return to the path of God[19]: «Repent, for the Kingdom of heaven is at hand» (4:17).

In 4:18-22, Matthew uses the verb ἀκολουθέω twice (4: 20. 22). Both usages are to show the unconditional obedience of the disciples to the call of Jesus to follow him (Δεῦτε ὀπίσω μου, 4:19). Their obedience is manifested in their following of Jesus, leaving behind everything: «And immediately they (Peter and Andrew) left their nets and *followed* him» (v. 20); «And they, immediately, having left the boat and their father *followed* him» (v. 22). They leave practically everything that they have (nets, boat and their father) and respond to the call of Jesus[20]. Matthew uses the verb ἀκολουθέω to describe their following of Jesus. Being called by Jesus, they surrender themselves to the person of Jesus and accept his leadership. This gesture of acknowledgement expresses their personal commitment to Jesus even at the cost of their livelihood (boat and net) and family (father).

5.1.3 The Meaning of ἀκολουθέω in Matt 8:18-22

A second passage that interests us is Matt 8:18-22[21]. Apart from the introductory setting (8:18), this short pericope[22] contains two parallel scenes that have a symmetric structure: a) an eager scribe's request to

---

associated with the discipleship theme. The people called are ordinary citizens of Galilee engaged in fishing, a major industry in the area. Jesus encounters them in their place of work, on the shore of the Lake of Galilee.

[19] See C.S. KEENER, *Matthew*, 148.

[20] Jesus' call to follow him was economically demanding (C.S. KEENER, *Matthew*, 152). It was a call to leave all earthly securities. Although the main occupation of the people around the lake of Galilee was agriculture (See R.A. HORSELY, *Galilee*, 194), fishing was a major industry of the people (see S. SAFRAI, «Home and Family», 728-792) and fish was an important item for the first century Palestinian diet (see J. NEUSNER, *Judaism*, 23). People were engaged in the fish business and it was a means of making money. Jesus' call to abandon their full-time livelihood is significant. Such an abandonment meant keeping oneself insecure economically as well as socially (C.S. KEENER, *Matthew*, 150).

[21] This passage has been an object of scholarly debate in the last few decades. See J.D. KINGSBURY, «On Following Jesus», 45-49; J. KIILUNEN, «Der Nachfolgewillige Shriftgelehrte», 268-279; U. LUZ, *Das Evangelium nach Matthäus*, 2, 23; W.D. DAVIES – D.C. ALLISON, *Matthew*, 2, 41, 53-54; R.H. GUNDRY, «On True and False Disciples», 433-441.

[22] This pericope can also be described as a discipleship pericope. In it Matthew explains to the readers still more about the discipleship theme. See M. HENGEL, *The Charismatic Leader*, 213.

Jesus to follow him (19-20), and b) a would-be disciple's[23] request to Jesus to follow him (vv. 21-22). Each scene is subdivided into two: a) a statement by the candidate (vv. 19, 21), b) a response from Jesus that speaks of the nature of discipleship (vv. 20, 22). Both scenes (8:19-20 and vv. 21-22) are related together with the key discipleship verb ἀκολουθέω.

In the first scene (vv. 19-20) Matthew presents a scribe (γραμματεύς)[24] who wants to follow Jesus: Διδάσκαλε, ἀκολουθήσω σοι ὅπου ἐὰν ἀπέρχῃ[25]. Unlike the previous scene we studied, here it is the candidate himself who takes the initiative, not Jesus. Such an initiative seems to reflect the rabbinic model of discipleship in which the candidate chose the master of his choice. Jesus replies to him: «Foxes have holes, and the birds of the air have nests; but the Son of man has nowhere to lay his head». This means, «following Jesus may cost a disciple even the most basic security such as a place to live»[26]. Discipleship is a call to share the master's destiny. Reference to foxes and birds speaks of the lifestyle of Jesus and the lifestyle the «would-be disciple» may be called upon to adopt. Reference to «foxes» and «birds» explains the wandering charismatic nature of Jesus' mission and the basic lifestyle of Jesus' model of discipleship, as opposed to the rabbinic institutional model. The mainstream society of Jesus' time regarded such a lifestyle as wretched, although it was sometimes considered to be the temporary lot of righteous heroes[27]. To be a follower of Jesus, therefore, is to find oneself in the same situation as that of Jesus[28]. Jesus' answer implies the cost of discipleship.

In the second scene (vv. 21-22) Matthew speaks of a would-be disciple's desire to follow Jesus. Contrary to the statement of the scribe, this disciple makes a request: ἐπίτρεψόν μοι πρῶτον ἀπελθεῖν καὶ θάψαι τὸν πατέρα μου, «Let me first go and bury my father» (8:21). But Jesus said to him, «Follow me, and leave the dead to bury their own dead»

---

[23] J.D. KINGSBURY, «On Following Jesus», 45-49.

[24] The Matthean insertion of γραμματεύς shows a possibility of his access to a source other than Q or perhaps it can mean somebody from the crowds who listened to Jesus, because Matthew's community included Christian Scribes (13:52; 23:54). Perhaps, Matthew is quoting a simple historical fact.

[25] He addresses Jesus as διδάσκαλος, «teacher». In Matthew the Pharisees and Sadducees often addressed Jesus as teacher (12:38; 22:16, 24, 36).

[26] See C.S. KEENER, Matthew, 274.

[27] C.S. KEENER, Matthew, 274.

[28] See K.E. BAILEY, Poet and Peasant, 24.

(8:22). This disciple wanted to follow Jesus on condition that Jesus allow him first to bury his father. This request could mean two things. First, it could mean that the father was dead, and he wanted to discharge his obligation towards the father and the family before leaving everything in order to become the disciple of Jesus. Secondly it could mean that the father was still alive, but it was the son's obligation to look after his father in his declining years, until his eventual death, which would mean postponing being a disciple of Jesus. Among these two interpretations, the second one seems to be more reasonable, as it would not have been easy for a man to get into a discourse with Jesus concerning discipleship while his father lay dead in the house. According to the Jewish customs, dead bodies were to be buried on the same day. Whatever be the case, the request sounds reasonable because it was the duty of a son to honor his father and mother (Gen 50:5; Tob 4:3; Sir 38:16), although a few teachers did insist that one should honor the teacher above one's parents[29].

Jesus' reply to this would-be disciple is instructive: Ἀκολούθει μοι καὶ ἄφες τοὺς νεκροὺς θάψαι τοὺς ἑαυτῶν νεκρούς. Burying the dead was considered an important religious duty and a violation of this obligation meant a violation of the law of Yahweh[30]. In spite of all these religious strictures and regulations, Jesus says «let the dead bury their dead». Scholars have variously interpreted the phrase «ἄφες τοὺς νεκροὺς θάψαι τοὺς ἑαυτῶν νεκρούς». According to M. Hengel and G. Vermes, the reference here is to the «spiritually dead»[31] (see Lk 15:24, 32; Eph 2:1). According to R.H. Gundry and B.R. McCane the reference is to the physically dead[32], while for L. Morris the expression is an indication to «those who are soon to die»[33]. Whatever be the meaning of the phrase, Jesus' statement underlines the fact that the call to discipleship is an absolute one that need not satisfy any canon of human responsibilities[34]. There must be nothing that takes precedence over the discipleship of Jesus. In the words of A. Stock, «the Commitment of discipleship brooks no suspension»[35].

---

[29] m. Baba Meṣi'a, 2:11.

[30] See Tob 4:3-4; 6:14; 1Macc 2:70.

[31] See M. HENGEL, The Charismatic Leader, 7-8; G. VERMES, The Religion of Jesus the Jew, 29; W.D. DAVIES – D.C. ALLISON, Matthew, 168.

[32] See R.H. GUNDRY, Matthew, 153; B.R. MCCANE, «Let the Dead», 41.

[33] L.L. MORRIS, The Gospel According to Matthew, 203.

[34] See K.E. BAILEY, Poet and Peasant, 26-27.

[35] A. STOCK, The Method and Message of Matthew, 139.

5.1.4 Meaning of ἀκολουθέω in Matt 9:9

A third discipleship passage that interests us is Matt 9:9. The Evangelist uses the verb ἀκολουθέω to speak of Matthew's following of Jesus: «As Jesus passed on from there, he saw a *man* called Matthew, sitting at the tax office; and he said to him 'follow me' (ἀκολούθει μοι), and he «rose and 'followed' him» (καὶ ἀναστὰς ἠκολούθησεν αὐτῷ) (Matt 9:9)[36].

Our attention rests on Matthew's use of the verb ἀκολουθέω. This is the second of the four instances where the imperative 'ακολούθει appears in Matthew[37]. The imperative ἀκολούθει here clearly refers to Jesus' invitation to become his disciple. The use of the present imperative indicates a continuous following[38].

It is Jesus who takes the initiative to invite Matthew to follow him (ἀκολούθει μοι). In response to the call of Jesus, Matthew «rose» (ἀναστάς) and «followed» (ἠκολούθησεν) him. Matthew uses the same verb to show Jesus' call of Matthew as well as Matthew's response to the call of Jesus. The Matthean account of the call of Matthew the tax collector here highlights two features: a call and a response. The response itself is again characterised by two factors: commitment and cost. Matthew's obedient listening to the call of Jesus and his following behind him express his commitment to Jesus, while the leaving of his livelihood (tax gathering) expresses the cost.

5.1.5 The Meaning of ἀκολουθέω in Matt 10:37-38

Matt 10:37-38 contains three parallel sayings of which the first two are expressed in a positive mode while the third one is expressed negatively. They are linked together by the conjunction καί. In order to emphasize the disciple's relationship to Jesus, Matthew first makes use of two positive modes, children's love for parents and parents' love for children, which manifest the most personal relationship found in human life. The pericope reads «He who *loves* father or mother more than me is not worthy of me; and he who *loves* son or daughter more than me is not worthy of me» (10:37).

---

[36] All three Synoptists report Jesus' call of the tax collector (Mark 2:13-17; Luke 5:27-32) who is called Matthew in the first Gospel (9:9), and Levi by Mark (2:14) and Luke (5:27). They portray him as sitting at the tax office when Jesus called him.

[37] Three other occurrences are found in 8:22; 10:38; 19:21.

[38] L.L. MORRIS, *The Gospel according to Matthew*, 219.

For Matthew the discipleship of Jesus demands greater love than for one's blood relationships. That is to say «love of Jesus must be given preference, because by it one's "worthiness" is measured»[39].

After having expressed the two positive modes, in verse 38 Matthew expresses a negative mode which speaks of the relationship between cross-bearing and discipleship: «καὶ ὃς οὐ λαμβάνει τὸν σταυρὸν αὐτοῦ καὶ ἀκολουθεῖ ὀπίσω μου, οὐκ ἔστιν μου ἄξιος». The demand for loyalty is further brought out by relating discipleship to cross-bearing[40]. Cross-bearing and doing God's (12:46-50) will form the innermost kernel of the discipleship of Jesus[41].

Discipleship of Jesus, in this context, is closely associated with suffering and cross-bearing. Matthew's context suggests that the disciple's cross stands for «persecution» to the point of martyrdom[42]. Carrying one's cross is to expose oneself to this possibility through open discipleship[43]. Taking up one's cross in Jesus' time literally meant marching on the way to the site of execution, shamefully carrying the heavy horizontal beam of one's own death instrument through the midst of a jeering crowd[44]. Such a background made Jesus' call really challenging.

5.2 *διακονοῦσαι αὐτῷ*

The verb διακονέω is generally accepted to be a discipleship verb in the NT. The words διάκονος and διακονία are closely associated with this verb. This verb appears 36 times in the NT[45]. It designates «to serve». The activities designated by the verb are expressed abstractly by the noun διακονία («service»)[46]. The one who executes the activities

---

[39] A. STOCK, *The Method and Message of Matthew*, 176.

[40] L.L. MORRIS, *The Gospel according to Matthew*, 268.

[41] A. STOCK, *The Method and Message of Matthew*, 176.

[42] R.H. GUNDRY, *Matthew*, 200.

[43] R.H. GUNDRY, *Matthew*, 200.

[44] See J. JEREMIAS, *The Parable of Jesus*, 218-219; ID., *New Testament Theology*, 24; C.S. KEENER, *Matthew*, 331; R.V.G. TASKER, *The Gospel According to Matthew*, 109.

[45] 21 times in the Synoptics and Acts; 3 times in John, 8 times in the Pauline corpus letters, once in Hebrews, and 3 times in 1Peter.

[46] The noun διακονία appears 33 times in the NT. It appears only once in the Gospels (Luke 10:40), 8 times in Acts, 22 times in the Pauline letters and twice in Hebrews.

is called διάκονος («servant»)[47]. In Christian Greek these three words can have a special meaning. The substantive διάκονος can refer to a Christian Deacon (Phil 1:1; 1Tim 3:8. 12)[48]. The verb διακονέω can mean «to serve» as a deacon (1Tim 3:10. 13).

The word group can also mean «to wait on someone at the table», (Matt 22:13; Mark 1:31; Luke 12:37; 17:8; John 2:5, 9: 12:2; Acts 6:2), «to take care» (2Cor 3:3), «help or support someone» (Matt 25:44; Mark 1:13; Mark 15:41; Luke 8:3)[49], «the service of the disciples in a comprehensive sense» (Matt 23:11; Mark 9:35; 10:43; Luke 22:26f; John 12:26; Matt 27:55), «charitable service in the congregation» (Acts 6:1; Rom 12:7; 1Pet 4:11), «ministry of the Church» (1Cor 12:5; 16:15; 2Tim 1:18; Heb 6:10), «ministry of the apostles, prophets, Evangelists, pastors, and teachers» (Eph 4:12), «leadership in the Church» (Eph 4:17; Col 4:17; 1Tim 4:6; 2Tim 4:5) and «the office of the deacon» (Phil 1:1; 1Tim 3:8, 10, 12f)[50].

6. The Biblical Background

Matt 27:51b-56 reflects several OT passages, the understanding of which will help us to interpret the text.

6.1 The Earthquake

An earthquake is an apocalyptic phenomenon closely associated with the manifestation of Yahweh (Judg 5:4; Psa 68:8; Isa 63:19). It can be a sign of divine judgement, of the last times (Judg 5:4; Isa 24:18; Ezek 38:19), and of God's blazing anger against His people (Isa 5:25). It is often accompanied by other cosmic elements such as fire, storm, thunder, and darkness (Psa 18:8-16; Joel 2:10; 2Sam 22:8-16; Jer 8:16; 8:8-9). The earthquake has a proleptic eschatological significance (1Enoch

---

[47] This noun appears 29 times in the NT: 8 times in the Gospels and 21 times in the Pauline letters.

[48] The feminine version of the word is also διάκονος and is applied to Phoebe, a «deaconess» of the Church at Cenchreae (Rom 16:1).

[49] W. BAUER, A Greek English Lexicon, 184.

[50] H.W. BEYER, «διακονέω», 81-91. While illustrating the use of this verb Beyer suggests that it did not carry very dignified or acceptable connotations in ordinary Greek usage where it designated «waiting at table». But this word in the Christian context gradually moved from a simple designation of «waiting at table» to refer to the heart of Christian discipleship. See also M.J. SELVIDGE, «Mark and Woman», 23-32.

1:6-8; 2Bar 27:7; 70:8; Rev 6:12)[51]. Matthew seems to associate the cosmic implications of the death of Jesus with those of the resurrection (28:2). Matthew's use of the aorist passive ἐσείσθη refers to God indirectly as the agent of this terrestrial phenomenon.

6.2 The Splitting of the Rocks (1Kgs 19:11)

From a structural point of view, the phrase πέτραι ἐσχίσθησαν, «the rocks were split», might be considered as a poetic parallelism to the phrase ἡ γῆ ἐσείσθη, «the earth was shaken». The rending of the rocks is found in association with divine manifestations described in 1Kgs 19:11: «Now there was a great wind, so strong that it was splitting mountains and *breaking rocks* in pieces before the Lord ...».

6.3 The Resurrection of the Dead (LXX Ezek 37:12)

The resurrection of the dead manifests God's power to raise the dead. Matt 27:53 reflects at least two OT passages concerning the resurrection. This text reflects the vocabulary used in LXX Ezek 37:1-14[52] and noteworthy is the relationship between Matt 27:53 and Ezek 37:12:

LXX Ezek 37:12	Matt 27:53
Yahweh speaks	
ἐγὼ *ἀνοίγω* ὑμῶν τὰ μνήματα	καὶ τὰ μνημεῖα *ἀνεῴχθησαν*
I will open your tombs,	and the tombs were opened
καὶ ἀνάξω ὑμᾶς *ἐκ τῶν μνημάτων* ὑμῶν	καὶ ἐξελθόντες *ἐκ τῶν μνημείων*
and bring you *from* your tombs,	and having come *out* from *the tombs*
καὶ *εἰσάξω* ὑμᾶς *εἰς τὴν γῆν* τοῦ Ισραηλ	εἰσῆλθον *εἰς τὴν ἁγίαν πόλιν*
I will bring you into the land of Israel	*they entered* into the *holy city*

There is a structural as well as a thematic correspondence between the two texts. Matthew uses similar words. The substantive μνήματα in Ezek 37:12 is equivalent to the Matthean μνημεῖα. The principal verbs in the text of Ezekiel are in the active indicative (ἀνοίγω) and future

---

51 C.S. KEENER, *Matthew*, 686; R. BAUCKHAM, «The Eschatological Earthquake», 224-233.

52 R.B. GARDNER, *Matthew*, 393; J. GNILKA, *Das Matthäusevangelium*, 477.

form (ἀνάξω, εἰσάξω). God is the subject. Matt 27:51b-53 contains similar verbs, but in the aorist passive form, used as a divine passive. This indicates God as the agent of resurrection.

A second biblical passage which might have shaped the Matthean view of the resurrection of the dead is LXX Isa 26:19, which reads, ἀναστήσονται οἱ νεκροί καὶ ἐγερθήσονται οἱ ἐν τοῖς μνημείοις, «The dead shall rise and the ones in the tombs shall be raised up». This corresponds to the second part of Matt 27:53, «καὶ πολλὰ σώματα τῶν κεκοιμημένων ἁγίων ἠγέρθησαν, «And many bodies of the fallen asleep saints were raised».

6.4 *The Gentiles' Confession (Psa 22:27-28)*

Matthew's description of the choral confession of the divine sonship of Jesus seems to reflect Psalm 22, in which the psalmist prays: «All the ends of the earth shall remember and turn to the Lord, and all the families of the nations shall worship before him. For dominion belongs to the Lord, and he rules over the nations» (Psa 22:28-29)[53].

This brief discussion on the various biblical passages reflected in Matt 27:51b-56 suggests to us how the death of Jesus and the various divine and human reactions to it are in harmony with the OT biblical passages.

7. Interpretation

In the preceding three sections of this chapter we have discussed some of the significant problems found in the text (27:51b-56), its compositional features, important vocabulary items and biblical parallels, all of which contribute to the interpretation of the passage.

7.1 *The Divine Reaction to the Death of Jesus as an Invitation to Believe in the Son of God (Matt 27:51b-53)*

The mention of an earthquake, rending of the rocks, opening of the tombs and the resurrection of the bodies of dead saints in relation to the death of Jesus are peculiar to Matthew. Scholars like R. Aguirre, W. Bieder, E. Fascher and M. Riebl consider Matt 27:51b-53 as a pre-

---

[53] J. GNILKA, *Das Matthäusevangelium,* 480; D. SENIOR, *The Passion,* 149; ID., «The Death of Jesus», 324.

Matthean poetic piece circulating in popular circles[54]. On the other hand A. Resch, H.W. Bartsch and P. Seidensticker hold the view that it is a fragment of the paschal tradition[55]. They arrive at this conclusion by basing their argument on the style and vocabulary used in Matthew[56]. D. Senior considers 27:51b-53 as Matthew's own composition[57].

Matthew employs a series of aorist passive forms of the verbs, such as ἐσείσθη, ἐσχίσθησαν, ἀνεῴχθησαν and ἠγέρθησαν. They can all be called divine passives, which suggest God as the agent of these actions[58]. Scholars have interpreted these signs differently. According to W. Hendriksen, these signs refer to nature's response to what happened to Jesus[59]. D. Patte understands them as an ultimate demonstration of the authority and power that Jesus exercised during his public ministry: unambiguously God's own power[60].

The different apocalyptic elements in the text speak of Matthew's apocalyptic motif[61]. The earthquake, an apocalyptic motif that Matthew adds to other passages in the Gospel as well (6:24; 28:2), is mentioned in relation to the day of God's appearance (theophany)[62]. It is a sign of the last judgement (Joel 4:14-17). According to Bornkamm, this «denotes specifically the invasion of the realm of the dead by the divine victor»[63] and marks the beginning of the travails of the last time (Matt 24:7-8). In Matthew the earthquake is not an isolated sign. It is related to a chain of different reactions. It leads to the splitting of the rocks,

---

54 R. AGUIRRE, *Exegesis*, 363-382; W. BIEDER, *Die Vorstellung*, 49-56; E. FASCHER, *Das Weib;* M. RIEBL, «Jesu Tod», 208-213.

55 See A. RESCH, *Agrapha*, 454-456; H.W. BARTSCH, *Das Auferstehungszeugnis*, 1-31; P. SEIDENSTICKER, *Die Auferstehung Jesu*, 38-58, 146-48.

56 On the issue of pre-Matthean style and vocabulary see R. AGUIRRE, *Exegesis*, 29-56.

57 He bases his argument on this by pointing out a similar example of parataxis found in Matthew 7:25. See D. SENIOR, «Death of Jesus», 312-329; ID., «Matthew's Special Material» 277-85.

58 J. GNILKA, *Das Matthäusevangelium*, 695; According B. M. Newman and P.C. Stine, in some languages it may be necessary to translate «God caused the earth to shake, and he split the rocks apart». See B.M. NEWMAN – P.C. STINE, *A Translator's Handbook*, 892.

59 W. HENDRIKSEN, *The Gospel of Matthew*, 975.

60 D. PATTE, *The Gospel according to Matthew*, 388.

61 R.E. BROWN, *The Death*, 1139.

62 H. FRANKMÖLLE, *Matthäus Kommentar 2*, 504

63 G. BORNKAMM, «σείω, σεισμός», 200

which in turn causes the opening of the tombs hewn in the rocks. The splitting of the rocks is closely associated with God's presence (1Kgs 19:11; Isa 48:21). The opening of the tombs allows the dead saints to come forth. The resurrection of the bodies is found in association with the end-time (Dan 12:1-4).

Noteworthy is Matthew's focus on the phrase μετὰ τὴν ἔγερσιν αὐτοῦ[64] in v. 53. In the composition of the passage we have found that the phrase μετὰ τὴν ἔγερσιν αὐτοῦ occupies a central position. Matthew's intention is clear. It seems that the Evangelist is trying to extend the eschatological symbolism to the resurrection of Jesus thus associating Jesus as the cause of the resurrection of the dead (1Cor 15:20). Jesus is «the first born from the dead» (1Col 1:18)[65]. This is in accordance with 1Thess 4:14: «If we believe that Jesus died and rose, so also [we believe] will God the ones who have fallen asleep through Jesus lead forth with him». In this manner Matthew seems to associate, though he does not say it clearly, our own resurrection with the death of Jesus[66], because the death of Jesus is life-giving. In Matt 26:28 the Evangelist seems to express the same faith interpretation of the death of Jesus, which speaks of death as a covenant for the remission of sins. Jesus is the life-giving and healing servant of God (Matt 8:17; 20:28). Matthew portrays it by showing that «the saintly dead of Israel's past rise at the death of Israel's Messiah»[67]. Commenting on the death of Jesus, Morris observes: «On the one hand Jesus' sacrificial death blots out sin, defeats the power of evil and death, and opens up access to God. On the other hand, Jesus' victorious resurrection and vindication promise the final resurrection of those who die in him»[68]. Matt 27:52-53 depicts the resurrection of the dead as taking place at the death of Jesus[69]. D. Senior sees an implied soteriology in Matthew's citing of

---

[64] Translation of this phrase is difficult. The problem here is with the translation of the substantive ἔγερσις. The word can be understood in a transitive as well as in an intransitive sense. Taking it in a transitive sense, it means «raising». Taking it in an intransitive sense it means «rising». Hence the phrase μετὰ τὴν ἔγερσιν αὐτοῦ may be translated either as «after the raising of him», or «after the rising of him». The first translation seems to be more correct. It indicates God as the agent of resurrection.

[65] See R.E. BROWN, *The Death of the Messiah*, 1139; H.H. HOBBS, *An Exposition of the Four Gospels*, 405.

[66] L.L. MORRIS, *The Gospel According to Matthew*, 725.

[67] J.P. MEIER, *The Vision of Matthew*, 34.

[68] See L.L. MORRIS, *The Gospel according to Matthew*, 725.

[69] According to some, Matthew mentions the resurrection of the saints before Jesus' resurrection by mistake. For McNeile, the resurrection of the saints was probably

eschatological phenomena such as the quaking of the earth, the opening of the tombs and the raising of the dead[70]. Here the Evangelist is telling his readers something about salvation.

By the inclusion of the apocalyptic material, Matthew, on the one hand, prepares us for the resurrection of Jesus and, on the other hand for our own resurrection. This marks the end of the old and the beginning of the new aeon[71], a new salvation economy[72]. The death of Jesus marks the beginning of the end-time: the time that will culminate in the coming of the Son of Man and of judgement; a time during which one needs to watch as is indicated in Matt 24 and 25.

7.2 The Human Response to the Death of Jesus as a Faith Response (Matt 27: 54-56)

A series of apocalyptic events (27:51b-53) leads to various human responses (27:54-56), which could be divided into two different categories: a) the response of the soldiers (v. 54), and b) the response of the women followers (vv. 55-56).

7.2.1 The Response of the Centurion and the Men with Him (Matt 27: 54)

The first human response to the death of Jesus is the reaction of the Gentile soldiers near the cross: Ὁ δὲ ἑκατόνταρχος καὶ οἱ μετ' αὐτοῦ τηροῦντες τὸν Ἰησοῦν ἰδόντες τὸν σεισμὸν καὶ τὰ γενόμενα ἐφοβήθησαν σφόδρα, λέγοντες, Ἀληθῶς θεοῦ υἱὸς ἦν οὗτος (v. 54)[73].

---

the sequel to the earthquake at Jesus' resurrection in 28:2 and was mistakenly placed here at Jesus' death. See A. MCNEILE, The Gospel according to Matthew, 424. See also F.D. BRUNER, Matthew, 1062.

Some others suggest that in the oral tradition, this scene was connected to the resurrection of Jesus and that when Matthew moved this general resurrection back to the death of Jesus, he inserted the phrase «μετὰ τὴν ἔγερσιν αὐτοῦ « to keep primacy of Christ as the first fruits of the dead». See J.P. MEIER, Matthew, 352; ID., The vision of Matthew, 34; J.C. FENTON, Saint Matthew, 444.

[70] D. SENIOR, «The Death of Jesus», 328.

[71] See R.B. GARDNER, Matthew, 393; G.T. MONTAGUE, Companion God, 317.

[72] A. STOCK, The Method and Message of Matthew, 429; O. DA SPINETOLI, Matteo, 655-657.

[73] It is generally accepted that for 27:54 Matthew depends on Mark 15:39. At the same time the author has used editorial freedom to bring significant changes to the text for his own theological purposes. Matthew makes four important changes to the Markan text.

After presenting a series of divine reactions, Matthew using the particle δέ (v. 54) shifts the scene from divine to human reactions. Matthew's repetition of the «earthquake» further links these human reactions to the divine reaction. The participle λέγοντες is dependent upon the phrase «feared exceedingly». In other words the divine fear engendered by the eschatological signs is the context in which the centurion and the men with him confess Jesus as the Son of God.

The confession of the Gentile soldiers in Matt 27:54 displays two elements. Their confession, on the one hand, sharply contrasts with the mockeries and humiliations with which they themselves reviled Jesus before his death on the cross (27:27-37). On the other hand it parallels the confession of the disciples in general (Matt 14:33) and Peter in particular (16:16) during the public ministry of Jesus. The soldiers' confession represents a fundamental reformation of attitude[74]. The various apocalyptic events change their attitude about Jesus. As a result they confess him as «the Son of God».

The second element deserves special attention as it contributes to the understanding of the Matthean concept of discipleship. The confession of the centurion and the men with him gives them a status alongside the disciples of Jesus as it closely parallels Matt 14:22-35, which contains three elements: a) a context of the divine manifestation (Jesus' walking on the sea, v. 25); b) a reaction of fear (they cried out of fear, v. 26) and 3) a solemn confession (Truly you are the Son of God, v. 33).

Similar to 14:22-35, Matt 27:51b-54 reflects the same elements: a) a context of divine manifestation (the earthquake and the things that happened, vv. 51b-53) b) a reaction of fear (they were filled with fear, v. 54) and c) a solemn Christian confession (Truly you are the Son of God, v. 54). Each element calls for special mention.

---

i) Matthew changes the Markan word ὁ κεντυρίων, a unique NT word, and copies a usual biblical form ὁ ἑκατόνταρχος.

ii) Matthew extends the centurion's «confession» to a choral confession by «the centurion and the men with him guarding Jesus». See L.L. MORRIS, *The Gospel according to Matthew*, 726.

iii) Matthew changes Mark's Ἰδὼν δὲ ὁ κεντυρίων ὁ παρεστηκὼς ἐξ ἐναντίας αὐτοῦ ὅτι οὕτως ἐξέπνευσεν, into Ὁ δὲ ἑκατόνταρχος καὶ οἱ μετ' αὐτοῦ τηροῦντες τὸν Ἰησοῦν ἰδόντες τὸν σεισμὸν καὶ τὰ γενόμενα ἐφοβήθησαν σφόδρα, λέγοντες, Ἀληθῶς θεοῦ υἱὸς ἦν οὗτος thus emphasizing σεισμός, «earthquake», as the principal factor.

iv) Matthew has the additional element of ἐφοβήθησαν σφόδρα. The usage here echoes a similar insertion in 17:6. See R.H. GUNDRY, *Matthew*, 576-77.

[74] L. SABOURIN, *The Gospel according to St Matthew*, 920.

a) *The Divine Manifestation*

In 27:54, Matthew seems to single out the earthquake for two reasons. First, because it is understood to be the principal phenomenon that caused reactions such as the splitting of rocks and the opening of tombs[75]. Second the concept of the earthquake is closely associated with the divine manifestations in Matthew (8:24). For the centurion and the men with him the earthquake and its attendant events constitute a revelatory atmosphere inspiring holy fear, as they lead them to the recognition of the identity of Jesus: Ἀληθῶς θεοῦ υἱὸς ἦν οὗτος (v. 54). This could be compared to the event of Jesus' walking on the sea that aroused fear in the disciples (14:26), and which led them to the recognition of the Lord, followed by their confession (Ἀληθῶς θεοῦ υἱὸς εἶ, 14:33)[76].

b) *The Reaction of Fear*

The second element concerns Matthew's use of the phrase ἐφοβήθησαν σφόδρα, «they were greatly afraid». The «earthquake and the things that happened» (σεισμόν καὶ τὰ γενόμενα) aroused in them great fear. The concept of fear, elsewhere in Matthew, is closely associated with the manifestation of divine power (17:6)[77]. Only on two occasions do we find the phrase ἐφοβήθησαν σφόδρα. Both thematically and structurally, the usage in Matt 27:54 is parallel to 17:6[78]:

---

[75] Scholars L. Sabourin, J. Morison, and W. Hendricksen hold the opinion that perhaps the rending of the temple curtain was caused by the earthquake. See L. SABOURIN, *The Gospel According to Matthew*, 920; J. MORISON, *A Practical Commentary*, 603; W. HENDRICKSEN, *The Gospel of Matthew*, 977; R.E. BROWN, *The Death*, 1145. Such an interpretation, instead of solving problems, seems to create more problems. These scholars base their arguments on the whole event as a historical narration. Looking for historical explanation leads us here to more complex problems. For example, if the earthquake caused the tearing of the temple curtain, then how did the temple remain intact? If the rocks were split, how did Joseph of Arimatthea find a tomb intact to bury to bury the body of Jesus? Besides, as argued above, Matthew on the literary level begins and ends the incident of the rending of the veil before the earthquake.

[76] D.R.A. HARE, *Matthew*, 324; D. SENIOR, *The Passion*, 147; A. STOCK, *The Method and Message of Matthew*, 429.

[77] D. SENIOR, *The Passion Narrative*, 326; E. LOHMEYER, *Das Evangelium des Matthäus*, 397; G. STRECKER, *Der Weg*, 234.

[78] See R.H. GUNDRY, *Matthew*, 578.

17:6 ἀκούσαντες ... ἐφοβήθησαν σφόδρα.
27:54 ἰδόντες   ...   ἐφοβήθησαν σφόδρα,

The immediate context for the usage of ἐφοβήθησαν σφόδρα in 17:6 is the divine manifestation, a voice from heaven that reveals the divine sonship of Jesus: Οὗτός ἐστιν ὁ υἱός μου ὁ ἀγαπητός, ἐν ᾧ εὐδόκησα· ἀκούετε αὐτοῦ (17:5). This divine voice speaks of the identity of Jesus as God's Son. This was a revelation to the disciples, a revelation that filled them with fear: «When the disciples heard this, they fell on their faces, and «feared greatly», ἐφοβήθησαν σφόδρα (Matt 17:6)[79]. The revelatory voice arousing fear leads them to the recognition of the Lord.

Matt 27:54 has a similar background. The death of Jesus is followed by extraordinary events, symbols of a divine reaction that aroused great fear in the centurion and the soldiers watching Jesus. Their fear was a reverential fear, a fear that led them to the acknowledgement of the true identity of Jesus[80].

The reaction of the Gentile centurion and the men with him parallels the reaction of the disciples in 17:6[81]. Both for the disciples and for the centurion along with the men accompanying him, the events that caused fear in them become also means of recognition of the true identity of the Lord, which finds its expression in the confession.

c) *The Solemn Christian Confession*

The third element that relates v. 54 to the theme of discipleship is the confession itself. The holy fear led the disciples to the confession: «'Αληθῶς θεοῦ υἱὸς εἶ (14:33). A similar fear now leads the centurion and the men with him to confess 'Αληθῶς θεοῦ υἱὸς ἦν οὗτος (27:54). Their confession gives them a status alongside that of the disciples of Jesus, as it is identical to the confession made by the disciples after Jesus' stilling of the storm in 14:33[82]. Both the disciples as well as the Gentiles recognize the divine sonship of Jesus. What God declared of

---

[79] D.C. ALLISON, *Matthew*, 636; F.D BRUNER, *Matthew*, 1064; R.H. GUNDRY, *Matthew*, 578.

[80] D. SENIOR, *Passion Narrative*, 327.

[81] D. SENIOR, *Passion Narrative*, 328.

[82] See L.L. MORRIS, *The Gospel according to Matthew*, 726; L. SABOURIN, *The Gospel according to Matthew*, 920. According to 14:33, which follows the episodes of Jesus' walking on the water and his stilling of the storm, the disciples worship Jesus and proclaim to him 'Αληθῶς θεοῦ υἱὸς εἶ, «Truly, you are the Son of God».

Jesus in 3:17 and 17:5, and what the disciples confessed of Jesus in 14:33 and 16:16[83], is now acknowledged by the Gentiles:

God's Declaration

Οὗτός ἐστιν ὁ υἱός μου ὁ ἀγαπητός, ἐν ᾧ εὐδόκησα (3:17).

Οὗτός ἐστιν ὁ υἱός μου ὁ ἀγαπητός, ἐν ᾧ εὐδόκησα· ἀκούετε αὐτοῦ (17:5).

The Disciples' Confession

Ἀληθῶς θεοῦ υἱὸς εἶ (14:33)

Σὺ εἶ ὁ Χριστὸς ὁ υἱὸς τοῦ θεοῦ τοῦ ζῶντος (16:16).

The Gentiles' Confession

Ἀληθῶς θεοῦ υἱὸς ἦν οὗτος (27:54)

The soldiers' confession of Jesus as the Son of God foreshadows the conversion of the Gentiles[84]. According to D. Senior «... the Gentile believers take their place alongside the *disciples* themselves»[85]. L. Sabourin thinks that the Gentiles' acceptance of the divine sonship of Jesus makes them candidates for discipleship and the first representatives of a future Gentile community[86]. J.P. Meier holds the opinion that the missionary mandate of the risen Lord in 28:16-20 is proleptically realized in the Gentiles' confession of the divine sonship of Jesus[87]. Through the confession, the Gentiles are becoming disciples[88]. Through their confession Matthew is re-affirming the identity of Jesus as the Son of God, which for Matthew is a mature knowledge of the purpose of Jesus' earthly ministry[89]. Placing this confession of the identity of Jesus in the mouth of the Gentile soldiers, Matthew seems to place all those Gentiles who will make a similar confession of faith along with the disciples (14:33), and Peter (16:16), who had made a confession to the Christ using the same words[90]. Unlike Peter, these

---

[83] D. SENIOR, *The Gospel of Matthew*, 166; F. D. BRUNER, *Matthew*, 1064.

[84] See SENIOR, *Passion Narrative*, 324; W. HENDRICKSEN, *The Gospel of Matthew*, 977; J.P. HEIL, «The Narrative Structure», 423.

[85] D. SENIOR, *The Passion Narrative*, 327.

[86] L. SABOURIN, *The Gospel According to Matthew*, 920.

[87] J.P. MEIER, *The Vision of Matthew*, 34.

[88] J.P. MEIER, *Matthew*, 352.

[89] A. STOCK, *The Method and Message of Matthew*, 429.

[90] R. FABRIS, *Matteo*, 556; C.S. KEENER, *Matthew*, 686; J. GNILKA, *Das Matthäusevangelium*, 478; E. LOHMEYER, *Das Evangelium des Matthäus*, 397; T. ZAHN, *Das Evangelium des Matthäus*, 706. D. SENIOR, *Passion Narrative*, 327; A. STOCK, *The Method and Message of Matthew*, 429.

Gentiles recognize Jesus in the cross, rather than ignoring it (16:21-22)[91]. In this manner the Gentile executioners become the first persons after Jesus' death to concur with Jesus' identity[92]. Thus the first Christian confession after the death of Jesus comes from the Gentiles[93] and it foreshadows the conversion of the Gentiles[94]. Matthew's presentation of a choral confession, unlike that of Mark's single centurion, refers to the fact that the entire body of the Gentile execution squad recognizes the identity of Jesus[95]. The astonishing apocalyptic events, such as the earthquake and the splitting of the rocks perhaps changed their hearts[96]. Matthew's signs offer more reasons for the Gentiles' confession than Mark[97]. Seeing and hearing Jesus produce conversion[98]. Ironically, the centurion and the men with him recognize without prompting what the Sanhedrin had denied: Jesus is God's Son (v. 54)[99]. Matthew here teaches the doctrine of conversion in this text[100]. The text here echoes the creation of a new community of disciples gathered from all nations (28:18)[101].

In this way we see that Matthew regards the Gentiles favorably. Jesus' mission is extended to all, the Gentile nations as well[102]. The

---

[91] C.S. KEENER, *Matthew*, 687.

[92] J. Pobee and D.C. Sim interpret the confession of the centurion more as a cry of defeat than as a Christian confession. See J. POBEE, «The Cry of the centurion», 91; D.C. SIM, «The Confession», 401-424. This proposal misses the greater emphasis on the Gentile mission in Matthew.

[93] It was a Gentile Magi that first honored Jesus' birth (Matt 2). In the same manner the Gentile soldiers are the first to honor Jesus' death. See F.D. BRUNER, *Matthew*, 1063.

[94] K. STOCK, *Il racconto*, 114-17.

[95] C.S. KEENER, *Matthew*, 688; J.P. MEIER, *The Vision of Matthew*, 205; R.H. GUNDRY, *Matthew*, 579.

[96] As Matt 27:35-36 witnesses, the soldiers are the people who crucified Jesus and who divided his garments. The same soldiers now seeing the earthquake and the things that happened, accept the identity of Jesus as the Son of God. Here Matthew's missionary and paranetic thrust is clear, that is to say, conversion and repentance are possible to any one. See J.P. MEIER, *The Vision of Matthew*, 205.

[97] C.S. KEENER, *Matthew*, 688.

[98] F.D. BRUNER, *Matthew*, 1063.

[99] See W. HENDRIKSEN, *The Gospel of Matthew*, 976; C.S. KEENER, *Matthew*, 688.

[100] E. LOHMEYER, *Das Evangelium des Matthäus*, 397; F.D. BRUNER, *Matthew*, 1063; See also K. STOCK, «Das Bekenntnis des Centurio», 289-301.

[101] R.B. GARDNER, *Matthew*, 393; J.P. MEIER, *The Vision of Matthew*, 205; D.A. HAGNER, *Matthew 14-28*, 853.

[102] Matthew's reference to the Gentiles appears virtually in every section of the Gospel: It starts with the infancy narrative (1:1-16, the genealogy; inclusion of the

passion and death of Jesus becomes the revelation to the Gentiles, and their redemption consists in believing in Jesus, which is to become his disciples (28:19). Discipleship includes responding to the call of Jesus and accepting the divine sonship of Jesus. The centurion and the soldiers saw the things that happened. Their seeing led them to confess: «Truly this was the Son of God». Thus the Gentiles under the cross, Jesus' own executioners, recognize his identity. While his own people had not believed, the centurion in charge of Jesus' execution and those with him recognized Jesus' identity the way Peter had some time before (16:16)[103]. To put it in different words, the centurion and the men with him confess to what the Jewish spectators and leaders mocked at just a short while before (27: 39-43)[104]. That is to say, the passion and the death of Jesus bring condemnation to those who refuse to believe in Jesus[105] while it brings salvation to those who accept his identity as the Son of God.

7.2.2 The Women's Response and their Discipleship of Jesus (Matt 27:55-56)

The second group of persons that witness the death of Jesus is the women who followed Jesus from Galilee (vv. 55-56). The centurion and the men saw the earthquake and the things that happened, which led them to the confession of Jesus as «the Son of God» (v. 54). The women who followed Jesus from Galilee seem to witness both the divine reactions as well as perhaps the confession of the Gentiles.

Gentile women; 2:1-2, story of the magi), can be found at the beginning of Jesus' ministry (4:12-16, Galilee of the Gentiles), at several points in his public ministry in Galilee (4:23-25, Jesus' healing ministry is extended to both Jews and Gentiles; 8:5-13, healing of the centurion' servant), during his final teachings in the temple of Jerusalem (22:1-14, Jesus' mission includes Jews and Gentiles; 24:14, universal proclamation of the Gospel throughout the world; 25:31-46, the parable of the sheep and goats), in the passion narrative (27:19, Pilate's wife, a Gentile woman attempts to rescue Jesus; 27:54, the confession of the centurion), and in the concluding scene of the Gospel (28:16-20). Here the Evangelist views the Gentiles as persons capable of exemplary faith in Jesus. The Gospel will be proclaimed to the Gentiles. This anticipates the inclusion of the Gentiles into the community. This shows both a conversion of the Gentiles on the one hand and an expansion of God's mercy on the other hand.

[103] C.S. KEENER, *Matthew*, 687.

[104] J.P. MEIER, *The Vision of Matthew*, 205; R.B. GARDNER, *Matthew*, 393.

[105] See U. VANNI, «La passione», 65-91. This article points out that the passion of Jesus became a punishment for the enemies of Jesus, while for the centurion and the soldiers, who confessed Jesus as the Son of God, it became a means of salvation.

This is the only reference in Matthew that speaks clearly of the women as «followers» of Jesus[106]. The text reads: Ἦσαν δὲ ἐκεῖ γυναῖκες πολλαὶ ἀπὸ μακρόθεν θεωροῦσαι, αἵτινες ἠκολούθησαν τῷ Ἰησοῦ ἀπὸ τῆς Γαλιλαίας διακονοῦσαι αὐτῷ· [56] ἐν αἷς ἦν Μαρία ἡ Μαγδαληνὴ καὶ Μαρία ἡ τοῦ Ἰακώβου καὶ Ἰωσὴφ μήτηρ καὶ ἡ μήτηρ τῶν υἱῶν Ζεβεδαίου. For these verses, Matthew depends of Mark 14:40-41.

Four editorial changes deserve special mention, as they lead us to the interpretation of the text. The first change concerns Matthew's replacing of the Markan imperfect (ἠκολούθουν) with the aorist form of the verb (ἠκολούθησαν). The second change concerns Matthew's changing of the phrase «ἐν τῇ Γαλιλαίᾳ» with «ἀπὸ τῆς Γαλιλαίας». The third change concerns Matthew's changing of the Markan imperfect διηκόνουν to the participle διακονοῦσαι, «ministering»[107]. The fourth change, closely related to the third one, is Matthew's combination of «following» and «serving:» (ἠκολούθησαν τῷ Ἰησοῦ ἀπὸ τῆς Γαλιλαίας διακονοῦσαι αὐτῷ), which for Mark are two separate activities (ἠκολούθουν αὐτῷ καὶ διηκόνουν αὐτῷ). Mark separates both these actions with a conjunction (καί, «and»).

a) *ἠκολούθησαν τῷ ʼιησοῦ*

Like Mark, Matthew also speaks of several women who followed Jesus from Galilee. The Evangelist's use of the aorist form ἠκολούθησαν calls our special attention to it as he uses the same verbal form (indicative aorist active) in different call passages to show the male disciples' following of Jesus:

The Male Disciples of Jesus

οἱ δὲ εὐθέως ἀφέντες τὰ δίκτυα   *ἠκολούθησαν* αὐτῷ (4:20)

οἱ δὲ εὐθέως ἀφέντες τὸ πλοῖον καὶ τὸν πατέρα αὐτῶν *ἠκολούθησαν* αὐτῷ (4:22)

καὶ ἀναστὰς   *ἠκολούθησεν* αὐτῷ (9:9).

The Women Followers

Ἦσαν δὲ ἐκεῖ γυναῖκες πολλαὶ ...*ἠκολούθησαν* τῷ Ἰησοῦ (27:55)

---

[106] C. S KEENER, *Matthew*, 689.

[107] W.C. ALLEN, *The Gospel According to Matthew*, 297; E. HAENCHEN, *Der Weg Jesus*, 541; R. ATWOOD, *Mary Magdalene*, 44.

Similar to the male disciples, the women also follow Jesus: ἠκολούθησαν τῷ Ἰησοῦ (27:55). Matthew employs the same vocabulary here. Now, does their following of Jesus indicate their discipleship of Jesus? The disciples' following of Jesus was clearly in response to a direct call from Jesus (Δεῦτε ὀπίσω μου, 4:19; ἐκάλεσεν αὐτούς, 4:21, Ἀκολούθει μοι, 9:9). And these persons follow Jesus immediately. Undoubtedly they are discipleship stories. In the case of the women, Matthew does not specify that the women's following of Jesus is in response to a direct call from Jesus. We have no description of Jesus' calling of any woman to follow him. But we have indication that some women followed Jesus. Whether Jesus called the women to follow him or not, their action of following Jesus (ἠκολούθησαν τῷ Ἰησοῦ) resembles the male disciples' action of following him (4:20, 22; 9:9). Although there is no direct call from Jesus, the fact that these women continued to follow Jesus implies certain elements of discipleship in it. Such a discipleship implication is further strengthened by two factors that we find in the Gospel: a) ἀπὸ τῆς Γαλιλαίας, and b) διακονοῦσαι αὐτῷ.

b) ἀπὸ τῆς Γαλιλαίας

The phrase ἀπὸ τῆς Γαλιλαίας refers to the place from where the women started following Jesus: «from Galilee». This description suggests that the women are Galileans, although Matthew does not say it specifically. This is important from a discipleship point of view. Significantly, Galilee is the place where Jesus started his ministry, calling the first disciples (Matt 4:18-22). It is also the place that symbolized for Matthew universal scope for the Church's mission (4:12-17)[108]. Jesus was «from Nazareth of Galilee» (Mark 1:9; Matt 2:23); much of his ministry was centered around Galilee and even «throughout Galilee» (Mark 1:39; Matt 4:23; see Luke 4:14). The disciples of Jesus are identified as «Galileans» (Acts 1:11).

Galilee was thus a part of Jesus' identity and Jesus was called «the Galilean» (Matt 26:69). Galilee signals a key missiological theme in the Gospel of Matthew, namely that God accepts the rejected ones of the world and commissions them as God's agents of change in the world[109]. Galilee was not a religious social center of power in the first

---

[108] D. SENIOR, Matthew, 341.
[109] P. HERTIG, «The Galilee Theme», 155-163.

century. Archeological evidence shows that the beautiful region of Galilee was mostly rural, largely Gentile, and densely populated with peasants. Dwelling places were small and clustered together[110]. Such living conditions often caused illness and a short life expectancy. Robberies and attacks from highwaymen were frequent[111]. Galilee had a mixture of cultures and ethnic groups, the principal reason for which was the international routes passing through it[112]. Culturally Galilee was dominated by the Greeks, and politically by the Romans[113]. Historically the people of the land were not only despised, but also exploited[114]. On Galilee V. Elizondo writes: «That God has chosen to become a Galilean underscores the great paradox of the incarnation, in which God becomes the despised, and lowly of the world. In becoming a Galilean, God becomes the fool of the world for the sake of the world's salvation»[115].

The Jews who lived in Galilee were considered inferior to the pious Jews of Jerusalem (John 1:46; 7:52). Pharisees and Saducees considered Galilean Jews with disdain due to their ignorance of the law and their laxity of religious observances[116]. In short Galilee was a place in which dwelt marginal people who were to become the center of God's activity. Jesus chose this land and the people there as the center of his mission.

The Twelve disciples of Jesus are called the Galileans, and therefore marginal people. Similarly Matthew portrays the women as those who followed Jesus «from Galilee». The women are therefore the marginal of the marginalised[117]. They are doubly marginalised; first because they are Galileans, secondly because they are women.

Matthew identifies the women as those who followed Jesus «from Galilee» (ἀπὸ τῆς Γαλιλαίας). After announcing the resurrection of Jesus, the angel of the Lord instructs the women to tell the disciples about Jesus' resurrection and his coming to Galilee. It meant for them a

---

[110] See H.C. KEE, «Early Christianity in Galilee», 16.

[111] S. FREYNE, *Galilee, Jesus and the Gospels*, 74, 145, 153.

[112] At the time of Jesus, Galilee was populated by Phonecians, Syrians, Samaritans, Arabians, Greeks, Romans, and Jews. See A. HENNESSY, *The Galilee of Jesus*, 18.

[113] P. HERTIG, «The Galilee Theme», 157.

[114] P. HERTIG, «The Galilee Theme», 157.

[115] V. ELIZONDO, *Galilean Journey*, 53.

[116] See R. A. HORSELY, *Sociology*, 120, 135-36.

[117] P. HERTIG, «The Galilee Theme», 157.

homecoming and a restarting of a new life with Jesus. For Jesus too, coming to Galilee would mean returning to his homeland (2:23) where most of his healing and preaching ministry had taken place (4:23; 21:11). The angel's message communicates to the readers that the resurrected one is the shepherd of the flock (9:36) and immediately he begins to gather the scattered Church (26:31-32; Heb 13:20)[118]. It is here in Galilee that the whole story of Jesus ends in a triumphant climax[119]. Thus Galilee reminds one of the whole theological program of Matthew (4:23-25)[120]. Matthew describes the women as having followed Jesus from Galilee (27:55). This probably refers to their continued physical following of Jesus from the origin of Jesus' ministry itself. Their presence at Golgotha (27:55) and later at the tomb of Jesus (27:61; 28:1-10) tell that these women followed Jesus till the end of his earthly ministry.

Now, let us see what Matthew may be implying when he says that the women followed Jesus «from Galilee»? According to Morris the phrase ἀπὸ τῆς Γαλιλαίας («from Galilee») indicates their «constant following» of Jesus[121]. Morris' interpretation of the phrase as indicating «constant following» gives us the impression that the women's following of Jesus was restricted to Jesus' journey.

D. Senior interprets ἀπὸ τῆς Γαλιλαίας as a topographical note, because «for Matthew, however, discipleship consists in taking part in the journey *from Galilee* to Jerusalem»[122]. Against this view one can argue that it is difficult to establish it because Jesus never teaches this. For the Gospel according to Matthew, doing the will of God is more essential to discipleship (12:46-50). However, Jesus' call implies a physical following of Jesus as a necessary discipleship feature. In this regard, Senior's observation is right.

L. Sabourin seems to hold a different view. He states:

> In Mt these women had followed Jesus from Galilee to Jerusalem. Matthew does not describe them, as does Mark, as women who (generally) followed Jesus, probably lest this should be understood to mean that they were disciples, a prerogative of the twelve[123].

A similar position is held by E. Lohmeyer who distinguishes the

---

[118] R.H. SMITH, *Matthew*, 333.
[119] R.T. FRANCE, *Matthew*, 407.
[120] See H. RILEY, *The First Gospel*, 98.
[121] L.L. MORRIS, *The Gospel According to Matthew*, 726.
[122] D. SENIOR, *Passion Narrative*, 331.
[123] L. SABOURIN, *The Gospel According to Matthew*, 921.

women's *Jüngerstum*, «discipleship», implied in Mark and their *Beglei-tung*, «accompaniment», of Jesus in Matthew, which leads them «from Galilee to Golgotha»[124]. B.M. Newman and P.C. Stine share a similar view: «There were also many women there who had followed Jesus from Galilee and taken care of his needs. They were watching all this from some distance away»[125].

We think that Matthew's identification of the women as following Jesus from Galilee is intentional. Galilee is the cradle of the disciple-ship of Jesus. The point where he chooses the apostles, inaugurating his public ministry, and where the risen Jesus will meet them after resur-rection. It is in Galilee that the risen Jesus commissions the apostles with the final commission (28:16-20), which is considered the apex of the Matthean discipleship theme. In this context, Matthew's identifica-tion of the women as having followed Jesus from Galilee should have been with a purpose. Their presence at the cross and later at the tomb shows that they followed Jesus continuously. Although Matthew does not call them disciples, unmistakable discipleship implications are cer-tainly undeniable. The following of Jesus is fundamental to the disci-pleship of Jesus (16:24).

The purpose of the women's following behind Jesus further strength-ens our view. They followed Jesus «serving him» (διακονοῦσαι αὐτῷ). This now draws our attention.

c) *διακονοῦσαι αὐτῷ*

If ἀκολουθέω in v. 55 refers to the following of Jesus, διακονέω re-fers to service rendered to Jesus. Matthew's use of the word διακονέω in association with ἀκολουθέω draws our attention.

Matthew uses this word to speak of the angel's service of Jesus after the temptations (4:11), Peter's mother-in-law serving Jesus (8:15), to characterize his mission and ministry (20:28), service to Jesus as the criterion for participating in the final salvation (25:44), and finally to designate the women followers' service of Jesus (27:55). In this final usage we note an interesting combination of two discipleship verbs: ἀκολουθέω and διακονέω. Both from a redactional as well as literary view point this usage conveys a discipleship message: «servanthood» as the essence of discipleship[126].

---

124 E. LOHMEYER, *Das Evangelium des Matthäus*, 398.
125 B. M. NEWMAN – P.C. STINE, *A Translator's Handbook*, 894.
126 J.D. KINGSBURY, *Matthew as Story*, 113.

Matthew follows Mark closely, with a slight, but significant change:

αἳ ὅτε ἦν ἐν τῇ Γαλιλαίᾳ ἠκολούθουν αὐτῷ καὶ διηκόνουν αὐτῷ (Mark 15:41)
ἠκολούθησαν τῷ Ἰησοῦ ἀπὸ τῆς Γαλιλαίας διακονοῦσαι αὐτῷ (Matt 27:55)

One significant change concerns Mark's insertion of the conjunction καί separating «following» and «ministering» as two separate activities. Matthew joins «following» and «ministering»: ἠκολούθησαν τῷ Ἰησοῦ ἀπὸ τῆς Γαλιλαίας διακονοῦσαι αὐτῷ.

Matt 16:24 reads: Εἴ τις θέλει ὀπίσω μου ἐλθεῖν, ἀπαρνησάσθω ἑαυτὸν καὶ ἀράτω τὸν σταυρὸν αὐτοῦ καὶ ἀκολουθείτω μοι (see Mark 8:34; Luke 9:23). A similar discipleship saying is found in John 12:26: ἐὰν ἐμοί τις διακονῇ, ἐμοὶ ἀκολουθείτω. In both the Synoptic and Johannine traditions the saying about following Jesus is a call for a willingness to imitate Jesus in suffering and death. The Synoptic tradition speaks of one who would *come after* Jesus; John speaks of one who would serve Jesus. The Synoptic Gospels speak of Jesus' service to others (Luke 22: 27) and of the need that the disciples should serve others (Mark 9:35). But they do not refer to the disciples as the servants of Jesus. But in Matt 27:55 (par Mark 14:41; see Luke 10:40) we note that the women who *followed* Jesus were said to have *served* him. There exists a close relationship between the «following» of Jesus and his «service». According to John to serve Jesus is to follow him unto death[127]. C.H. Dodd thinks that the Johannine verb διακονεῖν may represent a later adaptation of saying to the Church situation. He stresses that this saying belonged to more than one stream of tradition[128]. Following of Jesus involves the entire being and life of the follower. «Those who serve the Son must follow him both by their obedience to the will of the Father and their love for one another»[129]. Both Synoptics as well as John associate the following of Jesus with suffering and death[130].

8. Conclusion

We investigated Matt 27:51b-56 under four titles: the text, its composition, the important vocabulary, the biblical background, all of

---

127 C.K. BARRET, *The Gospel according to St. John,* 424.
128 C.H. DODD, *Historical Tradition,* 352-53.
129 S.B. MARROW, *The Gospel of John,* 209.
130 P.F. ELLIS, *The Genius of John,* 203

which led us to the interpretation of the text. As a concluding remark to this investigation we see various divine as well as human responses to the death of Jesus. The extraordinary events such as the earthquake, rending of the rocks and the resurrection of the holy ones refer to God's reaction to the death of His Son Jesus. In such reactions God seems to invite men and women, Jews and Gentiles to believe in Jesus (see Matt 3:17; 17:5). The death of Jesus and various extraordinary phenomena lead the Gentiles to the confession of the divine sonship of Jesus: Ἀληθῶς θεοῦ υἱὸς ἦν οὗτος. Their confession of the divine sonship of Jesus is juxtaposed to the disciples' own confession of Jesus in Matt 14:33 and 16:16. The death of Jesus and the various events that followed it, lead the Gentiles to the faith in Jesus.

In comparison to the Gentiles who confessed Jesus as the son of God, these women manifest no such external reactions. But a cluster of discipleship vocabulary that Matthew uses in order to describe the women and their activities in relation to Jesus speak of their discipleship of Jesus. They have followed Jesus physically serving him: ἠκολούθησαν τῷ Ἰησοῦ ἀπὸ τῆς Γαλιλαίας διακονοῦσαι αὐτῷ. Matthew does not say that these women followed Jesus because he called them to follow him. Neither does the Evangelist call them «disciples». However, their continued following behind Jesus, especially during his suffering and death, attributes to these women certain discipleship qualities.

CHAPTER IV

The Burial of Jesus and the Women's Role
(Matt 27:57-61)

1. Introduction

In this chapter we discuss Matt 27:57-61 by presenting its immediate
context, followed by a synoptic comparison, an etymological study, a
structural analysis and the biblical background of the text. Throughout
this investigation our attention rests especially on two factors: a) the
identity and the identifying activity of Joseph of Arimathea and b) the
identity and the identifying activity of the women in the Matthean burial narrative. Making use of the literary-critical analysis of the passage,
we seek to understand the role that these male and female characters
play in the Gospel of Matthew in general and in the Matthean burial
narrative in particular.

2. The Text (Matt 27:57-61)

⁵⁷Ὀψίας δὲ γενομένης ἦλθεν ἄνθρωπος πλούσιος ἀπὸ Ἀριμαθαίας,
τοὔνομα Ἰωσήφ, ὃς καὶ αὐτὸς ἐμαθητεύθη τῷ Ἰησοῦ· ⁵⁸οὗτος προσελθὼν τῷ
Πιλάτῳ ἠτήσατο τὸ σῶμα τοῦ Ἰησοῦ. τότε ὁ Πιλᾶτος ἐκέλευσεν ἀποδοθῆναι.
⁵⁹καὶ λαβὼν τὸ σῶμα ὁ Ἰωσὴφ ἐνετύλιξεν αὐτὸ [ἐν] σινδόνι καθαρᾷ ⁶⁰καὶ
ἔθηκεν αὐτὸ ἐν τῷ καινῷ αὐτοῦ μνημείῳ ὃ ἐλατόμησεν ἐν τῇ πέτρᾳ καὶ
προσκυλίσας λίθον μέγαν τῇ θύρᾳ τοῦ μνημείου ἀπῆλθεν.
⁶¹ἦν δὲ ἐκεῖ Μαριὰμ ἡ Μαγδαληνὴ καὶ ἡ ἄλλη Μαρία καθήμεναι
ἀπέναντι τοῦ τάφου.

3. Delimitation of the Text

The passage under our investigation is immediately preceded by the divine and human reactions to the death of Jesus (51b-56) and is followed by the scene about the setting of the guards at the tomb (27:62-66). It is a narrative unit, distinct in itself, yet related to the scene that precedes it (27:51b-56) and to the scene that follows it (27:62-66). Three different criteria, namely the theme, language, location and characters delimit Matt 27:57-61, thus making it distinct.

The first criterion that makes it a distinct narrative unit is the theme itself. There is a thematic difference between the passage that precedes (27:51b-56) and that follows the burial narrative (27:62-66). The preceding passage focuses on the human and divine reaction to the death of Jesus. The succeeding scene focuses on guarding of the tomb of Jesus (27:62-66). But the passage under our analysis concentrates on the burial of Jesus (27:57-61).

The second criterion that makes it a separate unit is the language. If the different divine (27:51b-53) and human reactions (vv. 54-56) to the death of Jesus are described to be dramatic, the burial of the body of Jesus follows as something natural. After the explosive and dramatic events that surround the death of Jesus, the burial narrative contains a silent and a reflective mood (27:57-61) which reflects the honor and the attention with which Joseph of Arimathea buries Jesus' body in the presence of the women followers of Jesus. That the body of Jesus receives a venerable burial by the hands of Joseph of Arimathea is confirmed by Matthew's use of a different vocabulary such as ἐνετύλιξεν, ἐλατόμησεν and προσκυλίσας.

The third criterion that makes it distinct is the set of characters involved in the scene. The dominant characters in the preceding scene were the centurion and the men with him (27:54), and the women who followed Jesus from Galilee (27:55-56). In the burial scene Matthew returns to the figure of Pilate and introduces a new figure, Joseph of Arimathea, ὃς καὶ αὐτὸς ἐμαθητεύθη τῷ Ἰησοῦ, who venerably buries the body of Jesus (vv. 57-61) while the women sit in front of the sepulcher of Jesus (v. 61). If the main characters in the scene that precedes it (27:54) and the scene that follows it contain mainly the opponents of Jesus (27:62-66), the scene about the burial narrative is dominated mainly by the male and female characters who were for Jesus.

4. Matt 27:57-61 in Comparison to Mark 15:42-47

A parallel presentation of the Markan and the Matthean texts shows that Matt 27:57-61 draws heavily upon Mark 15:42-47: [1]

Mark 15:42-47	Matt 27:57-60
⁴²Καὶ ἤδη ὀψίας γενομένης, ἐπεὶ ἦν παρασκευή ὅ ἐστιν προσάββατον,	⁵⁷ Ὀψίας δὲ γενομένης
⁴³ἐλθὼν Ἰωσὴφ [ὁ] ἀπὸ Ἀριμαθαίας εὐσχήμων βουλευτής, ὃς καὶ αὐτὸς ἦν προσδεχόμενος τὴν βασιλείαν τοῦ θεοῦ,	ἦλθεν <u>ἄνθρωπος πλούσιος</u> ἀπὸ Ἀριμαθαίας, τοὔνομα Ἰωσήφ, ὃς καὶ αὐτὸς <u>ἐμαθητεύθη τῷ Ἰησοῦ</u>·
τολμήσας εἰσῆλθεν πρὸς τὸν Πιλᾶτον καὶ ἠτήσατο τὸ σῶμα τοῦ Ἰησοῦ.	⁵⁸οὗτος προσελθὼν τῷ Πιλάτῳ ἠτήσατο τὸ σῶμα τοῦ Ἰησοῦ.
⁴⁴ὁ δὲ Πιλᾶτος ἐθαύμασεν εἰ ἤδη τέθνηκεν καὶ προσκαλεσάμενος τὸν κεντυρίωνα ἐπηρώτησεν αὐτὸν εἰ πάλαι ἀπέθανεν· καὶ γνοὺς ἀπὸ τοῦ κεντυρίωνος ἐδωρήσατο τὸ πτῶμα τῷ Ἰωσήφ.	τότε ὁ Πιλᾶτος ἐκέλευσεν ἀποδοθῆναι.
⁴⁶καὶ ἀγοράσας σινδόνα καθελὼν αὐτὸν ἐνείλησεν τῇ σινδόνι	⁵⁹καὶ λαβὼν τὸ σῶμα ὁ Ἰωσὴφ ἐνέτύλιξεν αὐτὸ [ἐν] σινδόνι καθαρᾷ
καὶ ἔθηκεν αὐτὸν ἐν μνημείῳ	⁶⁰καὶ ἔθηκεν αὐτὸ ἐν τῷ καινῷ αὐτοῦ μνημείῳ
ὃ ἦν λελατομημένον ἐκ πέτρας καὶ προσεκύλισεν λίθον ἐπὶ τὴν θύραν τοῦ μνημείου.	ὃ ἐλατόμησεν ἐν τῇ πέτρᾳ καὶ πρὸ σκυλίσας λίθον μέγαν τῇ θύρᾳ τοῦ μνημείου ἀπῆλθεν.
------------------------------	------------------------------
⁴⁷ἡ δὲ Μαρία ἡ Μαγδαληνὴ καὶ Μαρία ἡ Ἰωσῆτος ἐθεώρουν ποῦ τέθειται.	⁶¹ἦν δὲ ἐκεῖ Μαριὰμ ἡ Μαγδαληνὴ καὶ ἡ ἄλλη Μαρία καθήμεναι ἀπέναντι τοῦ τάφου.

---

[1] We limit this comparative study solely to the Gospel of Mark, the principal Matthean source, while making reference to the corresponding Gospel passages of Luke 23:50-56 and John 19:38-42 whenever it is found useful for our investigation.

Compared to Mark, Matthew's narrative is more concise and brief[2]. Among the various points of differences and agreements between Matthew and Mark on the burial of Jesus, two features call our special attention because of the particular discipleship nuance they share: a) the identity and identifying role of Joseph of Arimathea and b) the identity and identifying role of the women in the burial of Jesus.

4.1 *The Identity and the Identifying Activity of Joseph*

Matthew differs from Mark in his overall characterization of Joseph of Arimathea, such as his personal identity as well as his identifying role in the burial narrative.

4.1.1 The Identity of Joseph of Arimathea

The historicity of Joseph of Arimathea[3], the location of Arimathea[4] and the motivation of Joseph's burial of Jesus[5] have been points of dispute among NT commentators. All four evangelists speak of Joseph of Arimathea as the one who buried the body of Jesus (Matt 27:57; Mark 15:43; Luke 23:51 John 19:38). A majority of NT scholars holds the opinion that Joseph of Arimathea reverentially buried the body of

---

[2] D. Senior points out five special Matthean features in comparison to Mark 15:42-47: a) a different way of describing the time; b) a different way of identifying Joseph of Arimathea; c) a different manner in which the body of Jesus is secured; d) a different description for the shroud, the tomb and the stone; and finally e) a different conclusion to the burial story. D. SENIOR, «Matthew's Account », 1433-1448.

[3] For a discussion on the historicity of Joseph of Arimathea see G. O'COLLINS – D. KENDALL, «Did Joseph of Arimathea Exist», 237; S.E. PORTER, «Joseph of Arimathea», 971-972; W.B. BARRICK, «The Rich Man», 235-239.

[4] We know very little about the historical location of Arimathea. Some scholars believe Ἀριμαθαία to be the name of a village (modern Rentis) located about ten miles northwest of Lydda. There is also a tendency to identify Arimathea with Ramathaim of 1Sam 1:1. See W.D. DAVIES – D. C. ALLISON, *Matthew,* III, 648. See D. HILL, *The Gospel of Matthew,* 367; W.F. ALBRIGHT – C.S. MANN, *Matthew,* 354-55; S.E. PORTER, Joseph of Arimathea», 971-72. That the name of this place is attributed to Joseph here perhaps shows it as his place of origin. See D.J. HARRINGTON, *The Gospel of Matthew,* 404.

[5] I. BROER, *Die Urgemeinde und das Grab Jesus,* 175-83, 190-98; R.E. BROWN, «The Burial of Jesus», 233-245.

Jesus[6], although some scholars doubt the truthfulness of the NT accounts[7].

According to Mark, Joseph is a «respected member of the council» (εὐσχήμων[8] βουλευτής) while for Matthew he is a «rich man» (ἄνθρωπος πλούσιος)[9]. If for Mark «he was waiting expectantly for the kingdom of God» (ἦν προσδεχόμενος τὴν βασιλείαν τοῦ θεοῦ, 15:43), for Matthew he «also was a disciple of Jesus» (καὶ αὐτὸς ἐμαθητεύθη τῷ Ἰησου, 27:57)[10]. Thus, the Matthean Joseph has an identity that is different from the Markan Joseph.[11] Matthew presents Joseph clearly as a disciple of Jesus, who is also at the same time «a rich man»[12].

---

[6] See F.M. BRAUN, «La sépulture de Jesus», 34-52; K.P.G. CURTIS, «Three Points», 440-444; J. BLINZLER, *Der Prozess Jesu*, 289; J.S. KENNARD, «The Burial of Jesus», 227, 231; H. GRASS, *Ostergeschehen und Osterberichte*, 171.

[7] A. Loisy and C.A.H. Guignebert are of the opinion that the body of Jesus did not get any respectful burial, but that instead the soldiers threw it into a grave intended by the Jews for the corpses of criminals. See A. LOISY, *Le Quatrième évangile*, 894ff; ID., *Les Evangiles synoptiques*, 223; C.A.H. GUIGNEBERT, *Jésus*, 615.

G. Baldensperger speaks of a double burial: the first burial was carried out by the executioner somewhere near to Calvary, and the second burial was undertaken by Joseph of Arimathea. See G. BALDENSPERGER, *La Tombeau Vide*, 19. See also J. JEREMIAS, «Wo lag Golgotha und das Heilige Grab?, 141-173; J. SCHMID, *Das Evangelium nach Markus*, 297-301.

[8] The word εὐσχήμων means «prominent», «honorable» or «outstanding» (Acts 13:50; 17:12; 1Cor 7:35; 12:24). See J. SCHREIBER, «Die Bestattung Jesu», 143; R.E. BROWN, «Burial of Jesus», 233-245.

[9] Some NT scholars are of the opinion that the title ἄνθρωπος πλούσιος is an abbreviation of the Markan description of Joseph of Arimathea. They argue that being a «respected member of the council» (Mark 15:43), he should have been rich. See M.J. LAGRANGE, *Matthieu*, 534; S.E. JOHNSON, «The Gospel According to St. Matthew», 612; P. BONNARD, *L'évangile selon Saint Matthieu*, 408; C.H. GIBLIN, «Structural and Thematic Correlation», 406-420; W.B. BARRICK, «The Rich Man», 235-239; H.N. HENDRICKX, *Los Relatos de la pasión*, 174.

[10] See D. SENIOR, *Matthew*, 337; A. PLUMMER, *Matthew*, 406; A. STOCK, *The Method and Message of Matthew*, 431.

[11] See B.M. NEWMAN – P.C. STINE, *A Translator's Handbook*, 895.

[12] Matthew is here closer to John who clearly says that Joseph was «a disciple of Jesus, though a secret one because of his fear of the Jews...» (John 19:38). According to Montefiore, Matthew's presentation of Joseph «does not mean that he was a disciple of Jesus, or that he even expected Jesus to bring the Kingdom ... He may have been sympathetic towards Jesus and his teaching, but it does not follow that he was a regular disciple, though it was only natural that Mark's words would soon be understood in that sense». C.J.G. MONTEFIORE, *The Synoptic Gospels*, 391.

4.1.2 Identifying Role of Joseph

According to Matthew, Joseph goes to Pilate and asks for the body of Jesus, and Pilate immediately orders the body to be given to him (27:58). Whereas in Mark, Joseph had to «take courage» before approaching Pilate (15:43)[13]. Then it is said that Pilate «wonders if Jesus were already dead». He then summons the centurion to inquire if Jesus is truly dead and finally learns that he is dead (15:46). Since it was customary that a disciple bury the body of his master (14:12), these details seem unnecessary to Matthew who identifies Joseph as a disciple of Jesus.

As a conclusion to the comparative analysis of the Matthean and the Markan presentation of the identity and the identifying activities of Joseph of Arimathea, we see that compared to Mark, Matthew takes special interest in presenting Joseph as a disciple of Jesus who venerably buries the body of Jesus.

4.2 *The Identity and Identifying Activity of the Women*

In the description of the women's identity as well as their role Matthew and Mark show agreement as well as difference.

4.2.1 The Identity of the Women

Concerning the identity of the women in the burial narrative, Mark and Matthew agree principally on two main points. First, of the three women described as present at Golgotha looking on from afar in Mark 15:40, only two appear in the burial narrative (15:47). They are «Mary Magdalene and Mary [the mother] of Joses». Similarly, of the three women described as present looking on from afar in Matt 27:55-56, only two women appear in the Matthean burial narrative. They are «Mary Magdalene and the other Mary» (27:61). Here Matthew and Mark agree in narrowing down the number of the women from «three» to «two», both by way of elimination of the third name. Mark drops «Salome» (15:40) and Matthew drops «the mother of the sons of Zebedee» (27:56). Second, both Mark and Matthew have Mary Magdalene as the prominent female character who is mentioned always at the beginning of the name list.

---

[13] The fact that Matthew does not use τολμάω is perhaps to introduce the verb προσελθών, «approached», a verb which, according to R.H. Gundry, refers to a respectful approach (4:3; 8:14). See R. H. GUNDRY, *Matthew*, 580.

Mark and Matthew differ from each other on one point concerning the women's identity: while Mark identifies the second Mary at the tomb as ἡ Ἰωσῆτος («the [*mother*] of Joses», Mark 15:40, 47), Matthew identifies the second woman simply as ἡ ἄλλη Μαρία, «the other Mary», which is perhaps an abbreviation of the designation «Mary the mother of James and Joseph» in 27:56.

4.2.2 The Identifying Role of the Women

Mark concludes the burial scene with the notice of the women who «saw where he was laid» (ἐθεώρουν ποῦ τέθειται, 15:47; similarly Luke 23:55). Distinct from Mark, Matthew's burial scene concludes with the women as «sitting in front of the sepulcher» (καθήμεναι ἀπέναντι τοῦ τάφου, Matt 27:61). This becomes significant especially in regard to Matthew's presentation of the guards at the tomb in the immediately following scene (27:62-66), which would perhaps mean that the tomb of Jesus was never left unwatched[14]. This would be to defend the truthfulness of the resurrection of Jesus against the false accusation of the Jews that his disciples stole Jesus' body. On the other hand, the women's presence at the burial site (27:61) gives them knowledge of the site and thus enables them to return to the tomb on the first day of the week (28:1) and thus to become the first witnesses to the resurrection of Jesus (28:1-10)[15].

As a concluding remark to the comparative analysis of the Matthean and the Markan burial narratives, we observe that although Matthew follows Mark closely, Matthew makes certain significant changes especially concerning the characters in the burial scene. Matthew's description of the identity and the identifying activities of Joseph of Arimathea and the women has drawn our special attention. These redactional features interest us because of the discipleship nuance they contain. Unlike Mark, Matthew presents Joseph of Arimathea who has become a disciple of Jesus (καὶ αὐτὸς ἐμαθητεύθη τῷ ἰησου, 27:57). By burying the body of Jesus and thus fulfilling the duty of a disciple (Matt 14:12), Joseph expresses his discipleship. Similarly, Matthew takes special care

---

[14] J. KREMER, *Die Osterbotschaft*, 33; T.R.W. LONGSTAFF, «The Women at the Tomb», 278-281; E. KLOSTERMANN, *Das Matthäusevangelium*, 226; H.M. KELLER, *Jesus und die Frauen*, 120.

[15] See L. SABOURIN, *The Gospel according to St Matthew*, 922; A.J. LEVINE, «Matthew», 262.

to present the women followers of Jesus and their act of sitting in front of the tomb of Jesus (καθήμεναι ἀπέναντι τοῦ τάφου).

5. Etymological Study

Under this section we study two important verbs in Matt 27:57-61: μαθητεύω and κάθημαι. We will attempt to see how the verb μαθητεύω refers to the identity of Joseph of Arimathea, and how the verb κάθημαι refers to the identity of the women at the tomb.

5.1 Μαθητεύω

The first verb that we discuss under this section is μαθητεύω. This is a rare word in the NT and occurs principally in the Gospel of Matthew, where it appears only three times: μαθητευθείς, 13:52; ἐμαθητεύθη, 27:57 and μαθητεύσατε, 28:19[16]. The only other occurrence of this verb elsewhere in the NT is in Acts 14:21 (μαθητεύσαντες)[17].

The verb μαθητεύω draws on the noun μαθητής, «disciple»[18]. The verb μαθητεύω is understood in a transitive as well as intransitive sense. In a transitive sense μαθητεύω means «to make disciple». In an intransitive sense it means «to be or to become a disciple»[19].

The first occurrence of the verb μαθητεύω is found in 13:51-52: Συνήκατε ταῦτα πάντα; λέγουσιν αὐτῷ, Ναί. ὁ δὲ εἶπεν αὐτοῖς, Διὰ τοῦτο πᾶς γραμματεὺς μαθητευθεὶς τῇ βασιλείᾳ τῶν οὐρανῶν ὅμοιός ἐστιν ἀνθρώπῳ οἰκοδεσπότῃ, ὅστις ἐκβάλλει ἐκ τοῦ θησαυροῦ αὐτοῦ καινὰ καὶ παλαιά[20].

In 13:52, it seems better to understand this verb as a transitive passive having the meaning «being instructed». The verb μαθητεύω here

---

[16] See M. GRILLI, *Comunità e Missione,* 192-195.

[17] See R. MORGENTHALER, *Statistik,*118; D.A. HAGNER, *Matthew 14-28,* II, 887.

[18] W. CARTER, *Matthew and the Margins,* 552.

[19] M. J. WILKINS, *The Concept of Disciple,* 160.

[20] There exists a scholarly debate on the understanding and interpretation of the verbal form μαθητευθείς here. The debate centers on whether the verb μαθητευθεὶς derives from the deponent μαθητεύομαι («to be a disciple» or «to become a disciple») or from the transitive μαθητεύω («to make a disciple of», «to teach» or «to instruct»).

According to J.D. Kingsbury, a contextual reading of the text suggests that the aorist passive μαθητευθείς stems from the transitive μαθητεύω. He indicates two points in support of this position: a) the context does not suggest the meaning «being {becoming} a disciple» and b) key words like «explain» (13:36) and «understand» (13:51) do not favor the definition «be a disciple». J.D. KINGSBURY, *The Parables of Jesus,* 126-27.

contains some kind of discipleship indication especially in its use in association with the words συνήκατε and γραμματεύς, both of which are closely associated to the theme of discipleship in the Gospel. The verb συνήκατε, «understand» in Matthew is a distinguishing mark of a true disciple (13:51). When Jesus asks, «Have you understood (συνήκατε) all this (ταῦτα πάντα)», the disciples' affirmative answer ναί, «yes», shows Matthew's presentation of the disciples as «enlightened followers of Jesus»[21].

This understanding of the parables makes them γραμματεύς, «scribes» (13:52). The notion of the ideal scribe «trained for the kingdom of heaven» is important to Matthew for the understanding of discipleship. D. Orton's observation in this direction seems to be correct. According to him, Matthew communicates his vision of discipleship not only through those characters that bear the title «disciples», but also through another designation, namely «the scribes»[22]. However, this does not mean that all the scribes in Matthew are models of discipleship.

The second occurrence of the verb μαθητεύω is in 27:57. The verbal form that is found in the text is ἐμαθητεύθη which is a transitive passive[23]. A variant reading for this text is ἐμαθητευσεν which is an intransitive active.[24] The first reading, ἐμαθητεύθη, has stronger textual support and can be translated as «was discipled». Matthew substitutes the Markan phrase ὃς καὶ αὐτὸς ἦν προσδεχόμενος τὴν βασιλείαν τοῦ θεοῦ (15:43) «who also himself was waiting for the kingdom of God», with the phrase ἐμαθητεύθη τῷ Ἰησοῦ, literally, «was discipled to Jesus»[25].

---

21 J.D. KINGSBURY, *The Parables of Jesus,* 127-28.

22 D.E. Orton observes that a scribe in Matthew has the following five characteristics: a) he is the one imbued with wisdom and understanding; b) who has authority as a custodian of the community's values and true righteousness; c) who gives right teaching; d) who shows the insight and mission of a prophet and e) who creatively contributes to the life of the community through new insights and interpretation. See D.E. ORTON, *The Understanding Scribe,* 161-162.

23 This reading has the textual support of א C D θ λ *f*¹ 33. 700. 892 *pc.*

24 This reading is supported by b A B L W *f*¹³.

25 Scholars are divided on the interpretation of this verb in 27:57. Making a distinction between the substantive μαθητής and the verb μαθητεύω, Albright and Mann say that here Matthew employs the verbal form μαθητεύω, instead of the substantive μαθητής, in order to show that Joseph was not a disciple, but was only «taught by Jesus». W.F. ALBRIGHT – C.S. MANN, *Matthew,* LXXVII. On the contrary G. Strecker is of the opinion, that Matthew's use of the verb μαθητεύω is to show clearly that Joseph is a disciple of Jesus. G. STRECKER, *Der Weg,* 192.

The Matthean redaction of Mark suggests Matthew's intention to present Joseph as a disciple of Jesus. That Joseph was waiting for the kingdom of God as in Mark perhaps prompted Matthew to depict Joseph as a disciple of Jesus[26].

The third and last occurrence of the verb μαθητεύω in Matthew is found in 28:19. Here Matthew uses the aorist imperative μαθητεύσατε, «make disciples», the important command of Christ's final commission (28:16-20)[27], which according to O. Brooks «has controlled the entire design of the Gospel of Matthew»[28]. Paying particular attention to the narrative development of the themes «authority» and «teaching», Brooks rightly focuses on the one finite verb in the final commission: μαθητεύσατε, «make disciples»[29]. The final commission itself is given by means of one main imperative verb, μαθητεύσατε, «make disciples». Three syntactically subordinate participles are related to this main verb[30]. The first particple, πορευθέντες, precedes the main verb μαθητεύσατε. That is to say, the disciples are to «go» to «make disciples».

The two other participles βαπτίζοντες («baptizing») and διδάσκοντες («teaching»), which follow it, elaborate the main commission, i. e., μαθητεύσατε, «make disciples»[31]. The disciples are to «baptize» (Matt 3)[32] and «to teach» (4:23; 5:2.19; 7:28; 9:35; 11:1; 21:23; 26:55). According to D.A. Hagner, these words summarize the responsibility of the disciples: «to go, make disciples of all nations, baptize, and teach»[33]. Here Matthew seems to recapitulate and develop the most important themes of his Gospel[34]. According to J. LaGrand these words «summarize the chiasmic order of the narrative development of the whole Gospel: Jesus taught and finally suffered a humiliating death //

---

[26] On whether Joseph of Arimathea can be called a disciple of Jesus see G. STRECKER, Der Weg, 192; W.F. ALBRIGHT – C.S. MANN, Matthew, LXXVIII; B. PRZYBYLSKI, Righteousness, 110.

[27] C. L BLOMBERG, Matthew, 431.

[28] O. BROOKS, «Matthew xxviii 16-20», 2.

[29] O. BROOKS, «Matthew xxviii 16-20», 2; D.A. HAGNER, Matthew 14-28, II, 886.

[30] D.A. HAGNER, Matthew 14-28, II, 886; G. FRIEDRICH, «Die Formale Struktur», 137-183.

[31] C. ROGERS, «The Great Commission», 258-267; W. CARTER, Matthew and Margins, 552.

[32] Only in John 3:22; 4:1-2 do we read of Jesus' or his disciples' baptizing others.

[33] D.A. HAGNER, Matthew, II, 889.

[34] D.R. BAUER, The Structure of Matthew's Gospel, 109-128.

through baptism his disciples identify with his death in order to continue his teaching»[35].

As a concluding remark we note a strong discipleship nuance attached to all three occurrences of μαθητέω. This means that the verb μαθητεύω communicates specifically the Matthean concept of discipleship. This is further substantiated by Matthew's use of μαθητής in the Gospel.

5.2 *μαθητής*

After discussing the verb μαθητεύω in Matthew, we will now study the substantive μαθητής, which in Matthew is a technical word that designates a «disciple». In this word analysis we will study the concept of μαθητής in Jewish History, Greek literature, Gospel traditions in general and the Gospel of Matthew in particular.

5.2.1 Μαθητής in Jewish History

a) *Meaning of Μαθητής in a General Sense*

In Greek literature, in a very general usage, the word μαθητής designated a «learner» or a «pupil» who was normally engaged in some kind of learning, such as «gymnastics»[36] «writing»[37] or «medicine»[38]. In this context emphasis was laid mainly on learning[39]. In technical usage the word Μαθητής designated the one who «adopted the way of life of a cultural milieu which now characterises him, and of which he is now an adherent and representative»[40]. In this context emphasis was laid on adherence to a master. The word μαθητής was also employed to speak of the institutional pupil or student of the sophists[41].

---

[35] J. LaGrand, *The Earliest Christian Mission*, 237.
[36] Plato, *The Laws* 796. A. 8.
[37] Plato, *Euthydemus*, 276. A. 7.
[38] Plato, *The Republic*, 599. C. 4.
[39] K.H. Rengstorf, «Μαθητής», 416.
[40] M.J. Wilkins, *The Concept of Disciple*, 13.
[41] See K.H. Rengstorf, «Μαθητής», 11.

b) Μαθητής in the OT

The word μαθητής is absent in the LXX[42]. Similarly the equivalent תַּלְמִיד is absent in the Hebrew Bible with the singular exception of 1Chr 25:8 where the word designates an apprentice of a musician, a pupil engaged in some sort of learning. The word תַּלְמִיד is absent in the non-biblical writings discovered at Qumran as well[43]. We have no satisfactory explanation for the absence of this word in these writings. Perhaps this absence itself will contribute to the understanding of the uniqueness of this word in the NT to which we will make reference soon.

5.2.2 Μαθητής in Greek Literature

a) Μαθητής in the Writings of Philo

The word μαθητής appears for the first time in the writings of Philo of Alexandria (B. C. 25-A. D. 50) and the word could signify three things: a) someone who is engaged in some kind of learning in general[44]; b) someone who, though not perfect, is sufficiently advanced in learning to teach the masses[45]; and finally c) someone who is taught by God Himself and is now fully perfect[46]. Among the three designations, the third one is typical to Philo. On this J. P. Meier says: «He [Philo] typically uses this word within the context of his mystical views about the 'perfect' person who is directly taught by God»[47].

b) Μαθητής in the Writings of Josephus

The next important Jewish author who uses the word in his writings is Josephus. Even in the writings of Josephus μαθητής is not a very common word. In his voluminous writings this word occurs only on 15 occasions scattered throughout two of his works: a) *The Jewish Antiquities*; b) *Against Apion,* written about A.D. 93-94 and A.D. 100-105 respectively. Josephus understands it under three designations: a) in a

---

[42] The word μαθητής appears in three passages in the Codex Alexandrinus of the LXX (Jer 13:21; 20:11; 26:9 [MT 46:9].

[43] The absence of the word here is interesting especially against the background of the large amount of scribal activity and study of the scriptures at Qumran.

[44] PHILO, *De specialibus legibus* IV : 140. 3.

[45] PHILO, *Le posteritate Caini*, 132:2; 147:1.

[46] PHILO, *De sacrificiis Abelis et Caini*, 7:4; 64:10; 79:10.

[47] See J. P. MEIER, *A Marginal Jew*, 42.

general sense the word μαθητής signifies a learner, one who learns from others[48]; b) in a particular sense the word is used to describe various OT figures who have a student-master relationship[49]; c) besides these two usage, Josephus uses the word μαθητής to designate a person or a group of persons who follow a certain school of philosophical thought[50]. Among these three usages, the second is similar to the usage in the NT. Here Josephus uses the word μαθητής to recapitulate Elisha's relationship to Elijah. In *Jewish Antiquities* VIII:13. 7 and IX:3. 1 Josephus narrates how Elisha «followed» the prophet Elijah and became his disciple (μαθητής) and servant (διάκονος). While in *Jewish Antiquities* IX: 2. 4. we have the description of Elisha sitting in his house with *his disciples*. Again in IX: 6.1 we have the description of his sending of a *disciple* with a mission. Commenting on this, J.P. Meier says: «Josephus may be re-reading biblical passages in the light of the Pharisaic and nascent rabbinic movements with their schools–a phenomenon that in turn reflects Hellenistic cultural influence»[51]. We have evidence from the writings of Josephus that there existed the concept of μαθητής in the pharisaic movement[52].

This short etymological analysis of the word μαθητής suggests that Josephus' usage of the word μαθητής is the earliest of this kind that has a close parallel to its usage in the Gospel traditions. Such a parallelism is found only here in the Jewish history of the word μαθητής. Perhaps this contributes to the understanding of the uniqueness of Jesus' model of discipleship. That is to say that the NT use of the word μαθητής is neither a duplication of this word from the LXX, intertestamental literature, nor Dead Sea Scrolls. Commenting on the word in the Hebrew Bible, Septuagint and in Qumran, J.A. Fitzmyer suggests «discipleship in a "religious sense" may have emerged as a Christian phenomenon»[53].

---

[48] JOSEPHUS, *Jewish Antiquities* I: 11.3.

[49] Joshua is called a disciple of Moses (*Jewish Antiquities,* V: 5. 4); Elisha is called the disciple of Elijah (*Jewish Antiquities* VIII:13.7); Baruch is called the disciple of Jeremiah (*Jewish Antiquities,* X: 9. 1).

[50] Josephus contains three such usages (*The Life Against Apion* I: 2. 22; II: 41).

[51] J.P. MEIER, *A Marginal Jew,* 43.

[52] According to *Ant.* 13.10.5 §289 John Hyrcanus was a μαθητής of the Pharisees. Similarly in *Ant.* 15. 1.1. §3 we have evidence of the Pharisee Pollion and his disciple Samaias, who had followers of their own.

[53] J.A. FITZMYER, *Luke the Theologian,* 121.

5.2.3 Μαθητής in the Gospel of Matthew

Over against the absence of the word μαθητής in the Hebrew Scriptures, Septuagint and Qumran literature, its abundant attestations in the Gospels and Acts supported by multiple attestation of sources and forms are noteworthy.

Every Gospel source contains the reference to Jesus' call of the disciples. In Mark 1:16-20 we have a description of the call of the first four disciples: Peter, Andrew, James and John (see Matt 4:18-22). Mark 2:14 speaks of the call of the tax collector Levi (see Matt 9:9). Q tradition contains at least two clear occurrences of the word μαθητής (Matt 10:24/Luke 6:40; Matt 11:2/Luke 7:18-19). Besides these two clear occurrences there are several sayings of Jesus addressed to his audience concerning loyalty towards him (Matt 10:26-36/Luke 12:2-9, 51-53). J.P. Meier observes that such sayings make sense only if they are addressed to committed followers[54]. The Gospel of John contains 78 occurrences of the word μαθητής, which is more than any other book in the NT[55]. Undoubtedly Jesus had disciples around him and μαθητής was a technical word to designate a disciple of Jesus.

The Evangelist Matthew has a special interest in the word μαθητής[56]. Matthew uses this word more frequently than any other synoptic writer (Matthew 73, Mark 46 and Luke 37)[57]. Matthew uses the plural form (μαθηταί) of this word more often, while the singular form (μαθητής) is found only on three occasions (10:24, 25, 42).

E.R. Martinez's classification of different Matthean passages that contain the word μαθηταί is helpful in understanding various nuances

---

[54] J.P. MEIER, *A Marginal Jew*, III, 44.

[55] Josephus supports these attestations. Although he does not employ the word μαθητής to designate the disciples of Jesus, Josephus states that Jesus gained a «following» comprised of disciples of Jewish and Greek origin. See J.P. MEIER, *A Marginal Jew*, III, 44.

[56] Other than the reference to the disciples of Jesus, the word μαθητής in the NT is generally used to signify an «adherent» to a great leader or a movement (John 9:28), «disciples» of Pharisees (Matt 22:16), «disciples» of Paul (Acts 9:25), and «disciples» of John the Baptist (Mark 2:18). When it is in reference to the followers of Jesus, Matthew usually writes «*his* disciples» or «*the* disciples».

The use of the singular form is rare in Matthew while it is frequent in John and never in Mark. Only on three occasions does the singular form μαθητής appear in Matthew, all in chapter ten (10:24, 25, 42). In Matthew and Luke, it is found only on the lips of Jesus (Matt 10:24-25; 10:42; Luke 14:27; 6:40).

[57] John has 78 occurrences, while Acts uses it 28 times. See R. MORGENTHALER, *Statistik*, 118.

of the Matthean use of this word. He classifies the occurrences of this word (in its various forms) under three headings:

i) with the pronoun αὐτοῦ, σου or σου (οἱ μαθηταὶ αὐτοῦ): 5:1; (8:21); 8:23 (8:25); 9:10, 11, 14, 19, 37; 12:1, 2, 49; 13:36; (14:22); 15:2, 23, 32; 16:13, 21, 24; (17:10); 17:16; 19:23; 23:1; 24:1; 26:1, 18; (26:56); (27:64); 28:7, 8; (28:9, 10); 28:13).

ii) without any personal pronoun attached to the word (οἱ μαθηταὶ): 8:21; (8:25); 13:10; 14:15, 19, 22, 26; 15:12, 33, 36; 16:5, 20; 17:6, 10, 13, 19; 18:1; 19:10, 13, 25; 21:6, 20; 24:3; 26:8, 17, 19, 26, 35, 36, 40, 45, 56; 27:64.

iii) other relevant passages: 10:1, 2, 5; 11:1; 20:17, 24; 21:1; 26:14, 20, 47; 28:16[58].

After examining every individual reference to the word, Martinez discovers that up to chapter 10, Matthew uses the word μαθηταί always with a pronoun: οἱ μαθηταὶ αὐτοῦ or οἱ μαθηταὶ σου, while after chapter 10 Matthew frequently uses οἱ μαθηταὶ without any addition. In this latter instance the reference is usually to the Twelve. That is to say, after mentioning a definite group of disciples (10:1-4), Matthew uses the word οἱ μαθηταὶ, which indicates always a definite group of disciples, namely the Twelve unless a group of Two or Three is clear from the context[59]. The implication is that the technical expression οἱ μαθηταὶ in Matthew is reserved solely to the Twelve, whereas «his disciples» is indefinite and can refer to more or less, and this is unique to this Gospel as the other Gospels manifest no such exactitude of reference with the word μαθηταί. Significantly, Matthew never uses the expression οἱ μαθηταὶ, when speaking of other disciples such as the disciples of John the Baptist or of the Pharisees[60]. Because the expression in Matthew implies a definite group of disciples, the special group of «the Twelve». In the pre-Matthean traditions the words μαθηταί and δώδεκα are two separate concepts. But for Matthew οἱ μαθηταὶ meant δώδεκα so that he could replace δώδεκα with οἱ μαθηταὶ in editing his source (Matt 18:1 = Mark 9:35)[61]. Hence the expression is unique and definite in

---

58 E.R. MARTINEZ, «The Interpretation», 285.

59 E.R. MARTINEZ, «The Interpretation», 286.

60 To refer to the disciples of John, Matthew uses «his disciples» (μαθητῶν αὐτοῦ, 11:2; 14:12); to refer to the disciples of the Pharisees, Matthew uses the expression «their disciples» (μαθητὰς αὐτῶν, 22:16).

61 Albright and Mann hold the view that Matthew never refers to a wider group of disciples other than the twelve. See W.F. ALBRIGHT – C. S. MANN, *Matthew*, 355.

Matthew[62]. We think that Martinez' view on the Matthean expression οἱ μαθηται is correct. Such an interpretation is substantiated by a further observation on Matthew's concept of ὄχλοι in relation to «the disciples».

Matthew seems to draw a clear differentiation of μαθηταί from ὄχλοι. Matthew uses the word ὄχλοι more than any other synoptic writer[63]. At least on ten occasions where Matthew follows Mark, the Evangelist adds ὄχλοι (4:25; 7:28; 13:34, 36; 14:5; 21:8, 9, 10; 22:33). Matthew prefers the plural form ὄχλοι while Mark has a preference for the singular ὄχλος, although there is no substantial difference in their meanings (Mark 15:11; Matt 27:20)[64].

The identity of the ὄχλοι and their significance in relation to μαθηταί has often been variously interpreted by contemporary scholars. According to T.W. Manson, Jesus' teaching in Matthew is addressed to the disciples only, and not to the crowds[65]. For R.H. Gundry both groups are interchangeable as the audience of the sermon[66]. P. Bonnard finds no difference between these two groups.[67] According to P.S. Minear, μαθηταί are the primary audience of Jesus' teaching while ὄχλοι comprise the secondary audience[68]. J.P. Meier designates ὄχλοι to the outer circle of Jesus' followers, and μαθηταί to the inner circle[69].

However, we have seen in the course of our discussion that Matthew uses the expression οἱ μαθηταί solely for the «Twelve» disciples of Jesus (or two or three of them) who were distinct from the crowds that followed Jesus.

Does this identification limit the disciples of Jesus to the Twelve? Should the designation of «disciples of Jesus» be restricted to those first century twelve Palestinian Jews? The use of «the disciples» for a definite number would seem to answer «no» to this question. The issue

---

R. Pesch holds a similar position when he states «even in the replacement of «Levi» (Mark 2:14) with «Matthew» (Matt 9:9), Matthew has intentionally drawn an equation between μαθητής and δώδεκα. See R. PESCH, «Levi-Matthäus», 40-56. M. Hengel, who affirms indications of disciples in Matthew other than the twelve, holds an opposite view. See M. HENGEL, *The Charismatic Leader*, 163.

62 E.R. MARTINEZ, «The Interpretation», 291.

63 Matthew 49; Mark 38; Luke 41.

64 J.P. MEIER, *A Marginal Jew*, III, 22.

65 T.W. MANSON, *The Sayings of Jesus*, 47.

66 R.H. GUNDRY, *Matthew*, 136-137.

67 P. BONNARD, *Matthieu*, 54.

68 P.S. MINEAR, «The Disciples», 28-44.

69 J.P. MEIER, *A Marginal Jew*, 21-30.

is specifically on the limits of the term «discipleship». G. Strecker[70], W.F. Albright and C.S. Mann[71], and R. Pesch[72] deny a wider circle of disciples around Jesus. On the other hand, Hengel[73] and B. Przybylski[74] support the view that Jesus had disciples other than the twelve. The scholars who speak of a wider range of disciples of Jesus, base their arguments on Matt 8:19, 21, 10:24, 25, 42; 27:57; 28:19 where Matthew gives indications of a wider circle of disciples around Jesus. Such an interpretation is in tune with the other Gospels also. For example Mark 4:10-11 in conjunction with 4:34 also shows a wider group of disciples. Mark 2:15 gives indication of a large number of followers of Jesus (see John 4:1-2 and 6:60-71).

One feature that surprises is that despite the fact that several women followed Jesus, neither the word μαθητής nor any of its grammatical forms is anywhere used to designate the women followers of Jesus in the canonical Gospels. The only use of the feminine form μαθήτρια in the NT is found in Acts 9:36, where Luke uses it to describe Ταβιθά.

5.3 κάθημαι

The last word that deserves particular attention is κάθημαι, which has 91 occurrences in the NT[75]. The corresponding Hebrew word is יָשַׁב (Exod 18:14; Deut 6:7). The verb κάθημαι in a neutral or general sense means «to sit» or «to set down» (LXX Gen 18:1; 19:1; Lev 15:6; Zech 5:7), for instance on a «stool» (Gen 48:2), a «stone» (Exod 17:12), a «hill top» (2Kgs 1:9), the edge of a well (Exod 2:15), a «sea shore» (Matt 13:1; Mark 4:1), a «mountain» (Matt 5:1; 15:29; 24:3; Mark 13:3), the «ground» (11:16; Mark 10:46; John 9:8; Acts 3:10), in a «courtyard» (Matt 26:58; 26:69; Luke 22:55), by the cross (27:36)[76].

In the Hellenistic culture, the posture of sitting was a distinctive sign of a deity who often sat while the devotees stood to pray before it[77]. The concept of God's sitting on a throne is found in the history of Israel (1Kgs 22:19; 2Chr 18:18; Dan 3:55; Isa 6:1), a concept that is carried

---

[70] G. STRECKER, Der Weg, 192.

[71] W.F. ALBRIGHT – C. S. MANN, Matthew, 355.

[72] R. PESCH, «Levi-Matthäus», 40-56.

[73] M. HENGEL, The Charismatic Leader, 81-82.

[74] B. PRZYBYLSKI, Righteousness in Matthew, 108-10.

[75] Gospels 47, Acts 7, and Epistles 4; Revelation 33.

[76] G. SCHNEIDER, «κάθημαι», 440-444.

[77] This notion is supported by the archaeological evidence from Egypt, the Near East, and the Hellenistic world. See G. SCHNEIDER, «κάθημαι», 441.

forward to the NT (Matt 23:22) in which Christ is illustrated as en-throned along with the Father (Rev 5:13). The same verb is used in or-der to illustrate the posture of judges while administrating judgment (Exod 11:5; 12:29) and teachers to teach (Matt 5:15; 13:1; 15:29; 24:3; 26:55; Mark 4:1; 9:35; 13:3; Luke 5:3; John 5:3; 8:2).

In the OT, sitting was also considered to be an act of grief and mourning (Job 2:12, 14; Psa 137:1) which was held as a customary role of women in antiquity[78]. In the NT, «sitting» was also considered a normal gesture of the women who mourned the dead (see John 11:20, 29, 31; Matt 27:61).

Mary's sitting at the feet of Jesus (Luke 10:39) was a sign of humil-ity, and of being an attentive student[79]. Sitting also expressed one's dis-position when at a divine service and of listening to a teacher. For ex-ample Jesus customarily sat down to teach, whether in the open air (Matt 5:1; 13:1-2) or in the temple court (Matt 26:55). There is evi-dence that one sat while waiting for an oracle[80]. It was customary for a teacher to stand to read the scriptures and to sit to expound them (Luke 4:16-21). It was a normal gesture of people to sit in a synagogue (Acts 13:14)[81].

We find various nuances attached to the verb κάθημαι in the OT as well as in the NT. Among them what helps our investigation of the concept of discipleship in the Gospel of Matthew is perhaps its use in the context of a divine service (i.e., that synagogue service) and lament-ing the dead, which was a recognized religious duty assigned to the women of first century Judaism.

6. The Compositional Features

Matt 27:57-61 is composed of two scenes: a) Joseph's burial of the body of Jesus (27:57-60) and b) the women's witness to Joseph's burial of Jesus' body (27:61).

---

[78] L.A. BENTZ, «Jesus' Death and Resurrection», 251-74; B.W. PORTER, «With Our Backs to the Grave», 232-235. W. SHULLENBERGER, «The Other Mary», 241-245. R. STRELAN, «To Sit is to Mourn», 31-45.

[79] See R.T. FRANCE, «Κάθημαι», 587-589.

[80] W.D. DAVIES – D.C. ALLISON, Matthew, III, 652.

[81] J. ELBOGEN, Der jüdische Gottesdienst, 384-398.

6.1 Scene One: The Burial of Jesus by Joseph of Arimathea (Matt 27:57-60)

Matt 27:57-60 has the following structure:

⁵⁷'Οψίας δὲ γενομένης

ἦλθεν   _ἄνθρωπος πλούσιος_   ἀπὸ 'Αριμαθαίας, τοὔνομα 'Ιωσήφ,
   ὃς καὶ αὐτὸς   _ἐμαθητεύθη_ τῷ 'Ιησοῦ

⁵⁸ οὗτος   προσελθὼν   τῷ Πιλάτῳ
   ἠτήσατο   _τὸ σῶμα_   τοῦ 'Ιησοῦ.
   τότε ὁ Πιλᾶτος   ἐκέλευσεν   ἀποδοθῆναι.

⁵⁹ καὶ λαβὼν   _τὸ σῶμα_   ὁ 'Ιωσήφ
   ἐνετύλιξεν   αὐτὸ [ἐν]   σινδόνι _καθαρᾷ_
⁶⁰ καὶ ἔθηκεν   αὐτὸ ἐν   τῷ _καινῷ_ αὐτοῦ μνημείῳ

ὃ ἐλατόμησεν ἐν τῇ πέτρᾳ καὶ προσκυλίσας λίθον μέγαν τῇ θύρᾳ τοῦ μνημείου ἀπῆλθεν.

Having first indicated a temporal factor 'Οψίας δὲ γενομένης, Matthew introduces Joseph of Arimathea, a disciple of Jesus, who comes to Pilate, and requests the body of Jesus. Having obtained the necessary permission he takes it, wraps it in a burial sheet, buries it, rolls a large stone at the entrance of the tomb and goes away. A literary criterion that justifies treating 27:57-60 as a scene in itself and separate from 27:61 is provided by the inclusion formed by the explicit notices of Joseph's entrance into and exit from the scene: Joseph «came» (ἦλθεν) and «departed» (ἀπῆλθεν)[82].

Matthew presents Joseph's action of the burial of Jesus in a progressive manner as indicated in Matthew's application of various verbs: ἦλθεν, (ἔρχομαι) προσελθὼν (προσέρχομαι), ἠτήσατο (αἰτέω) λαβὼν (λαμβάνω), ἐνετύλιξεν (ἐντυλίσσω), ἔθηκεν (τίθημι), προσκυλίσας (προσκυλίω) and ἀπῆλθεν (ἀπέρχομαι).

6.2 Scene Two: The Women Witness the Burial of Jesus (Matt 27:61)

The prominent characters in the second part of the burial scene are the two women, Mary Magdalene and the other Mary, who sit opposite

---

[82] See J. P. HEIL, «The Narrative Structure», 426; ID., The Death and Resurrection of Jesus, 109.

the tomb witnessing Joseph's burial of the body of Jesus. This verse has the following structure:

[61] ἦν δὲ ἐκεῖ
Μαριὰμ ἡ Μαγδαληνὴ
καὶ ἡ ἄλλη Μαρία
καθήμεναι ἀπέναντι τοῦ τάφου.

The phrase ἦν δὲ ἐκεῖ marks a different unit introducing the female characters in the scene. In this scene Matthew identifies two women, «Mary Magdalene and the other Mary», as witnessing Joseph's burial of the body of Jesus: καθήμεναι ἀπέναντι τοῦ τάφου (27:61).

6.3 Scenes One and Two Taken Together (Matt 27:57-61)[83]

[57] Ὀψίας δὲ γενομένης

ἦλθεν ἄνθρωπος πλούσιος	ἀπὸ Ἀριμαθαίας, τοὔνομα Ἰωσήφ,
ὃς καὶ αὐτὸς	ἐμαθητεύθη τῷ Ἰησοῦ·

[58] οὗτος   προσελθὼν   τῷ Πιλάτῳ
ἠτήσατο   τὸ σῶμα   τοῦ Ἰησοῦ.
τότε ὁ Πιλᾶτος   ἐκέλευσεν   ἀποδοθῆναι.

[59] καὶ λαβὼν   τὸ σῶμα   ὁ Ἰωσὴφ
ἐνετύλιξεν   αὐτὸ [ἐν]   σινδόνι καθαρᾷ

[60] καὶ ἔθηκεν   αὐτὸ ἐν   τῷ καινῷ αὐτοῦ μνημείῳ
ὃ ἐλατόμησεν ἐν τῇ πέτρᾳ καὶ προσκυλίσας λίθον μέγαν τῇ θύρᾳ τοῦ μνημείου
ἀπῆλθεν.

[61] ἦν δὲ ἐκεῖ	Μαριὰμ ἡ Μαγδαληνὴ καὶ ἡ ἄλλη Μαρία
	καθήμεναι ἀπέναντι τοῦ τάφου.

The composition of the passage highlights the male and female followers of Jesus surrounding the body of Jesus. The two extreme segments (vv. 57, 61) seem to be parallel to each other as they introduce different characters: Joseph of Arimathea (27:57-60) and the women (27:61).

---

[83] See R. MEYNET, Jésus passe, 293.

Joseph of Arimathea is identified as ἐμαθητεύθη τῷ 'Ιησοῦ, while the women are identified as καθήμεναι ἀπέναντι τοῦ τάφου. Joseph of Arimathea is described as reverentially burying the body of Jesus, and Mary Magdalene and the other Mary are described as simply sitting opposite the sepulcher. The two named characters, Joseph of Arimathea and Mary Magdalene, are identified with the location of their origin: Joseph is from Arimathea (ἀπὸ 'Αριμαθαίας), Mary is from Magdala (ἡ Μαγδαληνὴ).

In the compositional features of Matt 27:57-61 we noted that, presented within two scenes, «Joseph of Arimathea» reverentially buries the body of Jesus while «Mary Magdalene and the other Mary» sit in front of the tomb of Jesus in constant vigil.

7. Biblical Background

At least two OT texts, Deut 21:22-23 and Isa 53:9, seem to have influenced the Matthean text on the burial narrative. Besides these two texts, we see also how Matthew maintains similarity of concepts between the burial of Jesus and the burial of John the Baptist in 14:12.

7.1 *The Burial of the Body before Sunset (Deut 21:22-23)*

According to the Mosaic law a criminal's body must not remain hanging exposed on a tree through the night. Especially in Judaea, it was considered a serious affront to Jewish law and custom and actually a violation of the law to leave a corpse overnight after crucifixion without burial: «his body shall not remain all night upon the tree, but you shall bury him the same day, for a hanged man is accursed by God; you must not defile your land which the Lord your God gives you for an inheritance» (Deut 21:23)[84]. According to the Jewish law, the burial had to be completed by sunset which in this case also marked the beginning of the Sabbath on which no labor should be done[85]. According to the Levitical law one incurred ceremonial defilement from physical contact with dead bodies[86]. The time indication 'ὀψίας δὲ γενομένης,

---

[84] See W.L. LANE, *The Gospel according to Mark,* 577-78; L.L. MORRIS, *The Gospel according to Matthew,* 729; K.H. REEVES, *The Resurrection Narrative in Matthew,* 45; W. HENDRIKSEN, *The Gospel of Matthew,* 978; F.W. BEARE, *The Gospel According to Matthew,* 538; J.P. MEIER, *Matthew,* 354; G.T. MONTAGUE, *Companion God,* 318.

[85] Shab 23.5.

[86] JOSEPHUS, *Antiquities,* XVIII: 2. 2.

«when it was evening», therefore, refers to the urgency of the burial[87], thus explaining the hasty burial of the body of Jesus 'οψίας δὲ γενομένης and still before sundown as Mark makes clear.

7.2 In the Rich Man's Tomb (Isa 53:9)

The second OT text that is reflected in the Matthean burial narrative is Isa 53:9: «They made his grave with the wicked and his tomb with the rich (τοὺς πλουσίους) ...» The text of Isa 53:9 is recalled when the «rich man from Arimathea», Joseph, buries the body of Jesus[88]. The majority of scholars support the influence of Isa 53:9 on Matt 27:57-61[89].

7.3 The Disciples' Burial of John the Baptist (Matt 14:12)

In Matt 14:12, we see that the disciples of John the Baptist bury the body of their master. Parallel to this, Matthew presents Joseph of Arimathea, identified as a disciple of Jesus, who buries the body of Jesus (27:57-60) while the women who followed Jesus from Galilee witness to it (27:61). Thus both John the Baptist and Jesus are reverentially buried by their disciples.

8. Interpretation

From what has been said above there are grounds to think that the Matthean burial narrative (27:57-61) contains elements of male and female discipleship.

---

[87] Josephus in The Jewish War IV: 317 speaks of the necessity of the burial of the crucified malefactors. See L.L. MORRIS, The Gospel according to Matthew, 729; W. HENDRIKSEN, The Gospel of Matthew, 979.

[88] We have already made reference to Matthew's interest in the fulfillment of the OT prophecy (Matt 1:22-23; 2:5-6. 15, 17-18, 23; 3:3; 4:14-16; 8:17; 11:10; 12:17-21; 13:14-15; 26:54, 56; 27:9-10). See R. H. GUNDRY, The Use, 146; D. GRASSO, Il Vangelo di Matteo, 664.

[89] W.B. BARRICK, «The Rich Man», 235-39; W.C. ALLEN, A Critical and Exegetical Commentary, 298; A. PLUMMER, Matthew, 406; E. KLOSTERMANN, Das Matthäusevangelium, 226; J. SCHMID, Das Evangelium nach Matthäus, 377; F.V. FILSON, A Commentary, 298; R.H. GUNDRY, Matthew, 580; ID., The Use, 146, 204, 209; J. BREECH, «Crucifixion», 250; R. FABRIS, Matteo, 559; L. SABOURIN, Matthew, II, 922; J.P. MEIER, The Vision of Matthew, 206; W. HENDRIKSEN, The Gospel of Matthew, 979; R.H. SMITH, Matthew, 329; T. MONTAGUE, Companion God, 318; R. MEYNET, Jésus passe, 300; H.N. HENDRICKX, Los Relatos de la pasión, 174.

8.1 The Rich Disciple's Burial of Jesus, the Master (Matt 27:57-60)

Among the Synoptic writers Matthew alone calls Joseph of Arimathea a rich man and also at the same time a disciple of Jesus. This becomes clear in his alteration of the Markan description of Joseph of Arimathea as a εὐσχήμων βουλευτής («member of the Sanhedrin»)[90] to ἄνθρωπος πλούσιος («a rich man») who was also «ἐμαθητεύθη τῷ Ἰησοῦ» (literally, «discipled to Jesus»)[91]. Matthew's use of the verb μαθητεύω is worth noting. This refers to a larger extension of Jesus' disciples around him. For Matthew, discipleship of Jesus is not limited to the Twelve male disciples around him.

Interestingly Matthew describes this disciple, Joseph of Arimathea, as ἄνθρωπος πλούσιος («a rich man», 27:57), a description which is significant especially against the background of Matt 19:16-30 in which Jesus warns the disciples of the difficulty for rich people to enter the kingdom of God: «Truly, I say to you, it will be hard for a rich man to enter the kingdom of heaven. Again I tell you, it is easier for a camel to go through the eye of a needle than for a rich man to enter the kingdom of God» (vv. 23-24)[92]. If this is so, to be «rich» and to be a «disciple» of Jesus at the same time would seem to be difficult. In spite of this hard saying of Jesus, if Matthew identifies this rich man as a disciple, it must have been for an important reason: «With men this is impossible, but with God all things are possible» (v. 26). Hence in Matthew's identification of Joseph as a rich disciple, what becomes evident is the divine intervention in the burial of Jesus. Because, this man from Arimathea, one of the «wealthy allies of Jesus' movement»[93] is an actual disciple[94]. Clearly God is at work in the burial of Jesus. It is by the providence of God that Joseph of Arimathea, the rich man, becomes a disciple of Jesus[95], and it is by the grace of God that this man is there to bury the body of Jesus[96]. According to K.H. Reeves, Joseph's action here «meets with God's approval and is in accord with His evaluative

---

[90] Commenting on this change R. E. Brown says that given the early Christian experiences and the feeling toward the Sanhedrin, the invention of a Sanhedrist's acting piously toward Jesus is not likely. See R.E. BROWN, *The Death of the Messiah*, 1240.

[91] See R.H. SMITH, *Matthew*, 329.

[92] See D. PATTE, *The Gospel according to Matthew*, 391.

[93] See R.H. SMITH, *Matthew*, 329; C.S. KEENER, *Matthew*, 690.

[94] C.S. KEENER, *Matthew*, 329.

[95] See D.W. TORRANCE – T.F. TORRANCE, *A Harmony of the Gospels*, 216.

[96] A.W. MORRISON, *A Commentary on the Gospels*, III, 216.

point of view»[97]. God chose a man of noble rank among his own people to begin to cover the shame of the cross with his honorable burial of the body of Jesus[98].

Joseph's request to Pilate for the body of Jesus and Pilate's granting of the body to Joseph show that the body of Jesus is no longer in the hands of his enemies, but in the hands of a disciple who cares for it. Here Matthew narrates Joseph's burial of Jesus' body which recalls John's disciples' burial of their master's body[99]: «And his disciples came and took the body and buried it...» (Matt 14:12). Similarly a disciple of Jesus buries the body of Jesus, but with the added notion that this disciple is a rich man (27:57-60).

Joseph's discipleship of Jesus perhaps motivated him while his wealth enabled him to carry out the burial of Jesus' body in a new tomb[100]. By burying the body of Jesus in a «rock-hewn new tomb» Joseph shows great generosity and honor towards the body of Jesus[101]. His generosity and the honor extended to Jesus are manifested in three specific Matthean terms: καθαρός («clean»), καινός («new») and μέγας («great»)[102]. Matthew is the only one who uses the words «clean» and «new» with regard to the tomb of Jesus, and refers to the fact that the tomb belonged to Joseph. These features continue to emphasize Joseph's status as a rich man and thus to show the continuing care of this disciple toward the body of Jesus[103]. Joseph's rolling of a huge stone to the door of Jesus' tomb shows the completion of the burial[104].

---

[97] K.H. REEVES, *The Resurrection Narrative in Matthew*, 43.

[98] D.W. TORRANCE – T.F. TORRANCE, *A Harmony of the Gospels*, 216.

[99] According to the Jewish burial customs the son, especially the eldest (8:21) or close relatives would conduct the burial of the dead person, but a teacher like Jesus would often be buried by the disciples (Matt 14:12). See L.L. MORRIS, *The Gospel according to Matthew*, 727; K.H. REEVES, *The Resurrection Narratives*, 44; F.D. BRUNER, *Matthew*, 1068; W. CARTER, *Matthew and the Margins*, 539.

[100] F.D. BRUNER, *Matthew*, 1068.

[101] Normally the body of the executed criminals would not be allowed to be buried in family graves (*Sanh* 6:5) but thrown into the common graves. See L.L. MORRIS, *Matthew*, 727; R.E. BROWN, «The Burial of Jesus», 233-245.

[102] See J.P. MEIER, *Matthew*, 354-56; J.P. HEIL, *Matthew*, 355; L. SABOURIN, *Matthew*, II, 922. F.D. BRUNER, *Matthew*, 1069; E. LOHMEYER, *Das Evangelium des Matthäus*, 399; K.H. REEVES, *The Resurrection Narrative in Matthew*, 44.

[103] D. SENIOR, *The Passion of Jesus*, 152.

[104] K.H. REEVES, *The Resurrection Narrative in Matthew*, 44. R.H. GUNDRY, *Matthew*, 337; C.H. GIBLIN, «Structural and Thematic Correlation», 407- 408.

This act of Joseph affirms the reality of Jesus' death[105] and prepares for the subsequent resurrection scene in which the angel of the Lord rolls back the stone and sits on it in triumph after the resurrection (28:2).

We see something dramatic about the appearance (27:57) and disappearance of Joseph of Arimathea (27:61). It looks as if Joseph's coming to bury the body of Jesus and his going away after the burial, show that his whole life was a preparation for this one historical deed[106]. In the person of Joseph of Arimathea, Matthew presents the «only» male disciple in this Gospel who remained with Jesus at his death. Thus in the absence of the twelve male disciples of Jesus, Matthew offers to the readers a discipleship model in Joseph, who, risking all his wealth and status, stayed with Jesus. Thus, Joseph displays his commitment towards Jesus not through elaborate words but by decisive deeds, which is a hallmark of authentic discipleship in Matthew's Gospel[107]. Judas' betrayal of Jesus and the flight of the rest of the disciples at the arrest of Jesus highlight either their fear or their failure to comprehend Jesus' passion predictions that the son of man was to suffer, die, be crucified, and on the third day be raised up (16:21-28; 17:9. 22-23; 20:17-19). Joseph's action on the other hand shows his recognition of Jesus, his master.

8.2 *The Women's Vigilant Sitting in Front of the Tomb (Matt 27:61)*

After understanding the significance of a rich disciple's burial of Jesus' body, our effort in the present section is to understand the meaning of the presence and the posture of the two women at the tomb of Jesus. We will begin this discussion examining some of the scholarly views on the significance of the women at the tomb. This will be followed by an interpretation of their presence and posture of sitting in front of the tomb of Jesus.

According to Matthew, the only character group that witnessed to Joseph's burial of Jesus' body comprises the two women, whom Matthew identifies as «Mary Magdalene» and «the other Mary» (v. 61). Here Matthew does not say anything about any assistance to Joseph in burying Jesus' body. All that Matthew says about the women at the tomb is «καθήμεναι ἀπέναντι τοῦ τάφου» («sitting opposite the sepulcher», 27:61). The women's posture of sitting in front of the tomb and

---

[105] D. SENIOR, *Passion Narrative,* 337.

[106] R.H. GUNDRY, *Matthew,* 564; J.P. MEIER, *The Vision of Matthew,* 206.

[107] See D. SENIOR, *The Passion of Jesus,* 152.

its significance in the first Gospel has been interpreted differently by various commentators. R.H. Gundry is of the opinion that by placing the women in front of the tomb of Jesus, Matthew emphasizes the «historical reliability» of the tomb of Jesus, i. e., the women did not make a mistake in identifying the tomb on Easter morning (28:1)[108]. Expressing a similar view, Allison and Davies suggest that «the main point is that they know that he truly died and was truly buried, their testimony to his rising is all the stronger»[109]. The women's presence, according to Albright and Mann, is thus «to emphasize the identity of the person who died, was buried, and vanished from the tomb»[110]. The women's posture of sitting in front of the tomb tells us that they are faithful witnesses to both the death and the burial of Jesus. The witnessing role of the women's presence is emphasized by the scholars like L. Sabourin[111] J.P. Heil[112], A.J. Levine[113], R.H. Smith[114], K.H. Reeves[115], E.M. Wainwright[116], C.L. Blomberg[117], D. Senior[118], Garland[119] and L. Morris[120].

The scholars P. Gaechter, W. Grundmann, M.J. Lagrange, B.W. Porter, and C.L. Blomberg have interpreted the women's presence at the tomb of Jesus in terms of the lamentation of the dead[121], a religious role assigned to the women of first century Judaism[122]. According to them the women sit in front of the tomb to mourn the death

---

[108] R.H. GUNDRY, *Matthew*, 565. See F.D. BRUNER, *Matthew*, II, 1069.

[109] W.D. DAVIES – D.C. ALLISON, *Saint Matthew*, 652.

[110] W.F. ALBRIGHT – C.S. MANN, *Matthew*, 355.

[111] L. SABOURIN, *Matthew*, II, 922-923. See L.L. MORRIS, *The Gospel According to Matthew*, 727.

[112] J.P. HEIL, «Narrative Structure», 427.

[113] See A.J. LEVINE, «Matthew», 262.

[114] R.H. SMITH, *Matthew*, 329.

[115] K.H. REEVES, *The Resurrection Narrative in Matthew*, 44.

[116] E. WAINWRIGHT, «The Gospel of Matthew», 635-677.

[117] C.L BLOMBERG, *Matthew*, 423.

[118] D. SENIOR, *The Passion of Jesus*, 13, 15-152.

[119] D.E. GARLAND, *Reading Matthew*, 263.

[120] L.L. MORRIS, *The Gospel According to Matthew*, 727.

[121] See P. GAECHTER, *Das Matthäus-Evangelium*, 940; W. GRUNDMANN, *Das Evangelium nach Matthäus*, 568; M.J. LAGRANGE, *Matthieu*, 535; B.W. PORTER, «With our Backs to the Grave», 232-235; C.L. BLOMBERG, *Matthew*, 423.

[122] C. OSIEK, «The Women at the Tomb», 103-118; L.A. BENTZ, «Jesus' Death and Resurrection», 251-274; B.W. PORTER, «With Our Backs to the Grave», 232-235. W. SHULLENBERGER, «The Other Mary», 241-245. R. STRELAN, «To Sit is to Mourn», 31-45.

of Jesus. While the majority of the Matthean scholars interpret the women's posture as a sign of their lamentation, E. Cheney in a recent article has proposed a different interpretation[123]. The author admits sitting as an accepted posture of lamentation. She suggests various biblical as well as extra-biblical evidence that suggests «sitting» as a posture of lamentation, especially in the context of death and burial (Job 2:8, 13; Psa 137:1; 1Macc 1:27; Luke 10:13; t. Job 20:4, 17)[124]. Crying aloud and weeping (Gen 23:2; 43:30; 1Sam 30:4; 2Sam 1:24; Sir 22:11; Psa 137:1), sitting in sackcloth and ashes (Luke 10:13) beating the breast, etc., were some of the external signs of mourning the dead. According to her, although these women are supposed to lament, they manifest no sign of lamentation. Contrary to the traditional role of the women during a burial ritual, the women here do not lament, do not beat their breasts. That is to say the women do not do what they are ordinarily assigned or expected to do under such a circumstance: i. e., mourn the dead. This author interprets the women's non-lamentation as a sign of their discipleship.

She bases her argument on a piece of historical information on the custom of lamentation in the first century Judaism. It was customary that in «noble death» stories, family friends or disciples surrounded the dying person, during which time the women often lamented. The lamenting women were often then asked to leave the death chamber.[125] Naturally close male friends or attendants then surrounded the dying hero. It was not customary for the men to weep, because according to the contemporary customs, lamentation or grief was considered «womanish»[126] «irrational»[127].

---

[123] E. CHENEY, «The Mother», 13-21.

[124] See R.H. GUNDRY, *Matthew,* 565; A. OEPE, «καθίστημι, ἀκαταστασία, ἀκατάστατος», 446; W.D. DAVIES – D.C. ALLISON, *Matthew,* III, 652; W. CARTER, *Matthew and the Margins,* 539.

[125] The most classical example is the scene in Plato's writing about the death of Socrates: «So we went in and found Socrates just released ... And Socrates glanced at Crito, and said, "Crito, let her be taken home". So some of Crito's servants led her away weeping bitterly and beating her breast...». PHILO, *Phaedo,* translated by F.J. Church, *Plato's Phaedo,* 3.

[126] On this Plutarch states: «Yes, mourning is truly feminine, and weak, and ignoble, since women are more given to it than men, barbarians more than Greeks, and inferior men more than better men». Plutarch, *Mor,* 113.

[127] J.S. KLOPPENBORG, «Exitus clari viri», 106-120, here 111-112; K.E CORLEY, «Women and the Crucifixion», 200.

She cites examples from the Psalms[128] and Josephus[129] to substantiate her view. Now, from the contemporary social and cultural settings of first century Judaism one would expect the male disciples of Jesus to be at his side and the women to mourn. But contrary to the normal customs, the male disciples and the family members of Jesus are absent. According to Cheney, Matthew offers a different model here. Given that they restrain from grief and courageously stand by Jesus, these women seem to do what the male disciples of Jesus should have done. Matthew here seems to go beyond the existing gender restrictions and present the women as having «followed» Jesus constantly (27:55-56) and cared for him by being with him till the end (27:61). According to Cheney, the women's action here seems to illustrate their discipleship in the Gospel.

We see some kind of forced exegesis here. Just because of the fact that the text does not describe lamentation, we cannot say that the women are not lamenting. Because, the fact that something is not described does not deny it. For example, at the funeral of the son of the widow of Nain Luke 7:11-17 there is no description of lamentation except for the mother. It is unlikely that the others did not lament too. Perhaps, all that one can legitimately say in Matt 27:61 is that the women are not described as giving the normal external signs of mourning except sitting[130]. To base the women's discipleship of Jesus, just on the absence of lamentation seems to have no strong basis.

Perhaps, we can speak of the women's sitting in front of the sepulcher and their discipleship of Jesus from a different point of view. In 27:57-60 we are told that Joseph of Arimathea buries the body of Jesus in the μνημεῖον while the women are described as sitting in front of the τάφος. In this context, to sit in front of the τάφος implies sitting in front of the body of Jesus himself, their master, whom they have followed and served[131]. That means, the women still remain faithful to Jesus.

---

[128] The Psalms also contain examples of family and friends as onlookers, if only from a distance. See Psa 38:11; 88:8. A.Y. COLLINS, «The Genre», 14; W. MUNRO, «Women Disciples in Mark», 226; A. TOYNBEE, *Study of History,* 421.

[129] The first example concerns Josephus' description of the death of Moses in which a crowd seems to weep, while the women particularly weep and beat their breasts. See JOSEPHUS, *The Jewish Antiquities,* IV: 320-26.

[130] See C. OSIEK, «The Women at the Tomb», 100-101; S. HEINE, «Eine Person», 185; W. CARTER, *Matthew and the Margins,* 539.

[131] Although the words μνημεῖον and τάφος are synonymous, Matthew assigns particular theological significance to each. According to J.P. HEIL, when the focus is

They are at still at his service. Such an explanation is in harmony with vv. 55 in which the women are described to have followed Jesus serving him, which are two discipleship features for someone to be called disciple of Jesus. Although a similar notion is found in Mark, it looks more deliberate and clear in Matthew[132].

9. Conclusion

In this chapter we have been attempting to understand the role of the male and female characters in the Matthean burial narrative. We discussed the identity and the identifying activities of Joseph of Arimathea as well as that of the women. We have seen how Matthew takes special interest to portray these characters as disciples of Jesus. In the absence of the Twelve disciples of Jesus, Matthew presents a rich disciple who venerably buries the body of Jesus, thus manifesting the special divine intervention in the burial of Jesus.

Parallel to Joseph of Arimathea, Matthew presents two women as sitting opposite the tomb of Jesus. Contrary to the contemporary burial customs and the role assigned to the women in the burial rites, these women are presented as silently sitting in front of the body of Jesus in the tomb. Their sitting posture in front of the tomb suggests that they are still faithful to their master, and that they still remain at the service of their Lord.

As a concluding observation we see that in the absence of the Twelve, Matthew presents the male and female characters who play those roles which otherwise the Twelve disciples should have played. It is true that Matthew does not call these women disciples. But their sitting in front of Jesus' body, which is in harmony with vv. 55, attribute to them discipleship qualities. In comparison to Judas who betrayed him (26:48-50), the other Eleven male disciples who fled (26:56)[133], and Joseph of Arimathea who departed after the burial (27:60), the women alone are presented as constantly and faithfully standing by Jesus in the hour of Jesus' passion and death (27:55-56, 61).

---

away from the tomb then Matthew uses the word μνημεῖον, but when the focus is towards the tomb, then Matthew uses the word τάφος. J.P. HEIL, «Narrative Structure», 426; L. SABOURIN, *Matthew*, II, 922.

[132] In Mark, too, women are presented as disciples. T.J. WEEDEN, *Mark-Traditions in Conflict*; K.E. CORLEY, *Private Women*; 84-85; J.D. CROSSAN, *Who Killed Jesus?*, 105-106.

[133] C. S. KEENER, *Matthew*, 688.

CHAPTER V

The Resurrection of Jesus and the Women's Role (Matt 28:1-10)

1. Introduction

The present chapter discusses the role of the women in the
resurrection narrative of Matthew (Matt 28:1-10), which consists of
two interrelated passages: a) the empty tomb narrative (28:1-8), and b)
Jesus' appearance to and commissioning of the women (9-10). We begin our investigation with a Synoptic comparison. This will be followed
by a compositional analysis, a close reading of the text and a study of
the biblical background, all of which will guide us to the interpretation
of the text[1].

---

[1] Other multi-faceted problems associated with the resurrection of Jesus such as the
historicity of the empty tomb and the bodily nature of the resurrection are not within
the scope of our research. The extent of recent literature on the resurrection narratives
speaks for the attention given to these issues. For some of the detailed discussions on
the resurrection narratives in general see W. MICHAELIS, *Die Erscheinungen;*
W. NAUCK, «Die Bedeutung», 243-267; F. NEIRYNCK, «Les femmes au tombeau»,
168-190; T.R.W. LONGSTAFF, «The Women at the Tomb», 277-282; B. OBERBOR-
DER, «Was sucht ihr», 225-240; H. VON CAMPENHAUSEN, «The Events of Easter», 42-
89; E. LAVERDIERE, «The Resurrection according to Matthew», 126-135; H. RITT,
«Die Frauen», 117-133; W. TRILLING, *Christusverkündigung,* 212-243; J. CABA,
Cristo, 159-184.

For a discussion specifically on the historicity of the empty tomb see R.H. STEIN,
«Was the Tomb Really Empty», 23-29; W. NAUCK, «Die Bedeutung des leeren Grabes», 243-267; W.L. CRAIG, «The Empty Tomb of Jesus», 173-200.

For a most recent study on the topic see D. MARGUERAT, *Résurrection.* This book
discusses the various means used to describe the resurrection, the question of the historicity of Jesus' resurrection, the significance of the open tomb of Jesus, the appearance of the risen Jesus as alive again, and the manner of Jesus' resurrection.

2. The Text (Matt 28:1-10)

¹Ὀψὲ δὲ σαββάτων, τῇ ἐπιφωσκούσῃ εἰς μίαν σαββάτων ἦλθεν Μαριὰμ ἡ Μαγδαληνὴ καὶ ἡ ἄλλη Μαρία θεωρῆσαι τὸν τάφον. ²καὶ ἰδοὺ σεισμὸς ἐγένετο μέγας· ἄγγελος γὰρ κυρίου καταβὰς ἐξ οὐρανοῦ καὶ προσελθὼν ἀπεκύλισεν τὸν λίθον καὶ ἐκάθητο ἐπάνω αὐτοῦ. ³ἦν δὲ ἡ εἰδέα αὐτοῦ ὡς ἀστραπὴ καὶ τὸ ἔνδυμα αὐτοῦ λευκὸν ὡς χιών. ⁴ἀπὸ δὲ τοῦ φόβου αὐτοῦ ἐσείσθησαν οἱ τηροῦντες καὶ ἐγενήθησαν ὡς νεκροί. ⁵ἀποκριθεὶς δὲ ὁ ἄγγελος εἶπεν ταῖς γυναιξίν, Μὴ φοβεῖσθε ὑμεῖς, οἶδα γὰρ ὅτι Ἰησοῦν τὸν ἐσταυρωμένον ζητεῖτε· ⁶οὐκ ἔστιν ὧδε, ἠγέρθη γὰρ καθὼς εἶπεν· δεῦτε ἴδετε τὸν τόπον ὅπου ἔκειτο. ⁷καὶ ταχὺ πορευθεῖσαι εἴπατε τοῖς μαθηταῖς αὐτοῦ ὅτι Ἠγέρθη ἀπὸ τῶν νεκρῶν, καὶ ἰδοὺ προάγει ὑμᾶς εἰς τὴν Γαλιλαίαν, ἐκεῖ αὐτὸν ὄψεσθε· ἰδοὺ εἶπον ὑμῖν. ⁸καὶ ἀπελθοῦσαι ταχὺ ἀπὸ τοῦ μνημείου μετὰ φόβου καὶ χαρᾶς μεγάλης ἔδραμον ἀπαγγεῖλαι τοῖς μαθηταῖς αὐτοῦ.

⁹καὶ ἰδοὺ Ἰησοῦς ὑπήντησεν αὐταῖς λέγων, Χαίρετε. αἱ δὲ προσελθοῦσαι ἐκράτησαν αὐτοῦ τοὺς πόδας καὶ προσεκύνησαν αὐτῷ. ¹⁰τότε λέγει αὐταῖς ὁ Ἰησοῦς, Μὴ φοβεῖσθε· ὑπάγετε ἀπαγγείλατε τοῖς ἀδελφοῖς μου ἵνα ἀπέλθωσιν εἰς τὴν Γαλιλαίαν, κἀκεῖ με ὄψονται.

3. Comparison of Matthew with the Other Evangelists

In this section we will study Matt 28:1-10 in comparison with the other Synoptic Gospels and John (Mark 16:1-8; Luke 24:1-12; John 20:1-18)[2]. This is to highlight the special Matthean features concerning the women in the resurrection narrative.

Considering the degree of variation between the different resurrection narratives in the Gospels, it is almost impossible to reconstruct a complete and harmonious historical account of these narratives. The Gospel texts here vary substantially in length, focus and detail. The most probable explanation to this divergence is the existence of multiple traditions behind the Gospel accounts. In this regard L.L. Morris' observation is pertinent: «each of the evangelists tells the story as best

---

Together with the majority of the scholars in defence of the reality of the empty tomb and the subsequent appearance of Jesus to the women, we accept the reality of these events. We look to explain the women's role in the resurrection narrative with particular reference to the discipleship theme of the Gospel.

[2] See B. LINDARS, «The Resurrection and the Empty Tomb», 116-135; C.A. PERRY, *The Resurrection Promise,* 20-27; P.B. MURRAY, *The Message of the Resurrection,* 43-49; P. PERKINS, *Resurrection,* 126; H.N. HENDRICKX, *Resurrection Narratives,* 4-52; S. GRASSO, *Matteo,* 669-74.

as he knows it without trying to harmonize it with what somebody else says»[3]. In spite of a great deal of variation between the different Gospel texts on the resurrection narrative, an interesting factor that gives unity to the Gospel accounts is the witnessing presence of the women (Matt 28:1-10; Mark 16:1-8; Luke 24:1-11; John 20:1-18)[4], which is the focus of our discussion in this chapter.

A comparative study of the Matthean resurrection narrative in relation to the other Synoptic Gospels helps us to identify and apprehend the Matthean salient features, especially concerning the Gospel's presentation of the women followers of Jesus and the discipleship theme in the Gospel. We make this study under the following three headings: a) a comparative analysis of Matthew and Luke; b) a comparative analysis of Matthew and Mark, and finally c) elements peculiar to Matthew.

3.1 A Comparative Analysis of Matthew and Luke (Matt 28:1-10; Luke 24:1-11)

A comparative study of the Matthean narrative of the resurrection with the Lukan highlights points of agreement and disagreement. Matthew and Luke agree on the following points: a) the beginning of the narrative with a time indication (εἰς μίαν σαββάτων, Matt 28:1a; τῇ δὲ μιᾷ τῶν σαββάτων, Luke 24:1a); b) the women being presented as the important characters (Matt 28:1; Luke 24:1); c) Mary Magdalene being mentioned as the first in the list of the women (Matt 28:1b; Luke 24:10); d) the women's immediate reaction of fear at the sight of the one whom they saw at the tomb (φόβου, Matt 28:4; ἐμφόβων, Luke 24:5); e) the similarity of expression in presenting the Easter message: (Matt 28:6, οὐκ ἔστιν ὧδε, ἠγέρθη γὰρ καθὼς εἶπεν; Luke 24:6, οὐκ ἔστιν ὧδε, ἀλλὰ ἠγέρθη. μνήσθητε ὡς ἐλάλησεν ὑμῖν); and finally f) that the women bring the Easter message to the Eleven (Matt 28:8; Luke 24:9-10).

Matthew differs from Luke mainly on the following seven points; a) Matthew presents the identity of the women at the onset of his narration (Matt 28:1), while in Luke the identity of the women is made known towards the end of the narration (24:10); b) Matthew speaks of only two women protagonists («Mary Magdalene and the other Mary», 28:1), while in Luke there are more than two women («Mary Magda-

---

[3] L.L. MORRIS, The Gospel according to Matthew, 733.
[4] See E.P. SANDERS, The Historical Figure of Jesus, 280; D. SPOTO, The Hidden Jesus, 242.

lene, Joanna and Mary the mother of James and the other women»,
24:10); c) the women in Matthew go to «see the tomb» (θεωρῆσαι τὸν
τάφον, 28:1), whereas in Luke the women go to the tomb taking the
spices, probably to anoint the body (24:1); d) Matthew gives no indication of the women entering the tomb; whereas in Luke the women enter
the tomb, which they find empty (24:3); e) Matthew narrates that there
was an earthquake, that the angel of the Lord came down from heaven,
rolled away the stone and sat on it, and then spoke to the women (28:2-
4), whereas in Luke two men in shining garments (angels, v. 23) inside
the tomb speak to the women who in fear have bowed down to the
ground (24:4-5); f) the first words of the angel in Matthew contain a
consolatory greeting (Μὴ φοβεῖσθε ὑμεῖς, 28:5), while the words of the
two men in Luke are a direct question (Τί ζητεῖτε τὸν ζῶντα μετὰ τῶν
νεκρῶν, 24:5); g) Matthew gives no indication of the angel reminding
the women of Jesus' words to them in Galilee predicting his passion,
death and resurrection, whereas this is the case in Luke (24:6-7).

3.2   A Comparative Analysis of Matthew and Mark
(Matt 28:1-10; Mark 16:1-8)

Matthew basically follows Mark in his presentation of the resurrection narrative. Still we can observe ten important points where Matthew
differs from Mark: a) the Matthean narrative contains two women only
(Μαριὰμ ἡ Μαγδαληνὴ καὶ ἡ ἄλλη Μαρία, 28:1), whereas in Mark
there are three women (Μαρία ἡ Μαγδαληνὴ καὶ Μαρία ἡ [τοῦ]
Ἰακώβου καὶ Σαλώμη, 16:1); b) Matthew describes the women as going
«to see the sepulcher», (θεωρῆσαι τὸν τάφον, 28:1), whereas Mark describes the women as going «to anoint him» (ἀλείψωσιν αὐτόν, 16:1);
c) Matthew eliminates the Markan women's conversation on the way
about the problem of finding someone to roll away the stone (Mark
16:3). But then he adds a note concerning the earthquake, the description of the angel descending from heaven, rolling away the stone and
sitting on it, and the presence of the guards at the tomb (vv. 2-4); d)
Mark speaks of the women entering the tomb and seeing a «young man
sitting on the right side, dressed in a white robe» who speaks to them
because of their amazement: μὴ ἐκθαμβεῖσθε (v. 6) whereas Matthew
has the angel of the Lord outside the tomb give a consolatory saluta-
tion: Μὴ φοβεῖσθε ὑμεῖς (v. 5); e) Mark describes the young man as
commanding the women to «go and tell his disciples and Peter» (16:7),
but Matthew avoids any special reference to Peter and mentions only
«his disciples» in general (28:7); f) Matthew adds that the women are
told to go quickly (ταχύ) to tell the disciples (28:7) and the women in

complete obedience go «quickly» (ταχύ) from the tomb and run to tell the disciples (28:8); g) in Matthew the women are to communicate to the disciples the resurrection message as well as where the risen Jesus will be seen (v. 7). The Markan women are instructed to communicate to the disciples only the message that Jesus is going ahead of them to Galilee where they will see him; h) the Matthean women's reaction to the angel is also different from the Markan description. According to Mark the women depart with «*fear and astonishment*» (16:8) while according to Matthew the women left with «*fear and joy*» (28:8); i) the Markan women say nothing to anyone, which is not the case in Matthew where they run to tell the disciples[5].

3.3 *Features Peculiar to Matthew*

The above comparative analysis of the different Gospel accounts helps us to identify certain Matthean salient features concerning the Gospel's presentation of the women: a) a double temporal indicator; b) the identity of the women («Mary Magdalene and the other Mary»); c) the purpose of the women's visit to the tomb («to see the tomb»); d) the risen Jesus' appearance to the women and their reaction to him[6]

---

[5] For more on the comparison between Matthew and Mark see J. P. MEIER, *Matthew*, 360; B. WITHERINGTON, III, *Women in the Earliest Churches*, 171-172; F.W. BEARE, *The Gospel according to Matthew*, 543; C.E.B. CRANFIELD, «The Resurrection of Jesus Christ», 167-172; M.D. GOULDER, «Mark 16,1-8 and Parallels», 235-240; C.A. PERRY, *The Resurrection Promise*, 20-28.

[6] Concerning the risen Jesus' post resurrection appearance Matthew and John agree on three factors: a) Both Matthew and John agree on the risen Jesus' appearance to the women/woman whom he commissioned with a message to communicate to the disciples (Matt 28:9-10; John 20:11-17; b) both agree that the women/woman faithfully carried out the message to the disciples of Jesus (see Matt 28:16-20; John 20:18); c) in both the women/woman are asked to communicate the message to the brothers of Jesus (τοῖς ἀδελφοῖς μου, Matt 28:10; John 20:17).

Concerning the risen Jesus' appearance, Matthew and John differ at least on the following five factors: a) John identifies Mary Magdalene as the only witness (v. 20:11), while Matthew identifies two women (28:9); b) although John describes Mary Magdalene as standing before the tomb of Jesus when Jesus appears to her (20:11), Matthew describes the women as having left the tomb to communicate the angel's message to the disciples when Jesus appears to them (28:8); c) Mary Magdalene in John does not immediately recognize Jesus (20:14), while in Matthew there is no sign of non-recognition (28:9); d) in Matthew Jesus clearly instructs the women to tell «my brethren» to go to Galilee (28:10). John contains no instructions for the disciples to go to Galilee; e) in Matthew we see an emphasis on not being fearful and on giving the disciples the message to go to Galilee (vv. 9-10). In John the emphasis is on Mary

and finally e) the double commission the women receive: one from the angel and the other from the risen Jesus.

4. The Compositional Features of Matt 28:1-10

Under this title we will discuss the major divisions of Matt 28:1-10, its delimitation, and finally its relation to the narratives of the aftermath of the death and burial (27:51b-61). Matt 28:1-10 is composed of two passages: a) the empty tomb episode (vv. 1-8); b) the risen Jesus' appearance to and the commissioning of the women (vv. 9-10).

4.1 *Passage One: The Empty Tomb Episode (Matt 28:1-8)*

4.1.1 The Factors that Delimit the Passage

Three factors, namely time, theme and characters, justify treating 28:1-8 as a passage distinct in itself, separate from what precedes (27:62-66) and what follows (28:9-10).

The first factor concerns «the time», which changes from «on the next day, after the day of preparation» (τῇ δὲ ἐπαύριον, ἥτις ἐστὶν μετὰ τὴν παρασκευήν, 27:62) to «after the Sabbath, towards the dawn of the first day of the week», ('Οψὲ δὲ σαββάτων, τῇ ἐπιφωσκούσῃ εἰς μίαν σαββάτων, 28:1).

The second factor concerns «the theme». The theme of the episode that immediately precedes tells us of the chief priests and the Pharisees before Pilate discussing the issue of guarding the tomb of Jesus (27:62-66). The episode that follows immediately, on the other hand, tells of Jesus' encounter with the women on their way to Galilee. The dominant theme of 28:1-8 is the reality of the empty tomb, and the women as the witnesses thereof. Although Matthew speaks of the soldiers at the tomb (vv. 2-4), the emphasis seems to fall on the women as the ones whom the angel invites to see the tomb.

The third factor concerns «the characters». If the enemies of Jesus dominate the immediately preceding scene (27:66), the risen Jesus and the women dominate the scene that immediately follows (28:9-10).

---

in her conversation with Jesus, on the fact that Jesus is going to go up to the Father and that Mary is to carry this message to the disciples (v. 17). For more on a comparative analysis of Matthew and John, see J. CABA, *Cristo,* 173; R. ATWOOD, *Mary Magdalene,* 130; W.D. DAVIES – D.C. ALLISON, *Matthew,* 658; G.T. MONTAGUE, *Companion God,* 323; G.S. KEENER, *Matthew,* 703-735; B. DE SOLAGE, *Christ est ressuscité,* 152-153; C.A. PERRY, *The Resurrection Promise,* 20-28.

Distinct from both these scenes, the angel of the Lord is described as the dominant character who announces the resurrection message to the women at the tomb, while the guards have become like dead men.

To conclude, we see at least three factors of time, location, theme and characters that justify treating Matt 28:1-8 as a passage distinct in itself. The different compositional features further substantiate this idea.

4.1.2 The Composition of the Passage

Matt 28:1-8 is composed of four short scenes that are mutually related to one another: a) the introductory scene: the women's coming to the tomb (v. 1); b) the concluding scene: the women's going away from the tomb (v. 8). Besides the introductory and concluding scenes, the passage comprises two central scenes: c) the angel's action and the guards' reaction (vv. 2-4); d) the angel's message to the women and the commissioning (vv. 5-7).

a) *The Introductory and Concluding Scene:*
The Coming and Going Away of the Women (v. 1, 8)

The introductory and the concluding verses form an inclusion:

¹Ὀψὲ δὲ σαββάτων, τῇ ἐπιφωσκούσῃ εἰς μίαν σαββάτων
ἦλθεν Μαριὰμ ἡ Μαγδαληνὴ καὶ ἡ ἄλλη Μαρία θεωρῆσαι <u>τὸν τάφον.</u>

----

⁸ καὶ <u>ἀπελθοῦσαι</u> ταχὺ ἀπὸ <u>τοῦ μνημείου</u> μετὰ φόβου καὶ χαρᾶς μεγάλης ἔδραμον
ἀπαγγεῖλαι τοῖς μαθηταῖς αὐτοῦ.

Synonymous and antonymous words forming a Semitic inclusion, give an indication of the interrelationship between the introductory and the concluding verses. Various vocabulary items call for special attention.

If the introductory scene describes the two women's coming (ἦλθεν) to the sepulcher, the concluding scene, tells of their going away (ἀπελθοῦσαι) from the tomb of Jesus. These antonyms (ἦλθεν and ἀπελθοῦσαι) have the same root verb (ἔρχομαι, ἀπ-έρχομαι).

If in the introductory scene the Evangelist uses the word τάφος, in the concluding scene he uses its synonym μνημεῖον to designate the tomb of Jesus.

If the phrase θεωρῆσαι τὸν τάφον (v. 1b) shows the purpose of the women's coming to the sepulcher, the phrase ἀπαγγεῖλαι τοῖς μαθηταῖς αὐτοῦ (v. 8b) speaks of the purpose of their going away from the tomb. Matthew begins the passage with the coming of the women, and he ends the passage with the women's going away from the tomb. An inclusion marks the passage.

b) *The Second Scene: The Angel's Action and the Guards' Reaction (vv. 2-4)*

The phrase καὶ ἰδοὺ gives an indication of a new scene which is composed of two parts: a) the angel's action (vv. 2-3) and b) the guards' reaction (v. 4). The scene has the following structure:

2 καὶ ἰδοὺ σεισμὸς ἐγένετο μέγας·
ἄγγελος γὰρ κυρίου *καταβὰς ἐξ οὐρανοῦ καὶ προσελθὼν*
ἀπεκύλισεν τὸν λίθον καὶ ἐκάθητο ἐπάνω αὐτοῦ.
3 ἦν δὲ ἡ εἰδέα αὐτοῦ   ὡς ἀστραπὴ
καὶ τὸ ἔνδυμα αὐτοῦ   λευκὸν ὡς χιών.

----

4 ἀπὸ δὲ τοῦ φόβου αὐτοῦ
ἐσείσθησαν οἱ τηροῦντες καὶ ἐγενήθησαν ὡς νεκροί.

The key root that unites the two parts is σεισ from σείω, designating a «shaking». Matthew uses the same root in order to show its effect on the guards: *ἐσείσθησαν οἱ τηροῦντες καὶ ἐγενήθησαν ὡς νεκροί* (v. 4). Experiencing the earthquake, the guards become like dead men, leaving the women as the main characters who can witness the event.

c) *The Third Scene: The Angel's Message to the Women and the Commissioning (Matt 28:5-7)*

Matthew arranges this scene under two parts: the first part describes the angel's message to the women (vv. 5-6), while the second part tells of the angel's commissioning of the women (v. 7). Both parts placed together form the following structure:

5 ἀποκριθεὶς δὲ ὁ ἄγγελος *εἶπεν* ταῖς γυναιξίν,
 <u>Μὴ φοβεῖσθε</u> ὑμεῖς, οἶδα γὰρ ὅτι Ἰησοῦν τὸν ἐσταυρωμένον ζητεῖτε·
6 οὐκ ἔστιν ὧδε, ἠγέρθη γὰρ καθὼς *εἶπεν·*
δεῦτε <u>ἴδετε</u> τὸν τόπον ὅπου ἔκειτο.

----

7 καὶ ταχὺ <u>πορευθεῖσαι</u>   <u>εἴπατε</u> τοῖς μαθηταῖς αὐτοῦ
ὅτι Ἠγέρθη ἀπὸ τῶν νεκρῶν,
καὶ ἰδοὺ προάγει ὑμᾶς εἰς τὴν Γαλιλαίαν, ἐκεῖ αὐτὸν <u>ὄψεσθε·</u>
ἰδοὺ *εἶπον* ὑμῖν.

Four factors give a structural unity to this scene. The first factor concerns the verb ἠγέρθη, a technical word that designates Jesus' resurrection (ἠγέρθη γὰρ καθὼς εἶπεν, v. 6a; Ἠγέρθη ἀπὸ τῶν νεκρῶν, v. 7b), and which forms the central message of the scene. The second element that unites both parts is the verb εἶπον («tell») which is used in every verse in the scene (vv. 5-7). Its presence at the beginning and at the end of the scene marks an inclusion. The third factor that gives a structural unity is the mention of Ἰησοῦς (v. 5b) and αὐτὸν ὄψεσθε (v. 7a). The fourth factor that adds to the unity of the text is Matthew's use of five imperatives, namely, Μὴ φοβεῖσθε, δεῦτε, ἴδετε, πορευθεῖσαι, and εἴπατε.

All four factors together make clear the central message, which is the resurrection of Jesus (ἠγέρθη). The resurrection is first announced to the women (ταῖς γυναιξίν), who in turn were to communicate it to Jesus' disciples (εἴπατε τοῖς μαθηταῖς αὐτοῦ).

d) The Four Scenes Taken Together as a Single Unit (Matt 28:1-8)

All the scenes put together form the following structure:

¹Ὀψὲ δὲ σαββάτων, τῇ ἐπιφωσκούσῃ εἰς μίαν σαββάτων
    ἦλθεν _Μαριὰμ ἡ Μαγδαληνὴ καὶ ἡ ἄλλη Μαρία_ θεωρῆσαι τὸν τάφον.

        ²καὶ ἰδοὺ σεισμὸς ἐγένετο μέγας·
        ἄγγελος γὰρ κυρίου καταβὰς ἐξ οὐρανοῦ καὶ προσελθὼν
        ἀπεκύλισεν τὸν λίθον καὶ ἐκάθητο ἐπάνω αὐτοῦ.
        ³ἦν δὲ ἡ ἰδέα αὐτοῦ ὡς ἀστραπὴ καὶ τὸ ἔνδυμα αὐτοῦ λευκὸν ὡς χιών.
        ⁴ἀπὸ δὲ τοῦ φόβου αὐτοῦ
        ἐσείσθησαν οἱ τηροῦντες
        καὶ ἐγενήθησαν ὡς νεκροί.

            ⁵ἀποκριθεὶς δὲ ὁ ἄγγελος εἶπεν _ταῖς γυναιξίν,_
            Μὴ φοβεῖσθε ὑμεῖς, οἶδα γὰρ ὅτι Ἰησοῦν τὸν ἐσταυρωμένον ζητεῖτε·
            ⁶οὐκ ἔστιν ὧδε, ἠγέρθη γὰρ καθὼς εἶπεν·
            δεῦτε ἴδετε τὸν τόπον ὅπου ἔκειτο.

    ⁷καὶ ταχὺ πορευθεῖσαι   εἴπατε τοῖς μαθηταῖς αὐτοῦ
    ὅτι Ἠγέρθη ἀπὸ τῶν νεκρῶν,
    καὶ ἰδοὺ προάγει ὑμᾶς εἰς τὴν Γαλιλαίαν, ἐκεῖ αὐτὸν ὄψεσθε·
    ἰδοὺ εἶπον ὑμῖν.
⁸καὶ ἀπελθοῦσαι ταχὺ ἀπὸ τοῦ μνημείου
μετὰ φόβου καὶ χαρᾶς μεγάλης ἔδραμον   ἀπαγγεῖλαι τοῖς μαθηταῖς αὐτοῦ.

The literary device that justifies Matt 28:1-8 as a passage distinct in itself is provided by the inclusion formed by the explicit notice of the women's entrance into (ἦλθεν Μαριὰμ ἡ Μαγδαληνὴ καὶ ἡ ἄλλη Μαρία θεωρῆσαι τὸν τάφον, v. 1b) and going away from (ἀπελθοῦσαι ταχὺ ἀπὸ τοῦ μνημείου, v. 8) the scene,[7] thus presenting them as important characters in the narrative along with the angel of the Lord who is the main protagonist[8]. The women's coming to see the sepulcher (v. 1), the angel's consolatory greeting (v. 5b), the resurrection announcement addressed solely to the women (v. 6), his invitation to see the empty tomb (v. 6b), his commissioning them to tell the disciples (v. 7) and finally their going away from the tomb to tell the disciples (v. 7) describe the important role the women play in the resurrection narrative (Matt 28:1-8). The women's importance is further emphasized when the risen Jesus appears first to them on their way to communicate the resurrection message to the disciples (vv. 9-10).

4.2 Passage Two: The Risen Jesus' Appearance to and the Commissioning of the Women (Matt 28:9-10)

We now discuss the second passage (vv. 9-10), the various factors that delimit it and its various compositional features.

4.2.1 The Factors that Delimit the Passage

Three important factors, namely, the context, location and characters, mark it as a separate unit. Using the phrase καὶ ἰδού, Matthew changes the scene from the empty tomb narrative (28:1-8) to the scene of Jesus' appearance to the women (vv. 9-10). There is a shift from Angelophany to Christophony[9]. The second factor concerns the location. The text is not very clear about the location of the event. Evidently the women are running away from the tomb to tell the disciples when the risen Jesus will appear to them. This gives an indication of a different location away from the tomb. The third factor concerns the characters. It is no longer the angel who appears and speaks to the women, but the risen Jesus himself. The risen Jesus is the central character, the women being the only audience of Jesus' appearance and message.

---

[7] R. MEYNET, Jésus passe, 367.
[8] S. GRASSO, Matteo, 217.
[9] F. NEIRYNCK, «Le femmes au tombeau», 168-190.

4.2.2 The Compositional Features

Matt 28:9-10 is composed of two parts: a) the risen Jesus' appearance to the women (v. 9) and b) the risen Jesus' commissioning of the women (v. 10). The following structural presentation helps us to understand this passage[10]:

28:9 καὶ ἰδοὺ *Ἰησοῦς* ὑπήντησεν αὐταῖς λέγων,
    Χαίρετε.
        αἱ δὲ προσελθοῦσαι ἐκράτησαν αὐτοῦ τοὺς πόδας
                καὶ προσεκύνησαν αὐτῷ.
10 τότε λέγει αὐταῖς ὁ *Ἰησοῦς,*
    Μὴ φοβεῖσθε·
        ὑπάγετε   ἀπαγγείλατε   τοῖς ἀδελφοῖς μου
        ἵνα ἀπέλθωσιν εἰς τὴν Γαλιλαίαν, κἀκεῖ με ὄψονται.

Two principal factors add to the structural unity of this passage. The first factor that gives unity to the text is the repetition of the name Ἰησοῦς (9a; 10a). Jesus is the central character. He is the one who takes the initiative to talk to the women[11]. The second factor that gives unity to the scene is the two imperatives that Matthew employs: a) Χαίρετε (v. 9b) and b) Μὴ φοβεῖσθε (v. 10a). If the first imperative is positive, the second imperative is negative. Both of them are addressed clearly to the women.

4.3 *Both Passages Taken Together (Matt 28:1-10)*

The passage about the angel's appearance to and the commissioning of the women (vv. 1-8) is closely related to Jesus' appearance to and the commissioning of the women (vv. 9-10). Two factors relate the passages together: the consolatory greeting (vv. 5, 9) and the commissioning of the women (vv. 7, 10).

The angel's consolatory greeting addressed to the women (Μὴ φοβεῖσθε ὑμεῖς, v. 5) seems to parallel the greeting of the risen Jesus (Μὴ φοβεῖσθε, v. 10).

The second factor that links the two passages is the double commission that the women receive: a) from the angel and b) from the risen Jesus:

---

10 See R. MEYNET, *Jésus passe*, 372.
11 L. SWAIN, *Reading the Easter Gospels*, 28.

Matt 28:7	Matt 28:10
καὶ ταχὺ πορευθεῖσαι	ὑπάγετε
εἴπατε	ἀπαγγείλατε
τοῖς μαθηταῖς αὐτοῦ	τοῖς ἀδελφοῖς μου

Jesus' commissioning of the women seems almost to be a doublet of the angel's own commissioning of the women. These two factors together suggest how these two passages are related to each other. Matthew uses the empty tomb episode and the appearance of Jesus to the women as two signs that explain the single reality of the resurrection of Jesus (Matt 28:1-10).

4.4 *Matt 28:1-10 in the Context of 27:51b-61.*

We would now like to look at how Matt 28:1-10 is related to Matt 27:51b-61, which we discussed in the third and fourth chapters[12]. This will help us to identify the significant role that Matthew assigns to the women in the death (27:55-56), burial (27:61) and resurrection narratives (28:1-10).

There exists a linguistic as well as a thematic correlation between Matt 27:51b-61 and 28:1-10[13]. Five elements help us to explain our position: a) the presence of the women (27:55-56, 61; 28:1); b) the presence of the guards (Matt 27:51b; 28:3); c) the description of the resurrection of the dead (27:52-53; 28:6); d) the rolling away of the stone (27:60; 28:2); e) the sitting posture of the women and the angel (27:61; 28:2).

---

[12] Scholars seem to hold divergent opinions on the passages on the passion, death and resurrection narratives. We enumerate some of them. According to D. Senior, the Matthean passion narrative ends with Matt 27:55-56 (see D. SENIOR, *The Passion,* 328). C.H. GIBLIN, explains the burial-resurrection narrative beginning with the coming of Joseph of Arimathea, omitting any reference to the women in vv. 55-56 («Structural and Thematic Correlation», 406-420). Other authors have interpreted 28:1-10 within the frame of 27:62-66 and 28:11-15. See P. GAECHTER, *Matthäus,* 945; X. LÉON-DUFOUR, *Résurrection,* 203-204; R. MEYNET, *Jésus Passe,* 370-371; J. CABA, *Cristo,* 161-176; N. WALTER, «Eine vormatthäische Schilderung», 415-429; D.J. HARRINGTON, *Matthew,* 408; S. GRASSO, *Il vangelo di Matteo,* 215.

[13] See R. PRENTER, «La Testimonianza», 65-74; R.H. SMITH, *Matthew,* 332.

4.4.1 The Presence of the Women

The first factor that suggests the interrelationship between these passages is the presence of the women at the cross and the tomb (27:55-56, 61; 28:1). Three elements, the identity of these women, their purpose for coming to the tomb of Jesus, and finally, a temporal indicator showing the time when the women come to the tomb, confirm this view.

The first element concerns the identity of the women. The women who have witnessed the death (27:55-56) and the burial of Jesus (27:61) now witness to the empty tomb and Jesus' appearance, which are two classical signs of the resurrection (28:1-10). Matthew mentions two women on all three occasions. Thus the identity of these women adds to the relatedness of the different passages on the death, burial and resurrection narratives.

The second feature concerns the purpose of the women's coming to the sepulcher. According to Matthew the women come to «see the sepulcher» (θεωρῆσαι τὸν τάφον, 28:1). The verb used is θεωρέω. The only other usage of this verb in Matthew is found in 27:55, where the women are described as watching from afar (ἀπὸ μακρόθεν θεωροῦσαι, 27:55). The verb θεωρέω here has as its object the events at Golgotha, namely perhaps the darkness and the earthquake. The rending of the temple veil and the bodies of the saints coming out of the tombs obviously could not be witnessed by them. As the two women have witnessed the earthquake (27:51b), so too they now probably witness another earthquake accompanied by the angel of the Lord descending from heaven, although the Evangelist does not specify it[14]. The Evangelist continues to portray these women as witnesses not only of Jesus' death (27:55) and burial (27:61) but also of the empty the tomb (28:1). The verb θεωρέω, which indicates the women's action, thus links the empty tomb episode with the preceding passages on the death and burial of Jesus. In this connection Matthew's use of the substantive τάφος (27:61; 28:1b) is also worth mentioning. In 27:61 the women are described as «sitting in front of the sepulcher» (καθήμεναι ἀπέναντι τοῦ τάφου, 27:61). The same women now come «to see the sepulcher» (θεωρῆσαι τὸν τάφον, 28:1b). In both instances, the word τάφος is used.

The third element concerns the time indicator of the women's coming to the tomb. Joseph of Arimathea, a disciple of Jesus, goes to Pilate to ask for the body of Jesus ὀψίας δὲ γενομένης (27:57). The phrase

---

[14] J.P. MEIER, *Matthew*, 360.

ὀψίας δὲ γενομένης indicates the time of the burial. The women come to see the tomb ὀψὲ δὲ σαββάτων, τῇ ἐπιφωσκούσῃ εἰς μίαν σαββάτων (28:1), which designates the time when the angel announces the resurrection of Jesus and invites the women to see the empty tomb. There is an explicit mention of a time indication. Jesus is buried in the «evening» (27:57) and the tomb is discovered empty on the morning of the third day after the death, as Jesus himself had predicted (26:32).

4.4.2 The Soldiers at the Tomb

The second factor concerns the presence of the guards under the cross and at the tomb. Matthew alone speaks of an earthquake in association with the death of Jesus (27:51b). Similarly Matthew alone speaks of an earthquake taking place at the resurrection of Jesus (28:3). In both instances the guards are described as present at the earthquake. On both occasions the response of the guards is one of fear (27:54; 28:4), but with a difference. In 27:54 the centurion and the men with him watching Jesus are frightened (ἐφοβήθησαν σφόδρα) seeing the earthquake (σεισμός) and the other things that happened . This fear led them to the first Christian confession: ᾽Αληθῶς θεοῦ υἱὸς ἦν οὗτος (27:54). In 28:4, too, there is a mention of fear: ἀπὸ δὲ τοῦ φόβου αὐτοῦ ἐσείσθησαν οἱ τηροῦντες καὶ ἐγενήθησαν ὡς νεκροί. In contrast to the guards who are shaken (ἐσείσθησαν) seeing the earthquake (σεισμός) and become like dead men (ἐγενήθησαν ὡς νεκροί, 28:4)[15], Matthew does not clearly speak of any such reaction on the side of the women[16]. But the angel's consolatory message («do not be afraid») indicates that the women were also frightened.

4.4.3 The Resurrection of the Dead

The third factor that unites both passages is the verb ἐγείρω (27:52; 28:6, 7), a technical word designating Jesus' resurrection in the Gospel. In 27:52 Matthew speaks of the resurrection of κεκοιμημένων ἁγίων ἠγέρθησαν. The phrase which follows immediately, μετὰ τὴν ἔγερσιν αὐτοῦ («after his resurrection»), refers to the resurrection of Jesus him-

---

[15] J. P. MEIER, *Matthew*, 361; G. LÜDEMANN, *Die Auferstehung Jesus*, 158-161; P. SEIDENSTICKER, *Die Auferstehung*, 87; N. WALTER, *Schilderung*, 417-422; G.T. MONTAGUE, *Matthew*, 321.
[16] D. PATTE, *The Gospel according to Matthew*, 395.

self. Later Matthew uses the same verb to speak of Jesus' resurrection (28:6, 7). There is a striking verbal similarity. In both instances Matthew employs the aorist passive form of the verb (ἠγέρθη), indicating God as the agent of the resurrection.

What Matthew indicates in 27:53 (μετὰ τὴν ἔγερσιν αὐτοῦ) is realized in 28:6 (ἠγέρθη γὰρ καθὼς εἶπεν). Evidently Jesus is the «first fruits of those who have died» (1Cor 15:20).

4.4.4 The Rolling away of the Stone

The fourth factor that links Matt 28:1-10 with 27:51b-61 is the angel's action of rolling the stone away from the tomb.

Only Matthew mentions how the stone is removed from the door of the tomb: the angel of the Lord «rolled back the stone» (ἀπεκύλισεν τὸν λίθον). Now the angel's action is described as opposite to the action of Joseph of Arimathea[17].

If Joseph of Arimathea closes the tomb of Jesus with a big stone and goes away, the angel of the Lord comes and rolls the stone away from the door of the tomb and sits on it (28:2)[18]:

προσκυλίσας λίθον μέγαν τῇ θύρᾳ τοῦ μνημείου ἀπῆλθεν (Matt 27:60)

προσελθὼν ἀπεκύλισεν τὸν λίθον καὶ ἐκάθητο ἐπάνω αὐτοῦ (Matt 28:2).

If the former closes the body of Jesus in the tomb and thus keeps Jesus' body in the realm of the dead (27:60), the latter opens the tomb of Jesus to free Jesus from Sheol and show that he is not there, giving evidence of the realm of new life (28:2)[19].

Matthew's repetition of several vocabulary items, namely ἀποκυλίω, προσκυλίω, λίθος, ἀπέρχομαι, and προσέρχομαι, adds to the interrelationship between Matt 28:1-10 and 27:51b-61.

---

[17] J. P. HEIL, «Narrative Structure», 430; ID., *The Death and Resurrection of Jesus*, 98.

[18] The angel's rolling away of the huge stone shows the power of God. See J.P. MEIER, *The Vision of Matthew*, 209; W.D. DAVIES – D.C. ALLISON, *Matthew*, 665.

[19] The purpose of rolling away the stone is not told specifically. In the Gospel of Peter the stone is rolled away in order to let Jesus out (Pet 9:37-10:42).

4.4.5 The Sitting Posture of the Angel and the Women (27:61; 28:2)

The fifth factor that adds to the unity of Matt 28:1-10 and 27:51b-61 is the verb κάθημαι. Matthew uses an identical verb to designate the posture of the women (27:61) as well as of the angel (28:2)[20]:

Matt 27:61 καθήμεναι ἀπέναντι τοῦ τάφου (women)
Matt 28:2 ἐκάθητο ἐπάνω αὐτοῦ (angel)

At the end of our discussion on the compositional features of Matt 28:1-10 and its relation to Matt 27:51b-61, we see how Matthew has indicated the women as significant characters that link together the various events concerning the death, burial and the resurrection of Jesus.

5. **A Close Reading of the Text**

Nowhere in the canonical Gospels do we come across any portrayal of the actual resurrection itself[21]. It may be a reminder that the meaning and reality of the resurrection resist every attempt at objectification[22]. But every Gospel (including Mark's long ending) does contain several accounts of incidents associated with the resurrection of the Lord. As we have already indicated above, the Gospel of Matthew contains two such incidents: a) the empty tomb episode (28:1-8) and b) Jesus' appearance to the women (vv. 9-10).

5.1 *The Empty Tomb Episode (Matt 28:1-8)*

The compositional features have highlighted four little scenes: a) the women's coming to the tomb (v. 1); b) the angel's actions and the guards' reaction (vv. 2-4); c) the angel's message of the resurrection of Jesus and the commissioning of the women (vv. 5-7), and d) the women's reaction to the angel's message and commission (v. 8). Each scene calls for our special attention as it helps us to understand the women's importance.

---

[20] Sitting is a posture that is common in the passion, death and resurrection narratives: Peter and the guards, 26:58; the future Jesus in glory, 26:64; Pilate, 27:19; the soldiers at the cross, 27:36; the two Marys at the tomb, 27:61.

[21] See R.N. LONGENECKER, *Life in the Face of Death,* 108; J.P. MEIER, *Matthew,* 360.

[22] T. LORENZEN, *Resurrection and Discipleship,* 174.

5.1.1 The Women's Coming to the Tomb (28:1)

Three factors call our attention in the introductory scene: a) a double temporal indicator; b) the identity of the women (v. 1b), and c) the purpose of the women's visit to the tomb.

5.1.2 A Double Temporal Indicator (v. 1a)

The first factor that deserves our attention is a double temporal indicator, which Matthew uses in order to introduce the scene: Ὀψὲ δὲ σαββάτων, τῇ ἐπιφωσκούσῃ εἰς μίαν σαββάτων[23]. NT scholars have variously interpreted this temporal indicator in Matthew[24].

Among the various scholars who have tried to give an interpretation of the double temporal indicator, L. Sabourin, E.L. Bode, K.H. Reeves, P. Benoit, W. Hendriksen, M. Green and M.R. Thompson call for special mention. L. Sabourin thinks that by using a double temporal indica-

---

[23] Divergent translations and the number of researches on this Matthean temporal indicator itself speak for the special attention given to this issue. We feel that a right understanding of this issue will help us to explain the time indication of the empty tomb event, and the women as the principal witnesses to it.

The two temporal indicators are ὀψὲ δὲ σαββάτων and τῇ ἐπιφωσκούσῃ εἰς μίαν σαββάτων. The first one, ὀψὲ δὲ σαββάτων, has been variously translated: «late on the Sabbath» (A.H. McNEILE, *The Gospel according to Matthew*, 429), «after the Sabbath» (L.L. MORRIS, *The Gospel according to Matthew*, 735). For a detailed discussion on the problems associated with the translation of the phrase ὀψὲ δὲ σαββάτων see K.H. REEVES, *The Resurrection Narrative*, 52-53; G.R. DRIVER, «Two Problems», 327-337.

The second temporal indicator, τῇ ἐπιφωσκούσῃ εἰς μίαν σαββάτων, has also been variously translated. D.A. HAGNER – E.L. BODE translate it as «at the dawn of the first day of the week», i. e., «Sunday morning». See D.A. HAGNER, *Matthew 14-28*, 868; E.L. BODE, «A Liturgical Sitz im Leben», 237-42.

For a further discussion on this double temporal indicator see J.M. WINGER, «When did the Women Visit the Tomb: Sources for Some Temporal Clauses in the Synoptic Gospels», 284-288; R.T. FRANCE, *Matthew*, 406; E. SCHWEIZER, *Good News according to Matthew*, 523; ID., *Jesus*, 79; W. GRUNDMANN, *Das Evangelium nach Matthäus*, 569; W. WIEFEL, *Das Evangelium nach Matthäus*, 489; H. FRANKMÖLLE, *Matthäus Kommentar 2*, 518.

[24] From among the various English translations, we prefer to use the RSV's translation: «Now after the Sabbath, towards the dawn of the first day of the week». Following are some of the other translations of this double temporal indicator: «Now late on the Sabbath, as it began to dawn towards the first day of the week», (NASB); «In the end of the Sabbath, as it began to dawn towards the first day of the week» (KJV); «After the Sabbath, as Sunday morning was dawning», (TEV). See J.P. MEIER, *Matthew*, 360; See also A. FEHRIBACH, *The Women*, 150.

tor Matthew combines the Markan phrase καὶ διαγενομένου τοῦ σαββάτου («and when the Sabbath was past», Mark 16:1a) with καὶ λίαν πρωΐ τῇ μιᾷ τῶν σαββάτων («very early on the first day of the week», 16:2a), i. e., the day of the Lord[25].

According to E.L. Bode, K.H. Reeves and P. Benoit, Matthew's intention is to add precision and intensity to the resurrection narrative[26]. Similarly W. Hendriksen maintains the position that by making use of a double temporal indicator Matthew probably wants to emphasize the exact time when the women went to the tomb of Jesus: in the evening, after the Sabbath, namely, the dawn of the day, Sunday morning[27], which M. Green calls symbolic of a dawning new age[28]. M.R. Thompson observes that by making reference to the exact time, Matthew emphasizes the fact that the women set out for the tomb exactly when the Sabbath rest has been completed[29].

In agreement with the opinions of E.L. Bode and W. Hendriksen, we think that Matthew's description of a double temporal indicator is probably to add precision and exactness to the resurrection narrative[30]. Making use of a double temporal indicator Matthew perhaps wants to make clear that the women visited the tomb of Jesus at the dawn of «the third day»[31] after the death of Jesus[32].

---

[25] L. SABOURIN, Matthew, 927.

[26] E.L. BODE, The First Easter Morning, 13; K.H. REEVES, The Resurrection Narrative, 52; See P. BENOIT, The Passion and Resurrection of Jesus, 246.

[27] See W. HENDRIKSEN, The Gospel of Matthew, 987.

[28] M. GREEN, The Message of Matthew, 313.

[29] M. R. THOMPSON, Mary Magdalene, 39.

[30] See W.L. CRAIG, «The Empty Tomb of Jesus», 173-200; ID., «The Historicity», 39-67; ID., «Did Jesus Rise from the Dead»?, 141-176; G.E. LADD, «The Resurrection and History», 247-156.

[31] Compare: 1Cor 15:4; Acts 10:40; Mark 8:31 (Par Matt 16:21; Luke 9:22), 9:31 (Par Matt 17:23;), 10:34 (Par Matt 20:19) Luke 18:33); Matt 27:63; Luke 24:7, 46. For a discussion on other texts that make reference to the «three days» see K. LEHMANN, Auferweckt am dritten Tag, 159-176. W.L. CRAIG, «The Historicity», 36-67.

In Jewish thinking, the reference to the third day had an important soteriological thrust: God would restore the sick nation on the third day (Hos 6:2); Moses met God on Mount Sinai on the third day (Exod 19:16).

[32] L. PACOMIO, Gesù, 252; A.M. HUNTER, The Work and Words of Jesus, 155; J. LAGRAND, The Earliest Christian Mission, 225-226.

5.1.3 The Identity of the Women (v. 1b)

The second factor that calls for our attention in the initial scene is the Matthean identity of the women at the tomb. Matthew mentions only two women: Μαριὰμ ἡ Μαγδαληνὴ and ἡ ἄλλη Μαρία. As elsewhere in the Gospel, Mary Magdalene is mentioned first in the list, a position that is confirmed by other Evangelists also[33]. The context suggests that the designation of ἡ ἄλλη Μαρία is presumably Μαρία ἡ τοῦ Ἰακώβου καὶ Ἰωσὴφ μήτηρ in 27:56, who is also identified as ἡ ἄλλη Μαρία in 27:61[34]. In Matthew these are the same women who followed Jesus from Galilee and who now witness to the death and burial of Jesus (27:55, 61). Matthew carefully preserves the names of «Mary Magdalene and the other Mary» as the principles of continuity regarding Jesus' death (27:56), burial (27:61) and the empty tomb (28:1-8).

5.1.4 The Purpose of the Women's Visit to the Tomb

The third factor concerns the purpose of the women's coming to the sepulcher. The specific purpose of their visit to the tomb is to the see the sepulcher (θεωρῆσαι τὸν τάφον, 28:1)[35]. That the women come pre-

---

[33] See G. O' COLLINS – D. KENDALL, «Mary Magdalene», 631-646.

[34] D. A. HAGNER, Matthew 14-28, 868; W.D. DAVIES – D.C. ALLISON, Matthew, 665.

[35] Unlike Mark (16:1) and Luke (24:1) Matthew does not say that the women come to anoint the body of Jesus with spices. On the significance of anointing see T.R.W. LONGSTAFF, «The Women at the Tomb», 278-281; W. LOCKTON, The Resurrection and the Virgin Birth, 32.

Matthew's omission of the women's intention of anointing the body of Jesus may be due to the following reasons. First, a symbolic anointing of Jesus has already been done at Bethany (Matt 27:6-13). Second, an anointing is perhaps impossible because of the guards at the tomb (27:62-66). Matthew's mention of the guards at the tomb would seem to explain the women's intention of simply seeing or visiting the tomb. They could not have done anything else in Matthew, because the guards would not permit them.

According to Matthew, the sole purpose of the women's visit is «to see the sepulcher». See R.E. BROWN, A Risen Christ in Eastertime, 27; P. PERKINS, Resurrection, 127; X. LÉON-DUFOUR, Résurrection de Jésus, 154; L.T. TISDALE, «Matthew 28:1-10», 63-68; R.H. FULLER, The Formation of the Resurrection Narratives, 74-75; M. DIBELIUS, From Tradition to Gospel, 297-298. See F.W. BEARE, Matthew, 542; L. SABOURIN, Matthew, 927.

Although we are told that the women come «to see the sepulcher», we do not know the reason for their coming. U. WILCKENS, Die Pericope, 30-41. F. NEIRYNCK, «Le femmes au tombeau», 176; J. LAGRAND, Earliest Christian Mission, 230; T. LONGSTAFF, «The Women at the Tomb», 278.

cisely to «see the sepulcher», according to W. Carter, makes them potential witnesses to the resurrection of Jesus[36]. This is in agreement with the women's identifying activity in 27:55 and their posture of vigilant sitting in front of the tomb in 27:61. Their coming to the sepulcher leaves open the possibility that during their following of Jesus from Galilee to Jerusalem they might have heard Jesus' predictions that he would be raised up on the third day (16:21; 17:22-23 and 20:18-19). This is more evident in Luke 24:6-8 in which two men in dazzling clothes say to the women: «Remember how he told you, while he was in Galilee, that the Son of Man must be handed over to sinners, and be crucified, and on the third day rise again».

To conclude, Matthew begins the scene introducing the time, the place of the event, and the main characters in the scene. The time is clearly defined: «after the Sabbath, toward the dawn of the first day of the week». The location is indicated: «the tomb of Jesus». The characters are also identified: «Mary Magdalene and the other Mary». Finally Matthew marks the intention of their visit to the tomb: «to see the sepulcher». In short, the Matthean narration is clear in describing the Matthean identity of the women at the tomb (v. 1), an identity that links the resurrection scene with the scenes on the aftermath of the death and burial scenes (27:55-56, 61).

5.1.5 The Appearance of the Angel and the Guards' Reaction (Matt 28:2-4)

Having first described the women's coming to the sepulcher on the Easter morning, Matthew describes the appearance of the angel and the guards' reaction. This scene contains two parts: a) the action of the angel of the Lord (vv. 2-3) and b) the guard's reaction to it (v. 4).

a) *The Action of Angel of the Lord (28:2-3)*

The first factor that deserves mention in this second scene is the descending of the angel of the Lord. As mentioned elsewhere, Matthew alone describes an earthquake that happened immediately after the death of Jesus (27:51b)[37]: «...καὶ ἡ γῆ ἐσείσθη καὶ αἱ πέτραι

---

[36] W. CARTER, «To See the Tomb», 201-215; J.P. HEIL, *The Death and Resurrection*, 98; F. NEIRYNCK, «Le femmes au tombeau», 176.

[37] D.A. HAGNER, *Matthew 14-28*, 869; R.E. BROWN, *A Risen Christ*, 27; E. WAINWRIGHT, «The Gospel of Matthew», 664.

ἐσχίσθησαν». Similarly an earthquake prepares for the opening of Jesus' tomb (28:2-4), giving the resurrection narrative an apocalyptic color that links it with the power of God's judgment on His son's crucifixion (27:51b-53). Similar to the apocalyptic thematic attached to the earthquake in Matthew[38], the angel's appearance also contains an apocalyptic color[39]: ἦν δὲ ἡ εἰδέα αὐτοῦ ὡς ἀστραπὴ καὶ τὸ ἔνδυμα αὐτοῦ λευκὸν ὡς χιών. According to Matthew the angel of the Lord appears «like lightning», (see Dan 7:10; Matt 17:2; Rev. 1:16; 10:1; 12:1) and his garment is as white as snow. The lightning probably symbolizes the end-time power of God (Rev 8:5; 11:19; 16:18). Heavenly beings are spoken of as wearing garments white as snow[40].

Noteworthy is also the fact that only Matthew mentions how the stone is removed: ἀπεκύλισεν τὸν λίθον. Having rolled the stone away from the door of the tomb, Matthew describes the angel as sitting on the stone (ἐκάθητο ἐπάνω αὐτοῦ). The angelic posture of sitting prefigures Jesus who, having triumphed over death, would ascend to his seat in his everlasting kingdom[41]. The rolled back stone manifests the failure of human effort, specifically of death, to keep the body of Jesus in the tomb and thus prevent the resurrection. Now God's opening of the tomb through the instrument of the angel frees Jesus from death and allows the women to look in and see that Jesus is not there[42] because he has been raised up. The tomb could no longer hold Jesus' body within it[43].

b) *The Guards' Reaction (28:4)*

The second factor that calls our attention is the Matthean mention of an «earthquake» (σεισμός) at the appearance of the angel. For fear of

---

[38] See U. Luz, *Jesusgeschichte des Matthäus*, 153.

[39] See E.L. Bode, *The First Easter Morning*, 51; E.M. Wainwright, *Shall We Look for Another*, 113.

[40] A variety of functions have been suggested for white clothes. There is evidence that the priests generally wore white linen. See N. Lewis, *Life in Egypt under Roman Rule*, 92. In ancient times it was customary that the worshippers wear white garments or linen. See R.K. Sherk, ed., *The Roman Empire*, 58. White was considered good while black was considered evil (Dio. Laert. 8. 1. 34). Converts often dressed in white (Rev 3:4-5; 19:8, 14), angels often appeared in linen (Rev 15:6) or white garments (1Enoch 71:1).

[41] T.C. Oden – C.A. Hall, *Mark*, 243.

[42] G.T. Montague, *Companion God*, 321.

[43] T.C. Oden – C.A. Hall, *Mark*, 243.

him the guards were shaken (ἐσείσθησαν, 28:4). Elsewhere in Matthew an earthquake-like experience (σεισμός) causes the disciples to fear and to call on the sleeping Jesus in the boat (8:24-26). Once Matthew speaks of earthquakes as occurring in the future time of tribulation before the end (24:7)[44]. Matthew alone mentions an earthquake after the death of Jesus causing the rocks to be rent and the tombs to be opened. Consequently, God causes the resurrection of many dead saints of Israel (27:51-54). Finally Matthew mentions an earthquake before the coming down of an angel and the opening of Jesus' tomb (28:2). As a result of their fear of the angel (ἀπὸ δὲ τοῦ φόβου, 28:4) the guards «became like dead men» (ἐγενήθησαν ὡς νεκροί). The guards having become like dead men, the women remain the only live characters. This allows the angel to address the women alone[45], emphasizing the key role they play in the resurrection narrative.

5.1.6 The Angelic Resurrection Message to the Women (28:5-7)

The third scene concerns the angel's words addressed solely to the women (ἀποκριθεὶς δὲ ὁ ἄγγελος εἶπεν ταῖς γυναιξίν, v. 5a), which consists of a consolatory greeting (v. 5), the resurrection announcement (v. 6) and a commission with a two-fold message (v. 7).

a) *The Angel's Consolatory Greeting to the Women (28:5)*

The first important factor concerns the angel's consolatory words. The immediate effect of the angel's appearance is seen on the guards (ἐσείσθησαν . . . καὶ ἐγενήθησαν ὡς νεκροί, 28:4), but the angel's words are directed only towards the women: ἀποκριθεὶς δὲ ὁ ἄγγελος εἶπεν ταῖς γυναιξίν (v. 5a)[46]. Here Matthew draws a contrast between the women and the guards. The guards, who stood to guard the tomb, have become like dead men[47], and by contrast the women, who were considered inferior witnesses in the contemporary social cultural world, become the sole witnesses. In contrast to the guards who have become like dead men, Jesus has been raised to life[48].

---

[44] W. CARTER, *Matthew and the Margins,* 544; D.C. ALLISON, *The End,* 47-48.

[45] G.T. MONTAGUE, *Companion God,* 321.

[46] J.P. MEIER, *Matthew,* 360; W. GRUNDMANN, *Matthäus,* 569; H. BLOEM, *Ostererzählung,* 11.

[47] According to the Gospel of Peter 8-11, the guards are presented as witnesses to the resurrection. U. LUZ, *Jesusgeschichte,* 153.

[48] See P.S. MINEAR, «Matthew 28:1-10», 59-63.

b) *The Angel's Resurrection Announcement to the Women (28:6)*

The second important factor concerns the resurrection announcement. Having consoled the women, the angel announces the resurrection message, which is also directed only to the women: Οὐκ ἔστιν ὧδε, ἠγέρθη γὰρ καθὼς εἶπεν· δεῦτε ἴδετε τὸν τόπον ὅπου ἔκειτο. The resurrection message consists of an assertion and an interpretation. First there is an assertion which is authoritative: Οὐκ ἔστιν ὧδε. Second, there is an interpretation of the assertion: ἠγέρθη γὰρ, «for he has been raised», which is also the reason why «he is not here»[49]. The expression ἠγέρθη (aorist passive) refers to God as the acting agent of Jesus' resurrection[50]. God raised Jesus. The phrase that follows, καθὼς εἶπεν, affirms that Jesus' resurrection has happened according to what Jesus himself had predicted (16:21; 17:23; 20:19). Further the phrase «δεῦτε ἴδετε τὸν τόπον ὅπου ἔκειτο», gives supporting evidence to it, thus inviting «the testimony of sight to confirm this declaration»[51]. This seems to correspond to the women's motive of coming: θεωρῆσαι τὸν τάφον (28:1)[52]. The angel invites the women to see the sepulcher (v. 6c), because they have come «to see the sepulcher» (v. 1). When we put together the angel's consolatory words to the women and the resurrection message, we get following structure for vv. 5-6[53]:

[5]Μὴ φοβεῖσθε ὑμεῖς,
οἶδα γὰρ ὅτι
Ἰησοῦν τὸν ἐσταυρωμένον ζητεῖτε·

[6]οὐκ ἔστιν ὧδε,
ἠγέρθη γὰρ καθὼς εἶπεν·
δεῦτε ἴδετε τὸν τόπον ὅπου ἔκειτο.

The angel's words to the women including the commissioning are arranged in a sequential order as they consist of a 'comfort' (μὴ φοβεῖσθε ὑμεῖς, v. 5a), an «understanding» (οἶδα γὰρ ὅτι Ἰησοῦν τὸν ἐσταυρωμένον ζητεῖτε)[54], an «assurance» (ἠγέρθη γὰρ καθὼς εἶπεν·

---

[49] R. FABRIS, *Matteo*, 564; E.L. BODE, *The First Easter Morning*, 53.

[50] D.A. HAGNER, *Matthew 14-28*, 870.

[51] W.D. DAVIES – D.C. ALLISON, *Matthew*, 667.

[52] See F. NEIRYNCK, «Le femmes au tombeau», 176; U. WILCKENS, *Die Pericope vom leeren Grabe Jesu*, 30-41.

[53] See R.H. GUNDRY, *Matthew*, 589.

[54] ἐσταυρωμένον ζητεῖτε refers to the reality of the death of Jesus. H. FRANKMÖLLE, *Matthäus*, 520.

δεῦτε ἴδετε τὸν τόπον ὅπου ἔκειτο), and a «command» (καὶ ταχὺ πορευθεῖσαι εἴπατε τοῖς μαθηταῖς αὐτοῦ ... καὶ ἰδοὺ προάγει ὑμᾶς εἰς τὴν Γαλιλαίαν, ἐκεῖ αὐτὸν ὄψεσθε· ἰδοὺ εἶπον ὑμῖν)[55]: Jesus whom the women seek has been raised up and they will see him.

c) *The Angelic Commission of the Women (28:7)*

The third factor that merits our attention is the angel's commissioning of the women: καὶ ταχὺ πορευθεῖσαι εἴπατε τοῖς μαθηταῖς αὐτοῦ ὅτι Ἠγέρθη ἀπὸ τῶν νεκρῶν, καὶ ἰδοὺ προάγει ὑμᾶς εἰς τὴν Γαλιλαίαν, ἐκεῖ αὐτὸν ὄψεσθε· ἰδοὺ εἶπον ὑμῖν. Having consoled the women and having communicated the resurrection message, the angel of the Lord now commissions the women: καὶ ταχὺ πορευθεῖσαι εἴπατε τοῖς μαθηταῖς αὐτοῦ (28:7). The content of the commission is «to go quickly» (ταχὺ πορευθεῖσαι) «to his disciples» (τοῖς μαθηταῖς αὐτοῦ) and «tell» (εἴπατε) them «that he has been raised from the dead» (ὅτι Ἠγέρθη ἀπὸ τῶν νεκρῶν) by God, which became the cornerstone of the kerygma of the early Church (Acts 3:15; 4:10; 13:30; Rom 10:9; 1Cor 15:4-5, 42)[56]. The speed with which the women must go shows the urgency. They must immediately communicate to the disciples what has happened: «He has been raised up». Here Matthew seems to anticipate the reunion of the disciples with Jesus in Galilee and the final commission in 28:16-20, which is the climax of the entire Gospel, a discipleship story[57]:

28:7 καὶ ταχὺ πορευθεῖσαι   εἴπατε τοῖς   μαθηταῖς αὐτοῦ
28:19   πορευθέντες οὖν   μαθητεύσατε πάντα τὰ ἔθνη,

The angel's commission of the women consists of two messages that are to be carried to the disciples. The first message is ὅτι ἠγέρθη ἀπὸ τῶν νεκρῶν («that he has been raised from the dead»). The second message is καὶ ἰδοὺ προάγει ὑμᾶς εἰς τὴν Γαλιλαίαν. ἐκεῖ αὐτὸν ὄψεσθε («and behold he is going ahead of you to Galilee; there you will see him»)[58]. The content of the first message is the very reality of

---

[55] M. GREEN, *The Message of Matthew*, 313; D. PATTE, *The Gospel according to Matthew*, 395.

[56] G.T. MONTAGUE, *Companion God*, 320; W.D. DAVIES − D.C. ALLISON, *Matthew*, 666-667.

[57] J.D. KINGSBURY, *Matthew as a Story*, 57; J. NISSEN, *New Testament and Mission*, 26.

[58] H.N. HENDRICKX, *Resurrection Narratives*, 39.

Jesus' resurrection: ὅτι 'ηγέρθη ἀπὸ τῶν νεκρῶν. The content of the second message (προάγει ὑμᾶς εἰς τὴν Γαλιλαίαν ἐκεῖ αὐτὸν ὄψεσθε, 28:7) recalls Jesus' own words recorded in 26:32: μετὰ δὲ τὸ ἐγερθῆναί με προάξω ὑμᾶς εἰς τὴν Γαλιλαίαν[59]. These promising words are repeated by the risen Jesus in 28:10 and later realized in 28:16-17, when the disciples finally meet the risen Jesus in Galilee[60].

5.1.7 The Women's Reaction (28: 8)

The fourth and the final scene of the empty tomb narrative ends with the women's departing from the tomb of Jesus: καὶ ἀπελθοῦσαι ταχὺ ἀπὸ τοῦ μνημείου ... ἀπαγγεῖλαι τοῖς μαθηταῖς αὐτοῦ. Their response to the angel corresponds to the command of the angel:

καὶ ταχὺ πορευθεῖσαι   εἴπατε τοῖς μαθηταῖς αὐτοῦ ... (Matt 28:7)
καὶ ἀπελθοῦσαι ταχὺ   ... ἔδραμον ἀπαγγεῖλαι τοῖς μαθηταῖς αὐτοῦ (Matt 28:8)

The vocabulary of vv. 7-8 suggests that the women did precisely what the angel commanded them to do. They depart with fear and great joy, a response that is appropriate to the divine manifestation in Matthew (2:10; 14:26). They have fear, because they have experienced the divine majesty[61]. They have great joy because of the message of Jesus' resurrection which they received from the angel and which they have to communicate to the disciples immediately[62].

The women's reverential fear mixed with great joy refers to their recognition of the divine power in the resurrection of Jesus and the angel's authority to commission them.

---

[59] See W. HENDRIKSEN, *The Gospel of Matthew*, 987; R. FABRIS, *Matteo*, 564; J.P. HEIL, *The Death and Resurrection*, 101.

[60] W.D. DAVIES – D.C. ALLISON, *Matthew*, 668; P. GIBERT, *La résurrection du Christ*, 63-64.

For the significance of Galilee see, A. HENNESSY, *The Galilee of Jesus*, 20-38. For more on Galilee and Jesus see M. JOUETTE, «The Galileans», 243-257. R.A. BATEY, «Is not this the Carpenter?», 249-258; K. MACLEISCH, «The Land of Galilee», 832-65; G. O'COLLINS, *What are They Saying about Jesus*; E.S. MALBON, «Galilee and Jerusalem», 242-255. ID., «The Jesus», 363-277.

[61] W. TRILLING, *Das Evangelium nach Matthäus*, II, 340.

[62] W.D. DAVIES – D.C. ALLISON, *Matthew*, 668.

5.2 *The Appearance of Jesus to the Women (Matt 28:9-10)*

Matthew's Gospel records two appearances of the risen Jesus. Jesus' first appearance is to the women, who worship him and whom he instructs to communicate to «my brethren» that they will see him in Galilee (28:9-10). The second appearance is to the eleven disciples on a mountain in Galilee (28:16-20), where Jesus gives them a final commission. Both these appearances are typically Matthean[63].

5.2.1 The Risen Jesus' Greeting of the Women (28: 9a)

If the empty tomb narrative ends with the women's going away from the tomb, the appearance story begins with Jesus' meeting and greeting them on the way. The women who left the tomb «with fear and great joy» (μετὰ φόβου καὶ χαρᾶς μεγάλης), are met by Jesus whom they recognize immediately (contrast Luke 24:16; John 20:14). Jesus is the one who takes the initiative to meet and greet the women: χαίρετε («rejoice», «be glad»)[64]. Significantly, the first word spoken by the risen Jesus in Matthew, χαίρετε, is addressed specifically to the women[65].

5.2.2 The Women's Reaction to the Risen Jesus (28: 9b)

Having described Jesus' meeting with the women (v. 9a), Matthew describes their immediate reaction: αἱ δὲ προσελθοῦσαι ἐκράτησαν αὐτοῦ τοὺς πόδας καὶ προσεκύνησαν αὐτῷ («And they came up and took hold of his feet and worshipped him»). These women recognize Jesus immediately and respond to him appropriately. Matthew describes their reaction towards the risen Jesus making use of three phrases:

προσελθοῦσαι αὐτοῦ («they came to him»)
ἐκράτησαν αὐτοῦ τοὺς πόδας («grasped his feet»)
καὶ προσεκύνησαν αὐτῷ («worshipped him»)

---

63 M.E. BOISMARD, *Synopse*, 446-447; E. SCHWEIZER, *The Good News according to Matthew*, 523; L. SABOURIN, *Matthew*, 391.

64 This greeting perhaps replaces the Hebrew or Aramaic *shalom*, meaning «peace». See M.E. BOISMARD, *Synopse*, 446; F. NEIRYNCK, «Le femmes au tombeau», 177; H.B. SWETE, *The Resurrection*, 11.

65 K.B. OBSORNE, *The Resurrection of Jesus*, 51.

a) προσελθοῦσαι αὐτοῦ

The verb ἔρχομαι in a very general sense means to «come» or «go»[66]. Some form of the participle προσελθών («approaching») before a finite verb (e.g., ἐκράτησαν, «they took hold») is found fifty-one times in Matthew and almost always points to a solemn moment[67]. This verb is used throughout the Gospel in order to describe the approach of the sick or other petitioners to Jesus (8:2, 5, 19, 25; 9:14, 20, 28; 13:10, 36; 15:30; 17:14; 18:21; 19:16; 20:20; 21:14; 26:7)[68]. Matthew uses the same verb in order to speak of the women's coming to Jesus in 28:9. The reason for their coming to Jesus is explained in the phrase which follows immediately: ἐκράτησαν αὐτοῦ τοὺς πόδας.

b) ἐκράτησαν αὐτοῦ τοὺς πόδας

The women who come to Jesus take hold of his feet. Matthew uses the verb κρατέω in order to express their reaction. In its first sense, this verb means «to be strong» or «to possess power»[69]. In the Synoptic Gospels, in general it designates «to arrest» (Mark 6:17; 12:12; 14:1; Matt 14:3) or «to seize» (Mark 3:21). This verb is also found used in a context of healing by Jesus (Mark 1:31, 5:41, Matt 9:25; Luke 8:54)[70]. What deserves our attention is Matthew's use of the verb κρατέω to express the women's reaction towards the risen Jesus[71]: ἐκράτησαν αὐτοῦ τοὺς πόδας. This has been variously interpreted. According to Frankmölle the women's action here refers to the *Leiblichkeit Jesus*[72]. That is to say, the risen Jesus has a body that can be touched, thus identifying the risen Jesus with the same Jesus who lived his earthly life (2:14, 21; 8:2-3, 15, 25; 9:25, 29; 14:31,36; 17:7; 18:2; 19:13,15; 20:34; 26:7, 12, 23, 26, 27, 49, 50, 67; 27:2, 26-31, 34, 35, 48, 59-60). On the women's action, G.T. Montague writes: «This gesture is theologically important for Matthew, for it shows that the women identify the risen Jesus as the same Jesus they had known in his earthly life, and they can physically touch him. Jesus is not a ghost; his body, however,

[66] See J. SCHNEIDER, «ἔρχομαι», 666-684.
[67] H.N. HENDRICKX, *Resurrection Narratives*, 41.
[68] D. SENIOR, *Passion Narrative*, 342.
[69] W. MICHAELIS, «κρατέω», 910-912.
[70] See F. FENNER, «Die Krankheit im NT», 90.
[71] W. MICHAELIS, «κρατέω», 911.
[72] H. FRANKMÖLLE, *Matthäus*, 528.

spiritualized, is still a body»[73]. According to L.L. Morris, W.D. Davies – D.C. Allison, in doing so the women symbolically recognized Jesus' kingship[74]. R.T. France is of the opinion that the women's action here designates an appropriate response of glad and reverent homage to Jesus, and the physical contact emphasizes the reality of the resurrection of Jesus[75]. We agree that the women's taking hold of Jesus' feet confirms their recognition of him as the risen Lord.

c) προσεκύνησαν αὐτῷ

The verb προσκυνέω means «to worship, do obeisance to, prostrate oneself before, do reverence to, welcome respectfully»[76]. Among the Synoptic Gospels, Matthew has the most frequent use of the verb προσκυνέω (Matt 2:2, 8, 11; 8:2; 9:18; 14:33; 15:25; 18:26; 20:20; 28:9, 17).[77] In Matthew it is often used in the context of epiphany stories (Matt 14:33; 28:17)[78]. The use of the verb προσκυνέω with (προσ)ἔρχομαι is common in Matthew[79]. Further, the verb προσκυνέω is frequently used with πίπτω «to fall down» (Matt 2:11; 4:9; 18:26; Acts 10:25; 1Cor 14:25; Rev 4:10; 5:14) or with a similar expression such as κρατέω τοὺς πόδας (28:9).

In Mark the verb προσκυνέω is used of a man with an unclean spirit who prostrates himself before Jesus (Mark 5:6) and of the soldiers who bend the knees in a mocking gesture in front of Jesus (Mark 15:19). In Matthew such usage sometimes refers to false worship (Matt 4:9), servile and vile homage (Matt 18:26). Sometimes it designates one's worshipful gesture or homage towards Jesus (Matt 14:33; 28:9, 17)[80]. Further it can designate an act of supplication (Matt 8:2; 9:18; 15:25; 18:26; 20:20) and adoration (Matt 2:1, 2, 11; 4:10)[81].

---

[73] See G.T. MONTAGUE, *Companion God*, 323.

[74] L.L. MORRIS, *The Gospel according to Matthew*, 739; See also W.D. DAVIES – D.C. ALLISON, *Matthew*, 659.

[75] R.T. FRANCE, *Matthew*, 409.

[76] W. BAUER, *Lexicon*, 723.

[77] Matthew13, Mark 2, Luke 3, John 11, Acts 4, 1Corinthians 1, Hebrews 2, and Revelation 24.

[78] See H. GREEVEN, «προσκυνέω», 763; C.S. KEENER, *Matthew*, 703.

[79] See Matt 2:2, 8; 8:2; 9:18; 15:25; 20:20; 28:9.

[80] J.M. NÜTZEL, «προσκυνέω», 174; See also H. GREEVEN, «προσκυνέω», 758-766; W.G. THOMPSON, *Matthew's Advice*, 214-215.

[81] B. WITHERINGTON, III, *Women in the Earliest Churches*, 173; F. NEIRYNCK, «Le femmes au tombeau», 178; H. GREEVEN, «προσεκυνέω», 764.

The women's gesture of worshipping Jesus becomes significant especially considering the disciples' own worship of Jesus in Galilee: καὶ ἰδόντες αὐτὸν προσεκύνησαν, οἱ δὲ ἐδίστασαν (28:17). Like the women, the disciples too worshipped Jesus (προσεκύνησαν). But in this latter instance, Matthew adds an element of non-recognition: οἱ δὲ ἐδίστασαν («but some doubted»)[82].

5.2.3 The Risen Jesus' Commission of the Women (28:10)

Matt 28:10 consists of Jesus' commissioning of the women: Μὴ φοβεῖσθε· ὑπάγετε ἀπαγγείλατε τοῖς ἀδελφοῖς μου ἵνα ἀπέλθωσιν εἰς τὴν Γαλιλαίαν, κἀκεῖ με ὄψονται. This is parallel to the angel's commissioning of the women in vv. 5-7[83]:

Matt 28:5-7	Matt 28:10
Μὴ φοβεῖσθε (v. 5)	Μὴ φοβεῖσθε·
πορευθεῖσαι εἴπατε τοῖς μαθηταῖς αὐτοῦ	ὑπάγετε ἀπαγγείλατε τοῖς ἀδελφοῖς μου
προάγει ὑμᾶς εἰς τὴν Γαλιλαίαν	ἵνα ἀπέλθωσιν εἰς τὴν Γαλιλαίαν,
ἐκεῖ αὐτὸν ὄψεσθε (v. 7)	κἀκεῖ με ὄψονται.

Jesus' commissioning of the women looks to be a doublet of the angel's own commissioning of them (28:7)[84].

Two elements draw our attention. The first element concerns the phrase μὴ φοβεῖσθε, which in Matthew is used by Jesus himself and is always addressed to the male-female followers of Jesus in a context of a theophany:

εὐθὺς δὲ ἐλάλησεν	[ὁ Ἰησοῦς] αὐτοῖς λέγων,	
	Θαρσεῖτε, ἐγώ εἰμι·	*μὴ φοβεῖσθε* (14:27)
καὶ προσῆλθεν	ὁ Ἰησοῦς καὶ ἁψάμενος αὐτῶν εἶπεν,	
	Ἐγέρθητε καὶ	*μὴ φοβεῖσθε* (17:7)
τότε λέγει αὐταῖς	ὁ Ἰησοῦς,	*Μὴ φοβεῖσθε* (28:10)

---

82 E.L. BODE, *The First Easter Morning*, 55.

83 See R. KÜHSCHELM, «Angelophanie», 556-565; H. FRANKMÖLLE, *Matthäus*, 528-530.

84 M.E. BOISMARD, *Synopse*, 446; F. NEIRYNCK, «Le femmes au tombeau», 183; W.D. DAVIES – D. C. ALLISON, *Matthew*, 659.

The second element concerns Jesus' commissioning of the women, which is similar to the angel's own commissioning. What interests us is the major difference that exists between the two commissions. If the angel of the Lord directs the women to go and tell «his disciples» (τοῖς μαθηταῖς αὐτοῦ, 28:7), the risen Jesus instructs them to go and tell «my brothers» (τοῖς ἀδελφοῖς μου, 28:10)[85]. Jesus calls the disciples the brothers[86]. Various interpretations have been given to this designation in 28:10. G.W. Trompf interprets it in terms of the Matthean theology of Christian brotherhood (18:15-35)[87]. A similar thought is shared by C.L. Blomberg who states: «Here Jesus portrays the Church as a brotherhood that manifests more equality than hierarchy, even if some functional differentiation between leaders and followers is clear from other Scriptures (cf. 1Peter 5:1-5; Heb 13:17)»[88].

For R.E. Brown: «This indicates that a new status will emerge for those who hear and believe in the resurrection: they become God's children and thus the brothers and sisters of Jesus»[89]. According to T.G. Long, Jesus' calling the disciples «brothers» indicates his forgiveness of their faults. In other words they remain laborers with him in the work of the Father[90]. Jesus acts mercifully as in the rest of the Gospel (Matt 9:6; 12:1-14). Commenting on τοῖς ἀδελφοῖς μου, H. Hendrickx writes: «That the risen Christ now speaks of "my brethren" and orders them to go to Galilee means a new foundation of the discipleship, which is related to what happened before in Galilee, and appears now as a final employment which will consist in making disciples of all nations»[91]. Jesus' sending of the women with a message to the disciples shows Jesus' initiative to be reconciled with the disciples, although they had abandoned him and fled during the passion[92].

---

[85] The address «my brothers» echoes earlier passages in the Gospel where the disciples of Jesus are described as the «family» of Jesus (12:49). See D. SENIOR, *Passion Narrative*, 342.

[86] J. FRIEDRICH, *Gott im Bruder?*, 233; G. STRECKER, *Der Weg*, 98; E. SCHWEIZER, *Good News according to Matthew*, 342.

[87] G.W. TROMPF, «The First Resurrection Appearance», 323.

[88] C.L. BLOMBERG, *Matthew*, 428.

[89] R.E. BROWN, *A Risen Christ*, 31.

[90] T.G. LONG, *Matthew*, 323; see also C.L. BLOMBERG, *Matthew*, 428.

[91] H.N. HENDRICKX, *Resurrection Narratives*, 43.

[92] K.B. OBSORNE, *The Resurrection of Jesus*, 52.

We may conclude that Jesus' appearance to the women is not a superficial insertion in the Markan source, but an element that gives the narrative clarity and precision. This gives a smooth transition between the account at the tomb (28:1-8) and Jesus' commission of the disciples in Galilee (28:16-20). By adding this particular material (vv. 9-10) Matthew highlights the central role that the women play in the Gospel[93].

For establishing the significant position that the women enjoy in the narrative, Matthew presents them as the first to experience the resurrection of Jesus: the first to come to see the tomb (v. 1); the only audience of the angel's resurrection message (v. 5); the first to be invited to see the tomb empty (v. 6); the first to be commissioned by the angel to communicate the resurrection message to the disciples (v. 7); the first to set out to spread the resurrection message (v. 8); the first to see the risen Jesus and finally the first to be commissioned by the risen Jesus (vv. 9-10).

6. **Biblical Background**

We will now try to trace out some of the biblical passages which have probably influenced Matthew in the composition of 28:1-10. In this regard four elements call for our special attention: the earthquake (v. 2); the angel's appearance (v. 3); Jesus' consolatory greeting (v. 10a), and finally Jesus' commissioning of the women (v. 10b).

6.1 *The Earthquake (Matt 28:2; Isa 29:6; Ezek 37:7)*

The earthquake, an apocalyptic image both in the OT (Isa 29:6; Joel 2:10; 3:16; Isa 13:13; Jer 4:24; 51:29) as well as in the NT (Rev 8:5; 11:13; 16:18; Matt 24:7; Mark 13:8; Luke 21:11)[94], refers to the apocalyptic nature of the resurrection of Jesus[95]. Matthew's mention of an earthquake in association with the resurrection of Jesus closely parallels the similar mention of an earthquake at the death of Jesus that is accompanied by the resurrection of the holy ones (27:51b-53). On both

---

93 See U. WILCKENS, *Resurrection*, 48-50.

94 W. WIEFEL, *Matthäus*, 489.

95 E.L. BODE, *The First Easter Morning*, 51; R.E. BROWN, *A Risen Jesus of Eastertime*, 28; J.P. MEIER, *Matthew*, 360-361; G.T. MONTAGUE, *Companion God*, 321; R. FABRIS, *Matteo*, 563; See J.P. MEIER, *Matthew*, 360; D.A. HAGNER, «Gospel», 113; D.C. ALLISON, *The End*, 48.

occasions it refers to divine intervention[96]. God is at work in the resurrection of Jesus.

6.2 *The Appearance of the Angel (Matt 28:3; Dan 7:9)*

The Matthean description of the angel's appearance (28:3) echoes Dan 10:6 and 7:9. Structural and lexical similarity suggest a theophany[97]:

ἦν δὲ ἡ *εἰδέα*   αὐτοῦ ὡς   ἀστραπὴ ... (Matt 28:3)
καὶ τὸ *πρόσωπον* αὐτοῦ ὡσεὶ ὅρασις ἀστραπῆς ...(LXX, Dan 10:6)

καὶ τὸ ἔνδυμα αὐτοῦ λευκὸν ὡς   χιών (Matt 28:3)
τὸ ἔνδυμα αὐτοῦ   ὡσεὶ   χιὼν λευκόν (LXX Theodotion, Dan 7:9)

Further, the Matthean description of the angel corresponds to the appearance of the transfigured Jesus to his disciples: «And he was transfigured before them, and his face shone like the sun, and his garments became white as snow» (17:2)[98]. Matthew uses similar language on both occasions (Matt 28:3 and 17:2)[99]:

Matt 28:3	Matt 17:2
καὶ ἔλαμψεν τὸ πρόσωπον αὐτοῦ ὡς ὁ ἥλιος,	ἦν δὲ ἡ εἰδέα αὐτοῦ ὡς ἀστραπὴ
τὰ δὲ ἱμάτια αὐτοῦ ἐγένετο λευκὰ ὡς τὸ φῶς.	καὶ τὸ ἔνδυμα αὐτοῦ λευκὸν ὡς χιών.

6.3 *Μὴ φοβεῖσθε ὑμεῖς (Matt 28:5; LXX Gen 15:1; 21:17; 26:23)*

The angel's consolatory greeting (Μὴ φοβεῖσθε ὑμεῖς) reflects a similar usage (Μὴ φοβοῦ) in the OT (God to Abram, LXX, Gen 15:1; the angel of the Lord to Hagar, 21:17; God to Isaac, 26:23) and in the

---

[96] R.E. BROWN, *The Death of the Messiah*, II, 1126; F.W. DANKER, «God With Us», 437-438; W. CARTER, *Matthew and the Margins*, 545; C.A. JARVIS, «Matthew 28:1-10», 59-63.

For earthquakes as instances of cosmic phenomena associated with the death of heroes see M.E. BORING, ed., *Hellenistic Commentary*, 161-162, 166-67; R.H. MATTHEW, *Matthew*, 332; D.J. WEAVER, «Matthew 28:1-10», 399-402; W.D. DAVIES – D.C. ALLISON, *Matthew*, 667; K. GREEN, *The Message of Matthew*, 314.

[97] J. Jeremias reduces OT theophany to two elements: the coming of God and repercussions in nature. According to him the theophanies tell more or less of Yahweh's coming in storm, thunder and lightning, ... etc. See J. JEREMIAS, *Theophanie*, 100; X. LEON-DUFOUR, *Résurrection de Jésus*, 191-194; J. CABA, *Cristo*, 165.

[98] J. CABA, *Cristo*, 165.

[99] D.J. HARRINGTON, *Matthew*, 408.

NT (the angel of the Lord to Zacharias, Luke 1:13.30, the angel of the Lord to the shepherds, 2:10). In all the instances, the phrase refers to a divine assurance given to the human beings.

6.4   ὑπάγετε ἀπαγγείλατε τοῖς ἀδελφοῖς μου (Matt 28:10; LXX Psa 22:22)

The Risen Lord's commission to the women with the message ὑπάγετε ἀπαγγείλατε τοῖς ἀδελφοῖς μου seems to reflect the words of the unjustly persecuted in Psa 22:22[100]:

διηγήσομαι   τὸ ὄνομά σου   τοῖς ἀδελφοῖς μου ... (Psa 22:22)
ὑπάγετε ἀπαγγείλατε   τοῖς ἀδελφοῖς μου ... (Matt 28:10)

The Gospel of Matthew builds on OT themes, some of them reflecting apocalyptic overtones since the Jewish apocalyptic writings refer to earthquakes and apparitions by angels to indicate God's intervention at the end of the world. These signs in Matthew reflect more of a theological and symbolic significance than a historical one[101].

7. Interpretation

Our analysis of the text brings us to a threefold interpretation of the women's role in the resurrection narrative: a) Major witnesses to the resurrection of Jesus; b) The first announcers of the resurrection message, and c) the women and the discipleship theme.

7.1 The Major Witnesses to the Resurrection of Jesus

By the word «witnesses» we mean those who have first hand knowledge of facts and events. By «major witnesses» we intend to refer to those persons whose testimony is of greater importance. By «resurrection» we mean the unique act by which God has transformed and raised from the dead forever the person Jesus to his right hand (Gal 1:1)[102].

The Synoptic writers portray many women headed by Mary Magdalene as witnesses to the resurrection of Jesus (Mark 16:1-8; Matt 28:1-10; Luke 23:56b–24:10), while John names only one woman (Mary

---

100 R.H. GUNDRY, *Matthew*, 590 W. WIEFEL, *Matthäus*, 489; H.N. HENDRICKX, *Resurrection Narratives*, 43; J. SCHNIEWIND, *Das Evangelium nach Matthäus*, 271.
101 See K.B. OBSORNE, *The Resurrection of Jesus*, 50.
102 G. O'COLLINS, *Interpreting the Resurrection*, 22-23.

Magdalene) as the witness to the empty tomb of Jesus (John 20:1-29). The canonical Gospels agree in presenting Mary Magdalene as the major witness.

Such a statement faces a challenge. It concerns the absence of the women in the oldest tradition known to us: καὶ ὅτι ὤφθη Κηφᾷ εἶτα τοῖς δώδεκα· [6]ἔπειτα ὤφθη ἐπάνω πεντακοσίοις ἀδελφοῖς ἐφάπαξ, ἐξ ὧν οἱ πλείονες μένουσιν ἕως ἄρτι, τινὲς δὲ ἐκοιμήθησαν· [7]ἔπειτα ὤφθη Ἰακώβῳ, εἶτα τοῖς ἀποστόλοις πᾶσιν· [8]ἔσχατον δὲ πάντων ὡσπερεὶ τῷ ἐκτρώματι ὤφθη κἀμοί (1Cor 15:5-8)[103].

According to this tradition, the risen Jesus appeared first to Κηφᾶς (the Aramaic name given to Simon, Greek Πέτρος), then to «the Twelve» (τοῖς δώδεκα)[104]. This tradition does not speak of Jesus' appearance to any woman. Does it mean that Paul was not aware of the appearance stories recorded by the Evangelists or that he was simply repeating an old tradition?

Scholars have given various reasons why Paul does not speak of the female characters, whom the canonical Gospels without exception portray as the major witnesses of the risen Jesus. F. Bovon understands the absence of the women in the oldest account of the resurrection tradition in terms of Paul's interest in compromising between the Judeo Christianity of Jerusalem, represented by Peter and James, and that of the Hellenistic world, represented by Paul himself. He argues that for Paul it was necessary to omit the name of Mary Magdalene from the kerygmatic list because of the social, religious and cultural setup of the time. He enumerates three possible reasons why Paul did not include the women as the first witnesses to the resurrected Jesus: a) the people from a Jewish background would not accept a woman's testimony; b) the Church was concentrating on setting up a ministry of males hostile to the prophetic ministry; c) the mention of a woman as the first to witness to the risen Jesus would detract from Peter and Paul, on whom the early Church was focussing[105].

M. Green shares a similar view when he writes: «Paul found this rather trying: the women are significantly absent from his list of resur-

---

[103] This text perhaps dates back to within a year or two of the events themselves, for it was 'traditional' by the time of Paul's conversion, which cannot have been later than the mid 30s. See P. GIBERT, *La Résurrection du Christ*, 18-35; C. KANNENGIESSER, *Foi en la résurrection*, 31-59.

[104] On the significance of this tradition in Paul's letter to the Corinthians, see J.M. SHAW, *The Resurrection of Christ*, 22-45; P. PERKINS, *Resurrection*, 222-223.

[105] F. BOVON, «Le privilège pascal», 50-62.

rection witnesses in 1Corinthians 15. This is not the supposed Pauline anti-feminism at work. He is simply giving evidence for the resurrection that would stand scrutiny in a court of law»[106].

T. Lorenzen holds: «Nevertheless, a healthy suspicion must also remind us that there was a tendency in the earliest churches to downplay the role of women, and to highlight the witness of male disciples»[107].

J.S. Stone comments: «The testimony of the women has been set aside deliberately, on the ground that it would have had little weight with the Corinthians, and might have been ascribed to hysteria»[108].

G. O'Collins lists a number of solutions to the issue. He notes that the disparity between the traditional material (1Cor 15) and the Gospel accounts on the presence of the women may be due to the multiple traditions that existed side by side, one subordinate to the other[109].

D.J. Goergen, who recognizes various traditions, states: «Thus there is the Jerusalem-centered tradition focussed on the tomb and associated with the women, and Galilee-centered tradition focussed on the appearances and associated with Peter and the Eleven»[110].

We think that Paul did not mention any woman because of the historical fact that in first-century Judaism women were not generally qualified to testify in a court of law[111]. This situation seems to have continued throughout the centuries[112], although occasionally the women at the tomb, especially Mary Magdalene, were considered very important in the growth of the Church. We have some good examples for this. Hippolytus of Rome (300 AD) refers to the women at the tomb of Jesus as «apostles»[113]. Pope Leo the Great calls Mary Magdalene a «figure of the Church» («... *Maria Magadalene personam Ecclesiae gerens* ...»[114]. Pope Gregory the Great (600 AD) refers to her as another Eve who reveals life to males[115].

The absence of the women in the oldest tradition known to us does not discredit the presence of the women in the resurrection accounts in

---

106 M. GREEN, *The Message of Matthew*, 314.
107 T. LORENZEN, *Resurrection and Discipleship*, 140.
108 J.S. STONE, *The Glory After the Passion*, 111.
109 G. O'COLLINS, *Interpreting the Resurrection*, 36.
110 D.J. GOERGEN, *The Death and Resurrection*, 141.
111 JOSEPHUS, *Jewish Antiquities*, IV: 8, 15.
112 See ORIGEN, *Contra Celsum*, 2: 55.
113 HIPPOLYTUS OF ROME, *De Cantico*, 24- 26.
114 LEO THE GREAT, *De ascensione Domini serm*, 2: 4.
115 GREGORY THE GREAT, *De apparitione Christi*, 189.

the canonical Gospels. It may be wrong to think that the primitive Church obviously did not place any value on the testimony of the women. Such a claim is hardly compatible with the fact that all four Gospels report Jesus' tomb to have been found empty by one or more women.

Our investigation of Matt 28:9-10 in the previous sections of this chapter reveals how the Evangelist Matthew presents Mary Magdalene and the other Mary as major witnesses to the resurrected Jesus. Both in the empty tomb event as well as in the appearance story these two women are presented as the major witnesses.

In a social-cultural-religious background that did not value the testimony of a woman in a court of law, Matthew's presentation of the women as the primary witnesses to the most important events in human history speaks for itself about the truthfulness of the reality of the resurrection of Jesus. Had the story been fabricated, the natural tendency would have been to avoid any mention of the women.

Presenting the women as the primary witnesses to the resurrected Jesus, the Evangelist Matthew seems to convey how «God perpetuates the supreme irony of having two women as the first witnesses to his Son's resurrection»[116]. Such portrayal points to the dawning of a new age of equality among women and men in Christ (Gal 3:28)[117].

7.2 The First Announcers of the Resurrection Message

The Gospel of Matthew does not state that the women communicated the message to the disciples. It only describes the mission given to the women to announce. But, the fact that the risen Jesus could meet the disciples in Galilee indicates that certainly the women might have communicated the message to them. Their announcement of the resurrection message is based on the divine authority of the angel's telling them: ἰδοὺ εἶπον ὑμῖν (28: 7)[118]. The angel's message in turn confirms the reality of Jesus' own prediction of his resurrection: ἠγέρθη γὰρ καθὼς εἶπεν (v. 6)[119].

The angel's commissioning of the women in Matthew (v. 7) is confirmed by Jesus' own commissioning (v. 10), both of which together

---

[116] M. GREEN, The Message of Matthew, 313.

[117] See C.L. BLOMBERG, Matthew, 426; See M. GREEN, The Message of Matthew, 312.

[118] J.P. HEIL, The Death and Resurrection, 100.

[119] See J. LAGRAND, The Earliest Christian Mission, 225.

correspond to the final commission (28:16-20) with which the Gospel of Matthew comes to its climax[120]. Similarity, the structure and vocabulary make them parallel to each other:

Matt 28:7	Matt 28:10	Matt 28:19
καὶ ταχὺ πορευθεῖσαι	ὑπάγετε	πορευθέντες οὖν
εἴπατε	ἀπαγγείλατε	μαθητεύσατε
τοῖς μαθηταῖς αὐτοῦ	τοῖς ἀδελφοῖς μου	πάντα τὰ ἔθνη

Every commission begins with an imperative to go, which indicates immediacy of action: πορευθεῖσαι (v. 7), ὑπάγετε (v. 10), πορευθέντες (v. 19). Every command assigns a task to be completed: εἴπατε (v. 7), ἀπαγγείλατε (v. 10) and μαθητεύσατε (v. 19). Every commission is oriented towards a specific audience: τοῖς μαθηταῖς αὐτοῦ (28:7); τοῖς ἀδελφοῖς μου (28:10); πάντα τὰ ἔθνη (28:19). The angel commissions the women to tell «his disciples», (τοῖς μαθηταῖς αὐτοῦ, 28:7). Jesus commissions the women to tell «my brothers» (τοῖς ἀδελφοῖς μου, 28:10)[121]. Finally Jesus commissions the Eleven to make disciples of «all nations» (πάντα τὰ ἔθνη, 28:19)[122]. According to J.D. Kingsbury, Matthew here follows a «domino principle», namely, tell others so that the others tell others[123]. That is to say, the angel tells the women (28:5-6), the women tell the Eleven male disciples (see 28:8, 10; 16-20) and the Eleven male disciples in turn will tell all the nations (28:16-20). Thus we see an enlargement of the audience of the resurrection mes-

---

[120] See D.J. GOERGEN, *The Death and Resurrection*, 136.

[121] According to LaGrand, the phrase τοῖς ἀδελφοῖς μου here refers to the disciples with special emphasis perhaps on Jesus' identification with the 'new generation' as suggested in the genealogy (J. LAGRAND, *The Earliest Christian Mission*, 231).

[122] Some authors have interpreted the word ἔθνη as designating «Gentiles». According to them Jesus' mission is exclusively to the Gentiles (See D.J. HARRINGTON, «Make Disciples», 110-123; U. LUZ, *Jesusgeschichte des Matthäus*, 156-157. We think that this is not a correct understanding. It is hard to take 25:32 as being exclusive since it refers to a final judgment of the whole world. We think that the word is to be translated as «all peoples» and «races». This includes the Jews also. Such an explanation becomes more meaningful especially against the background of the death and resurrection of Jesus. The effect of Jesus' death and resurrection is that all boundaries have disappeared. Now «all nations», «peoples» or «races» have access to the Gospel of the kingdom. J. NISSEN, *New Testament and Mission*, 27.

[123] J.D. KINGSBURY, *Matthew*, 57.

sage: women (v. 5) – τοῖς μαθηταῖς αὐτοῦ, v. 7 (τοῖς ἀδελφοῖς μου, v. 10) and then πάντα τὰ ἔθνη (28:18)[124].

What is revealed first to a nucleus of faithful female followers of Jesus («Mary Magdalene and the other Mary») is now revealed to the Eleven disciples through whom the whole world comes to know the resurrection message. That is to say, Jesus' resurrection remains the decisive starting point for the worldwide mission of the Church[125]. Significantly Matthew presents the women as the catalysts, the first announcers and the first Christian missionaries of the resurrection message. Although their mission seems to be limited to communicating the message to the Eleven apostles, the fact that they are assigned such an important role in the Gospel is very significant[126]. J.P. Heil holds:

> As substitutes for the disciples who have been absent, the faithful Galilean women serve as the reliable intermediaries who are to link the disciples with the reality of Jesus' death, burial and resurrection. Empowered by the divine authority of the angel, the previously passive women actively begin to fulfill their role as authentic messengers of Jesus' resurrection[127].

The social aspect of Easter is evident. Jesus' appearance to the women was not a private vision simply for the devotion and edification of the women involved. The angel of the Lord and the risen Jesus entrust them with a message of reconciliation. That is to say, even though the male disciples had fled and some even rejected Jesus, Jesus now takes the initiative to meet them in Galilee and thus to reconcile them to himself. Jesus' calling the disciples «brothers» is indicative of reconciliation.

The significance of the women's presence lies not simply in having experienced the extraordinary phenomena, but in having listened to the angelic word and communicated it to the disciples[128]. From the above

---

[124] The implication is that it is through the death of Jesus that his teaching has become accessible to the Gentiles who are now destined to become members of the people of God. The mention of the Gentiles in 28:19 evokes the promise made to Abraham in Gen 12:1-2, a promise which Matthew has already evoked at the very beginning of the Gospel, both with reference to Abraham in 1:1, 2, 17 and with the story of the wise men in 2:1-18. What God promised to Abraham–the gathering of all the Gentiles as the people of God–is what Matthew presents as being realized through Jesus' death. See L. SWAIN, *Reading the Easter Gospels*, 35-36.

[125] N. PERRIN, *The Resurrection*, 48-49.

[126] C.A. PERRY, *The Resurrection Promise*, 23.

[127] J.P. HEIL, *The Death and Resurrection*, 101.

[128] L. SWAIN, *Reading the Easter Gospels*, 28.

discussion what becomes clear is the presence, commission, and special placement of women in the resurrection tradition. That the role of the Twelve came to be more operational and influential cannot be denied. This does not devalue the role of the women in the resurrection event but rather enhances it[129].

7.3 The Women and the Discipleship Theme

Matt 27:55 records that many women had followed Jesus from Galilee, among whom the Evangelist specifies three: Μαρία ἡ Μαγδαληνὴ καὶ Μαρία ἡ τοῦ Ἰακώβου καὶ Ἰωσὴφ μήτηρ καὶ ἡ μήτηρ τῶν υἱῶν Ζεβεδαίου. He mentions only two of these in 27:61 and 28:1. A structural presentation of the identity of these women helps us to understand some special Matthean features concerning them:

Matt 27:56	Matt 27:61	Matt 28:1
Μαρία ἡ Μαγδαληνή	Μαριὰμ ἡ Μαγδαληνὴ	Μαριὰμ ἡ Μαγδαληνὴ
Καὶ Μαρία ἡ τοῦ Ἰακώβου καὶ Ἰωσὴφ μήτηρ	καὶ ἡ ἄλλη Μαρία	καὶ ἡ ἄλλη Μαρία
καὶ ἡ μήτηρ τῶν υἱῶν Ζεβεδαίου	----------------------	----------------------

Such a presentation indicates three features: a) Mary Magdalene as the prominent female follower b) the abbreviation of the description of the second Mary from «Mary the mother of James and Joseph» to «the other Mary» in 27:61 and 28:1, and finally c) the absence of «the mother of the sons of Zebedee» in 27:61 and 28:1.

7.3.1 Mary Magdalene

Mary Magdalene appears to be an important witness to the death, burial, and resurrection of Jesus. She is identified by the place of her origin, Magdala[130]. We have already seen how Matthew's Gospel

---

129 K.B. OSBORNE, *The Resurrection Narrative*, 52.

130 The city from which Mary Magdalene comes is believed to be situated at the southern end of the plain of Gennesaret, on the west shore of the Sea of Galilee to the north of Tiberias. The proper name of this city does not occur in the Bible. But a de-

closely follows Mark for its description of this Mary as the primary witness to the death, burial and resurrection of Jesus (Matt 27:56, 61; 28:1). Matthew, however, departs from the Markan story in citing the names and purpose of the women who accompanied Mary Magdalene. Similarly, Matthew alters the women's immediate reaction at the empty tomb. Matthew, like the other Evangelists, says nothing of her parentage, marital status or age. What is striking about this woman in the Gospels is her devotion to Jesus.

When Jesus faces his ultimate humiliation and suffering, it is Mary Magdalene's fearless loyalty that stands out in boldest relief. Like the other Synoptics, Matthew also places this woman always first in list, probably to indicate the prominence she enjoyed in the final events of Jesus' story: his death, burial and resurrection (27:55-56, 57-61; 28:1-10). She plays a leading role.

7.3.2 The Other Mary

The second feature that calls our attention concerns the second woman whom Matthew calls ἡ ἄλλη Μαρία in 27:61 and 28:1. Although it is not easy to determine whom ἡ ἄλλη Μαρία designates[131], on the basis of the structural presentation which we have proposed above, as well as the fact that she is the last mentioned Mary with Mary Magdalene in v. 56, we think that it designates Μαρία ἡ τοῦ Ἰακώβου καὶ Ἰωσὴφ μήτηρ, «the mother of James and Joseph»[132].

Like Mary Magdalene, this «other Mary» has also followed Jesus from Galilee, serving him (27:55-56), and witnessing to the burial of Jesus (v. 61). She is also with Mary Magdalene on the way to the tomb

---

rived adjectival form Μαγδαληνὴ occurs in the NT (Matt 27:56, 61; 28:1; Mark 15:40, 47; 16:1, 9; Luke 8:2; 24:10; John 19:25, 20:1, 18) exclusively as a description of Mary, «the one/woman from Magdala» (R.F. COLLINS, «Mary», 579).

[131] Mark identifies the second woman as the «mother of James the Little and Joses» (15:40) while Matthew calls her «the Mother of James and Joseph» (27:56) and later «the other Mary» (v. 61). Luke calls a Mary at the tomb with Mary Magdalene the «[mother/wife] of James» (24:10). It is also possible that she is identical to Mary the wife/mother of Clopas in John 19:25.

[132] Basing themselves on Matt 13:55, some have argued that Matthew may be referring to the mother of Jesus. See R.H. GUNDRY, *Matthew*, 579. However this position does not seem to be acceptable. If Matthew is speaking of the Mother of Jesus he would most likely have said so, thus avoiding this ambiguous expression. See D. HILL, *The Gospel of Matthew*, 356; B. MCNEILE, *The Gospel According to St. Matthew*, 425; A. PLUMMER, *Matthew*, 367; L.L. MORRIS, *The Gospel according to Matthew*, 729; D. SENIOR, *The Passion Of Jesus*, 152.

on the Easter morning, she too receives the angelic message and commission (v. 1-8), and witnesses the risen Jesus (vv. 9-10).

Matthew's incorporation of this woman in the death, burial and resurrection narratives is possibly to highlight the absence of the male disciples, including two of her own sons, namely James and Joseph. In the
absence of the male disciples, this woman together with Mary Magdalene functions not only as a substitute for the twelve disciples but also
as the witness to Jesus' death, burial and resurrection[133]. Thus she too
plays an important role in reuniting the scattered disciples with the
risen Jesus (28:16-20).

7.3.3 The Mother of the Sons of Zebedee

The third feature that calls our attention is the presence of the mother
of the sons of Zebedee in 27:56 and later her absence in 27:61 and 28:1.
This woman is understood as the mother of James and John, the two
sons of Zebedee, two of the twelve apostles of Jesus (4:21; 10:2;
26:37), who together with Peter formed the nucleus group of three
whom Jesus often kept close to him.

In this connection her presence at a distance from the cross (27:55-
56) as well as her absence at the burial site (v. 61) and the empty tomb
(28:1-10) calls for special mention.

We now enumerate some important interpretations. Speaking of Matthew's replacement of the Markan «Salome» (15:40) with «the mother
of the sons of Zebedee», N. Perrin claims that the Matthean redaction is
not «theologically significant»[134]. A. Stock and L. Morris understand
the presence of this woman in Matt 27:56 as highlighting perhaps the
esteem and honor in which she was held in the Matthean community[135].
D.B. Howell and J.D. Kingsbury give no explanation as to why she is
mentioned in 27:56[136]. M.E. Boring has interpreted her presence in
27:56 as highlighting the male disciples' absence and the women's
playing of those roles which otherwise the male disciples should have

---

[133] See J.P. HEIL, *Death and Resurrection*, 94.

[134] M. PERRIN, *The Resurrection according to Matthew*, 41.

[135] A. STOCK, *Method and Message*, 429-30, 432; L.L. MORRIS, *The Gospel according to Matthew*, 726-27, 729;

[136] D.B. HOWELL, *Matthew's Inclusive Story*, 158, 183; J.D. KINGSBURY, *Matthew
as Story*, 158.

played[137]. D. Patte and E.M. Wainwright interpret the presence of the mother of the sons of Zebedee against the background of her presence in 20:20-23[138].

After having made an exploration of various narrative texts in the Hebrew Bible, ancient Greek romance novels and ancient biographies that pertain to men's and women's travels, E. Cheney concludes: «The presence of the mother of the sons of Zebedee in Mt. 20.20-21 and Mt 27.56, I propose, functions altogether differently. The mother's appearance in these two settings as well as her absence in Mt. 27.61 and 28:1 contributes towards defining discipleship in the Gospel of Matthew»[139]. Cheney's proposal gives us some assistance in understanding the significance of this woman, her presence as well as her absence.

Matthew does not reveal the name of this woman, but identifies her as «the mother of the sons of Zebedee». This identification refers back to 20:20-23, in which the woman, accompanied by her two sons, approaches Jesus in order to request a favor from him: «Say that these two sons of mine may sit, one at your right and one at your left, in your kingdom» (20:21)[140]. It is the mother who makes the request[141], but Jesus' answer is addressed to the sons: «Οὐκ οἴδατε τί αἰτεῖσθε. δύνασθε πιεῖν τὸ ποτήριον ὃ ἐγὼ μέλλω πίνειν». And the sons, not the mother, reply affirmatively «Δυνάμεθα» (v. 22). Jesus replies to them speaking of the authority of the Father to decide who will sit on the right and left of Jesus (v. 23). Jesus then differentiates between the rulers of the Gentile world and his true disciples (v. 25). Matt 20:26-27 is discipleship indicative: «But it shall not be so among you; whoever wishes to be great among you shall be your servant, and whoever wishes to be first among you shall be your slave». According to Matthew, service marks the true characteristic of a follower of Jesus (v. 27-28). The mother's request as well as Jesus' answer reflects the intense

---

137 See N. PERRIN, *The Resurrection*, 29-31; J.C. ANDERSON, «Matthew: Gender and Reading», 17-20.

138 D. PATTE, *The Gospel according to Matthew*, 391-395; E.M. WAINWRIGHT, *Toward a Feminist Critical Reading*, 119.

139 E. CHENEY, «The Mother», 16.

140 In making the request, she seems to play the traditional role of a mother who tries to secure the future of her sons. See for example, the assistance that Rebekah gives Jacob (Gen 27), that Sarah gives to Isaac (Gen 21), and that Bathsheba gives Solomon (1 Kgs 2:19-25).

141 In the Gospel of Mark it is not the mother who asks Jesus, but the sons themselves who request this of Jesus (Mark 10:35-45).

kind of discipleship required of the disciples (12:46-50; 16:24; 19:29). After her initial appearance in 20:20-21, the mother of the sons of Zebedee does not appear until after the death of Jesus (27:56). It is probable that she together with her sons continued to follow Jesus to Jerusalem (Matt 20:29; 21:1). The continuous loyal following of Jesus by this woman seems to explain her presence in the passion of Jesus. Especially against the background of the absence of the disciples, James and John, it looks as if this mother has faithfully followed Jesus, accepting the cup of suffering that Jesus offered her sons James and John, and which they claimed to be willing to drink (Matt 20:22)[142]. While the sons have promised to follow Jesus, it is their mother who actually keeps the word and stands alongside Jesus, thus in a way substituting for her sons[143].

By presenting these women at the cross (27:55-56) and tomb (28:61; 28:1-10) Matthew continues to emphasize their faithfulness to Jesus, set in contrast to the failure of the male disciples. Like any other Evangelist the flight of the disciples at the arrest of Jesus is an important theme for Matthew also. Although some scholars have tried to explain the flight of the male disciples as merely legendary[144], the NT evidence strongly favors the fact that the male disciples fled at the arrest of Jesus. Historically speaking, the earliest record does not acknowledge the presence of any of the Twelve male disciples at the cross, at the burial or at the empty tomb (Mark 15:40–16:8)[145]. The absence of the male disciples of Jesus makes the women's presence more emphatic. In their absence Matthew presents the women headed by Mary Magdalene as true discipleship models. They have followed Jesus from Galilee (ἠκολούθησαν τῷ Ἰησοῦ ἀπὸ τῆς Γαλιλαίας, 27:55), serving him (διακονοῦσαι αὐτῷ, v. 55). They witnessed the burial of the body of Jesus sitting in front of the sepulcher (v. 61). On the third day they came «to see the tomb» (28:1). They became the first to receive the resurrection message (v. 6), the first to witness the risen Jesus (vv. 9-10), and finally the first to be sent (vv. 7, 10). The fact that Jesus meets the eleven disciples in Galilee gives the indication that the women

---

142 E. M. WAINWRIGHT, «The Gospel of Matthew», 635-677.

143 See C.C. KROEGER – E. STORKEY, *The Women's Study,* 68.

144 See W. MARXEN, *Der Evangelist Markus,* 52.

145 For a discussion on the flight of the disciples see T. LORENZEN, *Resurrection and Discipleship,* 121-122.

really carried out the double commission they received: from the angel
(v. 7) and from the risen Jesus (v. 10).

8. Conclusion

Matthew assigns the female followers of Jesus special significance
preserving them as the primary witnesses to the empty tomb event
(28:1-8) and Jesus' appearance (vv. 9-10), both of which designate the
reality of Jesus' resurrection. By presenting the same women as the
witnesses to the death (27:55-56), burial (27:61) and the resurrection of
Jesus (28:1-10), Matthew presents them as the link that connects the
death and resurrection narratives together.

It is both a persistent and puzzling fact of the Matthean resurrection
stories that it was to the women followers of Jesus that the resurrection
is first announced and to whom the risen Jesus first appears. Numerous
features give us indications of the prominence of the women in the resurrection narrative as they are the first to come to see the tomb (v. 1),
the first to whom the resurrection is announced (v. 6), the first to whom
the risen Jesus appears (vv. 9-10), the first to be commissioned by the
angel (v. 7) as well as the risen Jesus (v. 10), and finally the first to
communicate the resurrection message (v. 8, 16-20). The women's continued and constant presence with Jesus highlights the absence of the
male disciples who have abandoned Jesus. These female figures are
entrusted with a message of reconciliation, that even though the male
disciples have fled and one has even denied Jesus, Jesus now takes the
initiative to meet them in Galilee and thus to reconcile them to himself.

GENERAL CONCLUSION

At the end of this exegetical journey through the Gospel of Matthew and its contemporary social-religious background, let us now briefly look back to assess the objective we set at the beginning of this work, the means we used to reach it, the plan we worked out, and finally the conclusion we have drawn.

It is a historically indisputable fact that the historical Jesus, during his earthly ministry, had several disciples around him. Such a discipleship phenomenon was not the monopoly of Jesus, because in the Greco-Roman period Jewish rabbis, philosophical and religious leaders gathered around themselves persons who were identified as followers, adherents, students or disciples. Despite several similarities between the various contemporary discipleship models, the NT discipleship was unique for various reasons. Different factors such as a direct call from Jesus, an immediate and literal following behind Jesus leaving all earthly ties in keeping with doing the will of God were considered basic features of the discipleship of Jesus. Naturally, anyone who fitted into such categories could therefore be called a disciple of Jesus. A technical word that designates such a person in the NT is μαθητής.

One phenomenon that adds to the question of discipleship in the NT is the continued presence of a group of women who followed Jesus from Galilee, serving him. They remained faithful to him till the end. A question that we raised in the introductory pages of this dissertation, and an answer thatb we have been seeking throughout our exegetical journey concerns the identity of these women followers in relation to Jesus: Can we speak of the discipleship of women in Matthew?

The data available to us is extremely sparse. All the scholars who have written on the women in the NT and their position in the Church, base their arguments on these sparse references to the women in the Gospels. The sources being very rare, a normal tendency found among recent scholars is to put undue pressure on the available texts to draw certain presumed and sometimes unwarranted conclusions. Such an exaggerated exegesis has often led to interpretations that the Evangelist probably never intended to convey.

We have tried to reach the above-mentioned objective, through an exegetical, biblical-rhetorical, and theological study of Matt 27:51b-56; 57-61 and 28:1-10. A study of the social, religious and cultural background of Matthew, and various passages that speak of the women's role in Jesus' ancestry (Matt 1:1-17) and the public ministry (Matt 8:14-17; 9:20-22; 15:21-28; 26:6-13), in the first two chapters of this dissertation, prepared a background and foundation for our research.

In the general introduction we discussed the important studies on the theme of disciples and discipleship in the NT in general and in the Gospel of Matthew in particular. We found that the major result of these studies is a basic consensus on some of the features of the NT discipleship model. Attention was drawn to the scarcity of serious Catholic exegesis on the topic of women as disciples of Jesus in comparison to the mounting literature on the same in Protestant exegetical circles. This highlighted the significance of the present study.

The first chapter discussed the social and religious status of women with special reference to first century Judaism and to the early Christian communities. While in the surrounding social, religious and cultural background women suffered great marginality, in the kingdom of God which Jesus inaugurated women were considered equal to men.

The second chapter presents an analysis of five passages concerning the life and ministry of Jesus and the women's role in them (1:1-17; 8:14-17; 9:20-22; 15:21-28; 26:6-13). This analysis arrives at a conclusion that despite the androcentric social cultural settings of the contemporary society, the Gospel narratives reflect various positive portrayals of women. Matthew, who depends mostly on Mark for his narratives of the women, has significantly edited his source. Both in the editorial modifications as well as in the structural features of the first Gospel, the women occupy a significant place throughout the Matthean Gospel, especially concerning the ancestry, life and ministry of Jesus. In comparison to several male characters as well as to the apostles themselves, on many occasions the female characters receive a favorable presentation in the Gospel. They play important roles in the messianic ancestry (Tamar, 1:3; Ruth, v. 5; Rahab, v. 5; the wife of Uriah, v. 6, and Mary, v. 16). They are examples of service (8:14-17), faith (9:20-22; 15:21-28) and love (26:6-13). All these passages imply certain aspects of the discipleship theme in the Gospel. Strikingly, none of these passages call any woman a disciple of Jesus. However, Matthew attributes to these women certain discipleship qualities.

Chapter three discussed the death of Jesus and the women's role. Matt 27:51b-56. The earthquake, the splitting of the rocks, and perhaps the opening of the tomb led the centurion and the men with him to make the first Christian confession: «Truly this was the Son of God». In comparison to these Gentile characters, the role of the women seems to be passive. But importantly Matthew uses some discipleship vocabulary to describe their relationship to Jesus: Ἦσαν δὲ ἐκεῖ γυναῖκες πολλαὶ ἀπὸ μακρόθεν θεωροῦσαι, αἵτινες ἠκολούθησαν τῷ Ἰησοῦ ἀπὸ τῆς Γαλιλαίας διακονοῦσαι αὐτῷ (Matt 27:55). Special attention was drawn to Matthew's use of the discipleship vocabulary ἠκολούθησαν τῷ Ἰησοῦ, and διακονοῦσαι αὐτῷ. Both in comparison to the Gentile soldiers under the cross, and the apostles who have fled, the women followers of Jesus manifest extraordinary faithfulness to Jesus. Matthew presents them as true witnesses of Jesus' death. This is something revolutionary as it resists certain social religious cultural regulations that devalued the worth of women.

In chapter four we discussed Matt 27:57-61, which concerns the burial of the body of Jesus. We gave special attention to certain words such as μαθητεύω, μαθητής and καθήμεναι ἀπέναντι τοῦ τάφου. Such a vocabulary study gave us an indication of a wider group of disciples. The whole passage highlights the absence of the Twelve. In their absence Matthew introduces Joseph of Arimathea as the disciple who carries out the duty of a disciple towards Jesus the master. In comparison to Joseph of Arimathea who buries the body of Jesus reverently, the women look to be passive onlookers. But once again the presence of the women manifests their extraordinary devotion. They remain faithful to Jesus even after his death. Through these male and female characters Matthew gives an indication that the discipleship of Jesus is not limited to the Twelve. That is to say, Jesus had disciples, male as well as female, other than the Twelve.

The fifth chapter discussed the role of women in the resurrection narrative. They were the first to come to see the tomb (28:1); the first to receive the angelic message of Jesus' resurrection (vv. 5-6); the first to be sent by the angel (v. 7); the first whom the risen Jesus meets (v. 9); the first whom the risen Jesus sends to the disciples (v. 10); the first to communicate the early Christian kerygma (v. 8, 11; and see vv. 16-20). The importance assigned to the women towards the end of the Gospel is highly significant especially in a social cultural setting that did not give women equal status with men.

In short, within the social and cultural context of the first century Mediterranean world we may identify a mixture of different positions about women and their role in society.

The New Testament gives a different picture of women. There are no absolute negative remarks about the nature, abilities and potential of women compared to men on the lips of Jesus in contrast to various Jewish authors. This means that Jesus had an estimation of the worth and validity of woman. Jesus rejected those attempts to devalue the worth of a woman and her word of witness. We find that the Gospels present the women as true witnesses of the truth about Jesus and especially about his death, burial, and the resurrection. Thus Jesus and his community granted to women together with men, an equal right that women did not have in contemporary Jewish world. Jesus respected them. Jesus' ministry was not limited to men alone. It included many women whose specific status and identity in relation to Jesus remain disputed.

In the course of this exegetical discussion on women in the Gospel of Matthew and their discipleship of Jesus, we have already come across several features that are unique to Matthew, especially when it concerns the Evangelist's vision of their discipleship of Jesus. But the question we raised at the beginning of this dissertation is yet to be answered: Can we speak of a discipleship of women in the first Gospel?

Perhaps, a simple way to answer this question is to see if the female followers met with the various discipleship requirements, which we have already highlighted in the general introduction of this work. Seeking an answer to this question, we are faced with at least two difficulties: a) the lack of a technical word that designates a woman disciple, and b) the lack of a clear call from Jesus.

The first difficulty in considering the women as disciples of Jesus concerns the lack of an appropriate vocabulary. The Synoptic Gospels, especially Matthew, use the plural of the word μαθητής in order to designate   disciples. The singular form of this word would designate a «male disciple». The plural form of this Greek word, οἱ μαθηταί, may convey an inclusive sense unless it is specified otherwise, an example of which we find in Luke 19:37, perhaps in Matt 12:49, and often in Acts, e.g., 11:26; 6:1,7; 9:1. Surprisingly neither the singular μαθητής nor its feminine form μαθήτρια is ever used in reference to a woman in the Gospels. Even Luke, who is believed to be most favorable to women, does not use the word μαθήτρια to designate a female disciple of Jesus in the Gospel, but he does use it of Tabitha in Acts 9:36. The women do not otherwise receive such an appellation. The second difficulty lies in the absence of a specific call from Jesus. Nowhere in the canonical Gospels do we find a description of Jesus' call of a woman to follow him.

Even if the Gospel does not call women «disciples», and even if neither the Gospel of Matthew, nor any other of the canonical Gospels, contains the description of Jesus' call of a woman, there are several other features that suggest that women followed Jesus and their following implied discipleship. In Matthew it is not any specific appellation that determines this, but function. Accordingly, whoever does the will of Jesus' heavenly Father becomes identified as a disciple in his new family (12:46-50). This suggests that Matthew's vision of discipleship is inclusive. This is clear from Matthew's genealogy which includes four OT women and Mary, the mother of Jesus. God used all four OT women in the process of fulfilling His will for our salvation. Matthew intends to show how God chose these women to bring about the presence the Messiah. This reached its culmination through the obedience of Joseph and Mary, through their total dedication to God's will.

Matt 27:55-56 speaks of some women who followed Jesus from Galilee. These women's following of Jesus (ἠκολούθησαν τῷ Ἰησοῦ) from Galilee (ἀπὸ τῆς Γαλιλαίας) and serving him (διακονοῦσαι αὐτῷ) become more intelligible especially against the background of the Matthean discipleship teaching. This explains their sitting in front of the sepulcher of Jesus (27:61), their coming to see the tomb (28:1), the angel's appearance and communication of the resurrection message to them (vv. 5-6), the angel's sending them to the disciples (v. 7), the risen Jesus' appearance to (v. 9) and sending of them to the disciples (v. 10) and finally their communicating the resurrection message to the disciples. The final commission context heightens such a discipleship reading (vv. 16-20).

Jesus' attitude toward a woman's right to religious training and to be a disciple was perhaps shocking to the Jews. Such a view did not fit into any of the categories of his day. Jesus appears to be a unique and sometimes radical reformer of the views regarding women and their roles that were commonly held among his people. Jesus had a transformed vision of the old patriarchal schema coupled with an affirmation of women's roles in the community of believers. In exposing the transformed vision of Jesus and the resulting variety of roles and tasks that women did assume in Jesus' community, the Synoptic Gospels present various protagonists who encapsulate the variety of missions that Christian women had in the Apostolic Church. As a result of this variety in their tasks the Synoptic tradition portrays some as leading women, while others as domestic actively participating and promoting the gift of salvation in Jesus Christ along and together with the men of their time. Even when there is no description of Jesus' calling these women to follow him, it is clear that Jesus accepted their continued accompaniment and service. There is no reason to think that Jesus did not consider them as his disciples. Their role as disciples in the Gospel becomes evident especially in the absence of the Twelve male disciples who fled Jesus in the hour of his passion and death. Among the different circles of disciples, the women formed a circle close to Jesus. However, the Twelve male disciples formed the leadership circle of disciples.

In the social, religious and cultural context of those nations in which women are often counted as marginal characters always inferior to men, where they lack freedom of movement and education, the Gospel message is one of liberation and equality. Especially against the background of the rural areas of Asia in which a female embryo is sometimes even denied the right to be born, or the new born female babies are abandoned merely because of their sex, where the parents and family members at times even lament and express their grief at the birth of a baby girl, while celebrating the birth of boy, where women are prohibited to appear in public or mingle freely in the public areas, the message of the divine word is one of liberation.

ABBREVIATIONS

Abbreviations throughout this study adhere for the most part to those proposed by S. SCHWERTNER, *Internationales Abkürzungsverzeichnis für Theo logie und Grenzgebiete,* Berlin, New York 1976. For abbreviations concerning the biblical and extra-biblical literature we rely on *Biblica* 70 (1989).

AB	Anchor Bible
ABD	Anchor Bible Dictionary
AD	Anno Domini
AfricEccRev	*African Ecclesiological Review*
al.	*Alii* (that is, others)
AnBib	Analecta Biblica
ANRW	Aufstieg und Niedergang der Römischen Welt
ArbT	Arbeiten zur Theologie
ASTI	*Annual of Swedish Theological Institute*
ATANT	Abhandlungen zur Theologie des Alten und Neuen Testaments
ATJ	*Augsburg Theological Journal*
BC	Before Christ
BH	Biblische Handbibliothek
BHT	Beiträge zur historischen Theologie
Bib	*Biblica*
BibS	Biblical Series
BJRL	*Bulletin of the John Rylands University Library Manchester*
BJS	Brown Judaic Studies
BLit	*Bibel und Liturgie*
BLS	Bible and Literature Series
BS	Bollingen Series
BSac	*Bibliotheca Sacra*
BT	*The Bible Translator*

BTB	*Biblical Theology Bulletin*
BV	Biblica Victoriensa
BW	*Biblical World*
BZ	*Biblische Zeitschrift*
BZNW	Beiheft zur Zeitschrift für die neuetestamentliche Wissenschaft
c.	circa
CBQ	*Catholic Biblical Quarterly*
CJ	*Conservative Judaism*
CL	*Christianity and Literature*
CNT	Commentaire du Nouveau Testament
CSHJ	Chicago Studies in the History of Judaism
CTM	*Currents in Theology and Mission*
CW	*Catholic World*
DDR	*Duke Divinity School Review*
EC	Epworth Commentaries
Ed.	Edition/edited by/editor
EDNT	*Exegetical Dictionary of the New Testament*
EE	*Estudios ecclesiásticos*
EKKNT	Evangelisch-Katholischer Kommentar zum Neuen Testament
EL	Everyman's Library
ÉPROER	Études Préliminaires aux Religions Orientales dans l'Empire Romain
EQ	*Evangelical Quarterly*
EThL	*Ephemerides Theologicae Lovanienses*
EuntDoc	*Euntes Docete*
EWNT	*Exegetisches Wörterbuch zum Neuen Testament*
ExpTim	*Expository Times*
GRBS	*Greek, Roman and Byzantine Studies*
HBT	*Horizon Biblical Theology*
HeyJ	*Heythrop Journal*
HM	Hallische Monographien
HNTC	Harper's New Testament Commentaries
HR	*History of Religion*
HTKNT	Herders theologischer Kommentar zum Neuen Testament
HTR	*Harvard Theological Review*
IB	Interpreter's Bible
ICC	International Critical Commentary
ID.	Idem
IDB	*Interpreter's Dictionary of the Bible*

IEJ	*Israel Exploration Journal*
Int	*Interpretation*
IRT	Issues, Religion and Theology
ISBE	International Standard Bible Encyclopedia
ITQ	*Irish Theological Quarterly*
JAAR	*Journal of the American Academy of Religion*
JBL	*Journal of Biblical Literature*
JETS	*Journal of Evangelical Theological Society*
JJS	*Journal of Jewish Studies*
JR	*Journal of Religion*
JSNT	*Journal for the Study of the New Testament*
JSNTSS	*Journal for the Study of the New Testament Supplement Series*
JSOT	*Journal for the Study of the Old Testament*
JSOTSS	*Journal for the Study of the Old Testament Supplement Series*
JTS	*Journal of Theological Studies*
KD	*Kerygma und Dogma*
KJV	King James Version
KNT	Kommentar zum Neuen Testament
LB	Lire la Bible
LCL	Loeb Classical Library
LD	Lectio Divina
MS	*Mediaeval Studies*
NAC	New American Commentary
NCB	New Clarendon Bible
NCBC	New Century Bible Commentary
NGM	*National Geographic Magazine*
NIV	*New International Version of the Bible*
NKZ	Neue kirchliche Zeitschrift
NovT	*Novum Testamentum*
NRSV	New Revised Standard Version
NTC	New Testament Commentary
NTD	Neue Testament Deutsch
NTM	New Testament Message
NTS	*New Testament Studies*
OPA	Oeuvres de Philon D' Alexandrie
PAAJR	*Proceedings of the American Academy of Jewish Research*
Prot	*Protestantesimo*
PSB	*Princeton Seminary Bulletin*
QD	Quaestiones Disputatae
RB	*Revue biblique*

RHR	*Revue d'histoire des religions*
RivB	*Rivista Biblica*
RL	*Religion in Life*
RNS	Recherche Nouvelle Série
RNT	Regensburger Neues Testament
RthPh	*Revue de théologie et de philosophie*
RTR	*Reformed Theological Review*
RVV	Religionsgeschichtliche Versuche und Vorarbeiten
RW	*Reformed World*
SANT	Studium zum Alten und Neuen Testament
SBEC	Studies in the Bible and Early Christianity
SBLASP	Society of Biblical Literature Abstracts and Seminar Papers
SBLDS	Society of Biblical Literature Dissertation Series
SBLSS	Society of Biblical Literature Symposium Series
SBS	Stuttgarter Bibelstudien
SBT	Studies in Biblical Theology
SEÅ	*Svensk Exegetisk Årsbok*
SEA	Schriftenreihe der evangelischen Akademie
SJLA	Studies in Judaism and Late Antiquity
SNT	Studien zum Neuen Testament
SNTSMS	Society for New Testament Studies Monograph Series
SNTU	*Studien zum neuen Testament und seiner Umwelt*
SP	Sacra Pagina
SPSBL	Seminar Papers of the Society of Biblical Literature
ST	*Studia Theologica*
SWR	Studies in Women and Religion
TDGR	Translated Documents of Greece and Rome
TDNT	*Theological Dictionary of the New Testament*
TEH	Theologische Existenz Heute
THKNT	Theologischer Handkommentar zum Neuen Testament
TJT	*Toronto Journal of Theology*
TNTC	Tyndale New Testament Commentaries
TS	*Theological Studies*
TT	*Theology Today*
TU	Texte und Untersuchungen
TW	Theologische Wissenschaft
UNT	*Untersuchung zum neuen Testament*
USQR	*Union Seminary Quarterly Review*
v(v)	verse(s)
VT	*Vetus Testamentum*
WBC	Word Biblical Commentary

WLQ	*Wisconsin Lutheran Quarterly*
WMANT	Wissenschaftliche Monographien zum Alten Testament
WTJ	*Westminster Theological Journal*
ZAW	*Zeitschrift für die alttestamentliche Wissenschaft*
ZKT	*Zeitschrift für katholische Theologie*
ZNW	*Zeitschrift für neutestamentlichte Wissenschaft*

SELECTED BIBLIOGRAPHY

AGUIRRE, R., «La casa como estructura del Christianismo primitivo: Las iglesias domesticas», *EE* 59 (1984) 27-51.

————, *Exégesis de Mateo, 27, 51b-53: para una teología de la muerte de Jesús en el Evangelio de Mateo,* BV 004, Victoria, Spain 1980.

ALAND, B. – ALAND, K. – KARAVIDOPOULOS, J. – MARTINI, C.M. – METZGER, B.M. ed., *Greek-English New Testament,* Stuttgart 1994[8].

————, *Novum Testamentum Graece,* Stuttgart 1994[27].

————, *The Greek New Testament,* Stuttgart 1993[4].

ALBRIGHT, W.F. – MANN, C.S. *Matthew,* AB 026, New York 1971.

ALEXIOU, M., *Ritual Lament in Greek Tradition,* Cambridge 1974.

ALLEN, W.C., *A Critical and Exegetical Commentary on the Gospel according to St. Matthew,* ICC, Edinburgh 1997.

ALLISON, D.C., *The End of the Ages Has Come: An Early Interpretation of the Passion and Resurrection of Jesus,* Philadelphia 1985.

————, «Anticipating the Passion: The Literary Reach of Matthew 26:47–27:56», *CBQ* 56 (1994) 701-714.

ALTER, R., «A Literary Approach to the Bible», *Commentary* 60 (1975) 70-77.

ANDERSON, J.C., «Matthew: Gender and Reading», *Semeia* 28 (1983) 3-27.

————, «Mary's Difference: Gender and Patriarchy in the Birth Narratives», *JR* 67 (1987) 183-202.

ARCHER, L.J., «The Role of Jewish Women in Graeco-Roman Palestine», in A. CAMERON – A. KUHRT, ed., *Images of Women in Antiquity,* Detroit 1983, 273-287.

ARCHER, L.J., *Her Price is Beyond Rubies: The Jewish Woman in Graeco-Roman Palestine*, JSOTSS 060, Sheffield 1990.

ARGYLE, A. W., *The Gospel according to Matthew*, Cambridge 1963.

ASTOUR, M.C., «Tamar the Hierodule: An Essay in the Method of Vestigial Motifs», *JBL* 85 (1966) 185-196.

ATWOOD, R., *Mary Magdalene in the New Testament Gospels and Early Tradition*, New York 1993.

AVI-YONAH, M., ed., *Encyclopedia of Archeological Excavation in the Holy Land*, London 1978.

AYNARD, L., *La Bible au féminin, de l'ancienne tradition à un christianisme hellénisé*, LD 138, Paris 1990.

BAER, R.A., *Philo's Use of the Categories Male and Female*, Leiden 1970.

BAILEY, K.E., *Poet and Peasant: Through Peasant Eyes: More Lukan Parables, Their Culture and Style*, Grand Rapids 1980.

BALDENSPERGER, G., *Le tombeau vide*, Paris 1933.

BALZ, H., «ἅγιος», *EDNT* I, 16-20.

BARRETT, C.K., *The Gospel according to St. John: An Introduction with Commentary and Notes on the Greek Text*, London 1985[2].

BARRICK, W.B., «The Rich Man from Arimathea (Mt 27:57-60) and IQIsa[a]», *JBL* 96 (1977) 235-239.

BARTA, K.A., «Resurrection Narratives: Thresholds of Faith», *BT* 27 (1989) 160-165.

BARTH, G., «Das Gesetzesverständnis des Evangelisten Matthäus», in G. BORNKAMM – G. BARTH – H.J. HELD, ed., *Überlieferung und Auslegung im Matthäusevangelium*, WMANT 01, Neukirchen 1960, 15-54.

BARTON, C.A., «A Comparison of Some Features of Hebrew and Babylonian Ritual», *JBL* 46 (1927) 79-89

BARTON, S.C., *Discipleship and Family Ties in Mark and Matthew*, Cambridge 1994.

BARTSCH, H.W., *Das Auferstehungszeugnis: sein historisches und sein theologisches Problem*, Hamburg 1965.

BASS, D.C., «Women's Studies and Biblical Studies: An Historical Perspective», *JSOT* 22 (1982) 6-12.

BATEY, R.A., «Is not this the Carpenter?», *NTS* 30 (1984) 249-258.

BAUCKHAM, R., «The Eschatological Earthquake in the Apocalypse of John», *NovT* 19 (1977) 224-233.

BAUER, D.R., «The Literary Function of Genealogy in Matthew's Gospel», in D.R. BAUER – M.A. POWELL, ed., *Treasures New and Old: Recent Contributions to Matthean Studies*, Atlanta 1990, 461-463.

———, *The Structure of Matthew's Gospel: A Study in Literary Design*, *JSNTS* 031, Sheffield 1988.

BAUER, W., *A Greek English Lexicon of the New Testament and Other Early Christian Literature*, Chicago 2000³.

BEARE, F.W., *The Earliest Records of Jesus: A Companion to the Synopsis of the First Three Gospels*, Oxford 1962.

———, *The Gospel according to Matthew: A Commentary*, Oxford 1981.

BEARSLEY, P.J., «Mary the Perfect Disciple: A Paradigm for Mariology», *TS* 41 (1980) 461-504.

BEATTIE, D.R.G., «The Book of Ruth as Evidence for Israelite Legal Practice», *VT* 24 (1974) 251-267.

BENOIT, P., *The Passion and Resurrection of Jesus*, New York 1969; orig. French, *Passion et resurrection du Seigneur*, Paris 1966.

BENTZ, L.A., «Jesus' Death and & Resurrection», *Encounter* 58 (1997) 251-274.

BERGMANN, J., *Ich bin Isis: Studien zum memphitischen Hintergrund der griechischen Isisaretalogien*, Uppsala 1968.

BERMAN, S., «The Status of Women in Halakhic Judaism», in E. KOLTUN, ed., *The Jewish Women* New York 1976, 114-128.

BERTMAN, A., «Symmetrical Design in the Book of Ruth», *JBL* 84 (1965) 165-168.

BEST, E., *Disciples and Discipleship: Studies in the Gospel According to Mark*, Edinburgh 1986.

———, *Following Jesus: Discipleship in the Gospel of Mark*, JSOTSS 004, Sheffield 1981.

BETZ, H.D., «Spirit, Freedom and Law: Paul's Message to the Galatian Churches», *SEÅ* 39 (1974) 145-160.

———, *Nachfolge und Nachahmung Jesu Christi im Neuen Testament*, BHT 037, Tübingen 1967.

BEVAN, T.W., «The Four Anointings», *ExpT* 39 (1928) 137-139.

BEYER, H., «διακονέω, διακονία, διακονος», *TDNT*, II, 81-93.

BIALE, R., *Women and Jewish Law: The Essential Texts, their History, and their Relevance for Today*, New York 1995.

BIEDER, W., *Die Vorstellung von der Höllenfahrt Jesus Christi*, ATANT 019, Zürich 1949.

BIRD, P.A., «Women (OT)», in *ABD* VI, 957-961.

————, «Images of Women in the Old Testament», in N. K. GOTTWALD – D.R. BAUER – M.A. POWELL, ed., *The Bible and Liberation*, Orbis Books 1984, 252-288.

BLASS, F.W – DEBRUNNER, A., *A Greek Grammar of the New Testament and Other Early Christian Literature*, Chicago 1961.

BLINZLER, J., *Der Prozess Jesu: das Jüdische und das römische Gerichtsverfahren gegen Jesus Christus auf Grund der ältesten Zeugnisse*, Regensburg 1960².

BLOEM, H., *Die Ostererzählung des Matthäus:Aufbau und Aussage von Mt 27,57-28,20*, Zeist 1985.

BLOMBERG, C.L., «The Liberation of Illegitimacy: Women and Rulers in Matthew 1-2», *BTB* 21 (1991) 145-150.

————, *Matthew*, NAC 022, Nashville 1992.

BODE, E.L., «A Liturgical Sitz im Leben for the Gospel Tradition of the Women's visit to the Tomb of Jesus»?, *CBQ* 32 (1970) 237-242.

————, *The First Easter Morning: The Gospel Accounts of the Women's Visit to the Tomb of Jesus*, AnBib 045, Rome 1970.

BOISMARD, M.E – LAMOUILLE, A., *Synopsis Graeca Quattuor Evangeliorum*, Leuven 1986.

BONNARD, P.E., *L'Évangile selon Saint Matthieu*, CNT 001, Neuchâtel 1970.

BONSIRVEN, J., *Palestinian Judaism in the Time of Jesus Christ*, New York 1964; orig. French, *Le judaïsme palestinien au temps de Jésus-Christ*, Paris 1950.

BORING, M.E., ed., *Hellenistic Commentary to the New Testament*, Nashville 1995².

BORNKAMM, G., «σείω, σεισμός», *TDNT* VII, 196-200.

————, ed., «Die Sturmstillung im Matthäus Evangelium», in *Wort und Dienst, Jahrbuch der Theologischen Schule Bethel*, Bielefeld 1948, 49-54.

BOSETTI, E., *Yahweh Shepherd of the People: Pastoral Symbolism in the Old Testament*, Middlegreen 1993.

BOUCHER, M., «Women and Priestly Ministry: The New Testament Evidence», *CBQ* 41 (1979) 608-613.

BOUTTIER, M., «Complexio Oppositorum: Sur les Formules de I Cor xii. 13; Gal iii 26-28; Col iii. 10, 11», *NTS* 23 (1976) 1-19.

BOVON, F., «Le privilège pascal de Marie-Madeleine», *NTS* 30 (1984) 50-62.

BRATCHER, R.G., «A Note on υἱὸς θεοῦ (Mark xv.39)», *ExpTim* 68 (1956-57) 27-28.

BRAUN, F.M., «La Sépulture de Jesus», *RB* 45 (1936) 34-52.

BRENNER, A., «Naomi and Ruth», *VT* 33 (1983) 385-397.

BRIGHT, J., *A History of Israel,* Louisville 2000[4].

BROER, I., *Die Urgemeinde und das Grab Jesus: eine Analyse der Grablegungsgeschichte im Neuen Testament,* SANT 031, München 1972.

BROOKS, B.A., «Fertility Cult Functionaries in the Old Testament», *JBL* 60 (1941) 227-253.

BROOKS, O., «Matthew xxviii 16-20 and the Design of the First Gospel», *JSNT* 10 (1981) 2-18.

BROOTEN, B.J., *Women Leaders in the Ancient Synagogues: Inscriptional Evidence and Background Issues,* BJS 036, Chico, CA 1982.

————, «Jewish Women's History in the Roman Period: A Task for Christian Theology», *HTR* 79 (1986) 22-30.

BROWN, R.E., *The Gospel according to John,* I–II, AB 29 and 29A, New York 1966-70.

————, *The Virginal Conception and Bodily Resurrection of Jesus,* London 1973.

————, «The Gospel of Peter and Canonical Gospel Priority», *NTS* 33 (1987) 321-343.

————, «The Burial of Jesus (Mark 15:42-47)», *CBQ* 50 (1988) 233-245.

————, *A Risen Christ in Eastertime: Essays on the Gospel Narratives of the Resurrection,* Collegeville 1990.

————, *The Birth of the Messiah: A Commentary on the Infancy Narratives in Matthew and Luke,* London 1993.

————, *The Death of the Messiah: From Gethsemane to Grave: A Commentary on the Passion Narratives in the Four Gospels,* I–II, New York 1994.

————, *An Introduction to the New Testament,* New York – London – Toronto – Sydney – Auckland 1997.

BRUMFIELD, A.C., *The Attic Festivals of Demeter and the Agricultural Year,* Salem 1981.

BRUNER, F.D., *Matthew: A Commentary,* I–II, Dallas 1990.

BULTMANN, R.K., *History of the Synoptic Tradition*, Oxford 1963[2]; orig. German, *Die Geschichte der synoptischen Tradition*, Göttingen 1958.

————, *The Gospel of John: A Commentary*, Oxford, 1971.

BURKE, K., *Counter-Statement*, Los Angeles, London 1968.

BURKERT, W., *Ancient Mystery Cults*, Cambridge 1987.

BURKILL, T.A., «The Historical Development of the Story of the Syrophoenician Woman (Mark vii: 24-31) », *NT* 9 (1967) 161-177.

BURRUS, V., *Chastity as Autonomy: Women in the Stories of the Apocryphal Acts*, SWR 023, Lewiston – Queenston 1987.

CABA, J., *Cristo, mia speranza è risorto: studio esegetico dei «vangeli» pasquali*, Milano 1988.

CAIRD, G.B., «Paul and Women's Liberty», *BJRL* 54 (1972) 269-281.

————, *The Gospel of St. Luke*, Harmondsworth 1963.

CAMPENHAUSEN VON, H., ed., «The Events of Easter and the Empty Tomb», in *Tradition and life in the Church*, Philadelphia, 1968.

CAPPS, D., *The Childsong: Religious Abuse of Children*, Louisville 1995.

CARTER, W., «Matthew 28:1-10», *Int* 38 (1984) 59-63.

————, *Households and Discipleship: A Study of Matthew 19-20*, JSNTSS 103, Sheffield 1994.

————, «To See the Tomb: A Note on Matthew's Women at the Tomb (Matt 28:1)», *ExpTim* 107 (1996) 201-205.

————, *Matthew and the Margins: A Socio-Political and Religious Reading*, JSOTSS 204, England 2000.

————, *Matthew and Empire: Initial Explorations*, Harrisburg 2001.

CHARLESWORTH, J.H., *Graphic Concordance to the Dead Sea Scrolls*, Tübingen 1991.

CASALINI, N., *Libro dell'Origine di Gesù Cristo: analisi letteraria e teologica di Matt 1-2*, Jerusalem 1990.

CHENEY, E., «The Mother of the Sons of Zebedee», *JSNT* 68 (1997) 13-21.

CLARK, E.A. «Women», in E. FERGUSON, ed., *Encyclopedia of Early Christianity*, II, New York 1997[2], 1281-1283.

CLARK, K.W., «The Gentile Bias in Matthew», *JBL* 66 (1947) 165-172.

COATS, G.W., «Widows' Rights: A Crux in the Structure of Genesis 38», *CBQ* 34 (1972) 461-466.

COHEN, A., *Everyman's Talmud*, New York 1978.

COHEN, B., «Concerning Divorce in Jewish and Roman Law», *PAAJR* 21 (1952) 3-24.

COHEN, M.S., «Women in the Synagogues of Antiquity», *CJ* 34 (1980) 23-29.

————, «The Tallit», *CJ* 44 (1992) 3-15.

COLE, S.G., «New Evidence for the Mysteries of Dionysus», *GRBS* 21 (1980) 223-238.

COLLINS, Y., «The Genre of the Passion Narrative», *ST* 47 (1993) 3-28.

COLWELL, E.C., «A Definite Rule for the Use of the Article in the Greek New Testament», *JBL* 52 (1933) 12-21.

COOGAN, M.D., «Rahab», in E.M. METZGER, ed., *The Oxford Companion to the Bible*, New York 1993, 642.

CORLEY, K.E., «The Egalitarian Jesus: A Christian Myth of Origins», *Forum* 1,2 (1978) 291-315.

————, *Private Women, Public Meals: Social Conflict in the Synoptic Tradition*, Peabody 1993.

————, «Women and the Crucifixion and Burial of Jesus», *Forum* 1 (1998) 181-225.

CRAIG, W.L., «The Empty Tomb of Jesus», in R.T. FRANCE – D. WENHAM, *Studies of History and Tradition in the Four Gospels*, I–II, Sheffield 1981, 173-200.

————, «The Historicity of the Empty Tomb of Jesus», *NTS* 31 (1985) 39-67.

————, *Assessing the New Testament Evidence for the Historicity of the Resurrection of Jesus*, Lewiston 1989.

————, «Did Jesus Rise from the Dead?», in M.J. WILKINS – J.P. MORELAND, ed., *Jesus Under Fire*, Grand Rapids 1995, 141-176.

CRANFIELD, C.E.B., «The Resurrection of Jesus Christ», *ExpTim* 101 (1989-90) 167-172.

CROSBY, M.H., *The House of Disciples: Church, Economics, and Justice in Matthew*, Mary Knoll 1988.

CROSSAN, J.D., *Four Other Gospels: Shadows in the Contours of Canon*, San Francisco 1985.

————, *Who Killed Jesus? Exposing the Roots of Anti-Semitism in the Gospel Story of the Death of Jesus*, San Francisco 1995.

CULLMANN, O., «Πέτρα», *TDNT* VI, 95-99.

CURTIS, K.P.G., «Three Points of Contact between Matthew and John in the Burial and Resurrection Narratives», *JTS* 23 (1972) 440-444.

D'ANGELO, M.R., «Women in Luke-Acts: A Redactional View», *JBL* 109 (1990) 441- 461.

DA SPINETOLI, O., *Matteo: Il Vangelo della Chiesa,* Assisi 1983.

DALMAN, G.H., *Aramäisch-Neuhebräisches Handwörterbuch zu Targum, Talmud und Midrasch,* Frankfurt am Main 1922[2].

DANBY, H., *The Mishnah,* Oxford 1958.

DANKER, F.W., «God With Us: Hellenistic Christological Perspectives in Matthew», *CTM* 19 (1992) 433-439.

DAVIES W.D – ALLISON, D.C., *A Critical and Exegetical Commentary on the Gospel according to Matthew*, I-III, ICC, Edinburgh 1997.

DAVIES, W.D., *The Sermon on the Mount,* Cambridge 1966.

DAVIS, C.T., «The Fulfillment of Creation: A Study of Matthew's Genealogy», *JAAR* 41 (1973) 520-535.

DERMIENCE, A., «La péricope de la Cananéenne (Mt 15,21-28): Redaction et théologie», *EthL* 58 (1982) 25-49.

DERRET, J.D.M., «Law in the New Testament: The Syro-Phoenician Woman and the Centurion of Capernaum», *NT* 15 (1973) 161-186.

DE SOLAGE, B., *Christ est ressuscité: la Résurrection selon le Nouveau Testament,* Toulouse 1976.

DE STAGÉ, J. , *Mary and the Christian Gospel,* London 1976.

DEWEY, J., «Jesus' Healing of Women: Conformity and Non-conformity to Dominant Cultural Values as Clues for the Historical Reconstruction», *BTB* 24 (1994) 122-131.

————, «From Storytelling to Written Text: The Loss of Early Women's Voices», *BTB* 26 (1996) 71-78.

DIBELIUS, M., *Jesus,* Philadelphia 1939.

DIBELIUS, M – CONZELMANN, H., *The Pastoral Epistles,* Philadelphia 1972; orig. German, *Die Pastoralbriefe*, Tübingen 1955.

————, *From Tradition to Gospel*, New York 1965.

DODD, C.H., *The Interpretation of the Fourth Gospel*, Cambridge 1953.

————, *Historical Tradition in the Fourth Gospel*, Cambridge 1963.

DONAHUE, J.R., *Are You Christ,* SBLDS 10, Missoula 1973.

DOWNEY, G., *A History of Antioch in Syria: From Seleucus to the Arab Conquest*, Princeton 1961.

DOYLE, B.R., «Matthew's Intention as Discerned by His Structure», *RB* 95 (1988) 34-54.

DRIVER, G.R., «Two Problems in the New Testament», *JTS* 16 (1965) 327-337.

DUBISCH, J., «Culture Enters through the Kitchen: Women, Food, and Social Boundaries in Rural Greece», in J. DUBISCH, ed., *Gender and Power in Rural Greece*, Princeton 1986, 195-214.

DUNAND, F., *Le Culte d'Isis dans le bassin oriental del Mediterranée*, ÉPROER 026, Leiden 1973.

————, «Le Statut des Hiereiai en Egypte Romaine», in M.B. DEBOER, – T.A. EDRIDGE, ed., *Hommages a Maarten J. Vermaseren*, Leiden 1978, 352-372.

EDWARDS, R.A., «Uncertain Faith: Matthew's Portrait of the Disciples», in F.F. SEGOVIA, ed., *Discipleship in the New Testament*, Philadelphia 1985, 47-61.

————, *Matthew's Story of Jesus*, Philadelphia 1985.

EFROS, J., «Holiness and Glory in the Bible», *JQR* 41(1950/51) 263-277

EISSFELDT, O., *Einleitung in das Alte Testament: unter Einschluss der apokryphen und Pseudepigraphen sowie der Apokryphen und Pseudepigraphenartigen Qumran-Schriften*, Tübingen 1964.

————, *Hexateuch-Synopse: die Erzählung der fünf Bücher Mose und des Buches Josua mit dem Anfange des Richterbuches*, Darmstadt 1983.

ELBOGEN, I., *Der jüdische Gottesdienst in seiner geschichtlichen Entwicklung*, Hildesheim 1967.

ELIZONDO, V., *Galilean Journey: The Mexican American Promise*, Mary Knoll 1983.

ELLIOT, J.H., *A Home for the Homeless: A Sociological Exegesis of 1Peter: Its Situation and Strategy*, Philadelphia 1981.

ELLIS, E.E., «Paul and His Co-Workers», *NTS* 17 (1970-71) 437-452.

————, ed., *The Gospel of Luke*, Grand Rapids 1983.

ELLIS, P.F., *The Genius of John: A Composition-Critical Commentary on the Fourth Gospel*, Collegeville 1984.

EMERTON, J.A., «An Examination of a Recent Structuralist Interpretation of Genesis xxxviii», *VT* 25 (1975) 338-361.

————, «Judah and Tamar», *VT* 29 (1979) 403-415.

ENGELSMAN, J., *The Feminine Dimension of the Divine*, London 1979.

EPSTEIN, I., ed., *The Babylonian Talmud*, London 1935.

EVANS, M.J., *Woman in the Bible*, Exeter 1983.

FABRIS, R., *Matteo: traduzione e commento*, Roma 1982.

FALCONER, R., «1Timothy 2:14-15: Interpretative Notes», *JBL* LX (1949) 375-379.

FALLON, M.B., *The Gospel according to Matthew,* Kensington 1997.

FASCHER, E., *Das Weib des Pilatus (Matthäus 27,19): Die Auferweckung der Heiligen (Matthäus 27,51-53),* HM 020, Halle 1951.

FAUSTI, S., *Una comunità legge il vangelo di Matteo,* I–II, Bologna 1998.

FEHRIBACH, A., *The Women in the Life of the Bridegroom: A Feminist Historical-Literary Analysis of the Female Characters in the Fourth Gospel,* Collegeville 1998.

FENTON, J.C., *Saint Matthew,* London 1996.

————, *The Matthew Passion: A Lenten Journey to the Cross and Resurrection,* Minneapolis, 1996.

FILSON, F.V., *A Commentary on the Gospel according to St. Matthew,* London 1960.

FITZMYER, J.A., «The Use of Explicit Old Testament Quotations in Qumran Literature and in the New Testament», *NTS* 7 (1961) 297-333

————, *Essays on the Semitic Background of the New Testament,* SBT 005, Missoula 1974².

————, *Luke the Theologian: Aspects of His Teaching,* New York 1989.

FRANCE, R.T., ed., *A Bibliographical Guide to New Testament Research,* Sheffield 1979.

————, *The Gospel according to Matthew,* TNTC, Leicester 1985.

FRANKMÖLLE, H., *Matthäus Kommentar,* I–II, Düsseldorf 1997.

FREED, E.D., «The Women in Matthew's Genealogy», *JSNT* 29 (1987) 3-19.

FREEDMAN, H., *Midrash Rabbah,* London 1961.

FREYNE, S., *Galilee, Jesus and the Gospels,* Philadelphia 1988.

FRIEDRICH, G., «Die Formale Struktur von Mt 28:18-20», *ZTK* 80 (1983) 137-183.

FRIEDRICH, J., *Gott im Bruder? eine methodenkritische Untersuchung von Redaktion, Überlieferung und Traditionen in Mt 25, 31-46,* Stuttgart 1977.

FUCHS, A., «Entwicklungsgeschichtliche Studie zu Mk 1,29-31 par Mt 8:14-15 par Luke 4, 38-39. Mach über Fieber und Dämonen», *SNTU* A/6-7 (1981-82) 21-76.

FUCHS, L., *We were There,* New York 1993.

FUCHS, S., *The Expansion of Women's Rights during the Period of Mishnah*, Cincinnati 1974.

FULLER, R.C., «The Drink Offered to Christ at Calvary», *Scripture* 2 (1947) 114-115.

FULLER, R.H., *The Formation of the Resurrection Narratives*, New York 1971.

————, «In Search of the Earliest Passion Accounts», *Int* 45 (1991) 71-72.

GAECHTER, P., *Das Matthäusevangelium*, Innsbruck 1962.

GAGER, J.G., *Kingdom and Community: The Social World of Early Christianity*, New Jersey 1975.

GALOT, J., *Mission et ministère de la femme*, Paris 1973.

GARDNER, R.B., *Matthew*, BCBC, Scottsdale 1991.

GARLAND, D.E., *Reading Matthew: A Literary Theological Commentary on the First Gospel*, New York 1993.

GÄRTNER, B., *The Temple and Community in Qumran and in the New Testament: A Comparative Study in the Temple*, Cambridge 1965.

GIBERT, P., *La résurrection du Christ. Le témoignage Nouveau Testament: de l'histoire à la foi*, Paris 1975.

GIBLIN, C.H., «Structural and Thematic Correlation in the Matthean Burial-Resurrection Narrative (Matt xxvii. 57–xxviii. 20)», *NTS* 21 (1975) 406-420.

GILBERT, G.H., «Women in the Churches of Paul», *BW* 2 (1893) 38-47.

GILLMANN, F.M., *Women Who Knew Paul*, Collegeville 1992.

GNILKA, J., *Das Matthäusevangelium*, HTKNT, I–II, Freiburg 1986-1988.

————, *Jesus of Nazareth: Message and History*, Peabody 1997.

GOERGEN, D.J, *The Death and Resurrection of Jesus,* Wilmington 1988.

GOLDFELD, A., «Women as Sources of Torah in Rabbinic Tradition», in E. KOLTUN, ed., *The Jewish Woman: New Perspectives*, New York 1976, 257-271.

GOLDIN, J., «The Youngest Son or Where does Genesis 38 Belong», *JBL* 96 (1977) 27-44.

GOODBLATT, D., «The Beruriah Traditions», *JJS* 26 (1975) 68-85.

GORDIS, R., «Love, Marriage and Business in the Book of Ruth», in H.N. BREAM, ed., *A Light Unto My Path: Old Testament Studies in Honor of Jacob M. Myers*, Philadelphia 1974, 241-264.

GORDON, C.H., *The Common Background of Greek and Hebrew Civilizations*, New York 1965.

GOULD, E.P., *Critical and Exegetical Commentary on the Gospel according to St. Mark*, ICC, Edinburgh 1983.

GOULDER, M.D., «Mark xvi. 1-8 and Parallels», *NTS* 24 (1978) 235-240.

GRASS, H., *Ostergeschehen und Osterberichte*, Göttingen 1962[2].

GRASSO, S., *Il Vangelo di Matteo*, Roma 1995.

GREEN, H.B., *The Gospel according to Matthew in the Revised Standard Version*, Oxford 1987.

GREEN, M., *The Message of Matthew*, Nottingham 2000.

GREENBERG, B., «Female Sexuality and Bodily Functions in the Jewish Tradition», in J. BECHER, ed., *Women, Religion and Sexuality*, Geneva 1990, 1-44.

GREEVEN, H., «προσκυνέω», *TDNT* VI, 758-766.

GRILLI, M., *Comunità e Missione: le direttive di Matteo*, Frankfurt am Main 1992.

GROSSMAN, S., «Women and the Jerusalem Temple», in S. GROSSMAN – R. HAUT, *Daughters of the King: Women and the Synagogue*, Philadelphia 1991, 15-37.

GRUBER, M.I., «The Motherhood of God in Second Isaiah», *RB* 90 (1983) 351-359.

GRUNDMANN, W., *Das Evangelium nach Matthäus*, THKNT, I–II, Berlin 1968.

GUIGNEBERT, C., *Jésus*, Paris 1947.

GUNDRY, R.H., *The Use of the Old Testament in Matthew's Gospel: With Special Reference to the Messianic Hope*, SNT 018, Leiden 1975.

————, *Matthew: A Commentary on His Handbook for a Mixed Church under Persecution*, Grand Rapids 1994[2].

————, «On True and False Disciples in Matthew 8:18-22», *NTS* 40 (1994) 433-41.

GÜNTHER, W., «αδελφος», *NIDNTT* I, 254-258.

HAENCHEN, E., *Der Weg Jesu: Eine Erklärung des Markus-Evangeliums und der kanonischen Parallelen*, Berlin 1966.

HAGNER, D.A., *Matthew 1-13*, WBC 033A, Dallas 1993.

————, *Matthew 14-28*, WBC 033B, Dallas 1995.

HAGNER, D.A., «Gospel, Kingdom, and Resurrection in the Synoptic Gospels», in R.N. LONGENECKER, ed., *Life in the Face of Death: The Resurrection Message of the New Testament,* Grand Rapids, 1998, 99-122.

HALS, R.M., *The Theology of the Book of Ruth,* BibS 023, Philadelphia 1969.

HANNON, V.E., *The Question of Women and the Priesthood: Can Woman be Admitted to Holy Orders,* London 1967.

HARE, D.R.A., *Matthew: A Bible Commentary for Teaching and Preaching,* Louisville 1993.

HARLEY, J.B., «Did Paul Require Veils or the Silence of Women? A Consideration of 1Cor. 11:2-16 and 1 Cor. 14:33b-36», *WTJ* 35 (19772-73) 190-220.

HARNACK, A., «Probabilia über die Adresse und den Verfasser des Hebräerbriefes», *ZNW* 1 (1900) 16-41.

HARNER, P.B., «Qualitative Anarthrous Predicate Nouns: Mark 15:39 and John 1:1», *JBL* 92 (1973) 75-87.

HARRINGTON, D.J., ed., «Make Disciples of All the Gentiles», in *Light of All Nations: Essays on the Church in the New Testament Research,* Wilmington 1982, 110-123.

————, *The Gospel of Matthew,* SP 001, Collegeville 1991.

HARTMAN, G., «Die Vorlage der Osterberichte in Joh 20», *ZNW* 55 (1964) 197-220.

HATCH, E – REDPATH, H.A., *A Concordance to the Septuagint and Other Greek Versions of the Old Testament (including the Apocryphal Books),* I–III, Oxford 1897-1906.

HEFFERN, A.D., «The Four Women in St. Matthew's Genealogy of Christ», *JBL* 31 (1912) 68-81.

HEIL, J.P., «Narrative Roles of Women in Matthew's Genealogy», *Bib* 72 (1991) 538-545.

————, «The Narrative Structure of Matthew 27:55-28:20», *JBL* 110 (1991) 419-438.

————, *The Death and Resurrection of Jesus: A Narrative Critical Reading of Matthew 26-28,* Minneapolis, MN 1991.

HEINE, S., «Eine Person von Rang und Namen: historische Konturen der Magdalenerin», in D.A. KOCH – G. SELLIN – A. LINDERMANN, *Jesu Rede von Gott und ihre Nachgeschichte im frühen Christentum: Beiträge zur Verkündigung Jesus und zum Kerygma der Kirche,* Gütersloh 1989, 179-194.

HELFMEYER, «הָלַךְ», *TDOT* III, 388-403.

HENDRICKX, H.N., *Resurrection Narratives*, Manila 1978.

————, *Los relatos de la passion*, London 1984.

————, *The Miracle Stories of the Synoptic Gospels*, London 1987.

HENDRIKSEN, W., *The Gospel of Matthew*, Edinburgh 1989.

HENGEL, M., *Die Zeloten: Untersuchungen zur jüdischen Freiheitsbewegung in der Zeit von Herodes I. bis 70 N. Chr.*, Leiden 1961.

————, «Maria Magdalena und die Frauen als Zeugen», in O. BETZ, *Abraham Unser Vater: Juden und Christen im Gespräch über die Bibel*, Fs. O. Michel, Leiden 1963, 243-256.

————, *Nachfolge und Charisma: Eine exegetischreligionsgeschichtliche Studie zu Mt 8:21f. und Jesu Ruf in die Nachfolge*, BZNW 034, Berlin 1968.

————, *The Charismatic Leader and his Followers*, Edinburgh 1981.

————, *Giudaismo ed ellenismo*, Tübingen 1988.

HENNESSY, A., *The Galilee of Jesus*, Rome 1994.

HERLIHY, D., *Medieval Households*, London 1985.

HERTIG, P., «The Galilee Theme in the Gospel of Matthew: Transforming Mission through Marginality», *Missiology* 2 (1997) 155-163.

HEYOB, S., *The Cult of Isis among Women in the Graeco-Roman World*, ÉPROER 051, Leiden 1975.

HILL, D., *The Gospel of Matthew*, NCBC, London 1972.

HOBBS, H.H., *An Exposition of the Four Gospels*, Grand Rapids 1996.

HODGES, Z.C., «The Women and the Empty Tomb», *BSac* 123 (1966) 301-309.

HOH, J., «Der Christliche γραμματεὺς (Matt 13:52)», *BZ* 17 (1926) 256-269.

HOOKER, M.D., «Authority on Her Head: An Examination of 1Cor XI:10», *NTS* 10 (1963-64) 410-416.

————, *The Message of Mark*, London 1983.

HORSELY, R.A., *Sociology and the Jesus Movement*, New York 1994[2].

————, *Galilee: History, Politics, People*, Valley Forge, 1995.

HOSKYNS, E.C., *The Fourth Gospel*, London 1947.

HOWELL, D.B., *Matthew's Inclusive Story: A Study in the Narrative Rhetoric of the First Gospel*, JSNTSS 042, Sheffield 1990.

HUMMEL, R., *Die Auseinandersetzung zwischen Kirche und Judentum im Matthäusevangelium*, München 1963.

HUNTER, A.M., *The Work and Words of Jesus*, Philadelphia 1950.

HUTTER, M., «Ein altorientalischer Bittgestus in Mt 9:20-22», *ZNW* 75 (1984) 133-135.

ILAN, T., «The Attraction of Aristocratic Women to Pharisaism during the Second Temple Period», *HTR* 88 (1995) 1-33.

—————, *Jewish Women in Greco-Roman Palestine*: *An Inquiry into Image and Status*, Tübingen 1996.

IRVIN, D., «The Ministry of Women in Early Church: The Archaeological Evidence», *DDR* 45 (1980) 76-86.

JARVIS, C.A., «Matthew 28:1-10», *Interpretation* 42 (1988) 63-68.

JAUBERT, A., «Le Voile des femmes: 1Cor XI 2-16», *NTS* 18 (1972) 419-430.

JEREMIAS, J., «Wo lag Golgotha und das Heilige Grab? Die Überlieferung im Lichte der Formgeschichte», *Angelos* 1 (1925) 141-73.

—————, *Theophanie, Die Geschichte einer alttestamentlicher Gattung*, Neukirchen 1965.

—————, *Abba: Studien zur neutestamentlichen Theologie und Zeitgeschichte*, Göttingen 1966.

—————, *Jerusalem in the Time of Jesus: An Investigation into Economic and Social Conditions during the New Testament Period*, Philadelphia 1975; orig. German, *Jerusalem zur Zeit Jesu: Kulturgeschichtliche Untersuchungen zur neutestamentlichen Zeitgeschichte* Leipzig 1923-29.

—————, *New Testament Theology*, New York 1971; orig. German, *Neutestamentliche Theologie*, Gütersloh1971.

—————, *The Parables of Jesus*, New York 1972.

JOHNSON, M.D., *The Purpose of the Biblical Genealogies with Special Reference to the Settings of the Genealogies of Jesus*, SNTSMS 008, Cambridge 1969.

JOHNSON, S.E – BUTTRICK, A., *The Gospel according to St. Matthew*, IB, New York 1951.

JONES, I.H., *The Gospel of Matthew*, EC, London 1994.

JOSEPHUS, *Jewish Antiquities*, in T.E. PAGE – *al.*, ed., *Josephus*, LCL IV-IX, London 1961-1965.

—————, *The Jewish War*, in T.E. PAGE – *al.*, ed., *Josephus*, LCL II-III, London 1961.

—————, *The Life against Apion*, in T.E. PAGE – *al.*, ed., *Josephus*, LCL IX, London 1961.

JOUETTE, M., «The Galileans: A Neglected Factor in Johannine Community Research», *CBQ* 43 (1981) 243-257.

JUDGE, E.A., *The Social Pattern of Christian Groups in the First Century*, London 1960.

————, «St. Paul and Classical Society», *JAC* 15 (1972) 19-36.

KANNENGIESSER, C., *Foi en la résurrection, résurrection de la foi*, Paris 1974.

KARRIS, R.J., «The Background and Significance of the Polemic of the Pastoral Epistles», *JBL* 92 (1973) 549-564.

KEE, H.C., «Changing Role of Women in the Early Christian World», *TT* 49 (1992) 225-238.

————, «Early Christianity in Galilee: Reassessing the Evidence from the Gospel», in L.I. LEVINE, *The Galilee in Late Antiquity*, Cambridge 1992, 3-22.

KEENER, C.S., *Les évangiles synoptiques*, I–II, Ceffonds 1907.

————, *And Marries Another: Divorce and Remarriage in the Teaching of the New Testament*, Peabody 1991.

————, *Paul, Women and Wives: Marriage and Women's Ministry in the Letters of Paul*, Peabody 1992.

————, «Man and Woman», in G.F. HAWTHORNE – R. P. MARTIN, *Dictionary of Paul and His Letter*, England 1993, 683-692.

————, *Matthew*, Downers Grove – Leicester 1997.

————, *A Commentary on the Gospel of Matthew*, Grand Rapids 1999.

KELLER, H.M., *Jesus und die Frauen: Eine Verhältnisbestimmung nach der synoptischen Überlieferung*, Freiburg – Basel – Wien – Barcelona – Rom – New York 1997.

KENNARD, J.S., «The Burial of Jesus», *JBL* 74 (1955) 227-238

KENSKY, T.F., «Rahab», in C. MEYERS, ed., *Women in Scripture: A Dictionary of Named and Unnamed Women in the Hebrew Bible, the Apocryphal/Deuterocanonical Books, and the New Testament*, New York 2000, 140-141.

KERÉNYI, K., *Eleusis: Archetypical Image of Mother and Daughter*, BS 065, Princeton 1967.

KIILUNEN, J., «Der Nachfolgewillige Schriftgelehrte: Matthäus 8.19-20 im Verständnis des Evangelisten», *NTS* 37 (1991) 268-279.

————, *A Brief Commentary on the Gospel of Matthew*, New York 1992.

————, *The Origins of the Gospel according to Matthew*, Oxford 1946.

KINGSBURY, J.D., *The Parables of Jesus in Matthew 13: A Study in Redaction Criticism*, London 1969.

———, «The Verb *Akolouthein* (to Follow) as an Index of Matthew's View of His Community», *JBL* 97 (1978) 56-73.

———, *Matthew*, Philadelphia 1986.

———, «The Developing Conflict between Jesus and the Jewish Leaders in Matthew's Gospel: A Literary Critical Study», *CBQ* 49 (1987) 57-73.

———, «On Following Jesus: The "Eager" Scribe and the "Reluctant" Disciple (Matthew 8.18-22)», *NTS* 14 (1988) 45-59.

———, *Matthew as Story*, Philadelphia 1988[2].

KINUKAWA, H., *Women and Jesus in Mark: A Japanese Feminist Perspective*, Mary Knoll 1994.

KITTEL, G., «ἀκολουθέω», *TDNT* I, 210-216.

KLOPPENBERG, J.S., «Isis and Sophia in the Book of Wisdom», *HTR* 75 (1982) 57-84.

———, «Exitus clari viri: The Death of Jesus in Luke», *TJT* 8 (1992) 106-120.

KLOSTERMANN, E., *Das Matthäusevangelium*, Tübingen 1971.

KOLTUN, E., ed., *The Jewish Women*, New York 1976.

KOPAS, J., «Jesus and Women in Matthew», *TT* 47 (1990) 13-21.

KOSMALA, H., «Nachfolge und Nachahmung Gottes I. Im Griechischen Gedanken», *ASTI* II (1963) 47-49.

KOWALSKI, W., «The Call to Discipleship: A Challenge to Personal Commitment», *AfricEccRev* 36/6 (1994) 366-378.

KRAEMER, R.S., «Ecstasy and Possession: The Attraction of Women to the Cult of Dionysus», *HTR* 72 (1979) 55-80.

———, *Hellenistic Jewish Women: The Epigraphical Evidence*, SPSBL 25, Decatur 1986.

KRAEMER, R.S., «Non-literary Evidence for Jewish Women in Rome and Egypt», in M. SKINNER, ed., *Rescuing Creusa: New Methodological Approaches to Women in Antiquity*, Texas 1987, 85-101.

———, «Monastic Jewish Women in Graeco-Roman Egypt: Philo Judaeus on the Therapeutrides», *Signs* 14 (1989) 342-370.

———, *Her Share of the Blessings: Women's Religion Among Pagans, Jews, and Christians in the Greco-Roman World*, Oxford 1992.

KRAEMER, R.S., «Matt 8:14: Mother in Law of Peter (Simon)», in C. MEYERS, ed., *Women in Scripture: A Dictionary of Named and Unnamed Women in the Hebrew Bible, the Apocryphal/Deuterocanonical Books, and the New Testament*, Boston New York 2000, 408.

KREMER, J., *Die Osterbotschaft der Vier Evangelien: Versuch einer Auslegung der Berichte über das leere Grab und die Erscheinungen des Auferstanden*, Stuttgart 1968.

————, ἐγείρω, *EDNT* I, 372-376.

KROEGER, C.C – STORKEY, M.E., ed., *The Women's Study New Testament*, London 1995.

KÜHSCHELM, R., «Angelophanie and Christophanie in den synoptischen Grabesgeschichten Mk 16, 1-8 par. (unter Berücksichtigung von Joh 20,11-18)», in C. FOCANT, ed., *The Synoptic Gospels: Source Criticism and the New Literary Criticism*, ETL 110, Leuven 1993, 556-565.

KÜNG, H., *On Being a Christian*, New York 1976; orig. German, *Christ Sein*, München 1976.

KUSKE, D., «The Meaning of *matheteusate* in Matthew 28:19», *WLQ* 94 (1997) 115-121.

KUZMACK, L., «Aggadic Approaches to Biblical Women», in E. KOLTUN, ed., *The Jewish Woman*, New York 1976, 248-256.

LACHS, S.T., «The Pandora-Eve Motif in Rabbinic Literature», *HTR* 67 (1974) 341-345.

————, *A Rabbinic Commentary on the New Testament: The Gospel of Matthew*, New Jersey 1987.

LADD, G.E., «The Resurrection and History», *RL* 32 (1963) 247-256.

LAFAYE, G., *Histoire du culte des divinités d'Alexandrie. Sérapis, Isis, Harpocrate et Anubis hors de l'Égypte depuis les origines jusq'à la naissance de l'école néo-platonicienne*, Paris 1984.

————, «L'introduction du culte de Sérapis à Rome», *RHR* 11 (1985) 327-329.

LAGRAND, J., *The Earliest Christian Mission to «All Nations» in the Light of Matthew's Gospel*, Atlanta 1995.

LAGRANGE, M. -J., *Evangile selon saint Matthieu*, Paris 1948.

LANE, W.L., *The Gospel according to Mark*, Grand Rapids 1974.

LaVERDIERE, E., «The Resurrection according to Matthew», *Emmanuel* 93 (1987) 126-135.

LAWS, S.S, *A Commentary on the Epistle of James*, HNTC, San Francisco 1980.

LEANEY, R., «The Birth Narratives in St Luke and St Matthew», *NTS* 8 (1961-1962) 158-66.

LEHMANN, K., *Auferweckt am dritten Tag nach der Schrift. Exegetische und fundamentaltheologische Studien zu 1Kor 15, 3b-5*, QD, 038, Freiburg 1968.

LENSKI, R.C.H., *Commentary on the New Testament*, Columbus 1943.

LENTZEN-DEIS, F., *Die Taufe Jesu nach den Synoptikern: Literarkritische und gattungsgeschichtliche Untersuchungen*, Frankfurt am Main 1970.

LEON-DUFOUR, X., *Résurrection de Jésus et message pascal*, Paris 1971.

LEVINE, A.J., *The Social and Ethnic Dimensions of Matthean Salvation History: «Go Nowhere among the Gentiles...» (Matt. 10:5b)*, SBEC 014, Lewiston 1988.

————, «Matthew», in C.A. NEWSOM – S.H. RINGE, *The Women's Bible Commentary*, Louisville 1992, 252-262.

————, «Matt 9:20-22: Woman with a Twelve–Year Hemorrhage», in C. MEYERS, *Women in Scripture: A Dictionary of Named and Unnamed Women in the Hebrew Bible, the Apocryphal/Deuterocanonical Books, and the New Testament*, Boston – New York 2000, 408-409.

————, «Tamar», in C. MEYERS, ed., *Women in Scripture: A Dictionary of Named and Unnamed Women in the Hebrew Bible, the Apocryphal/Deuterocanonical Books, and the New Testament*, Boston – New York 2000, 161-165.

LEWIS, N., *Life in Egypt under Roman Rule*, Oxford 1984.

LINCOLN, B., «The Rape of Persephone: A Greek Scenario of Women's Initiation», *HTR* 72 (1979) 223-235.

LINDARS, B., «The Composition of John xx», *NTS* 7 (1960-61) 142-147.

————, «The Resurrection and the Empty Tomb», in P. AVIS, *The Resurrection of Jesus Christ*, London 1993, 116-135.

LOCKTON, W., *The Resurrection and the Virgin Birth*, Bombay 1924.

LOHMEYER, E., *Das Evangelium des Matthäus*, Göttingen 1956.

LOISY, A., *Le quatrième évangile*, Paris 1903.

LONG, T.G., *Matthew*, Louisville 1993.

LONGENECKER, R.N., *Life in the Face of Death: The Resurrection Message of the New Testament*, Cambridge 1998.

LONGSTAFF, T.R.W., «The Women at the Tomb: Matthew 28:1 Re-examined», *NTS* 27 (1981) 278-182.

LORENZEN, T., *Resurrection and Discipleship: Interpretive Models, Biblical Reflections, Theological Consequences,* New York 1995.

LORETZ, O., «The Theme of Ruth Story», *CBQ* 22 (1960) 391-399.

LÖSCH, S., «Christliche Frauen in Korinth», *TQ* CXXVII (1974) 216-261.

LOVE, S.L., «Women's Roles in Certain Second Testament Passages: A Macrosociological View», *BTB* 17 (1987) 50-59.

————, «The Household: A Major Social Component for Gender Analysis in the Gospel of Matthew», *BTB* 23 (1993) 21-31.

LÜDEMANN, G., *Die Auferstehung Jesu: Historie, Erfahrung, Theologie,* Göttingen 1994.

————, *Jesus nach 2000 Jahren,* Lüneburg 2000.

LUZ, U., «Die Jünger in Matthäusevangelium», *ZNW* 62 (1971) 141-171.

————, *Das Evangelium nach Matthäus Mt 1-7,* EKKNT 001, Zürich 1985.

————, *Jesusgeschichte des Matthäus,* Neukirchen 1993.

MACCINI, R.G., *Her Testimony is True: Women as Witnesses according to John,* JSNT 125, Sheffield 1996.

MACLEISCH, K., «The Land of Galilee», *NGM* 128 (1965) 832-865.

MALBON, E.S., «Galilee and Jerusalem: History and Literature in Marcan Interpretation», *CBQ* 44 (1982) 242-255.

————, «Fallible Followers: Women and Men in the Gospel of Mark», *Semeia* 28 (1983) 29-48.

————, «The Jesus of Mark and the Sea of Galilee», *JBL* 103 (1984) 363-377.

MALHERBE, A.J., *Social Aspects of Early Christianity,* Philadelphia 1983[2].

MALINA, B.J., *The New Testament World: Insights from Cultural Anthropology,* Louisville, KY 1981.

MALONE, M.T., *Women & Christianity,* I-II, Dublin 2000.

MANSON, T.W., *The Sayings of Jesus,* Grand Rapids 1979.

MARGUERAT, D., *Résurrection: Une histoire de vie,* Poliez-le-Grand 2001.

MARROW, S.B., *The Gospel of John: A Reading,* New York 1995.

MARTIN, F., *Encounter Story: A Characteristic Gospel Narrative,* DSS Dissertation, Rome 1977.

MARTIN, R.P., «Approaches to New Testament Exegesis», in I.H. MARSHALL, ed., *New Testament Interpretation: Essays on Principles and Methods*, Grand Rapids 1977, 220-251

MARTIN, W.J., «I Corinthians 11:2-16: An Interpretation», in W.W. GASQUE – R.P. MARTIN, ed., *Apostolic History and the Gospel*, Grand Rapids 1970, 231-41.

MARTINEZ, E.R., «The Interpretation of ói mathētai in Matthew 18», *CBQ* 23 (1961) 281-292.

————, *The Gospel Accounts of the Death of Jesus*, Excerpta ex dissertatione ad Lauream, Rome 1970.

————, *La sequela di Gesù Cristo nel vangelo secondo Marco*, Roma 1996.

MARTINEZ, F.G., *The Dead Sea Scrolls Translated*, New York 1992[2].

MARXEN, W., *Der Evangelist Markus: Studien zur Redaktionsgeschichte des Evangeliums*, Göttigen 1959.

MCCANE, B.R., «"Let the Dead Bury Their Own Dead": Secondary Burial and Matt 8:21-22», *HTR* 83 (1990) 31-43.

McDERMOTT, J.J., «Multipurpose Genealogies», *BT* 35 (6,97) 382.

MCKEATING, P., «Jesus Ben Sira's Attitude Toward Women», *ExpTim* 85 (1970) 85-87.

MCKELVEY, R.J., *The New Temple: The Church in New Testament*, London 1969.

MCNAMARA, J.K., *Sisters in Arms: Catholic Nuns Through Two Millennia*, London 1996.

MCNEILE, A., *The Gospel according to St. Matthew*, London 1915.

MEEKS, W.A., «The Image of Androgyne», *HR* 8 (1974) 165-208.

————, *The First Urban Christians: The Social World of the Apostle Paul*, New Haven 1983.

MEIER, J.P – R.E. BROWN, *Antioch and Rome: New Testament Cradles of Catholic Christianity*, New York 1983.

MEIER, J.P., «Matthew 15:21-28», *Int* 40 (1986) 397-402.

————, *Matthew*, NTM 003, Dublin 1984.

————, *A Marginal Jew: Rethinking the Historical Jesus*, I-III, New York 1991-2001

————, *The Vision of Matthew: Christ, Church, and Morality in the First Gospel*, New York 1991.

MERRIL, E.H., «The Book of Ruth: Narration and Shared Themes», *BSac* (1985) 130-141.

METZGER, B.M., *A Textual Commentary on the Greek New Testament: A Companion Volume to the United Bible Societies' Greek New Testament* by Bruce M. Metzger on behalf of and in cooperation with the Editorial Committee of the United Bible Societies' Greek New Testament Kurt Aland, et al., London, New York 1975[3].

MEYNET, R., *Jésus passe: testament, jugement, exécution et résurrection du Seigneur Jésus dans les évangiles*, Roma 1999.

MICHAELIS, W., «κρατέω», *TDNT* III, 910-912.

———, «μιμέομαι», *TDNT* IV, 650-674.

———, «θεωρέω», *TDNT* V, 315-367.

———, *Die Erscheinungen des Auferstandenen*, Basel 1944.

MILTON, H., «The Structure of the Prologue to St. Matthew's Gospel», *JBL* 81 (1962) 175-181.

MINEAR, P.S., «The Uniqueness of the Death», *ExpTim* 79 (1964-65) 55-59.

———, «The Disciples and the Crowds in the Gospel», *ATRSuppSer* 3 (1974) 28-44.

———, «Matthew 28:1-10», *Int* 38 (1984) 59-63.

MOLTMAN, W.E., *Liberty, Equality, Sisterhood: On the Emancipation of Women in Church and Society*, Philadelphia 1978.

MONTAGUE, G.T., *Companion God: A Cross Cultural Commentary on the Gospel of Matthew*, New York 1990.

MONTEFIORE, C.G – LOEWE, H., *A Rabbinic Anthology*, Philadelphia 1960.

MONTEFIORE, C.J.G., *The Synoptic Gospels*, I–II, New York 1968[2].

MORA, F., *Prosopografia Isiaca*, I–II, ÉPROER 113, Leiden 1990.

MORGENTHALER, R., *Statistik des neutestamentlichen Wortschatzes*, Zürich 1958-1982.

MORISON, J., *A Practical Commentary on the Gospel according to St. Matthew*, London 1883.

MORRIS, L.L., *The Gospel according to Matthew*, Grand Rapids 1992.

MORRISON, A.W., *A Commentary on the Gospels: Matthew, Mark and Luke*, Grand Rapids 1980.

MOULE, C.F.D., *An Idiom Book of New Testament Greek*, Cambridge 1959[2].

MOULTON, J.H – HOWARD, W.F., *A Grammar of New Testament Greek*, I–II, Edinburgh 1919-1926.

MOULTON, W.F — GEDEN, A.S. ed., *A Concordance to the Greek Testament according to the Texts of Westcott and Hort, Tischendorf and the English Revisers*, Edinburgh 1978[5].

MÜLLER, P. G., «ἀνοίγω», *EDNT* I, 105-106.

MULLINS, P., «The Public, Secular Roles of Women in Biblical Times», *MS* 43 (1998) 79-111.

MUNRO, W., «Women Disciples in Mark», *CBQ* 44 (1982) 225-241.

MURRAY, P.B., *The Message of the Resurrection*, Leicester, 2000.

MYLONAS, G.E., *Eleusis and the Eleusinisn Mysteries*, Princeton 1951.

NAUCK, W., «Die Bedeutung des leeren Grabes für den Glauben an den Auferstandenen», *ZNW* 47 (1956) 243-267.

NEBE, G., «πολός», *EDNT* III, 131-133.

NEIRYNCK, F., «Les femmes au tombeau: Étude de la rédaction matthéenne (Matt. Xxviii.1-10», *NTS* 15 (1968-79) 168-190.

————, «John and the Synoptics: The Empty Tomb Stories», *NTS* 30 (1984) 161-187.

NEUSNER, J., *The Idea of Purity in Ancient Judaism*, Leiden 1972-73.

————, *A History of the Mishnaic Law of Purities*, SJLA 006, Leiden 1975.

————, «From Scripture to Mishnah: The Origins of Tractate Niddah», *JJS* 29 (1978) 135-148.

————, *Judaism in the Beginning of Christianity*, Philadelphia 1984.

NEWMAN, B.M — STINE, P.C. *A Translator's Handbook on the Gospel of Matthew*, London 1988.

NICKELSBURG, G.E.W., *Jewish Literature between the Bible and the Mishnah: A Historical and Literary Introduction*, Philadelphia 1981.

NIDITCH, S., «The Wronged Woman Righted: An Analysis of Genesis 38», *HTR* 72 (1979) 143-149.

NISSEN, J. *New Testament and Mission: Historical and Hermeneutical Perspectives*, Frankfurt am Main 1999.

NOLAN, B.M., *The Royal Son of God: The Christology of Matthew 1-2 in the Setting of the Gospel*, Göttingen 1979.

NOTH, M., *The Laws in the Pentateuch and Other Studies*, Philadelphia 1966.

O'COLLINS, G — KENDALL. D., «Mary Magdalene as Major Witness to Jesus' Resurrection», *TS* 48 (1987) 631-646.

————, «Did Joseph of Arimathea Exist», *Bib* 75 (1994) 235-241.

O'COLLINS, G., *What are They Saying about Jesus: A Report on Recent Speculation About Jesus Christ and Its Implications for Christian Faith*, New 1983.

————, *Interpreting the Resurrection: Examining the Major Problems in the Stories of Jesus' Resurrection*, New York 1988.

O'DAY, G.R., «Surprised by Faith: Jesus and the Canaanite Woman», *Listening* 24 (1989) 290-301.

O'NEILL, J.C., «On the Resurrection of as an Historical Question», in S.W. SYKES – J.P. CLAYTON, ed., *Christ Faith and History,* Cambridge 1972, 205-219.

OBERBORDER, B., «Was sucht ihr den Lebendigen bei den Toten? Überlegungen zur Realität der Auferstehung in Auseinandersetzung mit Gerd Lüdemann», *KD* 46 (2000) 225-240

OBSORNE, G.R., «Women in the Ministry of Jesus», *WTJ* 51 (1989) 259-291.

ODEN, T.C – HALL, C.A., ed., *Mark,* Downers Grove 1998.

OEPKE, A., ἐγείρω, *TDNT* II, 333-339.

————, «καθεύδω», *TDNT* III, 431-437.

————, «καθίστημι, ἀκαταστασία, ἀκατάστατος», » *TDNT* III, 444-446.

OPOCENSKA, J., «Women at the Cross, at Jesus' Burial, and after the Resurrection: Mk 15:40; 16:10», *RW* 47 (1997) 40-48.

ORTON, D.E., *The Understanding Scribe: Matthew and the Apocalyptic Ideal,* JSNTSS 25, Sheffield 1989.

OVERMAN, J.A., *Matthew's Gospel and Formative Judaism: The Social World of the Matthean Community,* Minneapolis, 1990.

PACOMIO, L., *Gesù: i 37 anni che venti secoli fa cambiarono il senso della storia e i nostri destini*, Casale Monferrato 1996.

PATTE, D., *The Gospel according to Matthew: A Structural Commentary on Matthew's Gospel*, Philadelphia 1987.

PAUL, A., *L'Évangile de l'enfance selon Saint Matthieu,* LB 017, Paris 1968.

PERITZ, I. J., «Women in the Ancient Hebrew Cult», *JBL* 17 (1898) 111-147.

PERKINS, P., *Resurrection: New Testament Witness and Contemporary Reflection,* Garden City 1984.

PERRIN, N., *The Resurrection according to Matthew, Mark, and Luke*, Philadelphia 1977.

PERRY, C.A., *The Resurrection Promise: An Interpretation of the Easter Narratives,* Grand Rapids: Michigan, 1986.

PESCH, R., «Levi-Matthäus [Mc 2:14; Matt 9:9; 10:3]. Ein Beitrag zur Lösung eines Alten Problems», *ZNW* 59 (1968) 40-56.

———, ed., «Die Heilung der Schwiegermutter des Simon-Petrus: Ein Beispiel heutiger Synoptikerexegese», in *Neuere Exegese - Verlust oder Gewinn*, Freiburg 1968.

———, *Das Markusevangelium*, HTKNT, I-II, Freiburg 1976-1977.

PETERSEN, N.R., *Literary Criticism for New Testament Critics*, Philadelphia 1978.

PFEIFFER, R.H., «A Non-Israelite Source of the Book of Genesis», *ZAW* 48 (1930) 70-72

———, *Introduction to the Old Testament*, London 1952.

PHILO, *De opificio mundi*, in R. ARNALDEZ — J. POUILLOUX — C. MONDE-SERT, ed., *Philon d'Alexandrie*, OPA I, Paris 1961.

———, *De sacrificiis Abelis et Caini*, in R. ARNALDEZ — J. POUILLOUX — C. MONDESERT, ed., *Philon d'Alexandrie,* OPA IV, Paris 1966.

———, *De posteritate Caini*, in R. ARNALDEZ — J. POUILLOUX — C. MON-DESERT, ed., *Philon d'Alexandrie*, OPA, VI, Paris 1972.

———, *De virtutibus*, in R. ARNALDEZ — J. POUILLOUX — C. MONDESERT, ed., *Philon d'Alexandrie*, OPA XVI, Paris 1962.

———, *De aeternitate mundi*, in R. ARNALDEZ — J. POUILLOUX — C. MONDESERT, ed., *Philon d'Alexandrie*, OPA XXX, Paris 1969.

———, *In Flaccum*, in R. ARNALDEZ — J. POUILLOUX — C. MONDESERT, ed., *Philon d'Alexandrie*, OPA XXXI, Paris 1967.

———, *De specialibus legibus I et IV*, in R. ARNALDEZ — J. POUILLOUX — C. MONDESERT, ed., *Philon d'Alexandrie*, OPA XXV, Paris 1970.

PILCH, J.J., *Healing in the New Testament: Insights from Medical and Mediterranean Anthropology*, Minneapolis 2000.

PLUMMER, A., *An Exegetical Commentary on the Gospel according to St. Matthew*, London 1909.

POBEE, J., «The Cry of the centurion – A Cry of Defeat», in E. BAMMEL, ed., *The Trial of Jesus*, London: SCM, 1970, 91.

POLANYI, K., *The Great Transformation: The Political and Economic Origins of Our Time*, Boston 1957.

POMEROY, S.B., *Goddesses, Wives, Whores and Slaves: Women in Classical Antiquity*, New York 1975.

PORTER, B.W., «With Our Backs to the Grave: [Psalm 90:5, Matt 27:61, Luke 24:9]», *PSB* 1- 4 (1978) 232-235.

PORTER, S. E., «Joseph of Arimathea», *ABD* III, 971-972.

PRENTER, R., «La Testimonianza biblica della risurrezione di Gesu é la critica storica moderna», *Prot* 18 (1963) 65-74.

PROCKSCH, «ἅγιος», *TDNT* I, 88-115.

PRZYBYLSKI, B., *Righteousness in Matthew and his World of Thought*, MSSNTS 41, Cambridge 1980.

PUDUSSERY, P.S., *Discipleship, a Call to Suffering and Glory: An Exegetico-Theological Study of Mk 8,27-9,1; 13,9-13 and 13,24-27*, Roma 1987.

QUINN, J. D., «Is RAXAB in Mt 1,5 Rahab of Jericho?», *Bib* 62 (1981) 225-228.

RABBI TECHORESH, «Regarding the Education of Girls» [Hebrew], *Noam* 12 (1969) 77-81.

REEVES, K.H., *The Resurrection Narrative in Matthew: A Literary-Critical Examination*, Lewiston 1993.

REICKE, B., «προΐστημι», *TDNT* VI, 700-3.

REID, B.E., *Choosing the Better Part? Women in the Gospel of Luke*, Collegeville 1996.

RESCH, A., *Agrapha: Aussehrkanonische Evangelienfragmente*, TU 005, Leipzig 1906.

REUMANN, J., «Psalm 22 at the Cross: Lament and Thanksgiving for Jesus Christ», *Int* 28 (1974) 39-58.

RIEBL, M., *Auferstehung Jesu in der Stunde seines Todes? Zur Botschaft von Mt 27, 51b-53*, SBS 008, Stuttgart 1978.

————, «Jesu Tod und Auferstehung-Hoffnung für unser Sterben», *BLit* 57 (1984) 208-213.

RILEY, H., *The First Gospel*, Macon 1992.

RINALDI, G., «Il Messianismo tra "le Genti" in S. Matteo», *RivB* 2 (1954) 318-328.

RINGE, S.H., «A Gentile Woman's Story», in L.M. RUSSEL, *Feminist Interpretation of the Bible*, Philadelphia 1985, 65-72.

RITT, H., «Die Frauen und die Osterbotschaft Synopse der Grabesgeschichten (Mk 16, 1-8; Mt 27, 62–28, 15; Lk 24, 1-12; Joh 20, 1-8», in G. DAUTZENBERG, ed., *Die Frau im Urchristentum*, QD 095, Freiburg 1983, 117-133.

ROBBINS, V.K., «The Woman Who Touched Jesus' Garment: Socio-Rhetorical Analysis of the Synoptic Accounts», *NTS* 33 (1987) 502-515.

ROBERTSON, A.T., *A Grammar of the New Testament in the Light of Historical Research*, Nashville 1934[4].

ROBINSON, D.W.B., «Who Were the Saints», *RTR* 22 (1963) 45-53

ROBINSON, T.H., *The Gospel of Matthew*, London 1928.

RODGER, L., «The Infancy Stories of Matthew and Luke: An Examination of the Child as a Theological Metaphor», *HBT* 19 (1997) 58-81.

ROGERS, C., «The Great Commission», *BSac* 130 (1973) 258-267.

RUDOLF, K., *Gnosis: The Nature and History of an Ancient Religion*, trans. R. M. WILSON, Edinburgh 1983; orig. German, *Die Gnosis: Wesen und Geschichte einer spätantiken Religion*, Leipzig 1977.

RUETHER. R – MCLAUGHLIN, E., ed., *Women of Spirit: Female Leadership in the Jewish and Christian Traditions*, New York 1979.

RUSH, A., *Death and Burial in Christian Antiquity*, Washington DC 1941.

SABOURIN, L., *L'Evangile selon saint Matthieu et ses principaux parallèles*, Rome 1978.

SAFRAI, S., «Home and Family», in S. SAFRAI, ed., *The Jewish People in the First Century: Historical Geography, Political History, Social, Cultural, and Religious Life and Institutions*, I–II, Assen 1974-76.

SALDARINI, A.J., «Rabbinic Literature and the NT», *ABD* V, 602-604.

————, *Matthew's Christian-Jewish Community*, CSHJ, Chicago 1994.

SANDERS, E.P., *The Historical Figure of Jesus*, New York 1993.

SAWYER, D.F., *Women and Religion in the First Christian Centuries*, London 1996.

SCHABERG, J., *The Illegitimacy of Jesus: A Feminist Theological Interpretation of the Infancy Narratives*, San Francisco 1987.

SCHMID, J., *Das Evangelium nach Markus*, RNT 002, Regensburg 1958.

————, *Das Evangelium nach Matthäus*, RNT 001, Regensburg 1959[4].

SCHMITT, J.J., «The Motherhood of God and Zion as Mother», *RB* 92 (1985) 557-569.

SCHNACKENBURG, R., *Das Johannesevangelium*, I–III, HTKNT 004, Freiburg 1984-1986.

SCHNEIDER, F., «ἔρχομαι», *TDNT* II, 666-684.

SCHNEIDER, F., «Die Frauen im Stammbaum Jesu nach Matthäus», *BZ* 23 (1979) 187-196.

————, «Μαρία, ας/ Μαριάμ», *EDTNT* II, 386-389.

SCHNIEWIND, J., *Das Evangelium nach Matthäus*, Göttingen 1984[13].

SCHOLER, D.M., «Women», in J.B. GREEN – S. MCKNIGHT, ed., *Dictionary of Jesus and the Gospels,* Downers Grove 1972, 880-887

SCHOTTROFF, L., *Let the Oppressed Go Free: Feminist Perspective on New Testament*, Louisville – Kentucky 1993.

SCHOTTROFF , W., «Frauen in der Nachfolge Jesu in neutestamentlicher Zeit», in SCHOTTROFF , W. – STEGEMANN, W., ed., *Traditionen der Befreiung* II, München 1980.

SCHREIBER, J., «Die Bestattung Jesu: Redaktionsgeschichtliche Beobachtungen zu Mk 15:42-47», *ZNW* (1981) 142-177.

SCHÜRER, E., *A History of Jewish People in the Age of Jesus Christ* (175 BC– A D 135), I-III, Edinburgh 1973-1987.

SCHÜRMANN, H., *Das Lukasevangelium*, I-II, HTKNT 003, Freiburg 1969.

SCHÜSSLER FIORENZA, E., «Word, Spirit and Power: Women in Early Christian Communities», in R. RUETHER – E. MCLAUGHLIN, ed., *Women of Spirit: Female Leadership in the Jewish and Christian Traditions*, New York 1979, 29-70.

————, *But She Said: Feminist Practices of Biblical Interpretation*, Boston 1992.

————, *In Memory of Her: A Feminist Theological Reconstruction of Christian Origins*, New York 1994.

SCHWARZ, G., «ΣΥΡΟΦΟΙΝΙΚΙΣΣΑ-ΧΑΝΑΝΑΙΑ», (Markus 7.26/Matthäus 15.22», *NTS* 30 (1984) 626-628.

SCHWEIZER, E., *Erniedrigung und Erhöhung bei Jesus und seinen Nachfolgern*, Zurich 1955.

————, *Matthäus und seine Gemeinde*, SBS 071, Stuttgart 1974.

————, *Jesus: The Parable of God. What do We Really Know About Jesus*, Edinburgh 1997.

SCROGGS, R., «Paul and the Eschatological Woman: Revisited», *JAAR 42* (1974) 532-537.

————, «The Earliest Christian Communities as Sectarian Movement», in J. NEUSNER, ed., *Christianity, Judaism and Other Greco-Roman Cults*, I–II, Leiden 1975, 1-23.

SCROGGS, R., «Woman in the New Testament», in *IDB* Supplementary Volume, Nashville 1976, 966-968.

SEGAL, J.B., «Elements of Male Chauvinism in Classical Halakhah», *Judaism* 24 (1976) 226-244.

————, «Popular Religion in Israel», *JJS* 27 (1976) 1-22.

————, «The Jewish Attitude Towards Women», *JJS* 30 (1979) 121-37.

SEIDENSTICKER, P., *Die Auferstehung Jesu in der Botschaft der Evangelien: ein traditionsgeschichtlicher Versuch zum Problem der Sicherung der Osterbotschaft in der apostolischen Zeit*, Stuttgart 1967.

SEIM, T.K., *The Double Message: Patterns of Gender in Luke and Acts*, Nashville 1994.

SELVIDGE, M.J., «Mark and Woman: Reflections on Serving», *Explorations* 1 (1982) 23-32.

————, «Mark 5:25-34 and Leviticus 15:19-20: A Redaction to Restrictive Purity Regulations», *JBL* 103 (1984) 619-623.

————, «Violence, Woman, and the Future of the Matthean Community: A Redactional Critical Essay», *USQR* 39 (1984) 213-223.

SENIOR, D., *The Passion Narrative according to Matthew: A Redactional Study*, Leuven 1975.

————, «The Death of Jesus and the Resurrection of the Holy Ones (Matt 27:51-53)», *CBQ* 38 (1976) 312-329.

————, *What are they Saying about Matthew?*, New York 1983.

————, *The Passion of Jesus in the Gospel of Matthew*, Wilmington 1989.

————, «Matthew's Account of the Burial of Jesus (Mt 27:57-61)», in Van SEGBROECK, ed., *The Four Gospels*, Leuven 1992, 1433-1448.

SHAW, J.M., *The Resurrection of Christ: An Examination of the Apostolic Belief and its Significance for the Christian Faith*, Edinburgh 1920.

SHERK, R.K., ed., *The Roman Empire: Augustus to Hadrian*, TDGR 006, Cambridge 1988.

SHULLENBERGER, W., «The Other Mary», *CL* 43 (1994) 241-245.

SIBINGA, J.S., «Ignatius and Matthew», *NovT* 8 (1966) 263-283.

SILVER, A., «May Women be Taught Bible, Mishnah and Talmud»?, *Tradition* 17 (1978) 74-85.

SIM, D.C., «The Confession of the Soldiers in Matthew 27:54», *HeyJ* 34 (1993) 401-424.

————, *Apocalyptic Eschatology in the Gospel of Matthew*, SNTSMS 88, Cambridge 1996.

SMITH, M., *Jesus the Magician*, San Francisco 1978.

SMITH, R.H., *Matthew*, Minneapolis 1989.

SMYTH, K., «Matthew: 28 Resurrection as Theophany», *ITQ* 42/44 (1975) 173-180.

SOARES-PRABHU, G.M., *The Formula Quotations in the Infancy Narrative of Matthew: An Enquiry into the Traditional History of Mt 1-2*, AnBib 063, Rome 1976.

SPOTO, D., *The Hidden Jesus a New Life*, New York 1998.

STAGG, E – STAGG, F., *Woman in the World of Jesus*, Philadelphia 1978.

STAMBAUGH, J.E – BALCH, D.L., *The New Testament in its Social Environment*, Philadelphia 1986.

STAUFFER, E., *Jesus and His Story*, New York 1960; orig. German, *Jesus: Gestalt und Geschichte*, Bern 1957.

STEIN, R.H., «Was the Tomb Really Empty», *JETS* 20 (1977) 23-29.

STENDAHL, K., *The School of St. Matthew and Its Use of the Old Testament*, Philadelphia 1968[2].

————, «Quis et Unde? An Analysis of Matthew 1-2», in G. STANTON, ed., *The Interpretation of Matthew*, IRT 003, Edinburgh 1995, 69-80.

STOCK, A., *The Method and Message of Matthew*, Collegeville 1994.

STOCK, K., «Das Bekenntnis des Centurio: Mk 15,39 im Rahmen des Markusevangeliums», *ZKT* 100 (1978) 289-301.

————, *Il Racconto della passione nei vangeli sinottici*, Roma 2000.

STONE, J.S., *The Glory After the Passion: A Study of the Events in the Life of Our Lord from His Descend into Hell to His Enthronement in Heaven*, New York 1913.

STRACK, H. L. –STEMBERGER, G., *Introduction to the Talmud and Midrash*, Edinburgh 1991.

STRANGE, J.E., «Magdala», *ABD* IV, 443-444.

STRECKER, G., *Der Weg der Gerechtigkeit: Untersuchung zur Theologie des Matthäus*, Göttingen 1971.

STRELAN, R., «To Sit is to Mourn: The Women at the Tomb (Matthew 27:61», *Colloquium* 31 (1999) 31-45.

SWAIN, L., *Reading the Easter Gospels*, Collegeville 1993.

SWETE, H.B., *The Resurrection of Our Lord after the Passion: A Study in the Earliest Christian Tradition*, London 1907.

SWIDLER, L. J – SWIDLER, A., ed., *Women Priests: A Catholic Commentary on the Vatican Declaration*, New York 1977.

————, «Jesus was a Feminist», *CW* 212 (1971) 177-183.

————, *Women in Judaism: The Status of Women in Formative Judaism*, Metuchen 1976.

————, *Biblical Affirmations of Women*, Philadelphia 1979.

————, *Yeshua: A Model for Moderns*, Kansas City 1988.

TAKÁCS, S.A., *Isis and Sarapis in the Roman World*, Leiden 1995.

TASKER, R.V.G., *The Gospel according to St. Matthew: An introduction and Commentary*, London 1969.

TAYLOR, V., *Gospel according to St. Mark*, London 1952.

TEMPORINI, H., *Die Frauen am Hofe Trajans: Ein Beitrag zur Stellung der Augustae im Principat*, Berlin 1978.

TETLOW, E.M., *Women and Ministry in the New Testament*, New York 1980.

THEISSEN, G., «Soziale Schichtung in der korinthischen Gemeinde: Ein Beitrag zur Soziologie des hellenistischen Urchristentums», *ZNW* 65 (1974) 232-272.

————, *Soziologie der Jesus Bewegung*, TEH 144, München 1977.

————, *The Miracle Stories of the Early Christian Tradition*, Edinburgh 1983; orig. German, *Urchristliche Wundergeschichten: ein Beitrag zur formgeschichtlichen Erforschung der Synoptischen Evangelium*, Gütersloh 1974.

————, «Lokal und Sozialkolorit in der Geschichte von der syrophönikischen Frau (Mk 7 24-30)», *ZNW* 75 (1984) 202-225.

————, *Frauen im Umfeld Jesu*, Sexau 1993.

THEISSEN, G. – MERZ. A., *Der historische Jesus: ein Lehrbuch*, Göttingen, 1999[2].

THIEMANN, R.F., «The Unnamed Woman at Bethany», *TT* 44 (1983) 179-188.

THOMPSON, M.R., *Mary of Magdala, Apostle and Leader*, New York 1995.

THOMPSON, W.G., *Matthew's Advice to a Divided Community: Mt 17,22-18,35*, AnBib 44, Roma 1970.

THOMPSON, W.M., *The Jesus Debate: A Survey and Synthesis*, New York 1985.

THRALL, M.E., *Greek Particles in the New Testament: Linguistic and Exegetical Studies*, Leiden 1962.

THURSTON, B., *Women in the New Testament: Questions and Commentary*, New York: Cross Road, 1998.

TISERA, G., *Universalism according to the Gospel of Matthew*, Frankfurt am Main 1993.

TOLBERT, M.A., «Introduction» [The Bible and Feminist Hermeneutics]», *Semeia* 28 (1983) 113-126.

————, «Mark,», in C.A. NEWSOM – S.H. RINGE, *The Women's Bible Commentary*, Louisville – Westminister 1992, 263-274.

TORRANCE, D.W – TORRANCE, T.F., ed., *A Harmony of the Gospels: Matthew, Mark and Luke*, I-III, Grand Rapids 1980.

TOYNBEE, A., *Study of History*, London 1956-57.

TREVETT, C., «Approaching Matthew from the Second Century: The Under-Used Ignatian Correspondence», *JSNT* 20 (1984) 59-67.

TRIBLE, P., «Ruth», in C. MEYERS, ed., in *Women in Scripture: A Dictionary of Names and Unnamed Women in the Hebrew Bible, the Apocryphal/Deuterocanonical Books, and the New Testament*, Boston – New York 2000, 146-147.

————, «Women in the OT», in *IBD*, 963-966.

TRILLING, W., *Das Evangelium nach Matthäus*, I-II, Leipzig 1962.

————, *Das Wahre Israel: Studien zur Theologie des Matthäus*, Leipzig 1975.

————, *Christusverkündigung in den synoptischen Evangelien: Beispiele Gattungsgemäßer Auslegung*, BH 004, Munich 1996.

TROMPF, G.W., «The First Resurrection Appearance and Ending of Mark's Gospel», *NTS* 18 (1972) 308-330.

TRUMMER, P., *Blutende Frau: Wunderheilung im Neuen Testament*, Freiburg – Basel – Wien 1991.

TURNER, N., *Christian Words*, Edinburgh: T & T Clark, 1980.

TWELFTREE, G.S., *Jesus the Miracle Worker*, Downers Grove 1999.

VANNI, U., «La passione come rivelazione di condanna e di salvezza in Matteo 26, 64, e 27:54», *EuntDoc* 27 (1-2, 1974) 65-91.

VERMES, G., *Jesus the Jew: A Historian's Reading of the Gospels*, Philadelphia 1973.

————, *The Religion of Jesus the Jew*, Minneapolis 1993.

VERSUPT, D.J., «The Faith of the Reader and the Narrative of Matthew 13.53-16.20», *JSNT* 46 (1992) 3-24.

VIDMAN, L., *Isis und Sarapis bei den Griechen und Römern*, RVV 029, Berlin 1970.

VITTONATO, G., «La risurrezione dei morti in Mt. xxvii, 52-52», *Sapienza* 9 (1956) 131-150.

VIVIANO, B.T., «Where was the Gospel according to Matthew Written», *CBQ* 41 (1979) 533-546.

VÖGTEL, A., «Die Genealogie Mt 1, 2-26 und die matthäische Kindheitsgeschichte», *BZ* 8 (1964) 239-262.

VÖLKEL, M., θεωρέω, *ETDNT* II, 146-147.

————, «κοιμάομαι», *EDNT* II, 301-302.

WAETJEN, H.C., «The Genealogy as the Key to the Gospel according to Matthew», *JBL* 95 (1976) 205-230.

WAINWRIGHT, E.M., *Towards a Feminist Critical Reading of the Gospel according to Matthew*, Berlin 1991.

————, «The Gospel of Matthew», in E. SCHÜSSLER FIORENZA, ed., *Searching Scriptures*, New York 1993-94, 635-677.

————, *Shall We Look for Another? A Feminist Rereading of the Matthean Jesus*, Mary Knoll 1998.

WALLACE-HADRILL, D.S., *Christian Antioch: A Study of Early Christian Thought in the East*, Cambridge 1982.

WALTER, N., «Eine vormatthäische Schilderung der Auferstehung Jesu», *NTS* 19 (1972/73) 415-429

WEAVER, D.J., *Matthew's Missionary Discourse*, JSNTSS 038, Sheffield 1990.

————, «Matthew 28:1-10», *Int* 46 (1992) 399-402.

WEEDEN, T.J., *Mark – Traditions in Conflict*, Philadelphia 1971.

WEGNER, J.R, *Chattel or Person? The Status of Women in the Mishnah*, Oxford 1988.

WENHAM, J.W., «Relatives of Jesus», *EQ* 47 (1975) 6-15.

————, «When were the Saints Raised? A Note on the Punctuation of Matthew xxvii-51-53», *JTS* 1 (1981) 150-152.

WESTERMANN, C – JENNI, E., ed., *Theologisches Handwörterbuch zum Alten Testament*, I–II, München 1971-1976.

WIEFEL, W., *Das Evangelium nach Matthäus*, THNT 001, Berlin 1998.

WILCKENS, U., *Die Pericope vom leere Grabe Jesu in der nachmarkinischen Traditionsgeschichte*, Fs. F. Smend, Berlin 1963.

WILCKENS, U., *Resurrectiion: Biblical Testimony to the Resurrection: An Historical Examination and Explanation*, Atlanta 1977; orig. German, *Auferstehung: das biblische Auferstehungszeugnis historisch Untersucht und Erklärt*, Stuttgart 1970.

WILD, R.A., *Water in the Cultic Worship of Isis and Sarapis*, Leiden 1981.

WILKINS, M.J., *The Concept of Discipleship in Matthew's Gospel: As Reflected in the Use of the Term μαθητής*, Leiden 1988[2].

————, *Discipleship in the Ancient World and Matthew's Gospel*, Grand Rapids 1995[2].

WILLIAMS, J.G., *Women Recounted: Narrative Thinking and the God of Israel*, BLS 006, Sheffield 1982.

WILSON, R.R., «Genealogy, Genealogies», *ABD* II, 930-932

WINGER, J.M., «When did the Women Visit the Tomb: Sources for Some Temporal Clauses in the Synoptic Gospels», *NTS* 40 (1994) 284-288.

WINK, W., *Engaging the Powers: Discernment and Resistance in a World of Domination*, Minneapolis 1992.

WIRE, A.C., «The Structure of the Gospel Miracle Stories and Their Tellers», *Semeia* 11 (1978) 83-113.

————, ed., «Gender Role in Scribal Community», in *The Social History of the Matthean Community: Cross Disciplinary Approaches*, Minneapolis 1991, 87-121.

WITHERINGTON, B., III, *Women in the Ministry of Jesus: A Study of Jesus' Attitudes to Women and Their Roles as Reflected in His Earthly Life*, SNTSMS 051, Cambridge 1984.

————, *Women in the Earliest Churches*, Cambridge 1988.

————, «Women (NT)», in *ABD* VI, New York 1992, 957-961.

WITT, R.E., *Isis-Hellas*, Cambridge 1966.

————, *Isis in the Greco-Roman World*, London 1971.

WOSCHITZ, K.M., «Erzählter Glaube: Die Geschichte vom starken Glauben als Geschichte Gottes mit Juden und Heiden (Mt 15,21-28 par)», *ZKT* 107 (1985) 319-332.

YADIN, Y., «Expedition D – the Cave Letters», *IEJ* 12 (1962) 227-257

YARON, R., «Aramaic Marriage Contracts – Corrigenda and Addenda», *JSS* 5 (1960) 66-70.

ZAHN, T., «Der Zerrissene Tempelvorhang», *ZKT* 13 (1902) 729-756

————, *Das Evangelium des Matthäus*, KNT 001, Leipzig 1922.

ZERWICK, M. – GROSVENOR, M., *A Grammatical Analysis of the Greek New Testament*, Roma 1988.

ZERWICK, M., *Biblical Greek*, English Edition Adapted from the Fourth Latin Edition by J. SMITH, Roma 1994.

ZUCKERMANDEL, M.S., *Tosephta*, Jerusalem 1937.

ZUCROW, S., *Women, Slaves, and the Ignorant in Rabbinic Literature and also the Dignity of Man*, Boston 1932.

ZUNTZ, G., *Persephone: Three Essays on Religion and Thought in Magna Graeca*, Oxford 1971.

INDEX OF AUTHORS

TABLE OF CONTENTS

TESI GREGORIANA

Since 1995, the series «Tesi Gregoriana» has made available to the general public some of the best doctoral theses done at the Pontifical Gregorian University. The typesetting is done by the authors themselves following norms established and controlled by the University.

Published Volumes [Series: Theology]

1. NELLO FIGA, Antonio, *Teorema de la opción fundamental. Bases para su adecuada utilización en teología moral*, 1995, pp. 380.

2. BENTOGLIO, Gabriele, *Apertura e disponibilità. L'accoglienza nell'epistolario paolino*, 1995, pp. 376.

3. PISO, Alfeu, *Igreja e sacramentos. Renovação da Teologia Sacramentária na América Latina*, 1995, pp. 260.

4. PALAKEEL, Joseph, *The Use of Analogy in Theological Discourse. An Investigation in Ecumenical Perspective*, 1995, pp. 392.

5. KIZHAKKEPARAMPIL, Isaac, *The Invocation of the Holy Spirit as Constitutive of the Sacraments according to Cardinal Yves Congar*, 1995, pp. 200.

6. MROSO, Agapit J., *The Church in Africa and the New Evangelisation. A Theologico-Pastoral Study of the Orientations of John Paul II*, 1995, pp. 456.

7. NANGELIMALIL, Jacob, *The Relationship between the Eucharistic Liturgy, the Interior Life and the Social Witness of the Church according to Joseph Cardinal Parecattil*, 1996, pp. 224.

8. GIBBS, Philip, *The Word in the Third World. Divine Revelation in the Theology of Jen-Marc Éla, Aloysius Pieris and Gustavo Gutiérrez*, 1996, pp. 448.

9. DELL'ORO, Roberto, *Esperienza morale e persona. Per una reinterpretazione dell'etica fenomenologica di Dietrich von Hildebrand*, 1996, pp. 240.

10. BELLANDI, Andrea, *Fede cristiana come «stare e comprendere». La giustificazione dei fondamenti della fede in Joseph Ratzinger*, 1996, pp. 416.

11. BEDRIÑAN, Claudio, *La dimensión socio-política del mensaje teológico del Apocalipsis*, 1996, pp. 364.

12. GWYNNE, Paul, *Special Divine Action. Key Issues in the Contemporary Debate (1965-1995)*, 1996, pp. 376.

13. NIÑO, Francisco, *La Iglesia en la ciudad. El fenómeno de las grandes ciudades en América Latina, como problema teológico y como desafío pastoral*, 1996, pp. 492.

14. BRODEUR, Scott, *The Holy Spirit's Agency in the Resurrection of the Dead. An Exegetico-Theological Study of 1 Corinthians 15,44b-49 and Romans 8,9-13*, 1996, pp. 300.

15. ZAMBON, Gaudenzio, *Laicato e tipologie ecclesiali. Ricerca storica sulla «Teologia del laicato» in Italia alla luce del Concilio Vaticano II (1950-1980)*, 1996, pp. 548.

16. ALVES DE MELO, Antonio, *A Evangelização no Brasil. Dimensões teológicas e desafios pastorais. O debate teológico e eclesial (1952-1995)*, 1996, pp. 428.

17. APARICIO VALLS, María del Carmen, *La plenitud del ser humano en Cristo. La Revelación en la «Gaudium et Spes»*, 1997, pp. 308.

18. MARTIN, Seán Charles, *«Pauli Testamentum». 2 Timothy and the Last Words of Moses*, 1997, pp. 312.

19. RUSH, Ormond, *The Reception of Doctrine. An Appropriation of Hans Robert Jauss' Reception Aesthetics and Literary Hermeneutics*, 1997, pp. 424.

20. MIMEAULT, Jules, *La sotériologie de François-Xavier Durrwell. Exposé et réflexions critiques*, 1997, pp. 476.

21. CAPIZZI, Nunzio, *L'uso di Fil 2,6-11 nella cristologia contemporanea (1965-1993)*, 1997, pp. 528.

22. NANDKISORE, Robert, *Hoffnung auf Erlösung. Die Eschatologie im Werk Hans Urs von Balthasars*, 1997, pp. 304.

23. PERKOVIĆ, Marinko, *«Il cammino a Dio» e «La direzione alla vita»: L'ordine morale nelle opere di Jordan Kuničić, O.P. (1908-1974)*, 1997, pp. 336.

24. DOMERGUE, Benoît, *La réincarnation et la divinisation de l'homme dans les religions. Approche phénoménologique et théologique*, 1997, pp. 300.

25. FARKAŠ, Pavol, *La «donna» di Apocalisse 12. Storia, bilancio, nuove prospettive*, 1997, pp. 276.

26. OLIVER, Robert W., *The Vocation of the Laity to Evangelization. An Ecclesiological Inquiry into the Synod on the Laity (1987)*, Christifideles laici *(1989) and Documents of the NCCB (1987-1996)*, 1997, pp. 364.

27. SPATAFORA, Andrea, *From the «Temple of God» to God as the Temple. A Biblical Theological Study of the Temple in the Book of Revelation*, 1997, pp. 340.

28. IACOBONE, Pasquale, *Mysterium Trinitatis. Dogma e Iconografia nell'Italia medievale*, 1997, pp. 512.

29. CASTAÑO FONSECA, Adolfo M., *Δικαιοσύνη en Mateo. Una interpretación teológica a partir de 3,15 y 21,32*, 1997, pp. 344.

30. CABRIA ORTEGA, José Luis, *Relación teología-filosofía en el pensamiento de Xavier Zubiri*, 1997, pp. 580.

31. SCHERRER, Thierry, *La gloire de Dieu dans l'oeuvre de saint Irénée*, 1997, pp. 328.

32. PASCUZZI, Maria, *Ethics, Ecclesiology and Church Discipline. A Rhetorical Analysis of 1Cor 5,1-13*, 1997, pp. 240.

33. LOPES GONÇALVES, Paulo Sérgio, *Liberationis mysterium. O projeto sistemático da teologia da libertação. Um estudo teológico na perspectiva da regula fidei*, 1997, pp. 464.

34. KOLACINSKI, Mariusz, *Dio fonte del diritto naturale*, 1997, pp. 296.

35. LIMA CORRÊA, Maria de Lourdes, *Salvação entre juízo, conversão e graça. A perspectiva escatológica de Os 14,2-9*, 1998, pp. 360.

36. MEIATTINI, Giulio, *«Sentire cum Christo». La teologia dell'esperienza cristiana nell'opera di H.U. von Balthasar*, 1998, pp. 432.

37. KESSLER, Thomas W., *Peter as the First Witness of the Risen Lord. An Historical and Theological Investigation*, 1998, pp. 240.

38. BIORD CASTILLO Raúl, *La Resurrección de Cristo como Revelación. Análisis del tema en la teología fundamental a partir de la* Dei Verbum, 1998, pp. 308.

39. LÓPEZ, Javier, *La figura de la bestia entre historia y profecía. Investigación teológico-bíblica de Apocalipsis 13,1-8,* 1998, pp. 308.

40. SCARAFONI, Paolo, *Amore salvifico. Una lettura del mistero della salvezza. Uno studio comparativo di alcune soteriologie cattoliche postconciliari,* 1998, pp. 240.

41. BARRIOS PRIETO, Manuel Enrique, *Antropologia teologica. Temi principali di antropologia teologica usando un metodo di «correlazione» a partire dalle opere di John Macquarrie,* 1998, pp. 416.

42. LEWIS, Scott M., *«So That God May Be All in All». The Apocalyptic Message of 1 Corinthians 15,12-34,* 1998, pp. 252.

43. ROSSETTI, Carlo Lorenzo, *«Sei diventato Tempio di Dio». Il mistero del Tempio e dell'abitazione divina negli scritti di Origene,* 1998, pp. 232.

44. CERVERA BARRANCO, Pablo, *La incorporación en la Iglesia mediante el bautismo y la profesión de la fe según el Concilio Vaticano II,* 1998, pp. 372.

45. NETO, Laudelino, *Fé cristã e cultura latino-americana. Uma análise a partir das Conferências de Puebla e Santo Domingo,* 1998, pp. 340.

46. BRITO GUIMARÃES, Pedro, *Os sacramentos como atos eclesiais e proféticos. Um contributo ao conceito dogmático de sacramento à luz da exegese contemporânea,* 1998, pp. 448.

47. CALABRETTA, Rose B., *Baptism and Confirmation. The Vocation and Mission of the Laity in the Writings of Virgil Michel, O.S.B.,* 1998, pp. 320.

48. OTERO LÁZARO, Tomás, *Col 1,15-20 en el contexto de la carta,* 1999, pp.312.

49. KOWALCZYK, Dariusz, *La personalità in Dio. Dal metodo trascendentale di Karl Rahner verso un orientamento dialogico in Heinrich Ott,* 1999, pp. 484.

50. PRIOR, Joseph G., *The Historical-Critical Method in Catholic Exegesis,* 1999, pp. 352.

51. CAHILL, Brendan J, *The Renewal of Revelation Theology (1960-1962). The Development and Responses to the Fourth Chapter of the Preparatory Schema* De deposito Fidei, 1999, pp. 348.

52. TIEZZI, Ida, *Il rapporto tra la pneumatologia e l'ecclesiologia nella teologia italiana post-conciliare,* 1999, pp. 364.

53. HOLC, Paweł, *Un ampio consenso sulla dottrina della giustificazione. Studio sul dialogo teologico cattolico luterano,* 1999, pp. 452.

54. GAINO, Andrea, *Esistenza cristiana. Il pensiero teologico di J. Alfaro e la sua rilevanza morale,* 1999, pp. 344.

55. NERI, Francesco, *«Cur Verbum capax hominis». Le ragioni dell'incarnazione della seconda Persona della Trinità fra teologia scolastica e teologia contemporanea,* 1999, pp. 404.

56. MUÑOZ CÁRDABA, Luis-Miguel, *Principios eclesiológicos de la «Pastor Bonus»,* 1999, pp. 344.

57. IWE, John Chijioke, *Jesus in the Synagogue of Capernaum: the Pericope and Its Programmatic Character for the Gospel of Mark. An Exegetico-Theological Study of Mk 1:21-28,* 1999, pp. 364.

58. BARRIOCANAL GÓMEZ, José Luis, *La relectura de la tradición del éxodo en l libro de Amós,* 2000, pp. 332.

59. DE LOS SANTOS GARCÍA, Edmundo, *La novedad de la metáfora κεφαλή – σῶμα en la carta a los Efesios*, 2000, pp. 432.

60. RESTREPO SIERRA, Argiro, *La revelación según R. Latourelle*, 2000, pp. 442.

61. DI GIOVAMBATTISTA, Fulvio, *Il giorno dell'espiazione nella Lettera agli Ebrei*, 2000, pp. 232.

62. GIUSTOZZO, Massimo, *Il nesso tra il culto e la grazia eucaristica nella recente lettura teologica del pensiero agostiniano*, 2000, pp. 456.

63. PESARCHICK, Robert A., *The Trinitarian Foundation of Human Sexuality as Revealed by Christ according to Hans Urs von Balthasar. The Revelatory Significance of the Male Christ and the Male Ministerial Priesthood*, 2000, pp. 328.

64. SIMON, László T., *Identity and Identification. An Exegetical Study of 2Sam 21–24*, 2000. pp. 386.

65. TAKAYAMA, Sadami, *Shinran's Conversion in the Light of Paul's Conversion*, 2000, pp. 256.

66. JUAN MORADO, Guillermo, *«También nosotros creemos porque amamos». Tres concepciones del acto de fe: Newman, Blondel, Garrigou-Lagrange. Estudio comparativo desde la perspectiva teológico-fundamental*, 2000, pp. 444.

67. MAREČEK, Petr, *La preghiera di Gesù nel vangelo di Matteo. Uno studio esegetico-teologico*, 2000, pp. 246.

68. WODKA, Andrzej, *Una teologia biblica del dare nel contesto della colletta paolina (2Cor 8–9)*, 2000, pp. 356.

69. LANGELLA, Maria Rigel, *Salvezza come illuminazione. Uno studio comparato di S. Bulgakov, V. Lossky, P. Evdokimov*, 2000, pp. 292.

70. RUDELLI, Paolo, *Matrimonio come scelta di vita: opzione – vocazione – sacramento*, 2000, pp. 424.

71. GAŠPAR, Veronika, *Cristologia pneumatologica in alcuni autori cattolici postconciliari. Status quaestionis e prospettive*, 2000, pp. 440.

72. GJORGJEVSKI, Gjoko, *Enigma degli enigmi. Un contributo allo studio della composizione della raccolta salomonica (Pr 10,1–22,16)*, 2001, pp. 304.

73. LINGAD, Celestino G., Jr., *The Problems of Jewish Christians in the Johannine Community*, 2001, pp. 492.

74. MASALLES, Victor, *La profecía en la asamblea cristiana. Análisis retórico-literario de 1Cor 14,1-25*, 2001, pp. 416.

75. FIGUEIREDO, Anthony J., *The Magisterium-Theology Relationship. Contemporary Theological Conceptions in the Light of Universal Church Teaching since 1835 and the Pronouncements of the Bishops of the United States*, 2001, pp. 536.

76. PARDO IZAL, José Javier, *Pasión por un futuro imposible. Estudio literario-teológico de Jeremías 32*, 2001, pp. 412.

77. HANNA, Kamal Fahim Awad, *La passione di Cristo nell'Apocalisse*, 2001, pp. 480.

78. ALBANESI, Nicola, *«Cur Deus Homo»: la logica della redenzione. Studio sulla teoria della soddisfazione di S. Anselmo arcivescovo di Canterbury*, 2001, pp. 244.

79. ADE, Edouard, *Le temps de l'Eglise. Esquisse d'une théologie de l'histoire selon Hans Urs von Balthasar*, 2002, pp. 368.

80. MENÉNDEZ MARTÍNEZ, Valentín, *La misión de la Iglesia. Un estudio sobre el debate teológico y eclesial en América Latina (1955-1992), con atención al aporte de algunos teólogos de la Compañía de Jesús*, 2002, pp. 346.

81. COSTA, Paulo Cezar, *«Salvatoris Disciplina». Dionísio de Roma e a* Regula fidei *no debate teológico do terceiro século*, 2002, pp. 272.

82. PUTHUSSERY, Johnson, *Days of Man and God's Day. An Exegetico-Theological Study of* ἡμέρα *in the Book of Revelation*, 2002, pp. 302.

83. BARROS, Paulo César, *«Commendatur vobis in isto pane quomodo unitatem amare debeatis». A eclesiologia eucarística nos* Sermones ad populum *de Agostinho de Hipona e o movimento ecumênico*, 2002, pp. 344.

84. PALACHUVATTIL, Joy, *«He Saw». The Significance of Jesus' Seeing Denoted by the Verb* εἶδεν *in the Gospel of Mark*, 2002, pp. 312.

85. PISANO, Ombretta, *La radice e la stirpe di David. Salmi davidici nel libro dell'Apocalisse*, 2002, pp. 496.

86. KARIUKI, Njiru Paul, *Charisms and the Holy Spirit's Activity in the Body of Christ. An Exegetical-Theological Study of 1Cor 12,4-11 and Rom 12,6-8*, 2002, pp. 372.

87. CORRY, Donal, *«Ministerium Rationis Reddendae». An Approximation to Hilary of Poitiers' Understanding of Theology*, 2002, pp. 328.

88. PIKOR, Wojciech, *La comunicazione profetica alla luce di Ez 2–3*, 2002, pp. 322.

89. NWACHUKWU, Mary Sylvia Chinyere, *Creation–Covenant Scheme and Justification by Faith. A Canonical Study of the God-Human Drama in the Pentateuch and the Letter to the Romans*, 2002, 378 pp.

90. GAGLIARDI, Mauro, *La cristologia adamitica. Tentativo di recupero del suo significato originario*, 2002, pp. 624.

91. CHARAMSA, Krzysztof Olaf, *L'immutabilità di Dio. L'insegnamento di San Tommaso d'Aquino nei suoi sviluppi presso i commentatori scolastici*, 2002, pp. 520.

92. GLOBOKAR, Roman, *Verantwortung für alles, was lebt. Von Albert Schweitzer und Hans Jonas zu einer theologischen Ethik des Lebens*, 2002, pp. 608.

93. AJAYI, James Olaitan, *The HIV/AIDS Epidemic in Nigeria. Some Ethical Considerations*, 2003, pp. 212.

94. PARAMBI, Baby, *The Discipleship of the Women in the Gospel according to Matthew. An Exegetical Theological Study of Matt 27:51b-56, 57-61 and 28:1-10*, 2003, pp. 276.

Finito di stampare
nel mese di Aprile 2003

presso la tipografia
"Giovanni Olivieri" di E. Montefoschi
00187 Roma • Via dell'Archetto, 10, 11, 12
Tel. 06 6792327 • E-mail: tip.olivieri@libero.it